Cultures of Devotion

Cultures of Devotion

Folk Saints of Spanish America

FRANK GRAZIANO

OXFORD

UNIVERSITY PRESS

2007

OXFORD
UNIVERSITY PRESS

Oxford University Press, Inc., publishes works that further
Oxford University's objective of excellence
in research, scholarship, and education.

Oxford   New York
Auckland   Cape Town   Dar es Salaam   Hong Kong   Karachi
Kuala Lumpur   Madrid   Melbourne   Mexico City   Nairobi
New Delhi   Shanghai   Taipei   Toronto

With offices in
Argentina   Austria   Brazil   Chile   Czech Republic   France   Greece
Guatemala   Hungary   Italy   Japan   Poland   Portugal   Singapore
South Korea   Switzerland   Thailand   Turkey   Ukraine   Vietnam

Published by Oxford University Press, Inc.
198 Madison Avenue, New York, New York 10016

www.oup.com

Oxford is a registered trademark of Oxford University Press

Library of Congress Cataloging-in-Publication Data
Graziano, Frank, 1955–
Cultures of devotion : folk saints of Spanish America /
Frank Graziano.
    p. cm.
Includes bibliographical references and index.
ISBN-13 978-0-19-517130-3
ISBN 0-19-517130-6
1. Christian saints—Cult—Latin America.
2. Latin America—Religious life and customs.
3. Folk religion—Latin America.   I. Title.
BX4659.L3G73 2006
235'.2098—dc22   2006005948

9 8 7 6 5 4 3 2 1

Printed in the United States of America
on acid-free paper

For the devotees, who restored my faith in faith

Vox populi, vox dei

Preface

Folk saints are deceased people, some of entirely constructed identity, who are widely regarded as miraculous and receive the devotion of a substantial cult, but who are not canonized or officially recognized by the Catholic Church. Tragic death or fame as *curanderos* (healers) are the principal catalysts of folk devotion. Some folk saints, such as Difunta Correa in Argentina and Niño Fidencio in Mexico, have huge national or international cults; most other folk saints have smaller, local followings. There are innumerable folk-saint devotions in Spanish America; the six featured chapters in this book offer a representative sample. The page references in the index provide easy access to the many other folk saints who are discussed in passing throughout the book.

Folk saints are known in Spanish America by many names, among them *santos populares, santos profanos, santos paganos, santos informales, santones, almas milagrosas, muertos milagrosos,* and *ánimas* or *animitas*. Also frequently used are the related terms *canonizaciones populares* (folk canonizations), *devociones populares* (folk devotions), *Catolicismo popular* (folk Catholicism), and *religiosidad popular* (folk religion or, literally, folk religiosity).

In all cases, I use the English word "folk" to translate the Spanish word *popular* (which literally denotes "of the people"). I do so to avoid suggesting popularity, because the phrase "popular saints" is easily misunderstood to mean canonized saints who are well liked and have large followings. The phrase "folk saints" avoids such connotations and better captures the idea of saints who originate within the traditions of common people.

I also use "folk saints" to denote a category of sainthood, in contradistinction to "canonized saints." Canonized saints are excluded from this study, as are folk saints in the process of canonization, precisely because my intent is to explore how Catholics conceive of their saints when beyond the purview of the Church. Among the folk saints who are excluded by virtue of their formal Church recognition are Ceferino Namuncurá (Argentina), Pedro Urraca (Peru), Melchora Saravia Tasayco (Peru), the Beatita de Humay (Peru), and, aside from a few mentions in passing, Dr. José Gregorio Hernández (Venezuela). Devotion to folk saints and to canonized saints have much in common, but to stay on target I have alluded to these similarities only when they are pertinent to the folk-saint themes under discussion.

I use the term "Spanish America" in reference to Spanish-language cultures anywhere in the Americas, including the United States. "Spanish American" is the implied qualifier of "folk saints" throughout this study, and therefore the rich and complex religious traditions of Portuguese-speaking Brazil are beyond the scope of this book. My study is also restricted by the vast size and multicultural composition of Spanish America, which makes a single scholar's comprehensive study of anything nearly impossible. All area-studies scholarship necessarily reflects the regional strengths of its authors; mine are Argentina and Peru. The greatest part of the research was conducted in these two countries, with additional work in Bolivia, Mexico, and the United States. This fieldwork was reinforced by the broad range of print and archival sources that are itemized in the bibliography and acknowledgments.

"Devotee" (*devoto* in Spanish) is used throughout this study as an inclusive, generic term to denote adepts of folk-saint devotions. More common in some areas of Spanish America are *promesero* or *promesante* (meaning one who makes a promise, in reference to the promises made when requesting miracles). Some devotions use saint-specific words, such as *Fidencistas* in reference to those devoted to Niño Fidencio. For uniformity, and to allow general discussion that includes multiple devotions, I use "devotee" in reference to all of these. "Shrine," similarly, is the generic term used for the sites (chapels, mausoleums, domestic altars) where devotion occurs.

The Spanish word *campesino* has no satisfactory equivalent in English. It is often translated as "peasant" or, more recently, "farmer," but both have misleading connotations. "Country person" better captures the idea (*campo*, at the root of *campesino*, denotes a rural area), but it is too clunky for repeated use. Throughout this study, I will use "campesino" (unitalicized) to denote poor rural dwellers.

The word *gaucho*, similarly, defies easy definition because it encompasses an entire cultural tradition. The usual definition, "Argentine cowboy," is a start, but it carries the entirely inappropriate baggage of what "cowboy"—as in "cowboys and Indians"—implies in the United States. I will use the Spanish term "gaucho" to denote men (the women are called *chinas*) or sometimes men and women collectively who belong to or who identify with the horse-riding, cattle-ranching traditions of Argentina. Many details of gaucho culture are included in the discussion, particularly in the chapters on San La Muerte and Gaucho Gil.

The word "cult" can suggest fanaticism or even deviant strangeness reminiscent of such groups as Heaven's Gate or the Manson Family. I use the term instead in its neutral sense to denote a collective of devotees. "Cult" for my purposes denotes a community loosely cohered by belief in a particular folk saint. "Gaucho Gil's cult" is therefore more or less synonymous with "devotees of Gaucho Gil" or "the devotion to Gaucho Gil." When the word "Church" appears capitalized, it is a shorthand means of denoting the Catholic Church. The lower-case "church" refers to the building where devotion occurs. I use the word "miraculous" as a less cumbersome alternative to "miracle-working." And I generally use the Spanish term "curandero" unitalicized after an initial translation or definition.

For the most part, I have narrated from the perspective of devotees, without such qualifiers as "devotees believe that" or "according to traditional beliefs." Thus, for example, "Miguelito's remains tried to escape from their tomb," rather than, "According to devotees, Miguelito's remains tried to escape from their tomb." This makes for a more fluid prose while at once leaving questions of faith open to the discretion of each reader. When qualifiers concerning devotee beliefs are used, is it generally to stress a certain point or to enhance the contrast between historical and folkloric versions of a particular issue. Many observations are qualified with "some devotees believe" or "many devotees relate" in order to underscore a lack of consensus within a particular devotion.

I trust that it is apparent in the text when I am expressing my own opinion rather than reporting on the beliefs and practices of devotees. I personally have little religious belief in anything, but I find the folk-saint devotions described in this book to be extraordinary creative responses to deprivation and the failure of institutions. Folk-saint devotions are, for me, of the highest cultural value because they spontaneously and poetically express the very human determination to persevere against adverse circumstances beyond one's control. They emerge in the interactions of desperation and hope, of vulnerability and resilience, and they offer a unique entry into the logic and cosmovision by which millions of Spanish Americans order reality and negotiate everyday life.

The myths at the beginning of the featured-saint chapters are composites derived from various sources. They intend not to be historically accurate but rather to reflect prominent versions of the myths as related by devotees. Factual and chronological errors are common. In these narratives and throughout the study, all dates from oral traditions and nonhistorical sources are unverifiable and necessarily approximate.

Endnotes have been kept to an absolute minimum and in general are limited to proper acknowledgment of print and archival sources. I note the work of scholars when I include an original insight or the findings of original research, but not when the borrowed information (such as folk-saint biographies) is available in multiple sources. For overviews of regional folk saints, I am particularly indebted to the titles in the bibliography by Félix Coluccio, María de Hoyos and Laura Migale, and Miguel Raúl López Breard, for Argentina; and by Angelina Pollak-Eltz, for Venezuela.

Most of the primary print sources are from the Argentine folkloric surveys conducted periodically from the 1920s to the 1960s by the folklore commission of the Consejo Nacional de Educación. These surveys are archived at the Instituto Nacional de Antropología y Pensamiento Lationamericano and the Instituto Nacional de Investigaciones Lingüísticas y Filológicas, which I identify in the endnotes as INAPL and INILFI, respectively. Citation data was not always complete at the archives; I include in the notes whatever information was available. The same is true regarding news clippings consulted at libraries, museums, and shrines. Devotees who are discussed and quoted in the text are identified by their first names only.

Unless otherwise indicated, all of the photographs were taken by me during the 2001–2003 field research. Several galleries of additional photographs are available on the Web site designed to accompany this book: www.culturesofdevotion.com.

Acknowledgments

I send my first thanks out to the countless devotees who received me at their homes and shrines and graciously shared their faith.

I am also indebted to the many institutions that aided my research. In Argentina, the Difunta Correa Administration at the San Juan provincial government office in Caucete and the staff at the complex in Vallecito were helpful and accommodating. The administrators of the Gaucho Gil shrine and, particularly, the staff of the museum were likewise generous during my work in Mercedes. I am also grateful to the archives, libraries, and museums where I conducted research, among them the Archivo General de la Nación, Buenos Aires; Museo Policial, Resistencia; Museo del Hombre Chaqueño, Resistencia; Archivo Histórico, Provincia del Chaco, Resistencia; Archivo Histórico, Provincia de San Juan, San Juan; Biblioteca Franklin, San Juan; and Casa Natal de Sarmiento: Museo y Biblioteca, San Juan.

Very special thanks are extended to César Eduardo Quiroga Salcedo and the Instituto Nacional de Investigaciones Lingüísticas y Filológicas in San Juan; and to Catalina Saugy, Rubé Pérez Bugallo, and the Instituto Nacional de Antropología y Pensamiento Latinoamericano in Buenos Aires.

In Peru, research was conducted in the archives of the magazine *Caretas* and of the newspaper *El comercio*, both in Lima. I am also grateful to ATV/Channel 9, and to Gustavo Buntinx and the Casa de Cultura of the Universidad Nacional Mayor de San Marcos, both in

Lima. I also conducted research in the library of the Pontificia Universidad Católica del Perú, in Lima; in the social sciences library of the Universidad Nacional de San Agustín, in Arequipa; and in the library and photograph collection at the Centro Bartolomé de Las Casas, in Cuzco. I am most grateful to the staff at all of these sites for their kind assistance.

My sincere thanks are also extended to the many individuals who helped me in various ways during my research abroad. Among them, in Argentina, are Milciades Aguilar, of the Casa de Corrientes in Buenos Aires; Sebastián Savino and Mítico Producciones in Buenos Aires; Santiago and Graciela Gómez, Alfredo Videla, and Chiquita Benítez, in Mercedes; Hugo Alarcón in Goya; and Oscar Romero Giacaglia in San Juan.

The many individuals in Peru to whom I am grateful include Alejandro Ortiz Rescaniere, Teodoro Hampe-Martínez, and Judith Vélez in Lima; Jean-Jacques Decoster, Jorge Morales Zea, and Abraham Valencia in Cuzco; and David Brooks and Chris Teal at the United States Embassy in Lima.

Elsewhere I am indebted to Takahiro Kato in Kyoto, Japan; Favio Giorgio and the Casa Municipal de Cultura in Vallegrande, Bolivia; Alberto Salinas, Antonio Zavaleta, and the Niño Fidencio Research Project in Texas; and Layng Martine, Amy Lyon, and Systems Cowboy Media in New York.

My research for *Cultures of Devotion* was supported by the John D. MacArthur Chair at Connecticut College and a joint fellowship from the American Council of Learned Societies, the Social Science Research Council, and the National Endowment for the Humanities. A semester of research in Argentina, Bolivia, and Peru was funded by the Fulbright-Hays Program of the United States Department of Education. I am sincerely grateful to each of these funders, without whom the project would have been impossible.

Finally, I reiterate my most sincere and enduring gratitude to my editor at Oxford University Press, Cynthia Read.

Contents

Cultures of Devotion

Introduction

All things are possible for one who believes.
                    —Mark 9:23

I arrived in Goya, a small town in northeastern Argentina, with little
more than a phone number and a vague idea. The number was for
someone named Hugo; an anthropologist friend in Buenos Aires had
given me the lead. Years earlier I had heard of devotion to San La
Muerte (Saint Death) and knew that someday my interest would send
me in pursuit. This was someday: January 2001. In a rented car I
negotiated laneless swarms of Buenos Aires traffic, headed up the
Uruguay River toward the province of Corrientes, and rang up Hugo
in Goya.

He wasn't home. The hotel was grim and the desk clerk—he
looked like maybe his name was "Bruno"—seemed depressed. I hit
the streets to walk off a lingering road-weary fatigue and, a few blocks
away, happened upon a *santería* (a store selling saint images and
other objects of devotion). It was there that I purchased my first San
La Muerte. The image, about two inches tall, is carved in human bone
to represent personified death, like the Grim Reaper: a standing
skeleton holding a scythe. I put the carving, wrapped, in my pocket. It
later made it through U.S. customs but, back home, I was afraid to
bring it in the house.

Hugo returned my call while I was out walking, then showed
up in the lobby to await my return. We sat on his patio sipping

mate (a kind of tea) and getting acquainted while I explained the purpose of my visit. Like the many locals to whom I was later introduced, Hugo was surprised, even shocked, by the topic of my research. San La Muerte? That was a pagan belief to be avoided. Fear factored into the avoidance, because many believe that San La Muerte is vengeful and dangerous, but the dominant idea was that such devotions were idiosyncratic superstitions more worthy of eradication than scholarly attention, particularly that of a foreigner. Some also expressed the unease that my study of San La Muerte would give Americans the impression that Argentines were freaky.

Hugo had no personal acquaintance with San La Muerte devotees, so we began asking around. People tended to point up the road. We then focused the search on a *curandera* (healer) called Pirucha, who used San La Muerte in her rituals; I had heard about her in Buenos Aires. No one knew Pirucha when we inquired at a neighborhood store, but we discovered by chance that another folk healer, who likewise cured using San La Muerte, lived across the street. He was known as Papi. Whatever sanity that Papi may have once enjoyed was now little more than a fading memory.

It took some convincing to get Papi to open the door. When he finally let us in, he wasted no time in throwing the bolts behind us. The hallway was

Papi seated before his San La Muerte altar in Goya, Argentina.

dark. I had the idea that I might be sacrificed together with some chickens. Papi mumbled an incoherent monologue, explaining with muted terror that San La Muerte had sentenced him to death, that he was doomed. He was so overtaken by fear that two weeks earlier he had attempted suicide. The gun slipped off Papi's sweaty forehead, however, and he was only grazed by the bullet. San La Muerte then sent invisible men to murder him on Christmas Eve, but Papi fasted to ward off the assault. The death sentence was thus still pending.

Papi excused himself abruptly and headed down the hallway, mumbling. I was certain that he was going for the gun, that his delusion had pegged us for San La Muerte's goons on a wetwork contract. Or perhaps he had hit on the idea of leaving this world in good company. My instinct was flight and my first gesture was toward the door, but Hugo seemed relaxed and unconcerned—"He's crazy, no?"—so I calmed myself down and waited.

Papi's strange paranoia was my first contact with San La Muerte devotion, and standing between that door and Papi's imminent return—between the sword and the wall, as they say in Spanish America—I had the horrifying conviction that I was in over my head, that I should have put my affairs in order, that I had consigned myself to the study of a Satanic cult of lunatics.

A couple of years later, in 2003, I scheduled another research trip to coincide with the annual celebrations of San La Muerte's feast days in August. It was on this occasion that I began to understand that my initial impressions were far off the mark. Devotees to San La Muerte, like those to other folk saints, are predominantly quite normal people, like anyone else, and have strong traditional and family values.

There are, nevertheless, aspects of folk devotion that situate its adepts in a world far removed from the rational, scientific, and largely faithless world in which many people—including myself—now live. The world of folk saint devotion, and more broadly of folk Catholicism generally, is one in which supernatural beings (gods, saints, souls, spirits) are a prominent presence in everyday life. They intermingle with humans and have causal influence—magical and miraculous—on even the mundane matters of one's day-to-day routine. It is precisely this propensity for supernatural interventions, this profoundly religious disposition in a secular world, that distinguishes the devotees' reality from that perceived by hard rationality.

The more usual relations with a distant, silent God (and even the personal but formal relations with canonized saints) are displaced in folk devotion by an intimate familiarity with saints who are conceived as otherworldly extensions of their communities. The relation between devotee and folk saint is comfortable and interactive: a dialogue, a reciprocal exchange. Innumerable devotees describe their folk saint as a close friend and steadfast companion, as someone who is with them always, and with whom they converse, as many put it, "in the same way I'm talking to you."

"You can also feel him in your head. You can actually feel him with you," explains a devotee of Niño Fidencio. Respect, awe, and even fear are maintained while, at the same time, the relations are cordial and informal. One can joke with folk saints, drink with them, enjoy an old-friend familiarity, and address them by nicknames (San La Muerte, for example, is *Flaquito*— "Skinny") that underscore the relaxed intimacy of the relation. In this perspective, folk saints are hierarchical intermediaries situated between a distant God and informal people for whom faith and familiarity come naturally.[1]

The special world in which devotees live is well illustrated by an incident that occurred while I was attending a San La Muerte fiesta in Posadas, the capital of Misiones Province in northeastern Argentina. The evening began with performers—some local, others from neighboring regions—giving thanks to San La Muerte in song and dance. The traditional music (*chamamé*) and the corresponding dance (*bailantas*) were prominent, but the wide range of other styles that were also represented evidenced a freedom of expression, the right of each devotee to pay homage and express gratitude to San La Muerte in his or her manner.

Several groups had already performed and a large crowd had gathered when Arabic music began to play, and a young woman in belly-dancing attire appeared before San La Muerte's chapel. Carolina, the daughter of a dedicated devotee whose life was saved by San La Muerte, had made the promise to repay a miracle by belly dancing for seven consecutive years at the annual fiesta. Her promise included the tailoring of custom outfits and the choreographing of original dances that she would debut for San La Muerte.

Carolina had completed the first part of her performance to great applause, whistles, and cheers, but just as she was beginning the second dance a violent storm blew in, seemingly out of nowhere. Black clouds exploded into bolts of lighting, heavy rain, and pellets of hail blown sideways by strange winds. The crowds dispersed in an instant, the musicians ran to protect the amplifiers and speakers, and Pelusa, who presided over the event, looked pensive, heartbroken, and stern.

After the storm had passed and the mood calmed, Pelusa emerged from her ponderous withdrawal and gestured for Carolina. The two had a talk— Pelusa did most of the talking. She reiterated her frequent counsel concerning San La Muerte's jealousy, and it was then revealed, as Pelusa had expected, that Carolina's promise of a debut had been broken. Carolina confessed that she had performed the dance earlier and—to make matters worse—at a

Carolina, "the girl who made it rain."

religious event not affiliated with San La Muerte. Pelusa explained that the storm had come in punishment for this transgression—San La Muerte would not accept the used offering—and because of Carolina the entire celebration, along with the tremendous expense, planning, anticipation, and labor that made it possible, were ruined in an instant. Such was San La Muerte's power. And Carolina's. Her guilt concealed a quiet pride. She was, as Pelusa put it, "the girl who made it rain." The crowds were gone, the bands were sent home, the stage was taken down, and the party that usually went until daybreak was rained out well before midnight.

Driving back that night to my hotel downtown I had the sudden realization—or reaffirmation, really, of an unattended realization—that people standing beside one another, sharing the same spaces and experiences, can live in realities that are entirely different. Our shared experience comes, like truth, in versions, as evidenced so clearly by conflicting eyewitness testimonies.

And our physical proximity to one another as we move together through this world belies the mental, psychological, and emotional distances established by our beliefs, values, and the means by which we understand what we perceive. In my mind the dancing belly and the approaching storm had absolutely no relation, certainly not a causal one, but all the devotees remaining at the fiesta subscribed without doubt or hesitation to Pelusa's explanation that the storm was caused by Carolina's transgression and San La Muerte's wrath.

Something about their behavior nevertheless gave me the impression that ultimately the devotees understood that their consensus was forged by the willing suspension of disbelief. It was *as if* Carolina had caused the storm, but the moral lesson was nevertheless valid and the cause as real as the effect. They live within that "as if," I thought, because through it their world makes sense to them. Things were related, on earth and on high, and less was left to meaningless chance. "It was the first time I saw ice fall from the sky," Pelusa wrote to me a year later, "but it was a blessing and a warning."

I thus began to look at the people beside me at the market, in a line, in a movie theater, in a crowd crossing a street—people who shared my world spatially but had been cured of cancer by an amulet made of bone, or possessed by the spirit of a dead curandero, or cursed by inverted black candles lit on a Friday. I refer not only to poor and uneducated campesinos but also to the teachers, medical and legal professionals, accountants, engineers, psychologists, government officials, and countless other highly educated Spanish Americans who have deep faith in folk saints. While they go about their highly rational professions, they also believe that the skeletal remains of Niño Compadrito are growing, that Sarita Colonia walked on water, or that the channeled spirit of Pancho Villa effects miraculous cures.

As fantastic as such beliefs may seem, they are no more arational than the manifestations of folk Catholicism generally (the Crucified Christ appears in a tortilla, the baby Jesus escapes from church to play with local children) or even those of orthodox devotion (church statues cry, sweat, and bleed; saints fly; trees bow to praise the Lord; the Eucharist is transubstantiated into Christ's body). In all of these instances reason is subordinate to faith, and reality is ordered accordingly.

The potential for miracles can be jeopardized if reason elbows in with its complications. As evidence of Difunta Correa's miraculousness a devotee called my attention to the huge crowds and the countless offerings at the shrine. Soon a funny expression, troubled, came over his face, after which he observed that Difunta Correa must be something like a computer in order to keep track of the thousands of petitions and promises made to her daily. A brief, ponderous silence followed as he sorted his ideas, and when he resurfaced, calmer now, he added that in matters of faith it is best not to think too carefully.

The Living Dead

Rather than the terrible finality that death implies for most people in the United States, even for those who believe in a hereafter, death in Spanish American Catholicism implies more a change of state and status than a permanent absence from the world of the living. The dead are actors in everyday life. They communicate with the living (often in dreams) to exert their influence and offer their guidance. Together the living and the dead constitute a kind of extended family, a community divided between this world and the next. Visits to graves often include full conversations, sometimes after knocking ("It's me Dad, sorry I'm late") to get the attention of relatives resting in peace. It is quite common for people to request favors and miracles of their dead parents, often the mother. In some beliefs this occurs after a one-year waiting period, so the soul has time to get right with God.

The dead assist and protect their family members on earth, serving as intermediaries and advocates (presuming they are in heaven) between humans and God; and the living, reciprocally, attend duly to the needs and demands of the dead, receiving benefits for their devoted attention or, when remiss, suffering reprisals for insufficient care. Because the dead are alive in death, they require nourishment, company, affection, rest, respect, and other common human needs.

The rituals vary regionally, but care for the dead is particularly evident on November 1 (All Saints Day) and November 2 (All Souls Day, also known as the Day of the Dead). On these occasions Spanish Americans clean graves, leave flowers, light candles, make offerings of the food and drink that were preferred by the deceased, and share a meal, often followed by a party, with the dead in the cemetery. In some regions, these offerings may later be taken by people in need, provided that they pray for the rightful owner of the food. Some people also ritually feed their dead every Monday—the day associated with souls—by leaving food on the table for the nourishment of the deceased. The essence or nutrients of the offerings are absorbed by the spirits of the dead (some say via the aroma), while the material substance of the food—useless to spirits—stays behind, sometimes to be eaten by children.

The devotion to folk saints is clearly indebted to, if not derived from, this special relation of the living and the dead. Indeed, many folk devotions begin through the clouding of the distinction between praying *for* and praying *to* a recently deceased person. If several family members and friends pray at someone's tomb, perhaps lighting candles and leaving offerings, their actions arouse the curiosity of others. Some give it a try—the *for* and the *to* begin intermingling—because the frequent visits to the tomb suggest that the soul of its occupant may be miraculous. As soon as miracles are announced, often by family members and friends, newcomers arrive to send up prayers, now *to* the miraculous soul, with the hope of having their requests granted.

Something similar occurs at the sites of roadside deaths, usually marked by a cross or small shrine. Passersby stop to light candles or leave offerings, and if they are granted a miracle (which can be nothing more than a trip without mishaps or the help of a stranger with a flat tire), then they spread the word, others arrive to request miracles, and a new saint emerges.

Folk saints, in short, are very special dead people, beyond the norm in their willingness or capacity to intercede on behalf of their communities. They perform on a grand scale the role that a dead relative performs for the family. Thus many of the traditions surrounding folk saints (most of whom are venerated in cemeteries) are elaborations of the rituals devoted to a family's own dead. Cults devoted to the dead and to folk saints hold in common the "living" presence of the dead in everyday life, often in the form of close companionship, dialogue as though with a living person, and communication in dreams; ritual care that includes (in addition to prayer) banquets, parties, and offerings of preferred food and drink that are received through absorption of their essence; redistribution of the food (or other goods) that are offered to the dead saint; reprisals for insufficient care; and the performance of miracles. Even such details from ritual care of the dead as the knocking on the tomb and the taking of offerings in exchange for prayer are repeated in some folk devotions. And folk saint fiestas extend the day-of-the-dead idea that the dead prefer—in lieu of mourning—the joyful celebration of gathered family and friends.

This affinity of folk sainthood and the dead occurs within the broader context of a preoccupation with death in hispanic Catholicism generally. The churches of Spanish America are replete with imagery of death and suffering. The ubiquitous grizzly images of Christ—tortured, crucified, dead—provide the centerpiece, and they are complemented by skulls, hellscapes, martyrdoms, flagellations, and bone reliquaries.

Death in folk devotions differs from that of church Catholicism, however, insofar as the iconography of Christ and the saints serve more as models for meaningful suffering, for penance, and for consolation (by comparison with greater suffering) than they do as vehicles for positive, practical change. Folk-saint devotees may subscribe to the Catholic ideas and the corresponding religious practices, but they generally visit folk-saint graves with the express purpose of alleviating suffering. Death is not privileged for morbid attraction or passive contemplation, but rather for deployment of its otherworldly powers to improve one's life in this world.

Saints

The word "saint" is used far more broadly than to designate only those exemplary people who have been canonized by the Catholic Church. Folk saints are encompassed by the term, of course, but religious statues and paintings are also referred to as "saints." Spanish American Catholics know that, in theory, the statues and paintings are not one and the same with the saint, that they are visual aids to facilitate devotion to saints in heaven. In practice, however, the distinction dissolves because some statues and paintings are themselves believed to be miraculous. By re-presenting the saint, making him or her an almost living presence among the faithful, these images assume something of an independent identity. It is for this reason that long lines form and ex votos accumulate around one image of a particular saint—the image believed to be miraculous—while other statues and paintings of the same saint remain virtually ignored. The image itself has the miraculous power, which is derived from but no longer dependent upon the saint in heaven.

This presence of a saint on high in an object on earth is reminiscent of holy relics. Preserved body parts—bones, teeth, hair—make a spiritual presence tangible. During the early Christianization of Europe, relics were offered to new converts to replace their pagan idols. The predilection for immediate, material access to otherworldly powers gradually shifted toward more sophisticated miraculous objects, such as paintings and statues, and by the late Middle Ages these had displaced relics as the predominant receptacles of spiritual power.

The images of some folk saints today, notably Niño Compadrito and San La Muerte (both made of bone), are decidedly relic-like. They are also similar to the miraculous "saints" (paintings and statues) in churches because their power resides in a this-worldly object that is associated with a saint in heaven. Both of these folk saints have a dual access to power—as magical amulets or miraculous images and as saints—and this contributes substantially to their appeal. San La Muerte, which began as an amulet and gradually evolved into a folk saint, is particularly suggestive in this regard, because the magical properties of San La Muerte as a bone object and the religious belief in San La

Muerte as a saint in heaven are interacting aspects of single composite that is doubly empowered.

Advocations of Christ are also regarded as saints. When I inquired in Vallegrande, Bolivia, for the saints of greatest local importance, the response was uniformly the Lord of Malta, which is an image of the crucified Christ. The same extension of "saint" was evident in Cuzco, Peru, where such Christ images as the Lord of Huanca and the Lord of Earthquakes are called saints. Similarly, trees in the Andes that grow branches in the form of a cross are sometimes dressed to resemble Christ—there is one in Cachimayo, near Cuzco—and are referred to as "saints."

One effect of this broadened usage of "saint" is a leveling and then reordering of the Catholic hierarchy. In theory, almighty God remains at the top of the pyramid, with the saints below, but in practice an informal pantheon of more or less equal saints is established. Hierarchical rearrangements are then based less on dogma than on reputations for granting miracles. As expressed in a 1950 testimony from Corrientes Province, God "has been substituted by images." Therefore, "If you want to see a wish granted, just request it of some saint: he can do anything. He is God made visible." And consequently, "there is no one who does not have a saint."[2]

Most folk saint devotees have learned their catechism and can readily recite the theological nuance of intercession. They explain that Difunta Correa or Sarita Colonia or Gaucho Gil are not themselves empowered to perform miracles because they are only intermediaries, situated been their communities and God. Saints intervene on behalf of their devotees and distribute divine graces, but the miracles are granted by God alone. It is for this reason that folk saints, like canonized saints, are often referred to as *abogados*. (The term is usually translated as "lawyers," and some of that meaning obtains, but in this context the word is best rendered by "advocates.") Like their canonized counterparts, folk saints provide access and expedition. Sarita Colonia is sometimes regarded as Christ's *tramitadora*, meaning a facilitator who tends to the dispatch and details once the miracle has been granted by God. Many devotees refer to folk saints as instruments of God, as channels for miracles, or—in the metaphor used by a Gaucho Gil devotee—as bridges to God.

In practice, however, the God who performs the miracles tends to disappear into the background. The request for miracles are made to the folk saints, the granted miracles are credited to the folk saints, and the thanks, including prayer and offerings, are directed to the folk saints rather than to God. The plaques that cover the walls of shrines do not read, for example, "Thank you, God, for the miracle, and thank you, too, Difunta Correa, for helping out"; they read: "Thank you, Difunta Correa." Devotees' perceptions may vacillate between the theological model of intercession and the urge for a pantheon of demigods, but in everyday devotion the folk saints are godlike in their awesome power to perform miracles.[3]

The deification of folk saints is also apparent when devotees explain that Niño Fidencio is an incarnation of Jesus Christ or the Holy Spirit, and that María Lionza is a "creole Goddess who will save Venezuela." One devotee expressed his conviction by negation when he reported that Niño Compadrito appeared in a dream, "revealing that he was not God." In other cases, such as that of Gaucho Gil, the links between the folk saint and God are established by myths that build a Christlike hero, and by iconography—in Gaucho Gil's case the cross is prominent—that embellish a folk saint's identity with attributes proper to Christ.[4]

Folk saints, like canonized saints in folk Catholicism, also seem an informal pantheon of deities by virtue of their specializations. Saints emerge for the fulfillment of specific needs held in common by members of a community. The assignment of specialties, which resembles indigenous (and also pagan Roman) belief in multiple deities with specific functions, provides a versatile, otherworldly alliance for remedy of the world's diverse problems. Along the border between the United States and Mexico, for example, Niño Perdido and Juan Soldado protect soldiers sent to war, and Jesús Malverde (the "narcosaint") protects marijuana smugglers. Mexico's Niño Fidencio, who was a curandero during his lifetime, is outstanding in health-related miracles. The Venezuelan folk saint Juan Bautista Morillo helps gamblers, but he takes a cut of the earnings. Devotees leave Morillo's cut in a box at the shrine, and boys with bubblegum on sticks fish some of it out for reinvestment. "We're going gambling, Morillo," say devotees as they light candles at the shrine, "and if we win we'll bring you back your share." Gambling is also a specialty of San La Muerte, who in addition (like St. Anthony) is a specialist in finding lost objects.[5]

Specialties can also be indexed by the nature of offerings, such as wedding gowns offered by grateful brides to Difunta Correa. At the end of the school year in Salta, Argentina, students offer their books and notebooks to Pedrito Sangüeso, who died as a child, to thank him for help in passing the grade. Similar offerings, along with toys and stuffed animals, are made to other folk saints associated with childhood, among them Miguel Angel Gaitán, Pedrito Hallado, and Enrique Gómez, all of them Argentine; María Francia in Caracas; Niño Compadrito in Cuzco; and Carlos Angulo, known as "Carlitos," in Hermosillo, Mexico.

Most folk saints are generalists who perform miracles concerning health, family, love, and employment. Even folk saints who are known for specialties, including those relative to aspects of their identities, tend to be generalists first. The identities and specialties of folk saints can also mutate to meet the changing needs of devotees. Since the economic collapse of 2001 in Argentina, Difunta Correa has developed a strength in miracles concerning employment and family crises resulting from poverty. In this instance, as in most others, the requests are conditioned by the devotees' socioeconomic condition: some request bread for their children, and others ask for a car, a visa, or admission to a university in the United States.

The malleable identities of folk saints further provide devotees with the opportunity to customize their miracle worker along the contours of personal disposition and need. If one is sick, Niño Compadrito appears as a doctor; if one has legal problems, he appears as a lawyer. María Lionza is a mother, a queen, a water goddess, a guardian of nature, and a patron of love, fortune, fertility, and harvest; devotees make their approach at the point that best corresponds with their personal need. The same is true of other syncretic folk saints with multiple identities, notably Maximón, also known as San Simón, in Guatemala. Sarita Colonia is venerated by prostitutes because she escaped an attempted rape; by domestic servants because she was mistreated by her employers; and by fishermen and dock workers because she died in the ocean. When I asked a family why they were drinking wine at Sarita Colonia's tomb, they responded that Sarita liked wine (there is no evidence of this, not even in myth), so they were offering her toasts with the hope of a miracle for their sick mother, who was lying on the ground beside them.

The many identities that folk saints have within their devotions contrasts sharply with the uniformity of perception from outside. Nondevotees tend to stereotype the folk saints and condescend to their devotees. When I asked nondevotees in many Peruvian cities about Sarita Colonia, for example, she was uniformly described as the patron saint of thieves, though thieves account for only a small percentage of Sarita's devotees. The cults to San La Muerte and Niño Compadrito are widely regarded as diabolical—as forms of witchcraft—but the great majority of devotees use these saints' powers to beneficent ends. Such negative views of the folk saints themselves tend to be accompanied by commentary on the ignorance of the devotees, on the superstitious and idiosyncratic nature of their beliefs, and on the exploitation of credulous and desperate people by profiteers.

The dismissal of a particular folk saint, however, does not imply a comprehensive rejection of folk devotions. Those who ridicule one folk saint may well embrace another, or even beg the pardon of the first at a time of special need. This became particularly clear to me during my conversations with Santiago, a former engineer who is now a shop owner in Cuzco. Santiago expressed a mocking disbelief in Niño Compadrito, describing him as a dressed-up monkey skeleton exploited by its owners to live off donations. At the same time, however, Santiago believed that his requests for miracles were granted by the recently deceased Daniel Estrada Pérez, a former mayor and local hero among some Cuzco residents. Santiago also carried a black, oval stone that, he explained, had fallen to earth during a meteor shower. He pointed out the elongated face of Estrada Pérez that had miraculously appeared on the stone, but I was unable to decipher it.

Santiago thus rejected an existing Cuzco folk saint as a farce, opting instead to create an individualized devotion that served his needs and that guaranteed his independence from others who might condition or exploit his faith. His disdain was not for folk devotion generally, but only for a particular folk saint whom he regarded as inauthentic.

Tragic Death

Tragic death in its broadest sense—including violent, accidental, sudden, painful, youthful, and unjust deaths—is the principal generator of folk devotions. Those who become folk saints were burned to death, killed in traffic accidents, shot and stabbed, struck by lightning, drowned, frozen in the mountains, murdered during rapes and robberies, or executed unjustly. Peru's Rosita de Pachacutec was raped at the age of eight and died a few days later; Carballito, a blind man from Argentina, was tied to a tree and left to die; and Anima de Guasare was a Venezuelan truck driver who was killed in a traffic accident. A series of Argentine singers became folk saints following their tragic deaths: Carlos Gardel died in a 1935 plane crash; Gilda died young in a 1996 bus accident; and Rodrigo Bueno died young in a 2003 auto accident (on the same day as Gardel's death, June 24). The folk saints known as the Almitas González, also Argentine, were three young boys murdered by their father.

Sometimes the tragedy is less explicit, or less dramatic, but the deaths evoke exceptional sorrow, compassion, and pity. Such is the case of the Argentine folk saints known as Los Lucas Hallao, who were twins found dead at a cemetery gate. A channeled spirit revealed that Niño Perdido, a folk-saint of Mexican origin now venerated in south Texas, died of hunger and exposure as a baby after his father beat his mother to death and then abandoned the home. The alcoholic Finado Arrieta was found dead, partially eaten by pigs and birds, with a wine bottle beside him. And the folk saint known as El Carrerito in Chimbas, Argentina, was shot by mistake while urinating under a tree.

In some cases the death is tragic only insofar as it is the consequence of a miserable, suffered life with which devotees identify. These folk saints die of hunger, neglect, or simply poverty. Others, notably Niño Fidencio, are said to have died of overwork and neglect as they selflessly dedicated their lives to people who needed them. The life of Sarita Colonia is increasingly elaborated along these same lines. Her brother is the principal advocate of this position, and he describes Sarita as a generous and abnegate girl debilitated by her service to the poor.

The tragedy is often compounded by death's violation of youth and innocence. It is not necessarily the form of death that makes it tragic; sometimes it is the timing—the stolen youth—and death's indifference to decency, charity, beauty, and goodness. Many devotees describe such deaths as unjust. Sarita Colonia—young, pure, kind—is a prime example. Evita Perón, who died young of cancer and was venerated as a folk saint for decades, similarly inspired sorrow because the suffering and the premature death were unbefitting to a person so loving and charitable. In these two cases, like those of many other female saints, the exaggeration of beauty (along with other positive attributes) make death's cruel injustice all the more horrible and shocking.

Virginity can be a primary consideration in the imputation of folk sanctity, particularly among young females. La Finadita Juanita (like Sarita Colonia) is miraculous because "having died without [sexual] sin God granted her this power." In many cases, female folk saints become "victims of their own beauty," as worded in a description of Difunta Correa, which is to say that their beauty attracts violent men who ruthlessly impose themselves sexually. The themes of innocence, purity, fidelity, and chastity are stressed in these narratives, which also feature male antagonists intent on overpowering and violating such ideals while female protagonists struggle for their preservation.[6]

In one version of Difunta Correa's story, a police chief falls desperately in love—or lust—with the young Deolinda (the woman's name; *difunta*—or the male form, *difunto*—means "deceased"). He and other policemen began to harass Deolinda and pressure her family, hoping to coerce her surrender to their designs. Deolinda married another man instead, expecting that matrimony would provide safe haven. Her husband and father were soon forcibly recruited into the troops of civil war, however, and Deolinda, left behind, was again vulnerable to unwanted attentions. Rather than succumbing to the forces closing in on her, Deolinda left San Juan with her infant son, traveling toward La Rioja by an indirect route to foil the pursuit of the policemen stalking her. It was thus that she met her terrible demise: forced into flight, she lost her way and died of thirst and exposure on the desert. This version of the narrative, which is gaining popularity, stresses the role of a male (and police) antagonist and provides a quest for the preservation of purity as the indirect cause of Difunta Correa's death. It thereby parallels Sarita Colonia's case, in which likewise a historical version was revised by folklore to stress the virtues of chastity and purity.[7]

Violence and sexuality also combine in the narratives of many other folk saints, particularly in Argentina. Juana Figueroa was murdered by her husband because he suspected her of being unfaithful; María Soledad was seventeen when she was raped, murdered, and disfigured by two young men; Almita Visitación Sivila was raped, murdered, mutilated, and partially eaten by a man who had made unwanted sexual advances; Pedrito Sangüeso was raped and murdered at the age of six by a pedophile; Finadita Juanita died when a rejected suitor thrust a sword through her body; Juana Layme was killed by her husband while protecting her daughter from his incestuous advances; La Finada Ramonita was strangled by a jealous lover; and La Degolladita was murdered, along with her fifteen-year-old daughter, by a husband who discovered her infidelities. In Chihuahua, Mexico, near the Texas border, there are remnants of devotion to Difunto Leyva, who in the early nineteenth century had an affair with a married woman and was burned to death by her husband. El Tiradito, the subject of a Tucson, Arizona, devotion dating back to the nineteenth century, was likewise involved with an unfaithful wife and was murdered by her husband. Some say that his own father murdered him because he was having an affair with his stepmother.

The tragedy and injustice of the death are sometimes redoubled by error. Almita Silvia had gone shopping for a wedding dress with a male cousin, who casually put his arm around her shoulder as they walked across Jujuy's central plaza. Rumors of infidelity began to circulate, and when they reached Silvia's fiancé he took misguided revenge and murdered her. Another folk saint known as El Soldadito Desconocido (the Unknown Soldier) is said to have been a poor American who joined the Peruvian army after World War II. One night after curfew, while returning to the barracks from a visit with his girlfriend, he was killed in error by a patrol.

As suggested by this last example, the deaths of male folk saints are also embellished with romantic details that intensify the tragedy. No one knows much about Enrique Gómez, known as Enriquito, save that he was hit by a train (some say a car) when he was fourteen years old. Devotees acknowledge that the circumstances are unknown, then add that Enriquito had quarreled with his mother over a girlfriend and ran out of the house to his tragic death. The fugitive Francisco López, adept at evading the authorities, could not resist a visit to his sweetheart, which gave police the opportunity to ambush him. One version adds that during his final agony, after his throat had been slashed by the police, López held a hand over his heart while his voice, whispering the name of his beloved, escaped from the hole in his throat.[8]

A similar story, now enhanced by betrayal, is told of José Dolores, a gaucho folk saint from San Juan. Dolores had found work on a ranch and fell in love with a young woman who lived there. Her mother objected and recruited the assistance of a police sergeant—an eager co-conspirator because he was in love with the same girl, who was his niece. The mother and uncle together plotted against Dolores, then invited him to the party where he was ambushed by the police. Dolores, gravely injured, managed to escape but finally collapsed against a tree (his shrine was later built beside it). When the police caught up with him they shot him in the back, and the sergeant cut off his head.

The corrupt and abusive authorities who populate these narratives are essential to the formation of folk saints. López, Dolores, and many other outlaws rise to sainthood in part because their stories represent, in the extreme, the everyday plight of poor people. Each executed hero is a hyperbole of a social group that is subjected to excessive force and sentenced to slow death by hard labor. The underclasses, like their folk saints, are pushed to the margins and suffer the injustices of social, political, and economic systems that privilege others at their expense.

Those who are courageous enough to challenge such oppression, to live outside of the law for the benefit of impoverished peoples, are deemed worthy of praise rather than punishment. They are folk heroes before they become folk saints, and their Robin Hood mission of protecting and providing for the poor is continued after death through miracles. The revolutionary Pancho Villa championed the causes of the poor (until he was assassinated in 1923) and today, as a folk saint, continues to do so for many Mexicans and Mexican Americans. His power, courage, and prowess are petitioned not for violent or insurrectional purposes, however, but rather to survive on the battlefield of everyday life. As expressed in one prayer, "I ask for your spiritual protection, so that you free me of all evil and give me the necessary strength and enough courage to face even the most difficult things that life presents."[9]

Such folk saints as Gaucho Gil, Gaucho Lega, Gaucho Cubillas, Bazán Frías, Bairoletto, and Isidoro Velázquez all developed reputations (greatly enhanced by post-mortem elaborations) as noble bandits. They stole from the rich out of necessity rather than greed, and they distributed the spoils among the poor. Many of the gauchos who become folk saints were forced outside the law for deserting civil wars into which they had been conscripted to kill other exploited people like themselves. If they stole now, it was to retrieve their stolen lives and to survive as best they could. They turned the corrupt system against itself and stood up as defiant avengers, settling scores with the public enemies to whom others meekly submitted out of fear. And in their almost magical evasion of police and soldiers, they made a mockery of oppressors and gave defeated people a measure of hope.

The noble outlaw's celebrity and life of crime generally end in a shootout or summary execution. Gaucho Lega was imprisoned for murder, escaped after twelve years of incarceration, and met his death two years later in a shootout with police. Gaucho Cubillas effectively evaded the police until they killed him in his sleep. Bairoletto was accused of murder, imprisoned, and released to a new life of crime that ended twenty years later in the usual bloodbath. And Bazán Frías, also a career criminal, was killed by police after he escaped from prison.

These unlikely candidates for sainthood, all of them Argentine, are complemented by several Venezuelan folk saints of a similar prototype. The Venezuelan cases, however, are more explicitly political. Santiago Melgar Contreras, who stole from the rich to give to the poor, was killed by Caracas police for leading an armed rebellion against the Marcos Pérez Giménez dictatorship. José Crisel Somoza, known as "Montenegro," has a similar story. Having abandoned a position with the police's secret anti-insurrectional forces, he joined a guerrilla group and stole from the rich to give to the poor until he was killed during a shootout in Guárico. The folk saint known as Machera, killed by police in Mérida at the age of twenty-two, was likewise a regional Robin Hood. José Antonio Orasma was imprisoned after murdering a rich, powerful, and detested landowner. Upon release, to avenge what he considered an injustice, he became a smuggler, cattle rustler, and allegedly the leader of a kidnap-and-ransom operation. The spoils of this decidedly classist struggle were shared with the poor until Orasma was finally killed by his enemies. The son of a landowner was accused of the crime but later was acquitted.

The execution makes the folk hero a martyr and, eventually, if miracles are granted, the martyrdom becomes the basis for sainthood. The spilled blood catapults the victim to heaven, the Robin Hood mission continues through miracles, and the execution ultimately benefits the oppressed community. The people are deprived a hero but awarded a saint.

At times these ideas gain figurative expression in folk saint narratives. Whether Jesús Malverde actually existed is uncertain, but he is believed to have been a noble bandit around Culiacán, in northwestern Mexico, in the early twentieth century. Malverde had been wounded in the leg and was dying of gangrene, so he instructed his partner to kill him, to cut off his head in order to collect the reward from the governor, and then to distribute the reward money to the poor. The funds of an inequitable system were thereby redistributed through Malverde's self-sacrifice. When his Robin Hood mission was no longer possible, the moribund Malverde found an alternative means to assist the poor. That mission continues after death through miracles. Oppression is transformed into social service.

Any crimes that may have been committed by folk saints are dismissed (the folk saint was innocent), interpreted as acts of saintly generosity, and neutralized by excessive punishment. The neutralization—a kind of purge—results from the immeasurably greater criminality of unwarranted or extrajudicial executions. The net effect is expressed in a 1921 report on Francisco López: "A dead man who was shot unjustly is venerated."[10]

The public execution or the display of brutalized corpses redoubles the horror—the shock of the kill—and combines with the perceived injustice to galvanize the folk saint's martyrdom. The nature of the crime is no longer important, because the nature of the punishment has overwhelmed it. It is for this reason that folk sainthood can accommodate rapists and murderers as readily as it does their victims. The two groups hold in common their respective tragedies: one the victim of a brutal crime, and the other the victim of a brutal punishment.

If abuse by authorities is lacking in a folk saint's narrative, then folklore makes the necessary compensations. Police and soldiers are the usual suspects. The attempted rape that results in Sarita Colonia's death is attributed to policemen or soldiers because they represent a system that is violating and rapacious toward marginal social groups. The idea is all the more compelling because police and soldiers in fact had nothing to do with Sarita's death. Their responsibility for this crime that never occurred is derived from the ideas and experiences of devotees who collectively, over time, build a saint as an extension of themselves. The devotees self-identify as victims of an inequitable and abusive society enforced by police and soldiers, and Sarita is fashioned accordingly. The abusive system is thus again turned against itself, because Sarita evades the rape, reaches heaven, and gains miraculous powers to protect her victimized community. A people's chronic sense of victimization is vindicated through its victimized folk saint.[11]

If a tragic death is lacking in a folk saint's story, then myths can make adjustments and compensations. Sarita Colonia actually died of malaria, not while escaping an attempted rape. Myths concerning Niño Compadrito, about whom nothing historical is known, relate that he was kidnapped as a child and tortured to death. San La Muerte, whose identity was also entirely constructed by folklore, starves to death in a leper's cell where he was imprisoned by jealous priests. When unknown corpses or skeletons are found, similarly tragic deaths are invented for them, miracles are requested, and new devotions commence if the results are positive.

A tragic death was also provided for Niño Fidencio in Mexico, who died of natural causes. The story is told in two related versions. In the first, Niño Fidencio had died but was going to resurrect, like Christ, on the third day. After two days he was prevented from resurrecting by jealous doctors who insisted on doing embalmment or autopsy procedures.

The alternative version relates that Niño Fidenco was sick and in need of rest after a long period of intense overwork. He had gone into a three-day trance to recharge his powers, leaving orders that his body was not to be touched, but his adoptive father, Enrique López de la Fuente, thought that he had died. In this version as in the first one, doctors were called to do an autopsy or embalm the body, and either by error or by evil intent they killed Fidencio by slitting his throat. (In some versions the doctors refuse to cut the body, fearing for their lives at the hands of followers, and veterinarians finally do the dirty work.) A photograph of the dead Niño Fidencio circulates widely among devotees, and many relate that the body's open mouth releases Fidencio's scream upon being murdered.

Tragic death is critical to folk sainthood not only because its shock arouses compassion, but also because it cancels debt in the economy of sin and atonement. Unjust or unwarranted deaths are a kind of purgatory on earth that cleanses sin and sends one's soul directly—or at least more quickly—to heaven. Excessive violence, stolen youth, the spilled blood of innocents, and other tragedies expedite the process of purification. They are, as one Gaucho Gil devotee put it, shortcuts to God. When I asked in San Juan why Difunta Correa is so miraculous, her devotees responded similarly that she suffered at the time of death and consequently is now close to God. Some describe her miraculous power as a reward granted by God in appreciation of the sacrifice and martyrdom. "Because she suffered during her death," explains a 1926 testimony, "God gave her the power of a Saint."[12]

The idea of a pure soul going straight to heaven is most explicit when death visits infants and young children. If they are baptized and thus cleansed of original sin before their deaths, these *angelitos* (little angels) are the epitome of purity and are admitted directly to heaven. Pedrito Hallado (*hallado* means "found") was a newborn abandoned in 1948 at the gate of a cemetery in Tucumán. He was baptized just before his death, his sinfree soul went directly to heaven, and from this privileged position beside God he performs miracles for his devotees. The folk saint Miguel Angel Gaitán, known as Miguelito or the Angelito of La Rioja, was similarly endowed with his powers. Miguelito died of meningitis in 1967, shortly before his first birthday, and went straight to heaven. On earth, however, his corpse kept trying to escape from its tomb. Miguelito's parents finally understood the message and put his mummy-like remains on display, in a glass-top coffin, so that Miguelito could visit with his devotees.

"Rebirth" can also open the gates of heaven by recuperating one's childlike purity. The Peruvian folk saint Víctor Apaza, from Arequipa, was sentenced to death for murdering his wife. He had converted earlier in his life to Evangelical Protestantism, but he returned to Catholicism shortly before facing a firing squad. On the day before his execution, Apaza made his confession and took communion. After midnight he took communion again, and right before his execution he received a blessing, kissed the crucifix, and returned the rosary he was wearing to the chaplain. In local legend he was holding a bible when he was shot. Apaza therefore died free of sin, in the likeness of an angelito, "clean before God." Innocent as a child and innocent (according to devotees) of the crime, Apaza's purity afforded entrance to heaven and at once made his tragic death all the more unjust.[13]

The implied penance that underlies Apaza's rebirth is explicit in the story of La Chavela (Isabel Escobar), also from Arequipa. According to tradition, La Chavela was a beautiful woman who had committed some crime—many say murder—against a husband or lover. She subsequently fled from Chile to Peru and arrived in Arequipa around 1918, when she was about twenty years old. Sad, down-and-out, alcoholic, and defeated, La Chavela supported her joyless life by singing for tips—often drinks and cigarettes—in low-life bars. "One pays for what one does," she would say, "and I am paying here." During this penitential existence she desired neither love nor sexual encounters, and she maintained her dignity by evading the advances of the many men who sought her favors. Those who imposed themselves were frightened off by the red spots that she painted around her pubis to feign a venereal disease. After some ten or fifteen years La Chavela died of her lifestyle, and a collection was taken for her burial. Rather than being dismissed as a worthless drunk, however, her life was viewed as a purifying penance and her avoidance of sexual relations as evidence of her seriousness of purpose. La Chavela thus gained access to God, and her down-and-out community gained an advocate in heaven. Instead of requesting songs, people began to request miracles.[14]

La Chavela's sins were neutralized by a kind of purgatory on earth, but in other cases—notably those of Apaza and the outlaw folk saints—the sins are purged by execution. The tragic deaths of executed folk saints are viewed as sacrificial, and accordingly, as in Christ's crucifixion, the sins are washed away with the spilled blood of innocents. The etymology of sacrifice, which means "to make sacred," captures the idea precisely: these folk become saints not so much by virtue of their lives (although folklore makes postmortem compensations) as by virtue of their deaths. Spilled blood is miraculous, particularly when it is spilled unjustly or by authorities regarded as abusive, illegitimate, or corrupt. True justice is recuperated on high when Christ, himself a victim, receives into sainthood these tragically dead people, misfits among them, because their deaths have purified their lives. The folk saint's tragic death is creatively reconceived as an affirmation of life. Just as guilt becomes innocence and the outcast becomes a saint, so too defeat is recast as victory and helplessness is channeled toward empowerment through miracles.

Folk Healers

Tragic death is the highway to folk sainthood, but fame as a curandero provides an alternate route. The outstanding example, Niño Fidencio, is from northern Mexico, a region that has also produced such curandero saints as Teresa Urrea and Don Pedrito Jaramillo. Pancho Sierra and Madre María were Argentine curanderos who became folk saints, and there are many others of local importance, such as Pedro Mariscal in Cachi (Salta), and La Finada Chabela in San Pedro (Jujuy). Among Venezuelans are Rosendo Mendoza, Flores Brito, Jacinta Flores, and María Catalina, as well as José Gregorio Hernández, a bona fide medical doctor who became a folk saint by virtue of his dedicated care of the poor.

A tragic death is not necessary for curanderos who reach sainthood by virtue of good deeds, but if a tragedy does occur (even if only in myth) it catalyzes the rapid development of the cult. Such was the case with José Gregorio Hernández, who was run over by a car in 1919. Another Venezuelan medical doctor, Pablo Valera, was also killed in a car accident and is today venerated in the cult of María Lionza. As noted earlier, Niño Fidencio's natural death was elaborated into a murder. Argentina's San La Muerte is attributed both fame as a curandero and slow death by starvation while imprisoned.

These tragic deaths give a boost to the devotion, but life accomplishments are crucial to the identity of curandero saints. Death is stressed for those who reach sainthood through tragedy, and life deeds are predominant for those who become folk saints through healing. Love of one's neighbor, imitation of Christ, selfless giving, abnegate dedication to the well-being of others, and effective alleviation of suffering are the characteristic attributes of curandero folk saints.

Health-related miracles are prominent in all folk saint devotions. Many folk saints who were curanderos during their lifetimes continue healing today, sometimes through mediums who channel their spirits. One may request well-being of Niño Fidencio directly, through prayer, or one may visit a medium (known as a *materia*) who is filled with Fidencio's spirit and heals with his powers. The same is true of Don Pedro Jaramillo, who, like Fidencio, is revered as a folk saint and is channeled as a spirit. Countless curanderos in Argentina heal with the powers of San La Muerte or Gaucho Gil; Sarita Colonia's sister, among others, conducts healing rituals using water and flower petals from Sarita's tomb, which she rubs onto the bodies of ailing devotees; and curanderos from as far away as Puno recruit the powers of Víctor Apaza for healing.[15]

In these last instances the spirits are not channeled. Instead, the curanderos make an appeal to the saint in heaven through rituals and prayers. Isabel, a curandera whom I met at the Gaucho Gil shrine, explained that she cures "in the powerful name of God the Father, the Son, and the Holy Spirit, and Lord San La Muerte and Antonio Gil," asking them to do their will through her. Isabel also explained that Gaucho Gil cured animals with the touch of his hands, and that his spilled blood cured his executioner. Blood that squirted from Francisco López's slit throat similarly cured the paralysis and rigidity in the hands of two of his executioners. These time-of-death cures—even before sacrifice expedites one to heaven—literalize the belief that innocent victims are miraculous.

Cures performed by the laying on of hands were prominent in antiquity and in the Middle Ages, when physical contact with an empowered person—sometimes a king by divine right—was sufficient to effect a cure. Faith healing is still an important aspect of many religions, notably Christian Science, Pentecostalism, and charismatic Catholicism. Christ himself rose to notoriety in part because of his health-related miracles. He healed a leper with his touch and words (Mark 1:40–42) and a blind man with his touch and saliva (Mark 8:22–25), and he felt spiritual power flowing out of him when a hemorrhaging woman cured herself by touching his garment (Mark 5:25–34).

A Catholic priest in Cuzco—one who had said masses for Niño Compadrito until he was censured by the bishop—surprised me when he related that he healed parishioners by laying on his hands. The power came from the Holy Spirit, he explained. When I pressed the issue—Why are some people cured, and others not?—he replied that the cure works if one really wants to be cured, if one is "psychologically" (his word) predisposed to the cure.

Curanderos are indeed folk psychologists, and some explain that a great part of the cure is simply listening and offering sound advice. "It's counseling and comforting and consoling," explained one curandero who channels the spirit of Niño Fidencio. Madre María was exceptional in this regard: "Her voice alone was a soothing balsam." One of her followers related that she conversed with her patients face-to-face, listening carefully, and then gave advice. He added: "One could almost say that she was the psychoanalyst of her times." A report from Corrientes in the 1950s generalized that observation by stating that curanderos, still called *médicos* (doctors) today, "generally try to study the psychological state of the patient, inspiring them with encouragement and faith."[16]

When Niño Fidencio was alive and working wonders in Espinazo, he was adept at using punishment, reward, fear, anticipation, humor, shock, entertainment, and other psychological strategies to effect his cures. Sometimes insight is the curandero's best asset. A woman suffering from migraines visited Don Pedrito Jaramillo, who prescribed cutting off her head and feeding it to the pigs. Her headaches went away. In other cases, the miracle of the cure seems predisposed by the nature of the illness. A message to Carlos Gardel at his tomb in Buenos Aires, for example, thanks the singer "for having cured me of depression listening to your tangos." Another devotee acquired a facial paralysis during a depression related to lost love but was cured after prayer to Sarita Colonia.

When curanderos channel the spirits of folk saints, notably in the devotions to Niño Fidencio and María Lionza, they provide for their patients a heavenly interlocutor who offers advice that is out of this world. The discourse is routed through a medium, but it belongs to a saint in heaven who takes personal interest in a devotee's problems. That recognition in itself can be half the cure. In cults in which spirits are not channeled, otherworldly advice comes to devotees directly, usually in dreams, and is readily heeded because its origin is supernatural. Even healing can occur in dreams. A woman who had an eye problem was cured in a dream by "Dr. Niño Compadrito, who was dressed like a doctor." He removed the malady from her eyes with his tiny hands, then reminded her that the arrangement was reciprocal, that he needed her help too.[17]

Many of the diverse people whom I interviewed—shrine owners, devotees, priests—explained that folk devotions are rooted in the fundamental human need for recognition, self-worth, and security. This need remains unfulfilled for most devotees, who struggle for survival on the margins of society. "Give me a sign," wrote one to Sarita Colonia, "I feel confused and need you to get better." These common sentiments were also expressed at the opening of a letter to Niño Compadrito: "I don't know where to go I don't know who to ask for the chance to get out of this misery and uncertainty of not knowing what will come tomorrow." Economic instability is conducive to and compounded by insecurity, uncertainty, disorientation, and dwindling self-esteem. The feeling that there is nowhere else to turn, which is often expressed by devotees, makes the folk saint shrine an extraordinary resource.

"Many people just need someone to talk to," shrine owners explain. They need someone who takes their individual importance into account, who cares enough to hear them out. The effectiveness of domestic shrine owners in counseling and consoling devotees directly affects the shrine's success and, perhaps, the miraculousness of the saint. Devotion to Niño Compadrito grew substantially because María Belén, then the owner of the effigy, offered compassionate consolation and advice to those who came to her in need. The highly regarded San La Muerte shrines also owe their success to owners, such as the late Porota in Barranqueras, who are empathetic and have strong interpersonal skills. Older women appear to excel at this potent combination of their own therapeutic personalities and a folk saint's otherworldly graces. Visits to the saint and the matron mutually enhance one another. The miracle results from the collaboration of their talents and powers.

That is why the "talking cure" is particularly effective in religious contexts: the consolation is backed up supernaturally. Aquiles, a carver of San La Muerte, talks devotees through crises by cellular phone while serving a life sentence in prison. His success in doing so owes to his compassion and insightfulness, but also to the mystique that imprisoned carvers enjoy among devotees. Intimacy with San La Muerte and the allure of his profession lend special resonance to the advice of Aquiles.

Oscar, who evokes Gaucho Gil for healing in Saladas, explained that people waste a lot of money on unsuccessful treatments by psychologists, then come to him and get well for free. He was eager to make this unsolicited comparison of himself and psychologists, and he repeated it, but he made no mention of the physical healing for which curanderos are more widely reputed. Perhaps his implication was that even the physical ailments treated by folk saint curanderos are to a great degree remedied psychologically.

Physical, psychological, and spiritual factors intermingle in the ritual purifications know as *limpias* (cleansings) or *la barrida* (literally "sweeping"). The purpose of these rituals is to extract various (but not clearly differentiated) impurities from the body, including diseases, evil spirits, curses, and psychological or spiritual maladies. Ritual cleansing is done by rubbing the body with prescribed objects—eggs are frequently used—that absorb impurities, or by "sweeping" the body with the branches of certain trees, bushes, or herbs. Candles are sometimes passed over the body and then burned in offering while beseeching well-being from a folk saint. Curanderos also jerk the body

Oscar cures using the powers of Gaucho Gil in Saladas, Argentina.

to *desalojar* (remove, literally dislodge) negative spirits or elements that have inhabited it.

Spiritual cures are a response to the belief that some maladies have non-biological causes, such as God, magic, envy, evil spirits, and curses. Curanderos generally heal their patients through some combination of religion (prayers and rituals), traditional medicine (herbs, salves), medical practices (surgery, tooth extraction), and folk psychology. One of the earliest documents of medical historiography, the Egyptian Papyrus Ebers (ca. 1500 B.C.), attests to the long history of spiritual and medical collaboration. The introduction to the document notes that "the Lord of All has given me words to drive away the diseases of all the gods and mortal sufferings of every kind." Remedies given later in the text, however, are more practical, suggesting that these words in themselves are insufficient. A crocodile bite, for example, is treated by laying raw meat on the wound. Contemporary curanderos, like these early Egyptian physicians, avail themselves of multiple remedies, even if the use of one belies the belief in another.[18]

The medical practices of curanderos are ritualized, however, and are thereby integrated into the religious context in which they occur. If the power to heal originates with God, then everything done in His name, even surgery, is essentially religious. The medical and the religious become inalienable aspects of a single, multifaceted procedure. A remedy for a snake bite, for example, might require slashing the wound with the sign of the cross, sucking out the venom, and then praying during ritual cleansings. In the cult to María Lionza there are actual or "open" operations, which are performed by a spirit who possesses the body of a medium-surgeon, and there are spiritual operations, which are performed without cutting open the body. During symbolic surgeries, a tiny slit is made, sometimes in the abdomen, and through it the possessed medium extracts the illness.

Mediums and curanderos heal not with their own powers but rather with the supernatural forces that flow through them. "Lord, I am only your instrument," wrote Niño Fidencio to God in 1929, and he similarly explained to reporters: "I only distribute the medicine that God put in my hands. He is the one who heals; I serve as his instrument and nothing more." All of the great curanderos have made similar statements, and today this conceding of power to God (rather than claiming it as one's own) is regarded as one of the two measures of a curandero's authenticity. "I don't have the power to heal," said Don Pedrito Jaramillo. "What heals is the power of God, through your faith."[19]

The other measure of authenticity concerns payment: a taboo prohibits that curanderos charge for healing, because they are God's instruments and doing God's work. Niño Fidencio believed that he would lose his curative powers if he were to charge his patients. Voluntary donations may be accepted, and this is the common practice today. If large sums are acquired, however, they are properly used not to enrich oneself but rather to improve one's service as a curandero, to help others in need, or to enhance the devotion (by building or expanding a chapel, for example, or by sponsoring an annual fiesta).[20]

In many regions the curanderos who charge for cures are considered frauds, as are those who profit from false remedies and other abracadabra paraphernalia that are marketed to desperate people. Some San La Muerte myths incorporate the taboo against charging into the narrative of the saint's origins. Papi, the curandero from Goya who feared for his life, got himself on San La Muerte's hit list precisely because he imposed obligatory charges for healing. Pirucha, the curandera I was searching for when I met Papi, explained that health-related sessions must be free or by voluntary donation, but curanderos may charge for other types of consultations, such as those concerning love, since these are a kind of luxury service. In all cases one must be charitable and not businesslike or exploitative, Pirucha explained, because San La Muerte served others selflessly even though he was very poor.[21]

Why Folk Saints?

Folk saint devotees are almost exclusively Catholic and have access to a multitude of canonized saints, all of whom are recognized as miraculous. Rather than contenting themselves with these diverse options, however, they supplement the canon by creating new saints—folk saints—despite the explicit disapproval of the Church. Why would Catholics prefer folk saints to canonized saints, even to the degree of tolerating censure and oppression in order to persevere in an unauthorized devotion?

As I listened to hundreds of devotees in five countries answer this and related questions, I came to understand that the reasons are rather standard. Those most mentioned by devotees include a preference for *lo nuestro* ("what is ours," meaning saints belonging to a given community and its culture); a desire for freedom of devotion, without the mediation, restrictions, and costs of clergy; and the belief that folk saints are more miraculous than canonized saints. Most devotees also point out that folk saints supplement Catholicism rather than replacing it. The general context for the emergence of folk saints is one of profound disillusion with religious and secular institutions.

Inclusion

Folk saints are informal additions to the Catholic canon, supplements that diversify and customize sainthood to suit particular needs. Inclusion is the rule, and devotion to folk saints thrives, in part, because it does not require abandonment of other religious beliefs or practices. Catholicism is not so much abandoned as expanded; it is stretched to encompass exceptional resources. Whereas Catholicism (like scholarship) defends a distinction between canonical and noncanonical or orthodox and heterodox, folk devotion intermingles these quite naturally and without reserve. The same is true of religion and magic. They flow back and forth into and over one another, as do high culture and popular culture, sacred and profane, sacraments and folk rituals, polytheism and monotheism, and indigenous and Roman Catholic religions. All of these constantly renegotiate their volatile and multiple interrelations. Amulets, black magic, spells, and secret potions mix freely with Catholic and quasi-Catholic prayers, rituals, and images. Folk devotion draws upon every resource in the arsenal.

The inclusive appeal to all available resources is particularly evident when devotees seek miracles concerning health. Those who request miraculous cures from folk saints generally do so in addition to consulting medical professionals and to praying to Christ, the Virgin, and canonized saints. Catholicism and medicine are the existing institutional resources, necessary but not sufficient, and the folk saint is a kind of secret weapon deployed as urgency warrants. The visits to medical doctors are often complemented by visits to curanderos, so that institutional and popular medicine interact together with institutional and popular religion.

Folk saint altars also evidence a spirit of plurality. With the occasional exception of San La Muerte, who in traditional veneration requires his own altar, devotees mix and match at will. Saints of all sorts are freely intermingled. In some cases the included Catholic images are purposefully selected; in others their presence reflects the chance inclusion of whatever was at hand. The latter was true of an altar in Resistencia, which was populated more or less at random by the statuettes left behind by a deceased mother. When I asked Pirucha why St. Joseph was on her San La Muerte altar, wondering if she might make reference to Joseph as patron saint of the dying, she looked at me with a strange expression of surprise—almost a snarl—and responded, "Because he is the father of the Lord." The wallet-sized images of Sarita Colonia allow for personal preference with a mix-and-match assortment of options on the flip side: St. Martin de Porres, the Lord of Miracles, St. Christopher, and St. Rose of Lima, among others.

Folk saints are also intermixed with one another, despite the belief that some are jealous and demand exclusive veneration. Generally a devotee has a favorite folk saint, and one or two others might be added to the favorite's altar. It is also quite common to see one folk saint represented at the public shrine of another, which in turn fosters double or multiple devotions among visitors. The José Dolores chapel in San Juan houses images of Gaucho Gil and Difunta Correa, the two brightest stars of Argentine folk sanctity, and in Peru, the shrine of Rosita de Pachacutec includes a prominent image of Sarita Colonia. A wide range of folk saint images are sold during Niño Fidencio fiestas in Espinazo, and many mediums channel these spirits in addition to Fidencio's. In other cases, the connections are more surprising, and unwitting. A young Peruvian woman was eager to show me a special prayer said to Niño Compadrito on the Day of the Dead, and it turned out to be a prayer to San La Muerte that I had seen many times in the Corrientes and Chaco Provinces of Argentina.

Folk devotions are characteristically receptive to outside influences, beliefs, and practices that are selectively and syncretically absorbed to the cult's advantage. Thus they are always changing, as they are designed and redesigned by and for the people who practice them. Many of the devotions, like

many of the devotees, are hybrids of indigenous, European, and African traditions. The syncretism attests to the devotees' capacity to reinterpret and appropriate, to dialectically transform the contributing factors into new cultures and
religious beliefs.

The Venezuelan cult to María Lionza well exemplifies this selective borrowing and assimilation of outside influences. This devotion is an amalgam of
indigenous beliefs and practices, western African and Afro-Caribbean religion,
popular Catholicism, and Kardecist spiritism. At the summit of a hierarchy
(that is reminiscent of the structure of Santería), María Lionza presides over a
pantheon of lesser saint-gods organized into courts. She is flanked at the
summit by the indigenous leader Guaicaipuro (sometimes spelled Guacaipuro)
and Negro Felipe, who together form an interracial trinity above which the
colors of the Venezuelan flag are represented. The assimilation of outside
influences is particularly evident in the lower courts, which include established
and emerging folk saints, heroes of Spanish American independence, and a
cast of such imported characters as John F. Kennedy, the pope, television
celebrities, and Mister Guillette [sic], who was derived from Gillette razor blade
advertisements.[22]

The racial representation at the summit and in the courts also attests to
an egalitarian inclusivity that is characteristic of folk devotions. Everyone is
welcome. Race and class are insignificant. Faith is all one needs. Even transvestites, who are stigmatized in Peruvian society at large, move about freely at
the biannual Sarita Colonia fiestas, with no apparent prejudicial treatment. San
La Muerte and Niño Fidencio cared for lepers, which are the paradigm of
ostracized humans. Folk saint devotions, like all social organizations, have
inner circles and certain implied hierarchies, but they otherwise tend toward
receptivity and equal access.

One afternoon at Sarita Colona's shrine a man entered, somewhat ten-
tatively, with a plaque to thank Sarita for a miracle. He was unknown to the
people who tend the shrine but was graciously received by one of them,
Arturo. The man explained his purpose, and Arturo helped him find a place
where the plaque could be affixed to the crowded walls. I was struck by how
collaboratively the decision was made—"Would you like it here? Or how about
here?" The devotee was timid and seemed amenable to any of the proposed
locations, but then Arturo noticed a vacant space at one of the most sacred
places in the shrine, where an older plaque had fallen off.

The newcomer couldn't believe his luck: his plaque would be situated on
the case that housed Sarita's photograph, just above her head. It was like a
second miracle. I too was struck by how this privileged location was made
available by chance to whoever happened to walk through the door at the right

moment. Arturo and the happy devotee proceeded to go about affixing the plaque, but then it turned out that the shrine was out of glue.

Lo nuestro

When explaining why they prefer a given folk saint to a canonized saint, devotees emphasize the close cultural relation that binds them to their devotion. The folk saint "is like us," they say, "one of us." This identification is established and maintained by a web of interrelations that includes heritage and traditions, a strong sense of place, problems held in common, and socioeconomic marginality. Regional pride, sometimes forged in opposition to incursion or domination by outsiders, also contributes to the preference for local folk saints. In some regions, such as northeastern Argentina, there is a strong sense of communal solidarity, almost a brotherhood, that fosters the emergence, defense, and sanctification of heroes with "blood of our blood."

As explained by Ramón, a San La Muerte devotee in Resistencia, folk saints have endured the same hardships as their people and therefore understand the requests that are made in prayers. They are more readily inclined to grant miracles (than, for example, a canonized saint from Italy) because the similar sufferings that they endured on earth are conducive to their empathy and compassion. These folk saints are native to "our land and our Guaraní region," Ramón adds, which he sees as the necessary basis for intimacy.

Another San La Muerte devotee, from Posadas, similarly explained that "going to church and praying to some well-painted, dressed-up saint does not conform with our way of thinking." The baroque sculpture and gilded clothing seem not only alien but almost obscene in contexts of devastating poverty. Folk saints are as humble as the folk who venerate them. A lyrical prayer addressed to Sarita Colonia asks for alleviation of poverty, because "you loved the poor/with the painful experience of your poverty."[23]

Devotees—humble, marginalized, voiceless—thus feel more comfortable making requests to one of their own. They know that their petitions will not be dismissed as insignificant, that their transgressions (perceived as consequences of their social condition) will be pardoned, and that their humble offerings will be accepted and respected. Even the way in which folk saints are addressed attests to their status as spiritual extensions of local communities. Whereas God and canonized saints accept prayers in any language, the pragmatics of communication must be considered when addressing folk saints. "I hope you can understand me when I write in English," a devotee wrote to Sarita Colonia on a Web site, and when English speakers converse (through a medium) with Niño Fidencio, they must do so with an interpreter.[24]

Folk saints are one with their people, but because they are dead and in heaven, with access to God, they are separated out from the crowd and endowed with the power to favor their constituents. In this sense they are something like "our man in the capital," which is to say a representative at a power center advocating for people who live on the periphery. In an alternative analogy, folk saints resemble *compadres* (ritual co-parents, or godparents), who are generally from higher social stations than their godchildren. As urgencies and special needs require, compadres protect, provide for, and intercede on behalf of the children consigned to their care.

In Spanish America it is difficult to make a bureaucratic hierarchy act in one's favor unless one has personal contact with someone in or close to power. One who works through established institutional channels without having (or buying) connections usually achieves nothing but exhaustion. If one has the right contact, however, then one discovers that a shortcut across the labyrinthine corridors of bureaucracy leads directly, miraculously, to a solution.

A similar structure obtains in folk devotions. One can negotiate religion through the bureaucratic Church—with its dogmatic priests, foreign saints, proscribed rituals, and expensive fees—or one can appeal to "one of us" who is close to God. In this perspective, folk devotion seems almost a transcendentalization of survival strategies derived from ineffective bureaucracy: the system does not work and one is helpless on one's own, but needs can be met by knowing the right person. The avenue of appeal is informal, unofficial, and nonbureaucratic; it bypasses institutional channels that have failed and makes its appeal directly to a friend on the inside.

And so it is not surprising that the needs brought to the attention of folk saints are predominantly those that ineffective government does not satisfy, notable basic health care and socioeconomic security. Folk saint devotions provide substitute satisfactions for deficiencies in secular as well as religious institutions. They offer improvised (and often symbolic) compensations for the lack of social services.

Folk saint devotions conform to devotees' social, political, and economic status as outsiders. The marginality of their social station, of their villages and neighborhoods, and of their ethnicities is replayed in the marginality of their religious beliefs. The informal economy in which they labor is complemented by the informal saint to whom they pray. All aspects of their lives evidence institutional failure and informal compensations, and their religion conforms to this pattern. Folk saints are a component of the larger package of marginality. Devotees live in a parallel society that stakes its claims and produces its miracles on the margins.

The creation of folk saints is also reminiscent of the evangelical concept of "inculturation." Rather than the Eurocentric imposition of Catholicism from above, with the intent of assimilating or extirpating local cultures, inculturation allows Catholicism the flexibility for expression in forms and terms consonant with the traditions of the recipients. Thus the faith can adapt one way in the Congo and another in Honduras, Korea, Ireland, or Poland. The chameleon-like face of Christ is evidence enough as it mutates to the look of locals.

Folk devotions are the results of a kind of reverse- or self-inculturation, which is to say that rather than the Church adapting Catholicism to local culture, the local culture adapts Catholicism to its own purposes. Folk devotions borrow aspects of Catholicism to produce unauthorized saints beyond Church control. The intent of Church inculturation is to bring outside cultures into the fold, seeking a confluence of local ways with those of the Church. Folk saints are produced, conversely, by liberating sainthood from the Church in order to build new devotions—new saints in the image of their makers—that belong exclusively to the people.

Protest can result if the folk saint's identity as "one of us" is threatened. Niño Compadrito revealed in a dream that he wanted blue eyes inserted into his eyeless skull, and the request was granted. This provoked an anxious reaction, including challenges to the authenticity of the revelation, because the blue eyes implied ethnic distance from the indigenous and mestizo devotees. Folk devotions can accept and assimilate outsiders, however, especially when their virtuous deeds or their suffering (including martyrdom) benefit local people or causes. San La Muerte is the best example, because myths establish him as a foreign Jesuit or Franciscan who dedicated his life to caring for sick and poor Guaranís until he was killed by jealous priests. Other outsiders, such as Niño Compadrito (when he is conceived as such), Niño Fidencio, and Che Guevara, are often believed to be *enviados de Dios*, meaning people sent by God to the aid of people in need. Their lifetime missions are sometimes accepted and sometimes rejected (locals killed Niño Compadrito and betrayed Che Guevara), but postmortem assimilation provides that the community benefit through miracles.[25]

The great majority of folk devotions are nevertheless homegrown. They begin among the rural and urban lower classes, and poverty is a prominent factor in establishing the "one of us" bond between saint and cult. Many versions stress how the poor San La Muerte spent his time among those in similar economic situations, including "a man who was very poor, very poor . . . even reaching the most extreme poverty." The repetitive, progressive stress underscores the importance of poverty in defining the saint and affirming the devotees' self-identification. When these ideas are politicized, poverty becomes mandatory—a requirement for admission—and those who have other entitlements need not apply. "You people who have money don't have the right to get involved with Sarita," a devotee explained to a middle-class man. "She belongs to us, to the poor, exclusively."[26]

The poverty of folk saints themselves is also represented as a qualifying credential or the attribute that authenticates sanctity. Gaucho Gil was "poor, very poor," and a "poor campesino, just like me." Niño Fidencio, of poor origins (some devotees say that as a child he lived in a cave), maintained his Christlike poverty despite the riches offered to him in gratitude for cures; and Sarita Colonia, a destitute migrant to Lima, shared the little she had with others who had even less. Sarita was buried in a common grave not because of poverty, according to her brother, but because she wanted to be close to the poor in death as she was in life. Today many consider her a "Patron of the Poor." Along the same lines, José Dolores is the "Protector of the Poor," and Jesús Malverde is "The Generous Bandit" and "The Angel of the Poor." When historical evidence indicates something other than poverty, then the appropriate apologies and compensations are made: "Although she belonged to a traditional and wealthy family, Deolinda [Difunta Correa] was humble and kind, with the gentle beauty of a geranium." In other cases, such as that of Madre María, the negative value of wealth is neutralized by distributing one's fortune among the poor.[27]

San La Muerte died of hunger, explained a devotee in Goya, and represents the perennial fear of countless Argentines who struggle for their daily

José Dolores is "Protector of the Poor" in San Juan, Argentina.

bread. Their neediness is epitomized by their starved-to-death saint, who provides for them what was deprived of him. Another Argentine folk saint, Difunto Pelado in San Juan Province, also died of hunger. The emaciated man who cares for the shrine, which is miles from nowhere on the desert, related Difunto Pelado's story and then asked me if I had anything to eat. I didn't, but I was so taken by this man's isolation and pitiable, Quixote-like profile that I returned the next day with two bags of groceries, liters of water, a barbecued chicken, a cake, and a couple of bottles of wine. That delivery bedazzled its recipient and undoubtedly entered the annals of Difunta Pelado's most prodigious miracles.

The cultural link between saint and devotees is also reinforced during the annual or biannual fiestas. Folk saint fiestas are celebrations, affirmations, and, in some cases, defenses of cultural identity. They contribute to defining a community and insulating it from dominant cultures, both secular and religious, in which devotees often feel inferior and exploited. The fiestas bring devotees together to immerse themselves in tradition, reaffirm life against the odds, recharge their hopes, and tap the natural and supernatural vitality of *lo nuestro*. They are occasions to see old friends and to make new ones, and they epitomize the sense of belonging, of solidarity, that devotees experience through sharing a faith deeply rooted in the culture that produced it. San La Muerte told one new devotee that she would make the pilgrimage to his annual fiesta, because "you are part of this place, and this place is part of you."

The interrelations of folk devotion and local culture are particularly prominent in northeastern Argentina. The *asado* (grilled meat) and *chamamé* (the local folk music) that characterize gaucho culture are the inalienable centerpieces of folk saint fiestas in this region. Popular culture and folk devotion intermingle as traditional dress, food, song, and dance are themselves, like the fiesta itself in its entirety, forms of religious offering and expressions of gratitude for miracles. One honors the saint and gives thanks by celebrating the feast day, and the good times thereby acquire devotional meaning.

In some cases the religious value of festivities is predisposed by the life story of a saint. Gaucho Gil was arrested at a dance celebrating the feast day of St. Baltazar, and consequently, according to some devotees, his fiesta should be celebrated with dance. The myths of another gaucho folk saint, Francisco López, formalize the mandate: the dying López specified that his miracles should be thanked by hosting dances. Dance was also prominent in Guaraní religious culture, which establishes a backdrop for these devotions.

Ramón, the San La Muerte devotee from Resistencia, was particularly insightful regarding the cultural determinants of folk saint offerings. Dance, song, drink, traditional foods, and cigarettes are offered, he explained, because

"You are part of this place and this place is part of you." The San La Muerte T-shirt and statuette are popular among new devotees who attend the annual fiesta in Empedrado, Argentina.

if we like them, and if the saints are one of us, then the saints must like them too. One can make an offering with relative certainty that it will be well received, because the saint, the devotee, and the offering are all integral to the same culture.

Ramón, whose nickname is "Chamamé" because of his passion for the music, then explained how devotees' preferences can be projected onto a saint. "I always say that San La Muerte likes chamamé," he said, "but I don't know that for sure. I think he likes it, but maybe it's only me. I think of him as a part of myself, so when I feel good, I think he feels good too." Ramón's reflections identify precisely how folk saint identities are constructed through interactions of cultural and personal preferences. Offerings to recently deceased folk saints, such as Frente Vital in Buenos Aires, are less speculative. Frente's friends know exactly what he liked—marijuana, beer, and Pronto Shake—and thus can make the appropriate offering with certainty. These offerings also conform to the collective taste of the microcommunity that the friends shared—and share—with Frente, so there is less room for error.

The concept of *convite* is also central to folk saint fiestas. To offer a *convite* is to invite or treat others to something (as in "I'll treat you to dinner"), usually food and drink. *Convite* is particularly important in cultures—such as the Guaraní-influenced culture of northeastern Argentina—that highly value reciprocity and that measure social worth, in part, through one's generosity in sharing and in giving assistance.

Local folk saint fiestas are regarded as legitimate when they are free, with each sponsor providing music, food, and drink in accord with the resources available. The public, mostly poor, enjoys the event without paying. The shrine owner who organizes the fiesta is technically a master of ceremonies, because the folk saint being celebrated is the true host. The expenses, often considerable, are also borne by the saint, which is to say by the cash reserves accumulated through donations offered at the shrine throughout the year. The devotee who organizes the event provides any additional funds necessary to meet to the expenses, and other devotees likewise make contributions (such as cash, meat, labor, and music) to assure the event's success. Some regional

Music and dance are prominent at the San La Muerte fiesta that Ramón—pictured here—hosts annually in Resistencia, Argentina.

shrines, such as the Gaucho Gil shrine in San Roque, sponsor raffles or other fund-raisers to subsidize the annual fiesta.

The idea of community sharing assumes a different form in the devotion to Sarita Colonia. Rather than squandering gratitude on expensive fiestas, penance, or frivolous offerings, Sarita's devotees arrive on feast days with gifts, usually food or drink, that they distribute to others at the shrine. In this way they thank Sarita for miracles, emulate her famed generosity, and participate, if only modestly or symbolically, in a community of mutual assistance. A public-awareness initiative at the Difunta Correa complex similarly endeavored to "raise consciousness among devotees, so that their offerings are at once a sign of gratitude and a help to their brothers." In Mexico, the custodian of the Jesús Malverde chapel himself took the initiative to recirculate offerings by distributing them to the poor. The sums were considerable, because Malverde, the "narcosaint," attracted cash donations from grateful drug dealers. Proceeds from the illegal drug trade—however small the percentage—thereby trickled down to the poor, with the Malverde shrine mediating this informal social service.[28]

This circulation of goods within a devotee community is also prominent at a San La Muerte shrine in Posadas. The annual fiesta begins with the free distribution of enormous quantities of food—some 350 pounds of grilled beef, along with trimmings, or hundreds of gallons of stew—after which even the pots are given away. Devotees leave bottles of whisky and wine as offerings to San La Muerte, and at the end of the fiesta the woman who presides at the shrine, Pelusa, distributes these randomly in the crowd. Cash from San La Muerte's reserves are also selectively distributed. During one fiesta, Pelusa asked devotees if 50 pesos (about $15) from San La Muerte's reserves should be given to a pregnant woman who was there. Everyone cheered in the affirmative, and the ecstatic recipient responded as though she had won the lottery. When I offered to match the award, Pelusa called for other pregnant women in the crowd, and then for more donations, so that all expecting mothers would receive at least something. The police at the fiesta eyed me wearily as they were obliged to dig deep for change.

Thus, however modestly, folk saint shrines offer an informal social service by recirculating cash and goods. This redistribution of wealth is reminiscent of the many folk saints who rose to notoriety through Robin Hood robberies and other crimes that benefited the poor. At the shrines wealth recirculates within an impoverished community rather than passing from rich to poor, but the spirit of giving and solidarity is similar.

Grass-roots efforts at mutual aid are undermined when devotions become large and institutionalized. Gaucho Gil's fiesta is attended by more than

100,000 devotees annually, which makes a free event out of the question. The traditional *convite* has thus yielded to traditional capitalism, which is to say a free-for-all driven by profit. At the same time, unknown sums of donated cash, along with jewels and other valuables, tended to disappear into the administration that was responsible for their management. As expressed by the parish priest of Mercedes, where the shrine is located, people seeking economic miracles from Gaucho Gil just get poorer, while a few people profit from their faith. Gaucho Gil stole from the rich to give to the poor, the priest continued, but the commission that ran the shrine stole from the poor to make itself rich. "They don't even respect the legend."

Thus the offerings of money and goods to folk saints are saved to sponsor fiestas, distributed to the poor, invested to improve the shrines, and stolen. The sums are relative to the size and means of the cult and therefore are usually modest, but they are nevertheless considerable from the perspective of the impoverished donors.

The unrealized plans at Víctor Apaza's tomb in Arequipa are typical of donation mismanagement. Contributions were deposited in a collection box and were solicited by Apaza's daughter for the purpose of building a mausoleum-chapel. The daughter and others involved were undoubtedly well intentioned as they raised the funds, but the promised shrine was never built. In such cases it is never clear what happens to the money. I would guess that the donations were insufficient to realize the project, and that the money gradually was depleted by perpetual urgent need until the project was forgotten. In the case of the Cajamarca folk saint Ubilberto Vásquez Bautista, similarly, a commission was formed to collect money to build a chapel, but the money that many deposited into a savings account disappeared without explanation.

The Difunta Correa shrine has been the most active in social-service functions, and for nearly a century. Reports from 1921 note that cash loans were frequent and that repayment was made with interest. The lending of wedding gowns was also popular, and the administration proactively sought additional gown donations in order to expand the service. (The belief that Difunta Correa punishes those who do not keep their promises encouraged the borrowers to return the gowns.) The Vallecito Cemetery Foundation, which managed the shrine until 2002, also drew from the considerable sums donated to Difunta Correa to benefit the local community. The record is uneven, and embezzlement is alleged, but substantial donations were made to schools, community centers, sports organizations, and hospitals. In 1978, during the dictatorship, the foundation presented a ceremonial flag, blessed by the local priest, to an elementary school in nearby Caucete while the police band played the national anthem.

Freedom of Devotion

When you go to church, a devotee explained at the Difunta Correa shrine, "you have to stand at a certain time, kneel at a certain time, put your hands in a certain way, shake hands at a certain time. Here you can do whatever you want."

Others similarly explain that in formal Catholicism "the priest has to approve everything," "the priest tells you what to do," and "the priest stands between you and God." These comments well represent the sentiments of innumerable devotees who prefer the freedom of devotion at folk saint shrines to the dogmatic oversight of clergy. Many also express dismay with the high cost of sacraments. Rolando, a Difunta Correa devotee, related that he complained to a parish priest about the fee for baptism because people cannot afford it and Jesus was baptized for free. The Church also charges for weddings, he continued—"with flowers, one price; without flowers, another price—they can't do that." People are having civil weddings instead, he explained, because what they save in Church fees covers the cost of the reception. "That's why people go to Difunta Correa," Rolando concluded.

Catholic priests are quite aware that Church dogma has a negative affect on parishioners, particularly in regions where folk Catholicism is prominent. When I asked the parish priest of Mercedes why locals go to the Gaucho Gil shrine rather than to church, he responded by saying that Catholicism is too restrictive, with too many norms and laws: "We don't allow people to express themselves freely." The Church is too conservative and dogmatic, too concerned with the rules pertaining to sacraments. At the Gaucho Gil shrine, conversely, "people come and do whatever they want. They feel free. There is no structure." The priest added that social, political, and economic conditions in Argentina impose a deep feeling of being oppressed, which in turn engenders a longing for freedom, for alleviation, that people find at the shrines. Folk devotion, he explained, is a response to this feeling of oppression.

The successful organization and normalization of folk saint devotions might ultimately be counterproductive. The devotions, like the saints, emerge outside of established institutions and are to a great degree anti-institutional. Their folk quality is undermined when they are regulated. Many devotees are attracted precisely by the informality, even the anarchy. The fervor of devotion tends to diminish with institutionalization, which generally results in a passionate core surrounded by rings of casual adepts. The Difunta Correa shrine has become a state-controlled recreation site that attracts as many picnickers as it does fervent devotees.

Institutionalization took a different turn when one branch of Niño Fidencio devotion organized into a church—the Fidencist Christian Church—that is officially recognized by the Mexican government. Most Fidencio devotees do not belong to this church and therefore are not restricted by its clergy and dogma. Even outside of the church, however, the spiritist nature of this devotion situates a medium (who channels Fidencio's spirit) between the devotee and the folk saint. The same is true of María Lionza's cult, also spiritist, although in both cases one may bypass the medium and take one's chances with direct prayer.

A different type of intermediary is evident in devotion to Víctor Apaza. Apaza's tomb-shrine is always covered with flowers, beneath which one can sometimes discern a tiny photograph of Apaza that was taken during his trial. Arriving devotees deliver their flower offerings to the *rezador* (a man who prays for tips), who arranges these among the other flowers covering the niche. He also places devotees' candles beside the photograph of Apaza, and they remain there while he prays. From time to time the rezador removes the candles to make the sign of the cross, or to tap them on Apaza's tomb, as though knocking.

Each devotee relates to the rezador the need for which Apaza's help is being solicited. Issues concerning health, work, family matters, legal problems, and adversity are common. The rezador's prayers are personalized and include the names of the parties involved. The prayers (and songs, including one to the Lord of Miracles) are Catholic, intermixed with the personalized petitions and other improvisations. Occasionally during the prayers the rezador takes a flask from his pocket and pours holy water on the hands of the devotee and on the flowers. After the prayer and a small tip, the devotee then goes to the nearby stations where candles are offered. Many devotees watch over their candles to be certain that they burn down completely.

This routinization of visits to Apaza, along with the mediating roles and special effects offered by the rezador, structure the devotion without restricting it or encroaching on individual freedom. One can well visit the shrine without recruiting the rezador, who in any case does not impose obligations or in any way condition requests made to Apaza. The same is true of most spiritist mediums: they assist without dominating. The flexibility essential to folk devotion is maintained. Implied protocols are established but not dogmatically enforced. The sacred pepper tree in Espinazo should be circled three times counterclockwise, but no one cares if one does something else. Bottles of water are a traditional offering to Difunta Correa, but one can offer whatever one pleases. Any rules, in short, are subject to improvisation and evasion. Mediums, curanderos, rezadores, shrine owners, and other folk saint intermediaries are valuable and tolerated only insofar as they are useful. Devotees otherwise find ways around them.

The protocols at domestic shrines are established not by doctrine, or even by convention, but rather by the disposition of each shrine owner. Some control and restrict devotees, others leave them alone, and most fall somewhere in between. The owner of a San La Muerte chapel in Empedrado, for example, has established rules that some devotees find disturbing. Images may not be placed on the altar, black candles and flags are prohibited, offerings of alcoholic beverages are forbidden, and music may not be played in the chapel. Devotees who arrive by tour bus from Buenos Aires seem largely untroubled by or oblivious to these regulations. Some locals who are familiar with other shrines, however, find the conditions to be excessive and are anxious to express their exception.

An interesting variation is presented by the San La Muerte shrine established by Pelusa in Posadas. Through the mentoring of devotees, the defining of fixed rituals and protocols, and the writing of a book on San La Muerte, Pelusa has established herself almost as a priestess. She imposes a structure of devotion that some might view as dogmatic. Tests of entrance and fulfillment of Pelusa-determined requirements eliminate uncommitted newcomers and casual devotees. The priestly oversight that one escaped at church thus reasserts itself informally through a shrine owner's efforts to systematize this quintessentially folk devotion. Pelusa's structure and control has an appeal to serious adepts seeking guidance, but others find her domination excessive and turn to alternatives.

These exceptions serve to reinforce the rule: pretty much anything goes. No one really knows exactly what is to be done. There are innumerable versions of everything. Beliefs, rituals, myths, and protocols are transmitted mostly by word of mouth and then customized by their recipients. What one holds to be true depends on which version happened to come one's way. Things must be done a certain way, but no one really knows why. When I asked, the response was usually, "It's the custom." But the customs vary from one region to the next, even one town to the next, depending upon the local culture, the influence and presence of formal Catholicism, the level of education, the access to information (including news media), and the contact with outsiders. Customs are flexible. You can have it your way. The rule is generally "whatever works."

On the wall beside Pirucha's San La Muerte altar there is a poster of Gilda and a rack of antlers. The tragically killed Gilda is an emerging folk saint, and powder scraped from the antlers is the active ingredient of a love potion that also cures heart disease. On a Sarita Colonia altar in Chaclacayo, I encountered images of Mexico's Santísima Muerte, of Karl Marx, and of several canonized saints, along with a skull that protected the home from intruders. Some advise feeding San La Muerte on Mondays with slices of onion, pumpkin, popcorn, candy, pork, chocolate cake, meringue, fruits, and hard liquor. Others, however, respond that candles and maybe some flowers are appropriate for San La Muerte's altar but that this "spiritual restaurant" is ridiculous and only "attracts flies." One devotee prescribes rituals for love (put three laurel leaves under your pillow with your left hand) whereas another responds that "the saint protects and guides us, he's not Cupid nor should he be used for this type of crap."[29]

Folk devotions, in short, provide broad latitude for individual preference. Each devotee assembles a collage of religious beliefs and practices that suits his or her sensibilities and needs. Free choice is exercised among multiple options, including whatever can be borrowed from Catholicism.

The Last Resort

First visits to folk saints are often made by people who have nothing to lose. Desperation conditions their quest, and they make their appeal to marginal, anti-institutional powers because all institutional resources have already failed them. Matías, a vendor at the Gaucho Gil shrine in Mercedes, explained that in times of crisis people will believe in anything, "anything that might save their lives." I myself have seen broken-down people, weak and whimpering, delivering themselves to folk saint altars in exhausted surrender, as though with the last energy in their bodies. They seem like refugees from a world emptied of meaning. They have been crushed by insurmountable anguish and appear now on their knees, with candles and streaming tears, to bet everything on this last hope.

A hierarchy of preferences (and of purposes) is suggested by a common sequence followed by people seeking medical cures. The quest usually begins with visits to doctors, curanderos, or both. If these are unsuccessful, then a priest is consulted and Catholic supernatural resources are petitioned. And if, despite these efforts, the problem persists, then, at the end of the line, a folk saint shrine is visited. Religious solutions are sought when practical, pragmatic solutions are lacking, and folk saints are sought when conventional religious resources are insufficient. Folk saints in these cases are the last resort, after conventional resources have failed. If the miracle is not granted, the patient is finished; sometimes that is why it is granted.

Many devotees relate that they first prayed to a folk saint after they were predisposed to blind faith by desperation. What had seemed ludicrous suddenly assumed awesome seriousness. If miracles are granted at this end of the line, on the brink of hopelessness, then their recipients becomes devotees for life. This conviction is accompanied by a reorganization of preferences: canonized saints (who failed the devotee) are relegated to secondary status behind the miraculous folk saint. Now the new devotees understand what others have always claimed: Folk saints are more able, or more willing, to fulfill the needs of their people. As expressed by a Niño Compadrito devotee, "in a short time he granted me the miracle that for three years no Saint could."[30]

At times folk saints are solicited because the Church is unable to help and medical professionals are undesirable or unaffordable. A man who heard voices in his head reported that his parents took him to their parish priest, but "the priest ran us off." By that he meant that the priest, once apprised of the problem, advised that the man needed a psychologist. The parents took the man to a medium instead, and in short order he was cured by Niño Fidencio.[31]

Even those who are deeply committed to formal Catholicism turn to folk saints during crises. The practices of a woman in Lima's El Agustino shantytown are typical. She usually prayed to the Virgin of Cocharcas but turned to Sarita Colonia ("although she is not yet a saint") in times of special need, "when I'm really in a bind."[32] In Mexico, a female sacristan told her priest of her plans to miss mass one Sunday to go to the Niño Fidencio shrine in Espinazo. Her daughter-in-law could not get pregnant and doctors could not help, she explained, so she was making the pilgrimage to request a miracle. The priest, surprised, asked if she was abandoning the Catholic faith. The woman replied that she was still Catholic, but that she needed help of a sort that the Church couldn't provide. She added: "Or maybe you can make my daughter-in-law get pregnant? I don't think so. That's why we're going there."[33]

Devotees relate that miracles only happen if one has absolute faith, and many use the phrase "faith moves mountains." As explained by Silvia, a Niño Compadrito devotee from Puno, "You have to believe in something so strongly and with such deep faith that you think the problem is already solved." When I asked Jorge, a lawyer from Cuzco, why Niño Compadrito had miraculous power, he responded that even a stone would perform miracles if one believed in it. The significance of this response is redoubled by its context: Jorge had been miraculously saved from a fatal illness by Niño Compadrito, after doctors had given up hope. Had his last resort been to the stone, rather than to Niño Compadrito, would the stone have likewise performed the miracle?

One is not cured by the folk saint, and much less by a curandero; it is one's own faith that effects the cure. The miracle does not happen automatically because one requests it; it happens because one's profound faith makes it happen. One invests oneself totally, everything one has left, and miracles emerge from this investment. There is a reciprocal, mutually reinforcing relation between one's faith and the saint's miraculous power. Niño Fidencio would ask his patients if they thought he could cure them, and when they replied in the affirmative he would add, "Then you will cure yourself." Madre María always said the same—that the cures were done by faith, not by her— and her principal disciple, Eleuterio Cueto, similarly maintained, "If you really have faith, you will cure yourself."

Faith fosters not only miraculous cures, but also a positive state of mind that might be miraculous in itself. Folk shrines give devotees a deep sense of peace, tranquillity, and well-being. Many describe the feeling as a recharging of their batteries, a replenishing of the reserves that get them through their difficult lives. Measures of hope, confidence, comfort, security, and stamina are restored by the belief that a supernatural power is protecting one, intervening on one's behalf. Folk saints are frequently described in the likeness of guardian angels, as protectors looking out always for devotees venturing through their precarious worlds.

Faith thus becomes a survival strategy in the struggle of everyday life. Horrors, pains, and hardships can be reinterpreted in a positive light, can become meaningful, and can even be viewed as miracles in themselves. Instead of complaining that there is nothing to eat but bread, devotees say that their saint makes sure that they always have food on the table, even if it is only bread. Miracle is a question of perception. Niño Fidencio told a breast cancer patient from Dallas that he would concentrate all of the cancer in one breast, so that doctors could surgically remove it and save her. "Two-and-a-half years ago they take my breast. You think I am not going to be thankful for all he has done for me?"[34]

Devotees explain that faith is all they have left, that it is the only thing that keeps them afloat. "People have to believe in something," they stress in reference to their folk saint. The more or less explicit follow-up relates that there is nothing else worthy of belief. Folk saints flourish in contexts of meaninglessness, hopelessness, corruption, and despair: they rise up out of these ashes. They put soul back into a soulless society. They introduce a last-chance principle of order to a world that seems out of control. And they reorder the chaos with a new design conducive to miracles and with devotees at the sacred center.

Doing Evil

Some devotees prefer folk saints because they grant certain types of miracles that canonized saints would never even consider. Success in crime and sending curses to enemies are the outstanding examples. Folk saints, many of whom were themselves criminals, understand these special needs and are not restricted by traditional moral standards. Many thieves ask Gaucho Gil for success in robberies because he, too, survived by stealing. One hunter periodically leaves him a cash gift in thanks for continued protection while poaching. Sarita Colonia, San La Muerte, Jesús Malverde, and many other folk saints also lend a hand in dubious enterprises, including muggings, hetero- and homosexual prostitution, drug dealing, and even murder.

The devotees' crimes, like those of their folk saints, are perceived (at least by their perpetrators) to be committed of necessity. Supernatural protection is requested, and granted, because the crimes are motivated by adverse circumstances—poverty, desperation—rather than by malice or greed. The crimes are seen as consistent with a certain concept of justice, a vengeful justice, particularly when perpetrated against wealthier classes regarded as exploitative. Folk saints protect criminal activity, devotees explain, because "we are victims of our reality/and piercing social inequality."[35]

Some folk saints lend themselves to uses reminiscent of witchcraft. Niño Compadrito, San La Muerte, and saints who were executed for crimes (such as Víctor Apaza and Ubilberto Vásquez Bautista) are outstanding in this regard. They grant miracles, which are generally requested by lighting black candles, that send harm, suffering, or death to one's enemies. The phrases *hacer el mal* (doing evil) or *el daño* (literally hurt, harm, or damage, here with the implication of a curse) are widely used by devotees to describe these practices.

Despite the admission of such phrases, those who use folk saints for assaults on their enemies view their actions as just and legitimate. Their adversaries have overpowered and injured them unjustly, so they take exceptional countermeasures to redress the offense. Rather than doing evil, they are exacting justice. Rather than being aggressive, they are retaliating defensively. They would not be doing so were it not absolutely necessary.

Most devotees got uncomfortable when I asked about black-candle rituals. All acknowledge that folk saints are used frequently for such purposes, and most are familiar with how it is done, but few claim to condone or practice these rituals. Those who spoke openly explained that they made black-candle petitions to clear their path of hostilities or to restore a disrupted status quo, rather than to seek malicious harm or personal gain. When I asked the rezador at the Víctor Apaza shrine about the purpose of black candles, he responded with a single word: "justice." I pressed the issue, and he came back with an example: "If your house is robbed, or if you are mugged, you get justice with a black candle." Justice is conceived almost as a synonym for revenge.

Formal Catholicism can also be used—with some manipulation—for the purpose of cursing enemies. Burning upside-down candles before Catholic saints is one way of doing so in the Andes. Priests can be recruited by asking them to celebrate a mass for the dead but providing the name of someone alive. The mass sends out the spell that dooms the unknowing victim.[36]

The Maintenance and Growth of Devotions

Folk saint devotions can be debilitated by religious or secular authorities, particularly if a tomb-shrine is removed or otherwise made inaccessible. The Peruvian devotions to El Soldadito Desconocido in Callao and to La Chavela in Arequipa both disappeared after the tombs were removed. Embezzlement can also weaken a devotion. As the Difunta Correa and Gaucho Gil shrines well evidence, however, a resilient cult can grow rapidly despite years of theft. Church repression, similarly, can quash a cult but can also strengthen its resolve. In the last analysis, a folk saint's reputation for miracles is the only absolute factor in the growth or demise of a devotion. If the scores are high in the area of miracles, the rest tends to work itself out. New devotions constantly emerge; some endure and must disappear. Critical mass at one point does not guarantee longevity, and the popularity of saints rises and falls with perceptions of miraculousness.

Devotees arrive at shrines by many routes and for multiple reasons. The factors contributing to the maintenance and growth of folk devotions may be summarized as follows:

- *Desperation.* Folk saint devotions flourish when people are struggling to meet basic needs. They therefore emerge in the lower classes, later attracting others who for various reasons (usually health crises) seek miracles.
- *A tradition of devotion in extended families.* Early and regular exposure to shrines, to myths, and to anecdotes concerning miracles are conducive to new generations of devotion. Some parents dedicate their children to a folk saint at birth or in early childhood, particularly when the children were conceived or saved from death thanks to miraculous intervention.

- *Recommendations by current devotees.* In times of crisis, many people are brought or sent to shrines by friends and coworkers who have received miracles. Word-of-mouth recommendations contribute significantly to the growth of cults.
- *Media.* Movies, miniseries, talk shows, and news reports spread the good news among broad audiences, and the effect is redoubled by word-of-mouth. Some individuals enticed by media accounts travel across their countries or internationally to visit a shrine. Newspaper and magazine articles often include versions of folk-saints narratives, and these versions—authorized by print and widely circulated—can challenge versions that were originally more prominent among devotees.
- *Fiestas.* The annual or biannual folk saint fiestas are times for renewal of faith, of vows, of friendships, and of stamina to continue the struggle of daily life. Recharged devotees return from pilgrimages with news of wonder-working saints that spreads throughout the community. The fiestas attract devotees and nondevotees alike, and the latter are sometimes the majority. Nondevotees attend out of curiosity, with friends, or simply for the fun of the party, but in the process they assimilate and become comfortable with a particular devotion. Many return later, on their knees, in hopes of receiving a folk saint's help during a crisis. Attendance by nondevotees is encouraged by open invitations to fiestas that are announced through the local media.
- *Oral traditions.* The frequent telling and retelling of myths, legends, anecdotes, and miracle stories contributes to the common knowledge that folk saints are available in times of need. In many regions, folk saints are an inalienable resource of one's culture and community. "It's like water absorbed by plants," explained the father of soccer star Diego Maradona in reference to Gaucho Gil devotion. "We carry it in our blood."[37]
- *Music.* Songs that thank or honor a folk saint, particularly when they are recorded by well-known artists, help to spread the word and to assimilate the devotion to broader cultural practices. Along with dance, songs also integrate the festive and religious aspects of the fiestas.
- *Print sources.* The many booklets written on folk saints are read, consulted, and quoted by devotees. The texts are often incomplete or incorrect, but the content is taken as authoritative because it is published. When I asked devotees questions to which they had no answers, they sometimes directed me to these texts. Some newcomers enter a devotion through the how-to aspects of these booklets.

- *Shrine owners.* The tutelage offered by domestic shrine owners is critical to the growth of folk saint cults. This is particularly true when strong interpersonal skills—generally sympathetic listening suffices—comfort devotees in crisis. Many devotees visit shrines for consolation and encouragement; the folk saint communicates, in effect, through the trusted shrine owner who listens, cares, and advises. Some shrine owners also act as mediators, praying to their saint on behalf of devotees who are too timid or fearful to make the request themselves, or who believe that the saint is more likely to grant the request if it comes from the shrine owner.

- *Shrine locations.* Being located along highways ensures regular traffic to the shrines of Gaucho Gil and Difunta Correa, especially because it is believed that passersby who do not pay their respects will have an ill-fated journey. This belief is derived from the broader tradition of stopping at roadside crosses erected in remembrance of people killed in traffic accidents. Proximity to a railroad line also contributed to the growth of Difunta Correa's shrine, as it did to Niño Fidencio's shrine in Espinazo. Today, conversely, the isolation of Espinazo (the railroad no longer serves it) contributes indirectly to the cult and perhaps to its growth as the "sacrifice" of pilgrimage has become integral to petitioning or giving thanks for miracles.

- *Secondary shrines.* The multiple roadside, regional, and domestic shrines constructed for some folk saints, particularly those in Argentina, facilitate access for current and new devotees unable to make the journey to the principal shrines.

- *Spiritism.* The many missions (organized devotional groups) and mediums for spiritist folk saints such as Niño Fidencio assure access and advocacy across wide geographical areas.

- *Famous devotees.* Sports stars (such as Diego Maradona), musicians, and other public figures stimulate new devotion when they publicly endorse a folk saint. Politicians sometimes show up at folk saint shrines, looking devout and shaking hands.

- *The Church.* Although the Catholic Church as an institution discourages folk saint devotion, individual priests, particularly those trained in the ideas of Vatican II, have on occasion fostered the growth of a devotion. The two most important shrines in Argentina, those of Difunta Correa and Gaucho Gil, were both developed with significant encouragement and participation of Catholic priests. The Church's opposition to devotion can also contribute to the growth of folk saint cults, because it unites devotees against a common adversary and creates an anti-institutional faith—appealing to many—that becomes all the more fervent in defiance. Church oppression of popular devotion is a critical aspects of some folk saint narratives, and it helps define these devotions as alternative, self-defined, and nonbureaucratic. Devotion also spreads through Catholic masses for the dead—dead folk saints—that are requested by devotees and heard by others.

- *Migration.* Migration from rural areas to major cities and capitals is an important factor in the dissemination of folk devotions. People migrate with their cultures and beliefs intact, and the new urban shrines that they establish, such as Gaucho Gil's "Tree of Faith" in Buenos Aires, foster devotion among other migrants. When these migrants—now "people from Buenos Aires"—later return by the busload for fiestas in their native provinces, their presence enhances the prestige of the shrines and thereby further stimulates devotion.

- *Patronage.* Devotion among truck, bus, and taxi drivers, many of whom prominently display images and slogans (such as "Visit Difunta Correa"), offer constant, mobile exposure to the folk saints who are patrons of drivers and travelers. Difunta Correa (whose devotion was first spread by livestock drivers) and Sarita Colonia have most benefited from this kind of exposure.

- *Lack of access to social services.* Miraculous solutions are sought because institutional solutions are lacking. The need for medical care is conspicuous. Curanderos are a major point of entry into folk devotions. Many devotees seek the help of Niño Fidencio, even in the United States, because "we poor people can't afford a doctor."[38]

- *Fear of reprisals.* Attrition in folk saint devotions is reduced by fear of reprisals. Devotees to Niño Compadrito, for example, often show up at the shrine in a nervous state after having been visited in dreams and censured for their slack devotion. Many other folk saints, particularly San La Muerte, are said to punish those who fail to keep their vows.

- *Web sites.* Folk saint Web sites provide devotees with a forum for announcements, for discussion, and for guidance concerning petitions and rituals. They also provide newcomers from around the world with ready access to a devotion. Some sites, notably the site of Difunta Correa, are used to promote religious tourism. The sites have limited range, however, because many or most folk saint devotees do not have access to computers or the skills to operate them.

- *Critical mass.* The thousands of plaques, offerings, and devotees at major shrines are viewed as indisputable evidence of a folk saint's miraculousness, and they therefore contribute to their cult's expansion. "It's hard to imagine that all these people are wrong," said a newcomer at the Difunta Correa complex. Another pointed to three buses from Uruguay to make the same point.

- *Recognition.* Folk saints who have substantial cults and are strongly identified with a region sometimes attract nods of recognition from government authorities. Such recognition reinforces the folk saint's legitimacy and consequently fosters growth of the cult. Neighborhoods are named after Gaucho Gil (Corrientes, Posadas) and Sarita Colonia (Callao), a street is named after José Dolores (San Juan), and a market and neighborhood are named after La Chavela (Arequipa). The town name "Vallecito" is gradually being displaced by "Difunta Correa" on regional maps in San Juan. The prison in Callao is informally known as "Sarita Colonia," and outside of it I saw a police patrol car with "Sarita Colonia" (designating the neighborhood) on its doors. In the private sector, there are several bars, restaurants, stores, and associations that are named after folk saints.

- *Religious tourism.* The attendance of more than 100,000 people at major folk saint fiestas creates opportunities for lucrative business. Provincial government authorities have assumed the direction of Argentina's two major folk saint shrines, one provisionally (for now) and the other permanently. San Juan's director of tourism was the president of the foundation running the Difunta Correa shrine until it finally came under direct government management in 2002. The other major shrine, Gaucho Gil's, is heading in a similar direction. Tourist-oriented administration increases the number of visitors through events such as the annual Truckers' Day at the Difunta Correa shrine, but the nature of the visits tends to become less religious and more recreational. Other folk saint sites are promoted to tourists only rarely, and sometimes for special audiences. Sarita Colonia's shrine is described in a gay travel guide, for example, and at least one "spiritual" tour operator offers visits to Niño Compadrito.

- *Scholarship.* The presence of foreign scholars at folk saint shrines and fiestas has a significant effect on devotion. It elevates the prestige of folk saints among devotees and (somewhat puzzled) nondevotees because the foreign visitor is perceived as a guarantor. The importance of the cult is affirmed because a scholar from abroad came to study it or—as some devotees see it—to pay homage to the folk saint. Foreign scholars also attract the press, which publicizes their interest in a folk saint. During San La Muerte fiestas my presence was announced from the stage by musicians; at the Gaucho Lega shrine in Saladas my business card, still hot from my wallet, was rushed to the front and center of the altar; and at most other shrines I was received graciously because my presence was regarded as honorific, if not miraculous. The work of scholars can also have a profound effect on the development of myths, as discussed in the chapter on Niño Compadrito.

- *Politics.* Political instability in general can stimulate the growth of cults, and certain events tend to bring rapid growth. The end of the Argentine dictatorship in 1983, for example, brought greater religious freedom that facilitated folk saint devotions. The Catholic Church was retreating from liberation theology at about the same time, which created opportunities for folk Catholicism.

- *Factions.* The division of larger devotions into factions can debilitate a cult or, conversely, invigorate its growth as the rivals work off of one another dialectically. Competing factions are particularly evident in María Lionza's cult, in which rival groups accuse one another of falsity; and in Niño Fidencio's cult, which is divided into followings of prominent leaders. One of these groups has incorporated as a state-recognized church, which has widened the divide between factions.

Miracles

The word "miracle" is used broadly in folk devotions. "Favors," which is also commonly used, is perhaps more accurate, at least when "miracle" is understood as an extraordinary divine intervention in human affairs. Requests for folk saint miracles mostly concern health, work, love, and family, but they can encompass almost anything and often include protection against the dangers and difficulties of everyday life. Whatever any human being might want or need is likely to appear on the wish list. One man asked a folk saint for a girlfriend who looked like Jenna Jameson or Pamela Anderson, and another provided a list of three local girls, conceding that he would be happy with any one of them.

Devotees request success in business, a change of government, money for the phone bill, luck in gambling, release from prison, admission to the university, safe passage across the border, cancellation of debts, normal pregnancy, lowering of a mother's bilirubin levels, the shrinking of an uncle's tumor, the return of a wayward husband, abstinence from drugs, better drug sales, and simply the strength to go on. Niño Compadrito reunites broken families, helps with one's studies, and removes adversaries from one's path. Gaucho Gil lends a hand in setting up a home, in healing a broken heart, in quitting smoking, and in evading tax authorities. Sarita Colonia helps out with marital problems, protects transvestites, guides illegal immigrants, and puts bread on the table. One man recently released from prison thanked San La Muerte for his freedom, then went on to ask for a good job, for the willpower to lose weight, and for boxing skills that would gain him respect and make him "very powerful like you are."

Such multiple requests are common, and written petitions are often a kind of shopping list of desires. Letters are left for folk saints (as for canonized

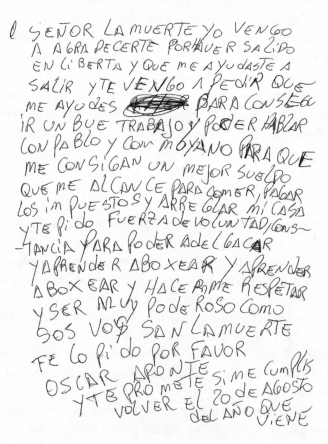

This note thanks San La Muerte for release from prison and then itemizes the devotee's requests. The note concludes with a promise to return for the next annual fiesta if the requests are granted.

saints) on altars, walls, and tombs; in special "mailboxes" provided for this purpose; or with shrine owners who convey the message. In one letter a woman asked Niño Compadrito for moral support and the strength to carry on, for a more harmonious home life, for her brothers' success in finding employment, and for her family's acceptance of her desire to marry someone named Rubén. Another devotee asked for a favorable outcome of his trial, for work, for protection of his children, and for good health. A third asked for approval of a loan application so he could buy a Volvo, guidance at work, and freedom from all misfortune. He then concluded: "Solve all my problems until my wife returns to me."

One of Sarita Colonia's devotees wrote to her: "I always have your image under my pillow (for sweet dreams), in my car (to travel far), on my motorbike (so I don't wipe out), and in my night table next to my box of condoms (for good luck with latinas and white girls)." Sometimes a general request is made in lieu of—or in addition to—a list of specifics. One Gaucho Gil devotee concluded his petition with "whatever," leaving the exact nature of the miracle to the discretion of the saint, and another wrote: "Please I want to be happy help me."[39]

For some devotees, particularly those stopping to visit Gaucho Gil or Difunta Correa, thanks are given because nothing happened, which is taken as evidence of miraculous protection. Sarita Colonia is also well known for such protective services. All the houses in a given neighborhood have been robbed, for example, except the house displaying Sarita's image on the door. A woman who passes daily through a dangerous area of drug addicts and thieves commends herself to Sarita's care and always makes it home unscathed. A transvestite handing out images of Sarita at her December fiesta explained that his offering was made in thanks for getting through the year without being attacked. For a safe day and good fortune in whatever they may be doing, countless devotees commend themselves to their folk saint before leaving home in the morning.

Health-related miracles are commonly cited as proof of a folk saint's miraculous powers. The most impressive miracle, that of being saved from death, is widely reported. Baffled doctors populate these narratives. The typical story begins with a grim medical diagnosis and doctors who regret that nothing can be done. The patient, desperate for help, visits a folk saint shrine as a last resort. The miracle is revealed upon return to the doctors, who discover in amazement that the terminal illness has inexplicably disappeared.

Most miracles actually involve more cooperation with the medical profession than these stories might suggest. Devotees request of folk saints that the medical tests come back negative, that the procedures be successful, or that the radiation destroy all the cancer. The miracles, that is to say, evidence a collaboration between folk saints and medical professionals. Science works because faith intervenes. One of the ministers of the Fidencist Christian Church, a woman from Monterrey, told me that Niño Fidencio had cured her of cancer; she then added gradually that the miracle had come with the help of radiation, chemotherapy, and surgery. A San La Muerte devotee from Goya had much the same story of a miraculous cure realized in the hospital. When operations are successful, it is often said that the folk saint guided the surgeon's hand. Some devotees bring their medications to shrines and touch them to a folk saint's tomb.

Folk saints also intervene to save devotees from accidental death. Characteristic is the story of a man who crashed his car into a telephone pole but inexplicably walked away unhurt. A moment after the crash he discovered the image of Sarita Colonia on the floor between his legs, looking up at him. One may suffer severe injury during accidents—this is the norm—but miraculous intervention saves one's life.

Punishment miracles are also common. These narratives, which seem addressed to nonbelievers as much as to devotees, relate how the saint's miraculous power turns against those who lack respect. The landowner on whose property Gaucho Gil was buried objected to trespassing devotees. As the shrine grew and was frequented by ever increasing numbers of people, the landowner had Gil's bones disinterred and buried in a cemetery. He did this to end the trespassing and to protect his livestock, but shortly afterward terrible things began to happen to him. The landowner was on the brink of madness and ruin when Gil appeared to him in a dream, asking that the remains be returned to their original grave. The landowner complied, his well-being was restored, and, as expressed in a testimony from 1950, he even received Gaucho Gil's thanks, "because his lambs are no longer stolen."[40]

Similar stories are told regarding other folk saints. The doctor who slit Niño Fidencio's throat accidentally pricked his finger while doing so, and he dropped dead as soon as he walked through the door of his office. Sarita Colonia was originally buried in the common grave, which was later cleared for construction of new pavilions. The worker in charge of removing Sarita's remains wounded his knee during excavation, was infected with gangrene, and lost the leg to amputation. He got the message, though, and quit his job in order to dedicate himself to building Sarita's shrine.[41]

I was often struck by the too-little, too-late quality of miracles. One married couple, for example, explained to me that two of their children had died, but that Difunta Correa gave them the strength and resignation to bear the loss. I wondered: Where was Difunta Correa when the miraculous cures were needed? Sarita Colonia's brother relates several specious miracles, but also that his only daughter, likewise named Sarita Colonia, was killed in a plane crash at the age of twenty-two. Where was Sarita when her namesake and the others on the plane needed miraculous rescue?[42]

Devotees explain that there are many reasons why miracles are not granted. It is because one does not deserve the miracle, or one did not request it properly, or one's faith is being tested by the saint. Misfortunes or sufferings can also be sacrifices exacted by the saint as punishments, in repayment for greater pains that were alleviated, or in purifying prepayment for miracles that will be granted later. Patience is also required, because the saint—providing miracles on a first-come, first-served basis—may have a backlog. If one perseveres with faith, the miracle will eventually be granted.

Some devotees, particularly those to San La Muerte, also explain that miracles fail to occur when a particular image's power is depleted and needs to be recharged. Such recharging is done by placing one's image on the altar of a San La Muerte reputed to be powerful, or else by taking it to church for new blessings. Saints, particularly those who are constantly working to fulfill miracles, get tired. They have very human needs for rest, recuperation, and recharge, along with the nourishment, gratitude, and loving care that also replenish them.

Images are often thought to be powerless until they have physical contact with their folk saint's shrine. This belief necessitates pilgrimage. It also boosts sales at the shrines, because the images purchased there are believed to be more powerful because of their prolonged contact. Objects charged through contact with the shrines, and particularly the tombs, make the miraculous power portable. If the contact is with the saint, or the bones of the saint, all the better. Inner-circle devotees used to wrap themselves in Sarita's blanket while requesting miracles. The practice was discontinued, however, because the threadbare blanket was being pulled to pieces by devotees sneaking off with authentic relics. When such prized relics are unavailable, images, flowers, shrine water, stones, and any saint-associated or shrine-acquired items suffice.

Devotees carry these charged images and objects in their pockets, wallets, and purses. Multiple contact is most desirable: a folk saint might be in one's wallet, worn around one's neck, and tattooed on one's body, while at once in one's heart, thoughts, and conversation. The greater the saturation, the greater the effect. Charged images and objects function, in effect, as amulets, and they are used for the same purposes: to ensure good luck, to ward off evil, and to protect bodies, homes, businesses, and cars.

The need for physical contact is a driving force of folk devotions. Touching and kissing express affection while at once putting devotees in direct, corporal contact with a folk saint's power. While I was at the José Dolores shrine in San Juan, a young couple, the woman holding a baby, systematically touched every image in the chapel. After touching each image they touched themselves, and often the baby, or signed themselves with the cross. The gestures imply a transfer mediated by their hands. Such touching can be seen at any shrine, because contact is the primary reason for being there. The tomb is most desirable, but anything at the shrine suffices. Life-size images of the saints make the contact more personal. The reclining Difunta Correa is touched constantly, and in Espinazo I saw devotees sucking on the huge thumb of a Niño Fidencio statue.

Washing with water from the shrines is at once cleansing and purifying. Drinking the water internalizes the folk saint's power. If the water is at the tomb, as at the shrines of Niño Fidencio and Sarita Colonia, it is all the more

Kissing, touching, and other forms of physical contact are essential to folk-saint devotion, here inside the Gaucho Gil shrine in Mercedes, Argentina.

imbued with power. Water from flower vases on or around a tomb is also highly valued.

Tattoos of saints and the surgical insertion of San La Muerte images under the skin make the contact permanent. More abstract but enduring contacts are made by tying ribbons (representing petitions) to shrines and by leaving such personal items as photographs, hair, and copies of identification documents. Mothers hang diapers and children's clothing at the shrines of two Venezuelan folk saints who were medical doctors. Once the diapers and clothes have absorbed sufficient miraculous power, the children are dressed in them to effect the cure.[43]

Visits to shrines are multiply efficacious: they place one in contact with the saint, they provide the opportunity for charging images and for acquiring relics, they fulfill promises, they renew faith, they foster a familiarity conducive to miracles, and they integrate one into the community of devotees. Many shrines are referred to as a "holy land," and organized groups make the pilgrimage in "missions" (Niño Fidencio devotion) or "caravans" (María Lionza devotion) so that the journey is as communal as the arrival. Many pilgrims travel to San La Muerte, Gaucho Gil, and Difunta Correa fiestas in buses hired by devotee groups and tour companies.

When folk saints fail to perform miracles, their images (often thought to be one and the same with the saint) are subject to insults, threats, punishment, burial, and even destruction. Some saints are tied up or hung upside down. This coercive punishment, which is lifted when the miracle is granted, is derived from folk Catholicism. The baby Jesus is taken from the arms of statuettes, for example, and held hostage until a miracle is granted. A poor woman who migrated to Lima said: "I asked St. Martin to cure my mother's disease. I begged him, crying; I lit candles at home, in church. But he didn't grant me the miracle. So I said to him: 'St. Martin, I'm taking your head so that you will grant what I have asked of you, and if you do I'll give you back your head.' But he didn't. My mother died."[44]

Others simply give up on a given saint and try another. A woman who posted a message on a San La Muerte Web site wrote that she was tired of making unfulfilled requests to San La Muerte: "I'm going to try Gaucho Gil. I've run out of patience." Another explained that he had made his requests some time ago but nothing happened, and asked, "How long does the saint take to respond?" A third requested success in gambling to improve his economic situation, but his bad luck remained unchanged. "I have many doubts regarding the effectiveness of this saint," he wrote. Some friends "told me that they didn't think he was so effective since if it were so simple there would be no hunger in Argentina and we would all be millionaires." And finally: "I learned about this saint through a television program and the person who was talking about the saint seemed very poor, which also makes me doubt."[45]

The Spiritual Contract

Devotion is structured by a spiritual contract that establishes mutual obligations for the folk saint and the devotee. The contract begins with a problem or need that the devotee presents to the saint with the hope of a miraculous solution. This request, also called a petition, is presented along with a promise, and it is for this reason that a devotee is often referred to as a *promesero* or *promesante* (one who makes a promise). A devotee might request success in finding a job, for example, and promise in return to make a pilgrimage to the shrine and offer candles. If the miracle is granted, then the promise—known in some regions as a *manda* (promise or vow of offering)—must be fulfilled. The fulfillment is often referred to as *pagar una manda* (paying off or for a promise or vow), and the offering itself as a *pago* (payment). Failure to uphold one's end of the bargain after receiving a requested miracle has consequences. The saint may undo the miracle or, in cases of more punitive saints, such as San La Muerte, may impose an additional punishment. More lenient saints simply withdraw their protection, which leaves devotees on their own in harm's way.

The practice of making payments to supernatural powers—in gratitude, in atonement, or simply to maintain good relations—has strong traditional antecedents in indigenous cultures. In the Peruvian Andes, regular offerings (again referred to as "payments") are made to mountain spirits and to the earth goddess Pachamama. Though these offerings can be accompanied by requests for specific benefits (health, work, and love, for example), they tend more toward installment or goodwill payments to maintain general well-being. Traditional payments to Pachamama are made primarily in early August, before sowing, with the hope of the earth's reciprocation through fecundity and bounty.

As new needs arise, however, tradition evolves and adapts. A distressed street vendor in Juliaca, finding herself in straits despite regular offerings to Pachamama, finally sought alleviation of her poverty through divine intervention in politics: "Although I made two payments to the earth this year so that she would protect us all, because she does not want us to suffer any more, what we earn isn't enough even though we are working hard. That is why we have prayed to the Holy Earth that the government will be changed."[46]

The similarity between indigenous rituals and folk saint devotions is most apparent in offerings to Tio ("Uncle"), the spirit of Bolivian mines. Regular offerings are made to the quasi-diabolical Tio to placate his wrath, to beseech his protection in the mines, and to gain his blessing for discovery and exploitation of new veins. Statues of Tio are situated at the various mine shafts and tunnels. Each Tio has his arms and mouth open to receive offerings. A huge erect penis is also characteristic, and (much to the delight of new miners) the mouths and penises of some Tios are connected so that drinks poured into the former squirt out the latter. Tios are offered coca, alcoholic drinks, and cigarettes, as well as the blood sacrifice of llamas and alpacas.

If regular payments are not made, then Tio doubly punishes: once with death, usually of miners, and again by withholding ore. In the Santa Rosita mine at Potosí, a mining firm discovered a huge vein of silver that had remained untapped after colonial exploitation. Some mine workers believed that the discovery was the result of a pact with Tio, which included the sacrifice of several human fetuses. The mining company made millions of dollars thanks to Tio, and some of the profits were invested in a fleet of buses. Accidents on the road soon resulted in dozens of deaths, however, because the company neglected to maintain its pact with Tio by sacrificing a red rooster on the first and last Fridays of each month.[47]

In folk-saint devotions, the obligations of the devotee and the saint are clearly established—this repayment in exchange for that miracle—at the time that the miracle is requested. The protocol varies, however, particularly in areas more influenced by indigenous traditions. Silvia, from Puno, made her first visit to the Niño Compadrito shrine bearing gifts. A second visit, likewise, was to present an offering, this time a custom-tailored outfit for the saint, but no request for a miracle was made on either occasion. When I asked Silvia why, she explained that she was building a relationship with Niño Compadrito and would make her request once she had established good rapport.

The exchange-based relations between devotee and saint are also less contractual once devotion becomes a way of life. Ramón, a dedicated devotee of San La Muerte, described a bond of ongoing, mutual care: "I take care of him and he takes care of me; it's reciprocal." As San La Muerte improves Ramón's financial situation, Ramón can afford luxuries for San La Muerte. Well-being advances in tandem, and Ramón's specific requests for miracles are integrated into this regimen of reciprocity.

The forms of offerings in exchange for miracles are as varied as the devotees themselves. Need-based faith is conditioned by poverty, and offerings are likewise in accord with one's means. The devotee establishes the terms, but repayment can nevertheless strain limited resources. This is particularly true when devotees overreach with the hope of inspiring a greatly needed miracle and then suffer the burden of debt service. The most common offerings are candles, flowers, plaques, banners, food, alcoholic drinks, cigarettes, visits to shrines, pilgrimages to distant shrines, votive artwork, attendance at fiestas, small cash donations, prayer, and Catholic masses said for the soul of the saint.

Grateful devotees also publish newspaper announcements, circulate chain letters, distribute food, provide saintly attire for images, perform dances, write and perform songs (often referred to as serenading the saint), name children after the saint, volunteer at a shrine, and get a saint's image tattooed on their bodies. Outside the chapel to San Simón in San Andrés Itzapa, Guatemala, fires burn to receive offerings (such as tobacco, copal, sugar, candles, and eggs) that are sometimes coded for specific purposes. Someone petitioning love, for example, offers sugar. Elsewhere, the recipients of substantial miracles, such as rescue from some life-threatening situation or illness, generally make greater offerings, particularly when they have the means. These include building a domestic or roadside shrine; contributing to the construction, expansion, or maintenance of an existing shrine; sponsoring a fiesta; and donating to a shrine a large sum of cash or such valuables as jewels and cars.

Many of these offerings conform to the ageless tradition of presenting an ex voto (a votive offering, from the Latin meaning "according to a vow") as acknowledgment of a miracle received. Because ex votos are public offerings, their accumulation on and around altars and images testifies to a saint's miraculousness and thus contributes to growth of the cult. Unlike candles or flowers, which are anonymous offerings, ex votos commemorate a miracle with a representation of the recipient (such as a photograph, an identification card, clothes, or a lock of hair) or of the miracle itself (such as narrative paintings or crutches that attest to a cure).

In addition to personal items of every sort, folk saint shrines are full of such ex votos as license plates, school texts and notebooks, trophies, sports-team paraphernalia, miniature models of homes and businesses, and legal documents, each of these relating to the miracle performed. Soldiers donate their uniforms, boxers their boxing gloves, musicians their instruments, and brides their wedding dresses. The tiny metal images known as *milagros* (literally "miracles") are also common in some regions. Traditional milagros represent body parts, and one pins a milagro of the ailing or healed part on or near a saint. Today milagros come in all forms—animals, cars, buses, airplanes, houses, crops, books, married couples—with each relating to the miracle received or requested.

In Andean traditions, the first cuttings of children's hair have for centuries been offered to *huacas* (local deities) and to saints. There are similar practices in folk Catholicism elsewhere. A 1951 report from western Argentina explains that the braids of children who had been cured miraculously were offered to the Virgin: "one often sees boys of 6 or 7 years old wearing braids until the mother judges that they are sufficiently long to make the offering."[48] Children's braids are also offered to folk saints, although some devotees object to the practice. One, at the Difunta Correa complex, suggested with some indignation that parents should make a sacrifice themselves (such as climbing to the shrine on their knees) rather than resorting to their children's hair.

The offering of stones to folk saints is a gesture of gratitude that even the poorest devotees can afford. Stones, which for centuries have been an offering in the Andes, today have special significance in the Mexican devotion to Jesús Malverde. Because Malverde was a thief, tradition holds that one must steal a stone from his shrine in order to get his attention. One returns the stone, with another as an offering, once the miracle has been granted. Stone offerings are also prominent in devotion to Juan Soldado in Tijuana, where likewise they are taken (but not stolen) upon making the petition and returned when the miracle is granted.

The offerings made by devotees often pay homage to a folk saint's identity. The poetic logic that guides these choices is reminiscent of the way canonized saints are attributed patronage. St. Lawrence, who was grilled alive, becomes the patron saint of cooks; Difunta Correa, who died of thirst, is offered bottles of water. Metaphorical inversions and extensions are common: "She who died of thirst gives all of us the water of hope." Some older devotees believe that candles offered to Gaucho Gil must be lit with the wick facing downward, because the saint was hanging upside-down when he was executed. The difficulty in lighting the candle this way attests to the devotee's seriousness of purpose and to the saint's willingness to receive the request. In Guatemala, tobacco is a common offering to Maximón (some say that the name is derived from the Mayan word for tobacco). The saint is represented with a cigar in his mouth, and many devotees smoke cigars at the time of making their petitions.[49]

Specific aspects of folk saints' lives also contribute to the choice of offerings and to the nature of devotion. An attendant in the San Pedro cemetery in Jujuy explained that Finada Chabela, a curandera who became a folk saint, never performed cures without drinking wine. In commemoration her devotees leave wine offerings when requesting miraculous cures. Another northern Argentine folk saint, La Telesita, wandered across the countryside and appeared unexpectedly in taverns to captivate gathered locals with her dancing. She was thus later venerated by *reza-bailes* (prayer-dances), themselves known as Telesitas, which intermix dance, devotion, and heavy drinking. The ritual, which can last all night, ends when the candle or candles lit at the beginning go out. A small effigy of Telesita is then burned in memory of her tragic death by fire.[50]

Dance and fiestas as a form of offering were also prominent in devotion to the gaucho saint Francisco López. Reports from Corrientes Province in the 1950s explain that López, who loved dance parties, will not accept prayer unless it is accompanied by dance. One woman, who kept a relic carved from the cross at López's tomb, typically sponsored a fiesta on the anniversary of López's death that entailed a prayer session followed by a night of dancing.[51]

Another report explained in more detail that López (like Gaucho Gil and José Dolores) was arrested at a dance. He was falsely accused of murder and robbery, was bound and deprived of water, and then eventually, when he was languishing from thirst, was summarily executed. His last words provided a mandate, while at once establishing a link between the thirst he suffered and the need for water that his supernatural powers would later alleviate: "They will kill me because of a false testimony, and when I'm dead I want you to have a dance for me instead of a wake. Also, whenever you need water or lose something, ask me for help in your prayers, because I will be close to God and from there will try to get for you everything that you ask of me."[52]

Offerings to folk saints tend to be valued in terms of their "sacrifice," which is to say what it cost one—more in pains than in money—to repay a saint for a miracle. There appears to be an inherent contradiction in suffering as a form of thanks to saints who alleviate suffering. This relation between miracles and sacrifice is clearly indebted to Catholicism, in which penance figures so prominently. God's graces can be acquired, or recuperated, through suffering, as epitomized by the crucifixion itself. When folk saints accept offerings that entail suffering, they do so not out of sadism but rather because suffering is viewed positively, as a means to purge and purify.

Devotees also regard sacrifices as demonstrations of sincerity, dedication, and seriousness of purpose. They are indices of true faith and gratitude, expressions of reciprocation for extraordinary gains. Miracles are more likely if the advance or the payoff signals the devotee's earnestness and worthiness. Repayment in pain is also to some degree imitative of Christ and of folk saints who in various ways sacrificed their lives for their people. Niño Fidencio worked tirelessly to serve the thousands who needed him, and because he suffered, "all those who want to follow him must suffer too." A medium from Texas added, "If you don't do a sacrifice, you don't get nothing." No pain, no gain.[53]

The most severe forms of sacrifice are physical. Typical hardships and sufferings include walking for miles in bare feet, climbing up stairs on one's back or knees, rolling uphill, and carrying heavy crosses. These acts of penance work off sin, pay off debt, express commitment, and offer voluntary, meaningful suffering in exchange for the alleviation of meaningless suffering—illness and injury—beyond one's control. Because they are public and often theatrical, such sacrifices attract the admiration and awe of some devotees (who see them as maximal expressions of faith) and the disapproval of others (who see them as excessive or as ostentatious spectacles).

Most devotees seek a proportional relation between the miracle and the sacrifice offered in exchange. The greater the miracle requested, the greater the sacrifice. A devotee at Difunta Correa's shrine explained that he asks for minor miracles daily and repays them by lighting a candle or saying a prayer. Now, however, he has traveled eight hours to the shrine to make a more substantial request. "If Difunta Correa gives me the miracle I am asking for," he said facetiously, "I'm going to have to come back [from home] on my knees." In other cases there is clearly a trade imbalance between the value of the miracle received and the offering made in gratitude. A San La Muerte devotee in Posadas, for example, explained that his life was miraculously spared during a mugging, and in gratitude he offered "two fingers" of a candle (the width of the fingers measure the amount of the candle to be burned).

Sacrifices are not limited to physical sufferings. They include any pains—in the broadest sense of the term—that express gratitude. The pilgrimages to distant shrines, sponsorship of fiestas, (unaffordable) expenses incurred by offerings, and other vow-related redirections of scarce resources are all considered sacrifices. Other hardships regarded as forms of sacrifice include, for example, the overnight walk from San Juan to the Difunta Correa shrine, the difficult conditions for camping in Espinazo during Niño Fidencio fiestas, and the painful insertion of San La Muerte images under one's skin. During a Sarita Colonia fiesta the sun was hot and the line to enter the shrine was endless. One woman got aggravated when another cut into the line to avoid waiting her turn. "You come here to make your sacrifice," said the aggravated woman, "and then you cut in line?"

Relations with the Church

Most canonized saints were first folk saints, but this does not imply that most folk saints will eventually be canonized. Indeed, it is highly improbable that any of the folk saints discussed in this book will ever be considered for canonization. They are of little interest to the Church because of their life-styles (as criminals or drunks), because there is insufficient historical information on their lives, or because they are entirely legendary (although other nonhistorical figures have been canonized).

Those folk saints who attract the attention of the Church have led virtuous lives in accord with saintly prototypes, sometimes in addition to having suffered a tragic death. Before Dr. José Gregorio Hernández was run over by an automobile in 1919, for example, he was a charitable man and model Christian, dedicated selflessly to providing medical treatment to the poor. Hernández never married, and he intended twice to become a priest but was persuaded instead to continue serving others through medicine. His cause for canonization was opened in 1949, and he was recognized as a venerable in 1985.

Many devotees are baffled by the Church's refusal to recognize their folk saint. How is it possible, they ask, that a soul so miraculous—more so than the saints in the churches—is not embraced by the Vatican? How can their own Church reject and even mock saints who have done so much for thousands of Catholics, who have earned their fervent devotion? And if some priests can recognize the value of folk saints, saying mass for them or blessing their images, then why can't others? Even thoughtful Ramón, the San La Muerte devotee in Resistencia, could not understand this paradox and felt as though the Church owed devotees an explanation.

As devotees pose these question to themselves, the respondents tend to divide into two groups. One group is hopeful and activist: it anticipates the eventual canonization of its folk saint and sometimes moves toward the mainstream in the hope of legitimization. An annual San La Muerte fiesta, for example, begins with praying of the rosary, and this is led by a shrine owner who has vowed to continue her struggle until the Church canonizes San La Muerte. A grateful Gaucho Gil devotee aspired to the same goal through prayer: "From my heart I am going to pray to God and to the Holy Father so that from Rome you will be Recognized by everyone and they will have FAITH in you and believe in you." Some devotees are less committed to canonization but share the belief that it is feasible and will happen sooner or later. When I asked such devotees if their folk saint was canonized, a common response was "not yet."[54]

These optimist and activist devotees contrast with others who are indifferent to canonization, who do not understand the difference between a folk saint and a canonized saint, or, at the far end of the spectrum, who prefer that their folk saint remain uncanonized. Sarita Colonia's countless devotees "already consider her a saint, which she is for them. They say that she does not need to go through the long delays and complicated process established by the Church and Canon Law." The folk saint "is a saint for us," say adepts of all devotions, thereby expressing their indifference to Church endorsement.[55]

Others believe that canonization would be detrimental. They implicitly object because through canonization they would lose ownership of a saint now exclusively theirs, born of *lo nuestro*. When their objection becomes explicit, it indicates a fear of losing access to miracles. A man in Lima told me that he was devoted to Sarita Colonia rather than to the Lord of Miracles because the latter already had more miracle requests than he could handle. The line to Sarita was shorter. Another devotee argued that "Sarita works miracles [for us] because she is not yet canonized. Because when the Church recognizes her as a saint, she will then be in the Heavenly Court, with the angels and other saints," and therefore "she will no longer remember us." José Gregorio Hernández used to frequently possess Venezuelan mediums for the purpose of spiritual cures, but now that he has been designated a venerable by the Church he sends his assistants instead.[56]

The divide between folk and formal Catholicism widens when Church authorities not only deny canonization, but also prohibit devotion, repress a cult, or speak out publicly against a given folk saint. The devotees take offense because they find their beliefs and their culture under attack (often by clergy from outside of their community), but also because they self-identify as Catholics and feel betrayed. They say Catholic prayers to their folk saints, they have Catholic imagery on the altars and in the chapels of their folk saints, they have masses said in Catholic churches for their folk saints, and they enjoy the collaboration of some priests. If they are Catholic and their folk saints are close to Jesus Christ, what's the problem? Why is their Church turning on them?

These questions circulated among puzzled devotees when devotion to Niño Compadrito came under Church assault in 1976. The devotees believed that their folk saint devotion was Catholic, and they argued the point in three ways: the shrine of Niño Compadrito was decorated with images and statues of saints and the Virgin, along with other Catholic paraphernalia and even an image of the pope; Catholic priests had come to the shrine and celebrated mass, which indicated that Niño Compadrito was compatible with Catholicism; and the great majority of Niño Compadrito devotees are dedicated Catholics, some of whom have held important positions in Cuzco churches and Catholic organizations. All of this proved that the devotion was Catholic and that the repression was unjustified. The shock to the cult was further aggravated by the manner of the archbishop of Cuzco, who took a hard-line approach reminiscent of colonial extirpations of idolatry.[57]

Other cults, such as Niño Fidencio's in 1990, have likewise been offended when Church authorities speak out against them. On March 19, 1976 (just prior to the coup that initiated the "dirty war"), the bishops of Argentina declared that Difunta Correa was "illegitimate and reprehensible" and asked Catholics to abandon this devotion. Orthodox lay Catholics also express their objections to folk saints, particularly when they feel that improper devotions are encroaching on sacrosanct terrain. In a letter to the editor of a Resistencia newspaper in 1986, two concerned citizens responded to an article that referred to San La Muerte as "Lord" and "King of Heaven." "This is in conflict with the teachings of the Bible," they wrote, which reserves these titles for Christ. A group of devotees met with a similar reaction in 1995 when they attempted to have devotion to San La Muerte officially recognized and included in the national registry of religions. The petition was denied because the devotion had insufficient organizational structure and was little more than a "folk superstition" based on "deformation of Christian beliefs."[58]

Sensitive and diplomatic statements made by Church authorities are better received, but they are also conducive to ambiguity and confusion. One common Church strategy seeks to curtail devotion without demeaning the folk saint or the cult. Monsignor Ricardo Durand Flórez, then bishop of Callao, explained to devotees that "we are not against Sarita Colonia" and "one may commend oneself to her." However, "what we are saying is that she cannot be given public cult because it would damage her cause." He later repeated that as long as there is public cult to Sarita Colonia, the cause for canonization cannot be pursued. This approach hopes to dissuade devotees without offending them. It does so by (deceptively) implying the possibility of Sarita's canonization, so that abandonment of her public cult seems in her best interest.[59]

Unsuccessful verbal campaigns against folk saints are sometimes followed by decisive actions. La Chavela often sang for tips at the San Camilo market in Arequipa, and after her death the vendors visited her tomb on Mondays, offering candles. This practice was sustained, in part, by the belief that failure to pay homage to La Chavela would result in poor sales. A bar crowd also visited La Chavela, toasting her at the grave. Church authorities were troubled by this improper devotion and intervened to eliminate it. The campaign began with defamations and prohibitions from the pulpit and in newspapers: it was scandalous that Catholics worshipped this sinner. When defamation failed, extreme measures followed. Under pressure from the Church, the cemetery housing La Chavela's grave was closed (parts of it were moved farther from the city) to deny devotees access to the tomb. The inaccessibility of the sacred site fatally damaged the devotion to La Chavela, which eventually disappeared completely.[60]

In Argentina, similarly, devotion to Francisco López inspired an aggressive reaction from the Church. López was "so popular and motivated such a scandalous cult" that the Church authorities, "jealous of this prestige," repressed it with the assistance of the police. Another archival report states that after a half-century of such scandal, the authorities intervened in 1910 (some give 1916 as the date) to put an end to the devotion. Under the orders of a priest who later became the bishop, López's remains were disinterred and removed to a cemetery in Corrientes. To fight this "idolatry," the shrine at López's tomb was demolished, but at midcentury the devotion was still booming. Today, López's cult has virtually disappeared. The assault on one saint, however, does not eliminate the urge conducive to the creation of others. Gaucho Gil, who was of lesser importance in the mid-twentieth century, has assumed now the position held earlier by López.[61]

Clergy who take a hard line against folk saint devotions are defending the faith against what they see as unorthodox deformations, but they are also responding to a challenge to the Church's monopoly on the supernatural. When they articulate their objections, the accusations generally include paganism, superstition, idolatry, magic, commercialism, and the reduction of religion to the exchange of payment for favors. From their perspective, folk saint devotions are a "mixture of religious beliefs with superstition and myths"; they evidence a "lack of development, profundity, and purity"; and they "reduce the Faith to a mere utilitarian contract."[62]

Though all of these accusations are essentially true, they likewise characterize devotion to canonized saints. Father Luis María Adis, the parish priest of Mercedes since 1991, recognized that Catholics also enter into utilitarian contracts with saints, the only difference being that these saints are approved by the Church. One clear example is devotion to San Expedito, a canonized saint who is popular in Corrientes and has a chapel in Bermejo, San Juan, near the shrine of Difunta Correa. As implied by his name (from the same root as "to expedite"), San Expedito is a generalist for the fulfillment of urgent needs—he gets the job done quickly. His cult is strong in many regions of Spanish America.

The magical aspects of folk saint devotion are also prevalent in the veneration of canonized saints. Adis gave the example of Catholics who camped out in line for weeks, waiting for the few seconds that they would touch a statue of San Cayetano (who is petitioned for bread and work). This quest for an "instantaneous solution," as he put it, is little different from the request made to folk saints. Adis also recognized that the commercial activity at folk saint shrines—which invites the accusations of scams exploiting ignorance—is also prevalent at major festivals honoring patron saints and at pilgrimage sites approved by the Church. The shrines of the Virgin of Luján and the Virgin of Itatí are far more commercial than most folk saint shrines, as is (among innumerable examples) the annual fiesta to the Lord of Miracles in Lima.

Father Adis, far from a liberal, might best be described as a moderate priest who understands the complexities of folk saints but nevertheless feels the responsibility to discourage unauthorized devotions. He will bless devotees' crosses and bottles of water, but when they ask for blessings of Gaucho Gil statuettes he offers a bit of catechism instead ("Now they know not to ask"). In 1995 he said the prayer for the dead at the shrine, despite his reservations; and in 1999 he prepared an outline for an (unproduced) brochure to catechize Gaucho Gil devotion. Earlier, when the bishop circulated a pastoral letter discouraging the devotion in 1992, parishioners told Adis that Gaucho Gil would punish him. Adis recognizes the relation of folk saint devotions to the cult to the dead—explaining that Catholics may request miracles from their deceased parents, as he does—but he draws the line when the cult goes public.

Some other moderate priests have a more relaxed, almost nonideological tolerance of folk saints: if they help people get through hard times, then why not? This position sometimes comes accompanied by a folkloric apology. Folk saints, like music, dress, foods, fiestas, and other folkloric expressions, are integral to local cultures and should be left alone. These priests avoid participation in folk saint cults but do not demean or repress them.

One simple but perhaps misguided remedy attempted by other priests is the diversion of folk saint devotees toward canonized saints with similar attributes. Much of the devotion to saints—both canonized and folk—entails petitions to specialists: this saint for one problem, that saint for another. Priests thus search for canonized alternatives, some of them long-forgotten saints from early or medieval Christianity, and encourage a switch from an unauthorized specialist to an authorized one. Crossovers to these replacement saints are viewed as positive, but the net effect is to perpetuate the simplistic, magical, contractual devotion that priests object to elsewhere. I was reminded of these switches when I asked a taxi driver in Jujuy if Almita Silvia was a canonized saint. He replied that she was not, but that if I was looking for that sort of thing I should try St. Rita (who also had an abusive husband).

In both folk saint devotion and folk Catholicism generally, devotees borrow supernatural resources from the Church and then do with them as they please. Many of the reports from Corrientes in the 1950s underscore precisely this mix of Catholicism with folk devotions. "They are Catholic people, but they practice the religion however they like, mixing sacred with profane." Another notes that some prefer canonized saints and others folk saints, but they are all used similarly for practical miracles via spiritual contracts. One man ended his remarks by describing the local religion as "Apostolic Roman Catholicism mixed with some practices of witchcraft."[63]

The distinction between folk saints and canonized saints is ultimately academic, because for millions of Spanish American Catholics miracles are the true measure of sainthood. The solemnly defended convictions of the Congregation of Rites have little relevance when miracles (or their absence) contradict them. It is for this reason that folk saint devotees are puzzled when their saints are attacked or their Catholicism is questioned. Saints perform miracles; Gaucho Gil performs miracles; therefore Gaucho Gil is a saint. This is what being Catholic means to them.

The mix of Catholicism with unorthodox practices is partially a consequence of unfinished catechism and the absence of priests in rural areas. When I asked a priest in Cuzco why Catholics pray to Niño Compadrito instead of to a canonized saint, he responded without hesitation: incomplete religious education and insufficient clerical guidance. Almost all of the reports from Corrientes Province in the 1940s and 1950s mention home altars to folk saints, and some describe them as compensations for the lack of a church. One report observed that locals "are in general religious and believe in God, but are also very superstitious. Due to the lack of Churches in these areas, the adults are almost entirely unfamiliar with the Religious Creeds because they did not have the opportunity to be raised in a religious climate."[64]

There is nothing new about clerical repression of folk devotions—for two thousand years the Church has been combating what it perceives to be superstition and heterodoxy. Early medieval Catholics used to flee the church in droves to escape the homily, and in response some bishops had the doors locked to keep the wayward faithful in their pews. Another tactic was the circulation of letters from Christ promising eternal punishment for those who did not obey divine law as prescribed by the Church.[65]

The results were nevertheless mixed, and the contentious issues of the past are remarkably similar to those of today. Consider, for example, this confessional interrogation: "Have you gone to pray anywhere except the church or someplace advised by the bishop or priest, that is, beside fountains, stones, trees, crossroads, and have you lit there for devotion a torch or candle; have you taken there bread or another offering and have you eaten it in quest of the health of your soul and your body?" St. Cesáreo de Arles went further, making shrine owners and witnesses the accomplices of offenders: "Whoever on his own lands, or in his house, or nearby has trees, altars, or any other vain thing where miserable people are accustomed to making vows, if you do not destroy it or cut it down, you become definitely a participant in the sacrileges that are committed there." He adds, "Stupid people, who never knew God, thought that gods were those who stood out above other men."[66]

Conquest of the Americas was followed by forced conversion, which often consisted only of rudimentary catechization and baptism. The cosmovision, gods, beliefs, rituals, and values of indigenous traditions did not simply disappear when the alien religion was imposed. They rather provided an understructure, a basis for cognition of Catholicism, and mix and match was the rule. The intermingling of Catholicism with traditional beliefs has continued into modern times, aided by continued limited understanding of (or interest in) theological doctrine and, more recently, by growing disillusion with the Church. The scarcity of priests is also conducive to do-it-yourself Catholicism.

Some clergy, particularly parish priests trained in the doctrines of the Second Vatican Council (Vatican II), are cognizant of this long view and are more tolerant of folk saint devotions. Whereas more conservative priests see superstition and paganism, these priests see deep faith that, however misguided, can be educated and encouraged toward orthodox practices. They view folk saint devotions as legitimate religious and cultural expressions that err for want of guidance. The verb used by many priests, *encausar* (to channel), captures the idea precisely: the priest's task is to steer or redirect devotees' true faith toward proper objects of devotion.

On occasion clergy visit folk saint shrines, and for diverse purposes. They say mass or offer blessings, they make gestures of peace and conciliation, they check out the competition (sometimes gathering information for later derogatory proclamations), and they gently attempt to "purify" the devotion. The usual visitors are priests, but symbolic appearances have been made by bishops and archbishops.

In November 1999, the archbishop of San Juan, Italo Severino Di Stéfano, visited the Difunta Correa complex. He was the first archbishop to do so, although he went only to the Catholic church at the complex and not to the shrine where Difunta Correa is venerated. The archbishop was explicit about the purpose of his visit—to try to channel devotion back toward the Church— but nevertheless his appearance stimulated the belief that Difunta Correa's canonization might be imminent.

In January 2005, similarly, the bishop of Goya, Ricardo Faifer, made an appearance at the Gaucho Gil fiesta. This visit, too, was a gesture of peace and an attempt to channel the devotion toward orthodox practices, but devotees again drew their own conclusions. The visits, blessings, and masses of priests are likewise ambiguous, because the theological nuances that justify them have little meaning to devotees. Any participation by a priest is easily misinterpreted as Church endorsement of the cult. When I asked the owner of a shrine in San Roque if Gaucho Gil was a canonized saint, he responded by saying that the shrine was blessed by the local priest.

Some more perceptive, or cynical, devotees see the priests' presence at folk saint shrines as an effort to control attrition, recuperate lost parishioners, and fill the pews. The majority of devotees hardly adhere to the requirements of Catholicism—such as attending mass—but they visit folk saint shrines frequently, happily, and of their own volition. When the Church's repression fails to stop this pattern of defections, then good-cop priests show up at the shrine with a new agenda. As Alfredo, a Gaucho Gil devotee, explained it, "If you can't defeat your enemy, make him your friend."

The cult of Niño Compadrito was actively repressed by an intolerant archbishop beginning in 1976, but before then some priests celebrated mass at the shrine. They did so at the request of devotees, again with the hope of steering the cult back toward the Church. The archbishop's prohibitions ended this practice, but when the cult reemerged in 1982, after the archbishop's death, devotee-requested masses were celebrated in churches. The bone effigy of Niño Compadrito was brought to the churches to hear the masses celebrated in his name, generally on or around his feast day.[67]

Most recently, it has been difficult for Niño Compadrito devotees to find a church willing to celebrate these masses. An annual mass for Niño Compadrito was traditionally celebrated in Cuzco's Franciscan church, but this venue eventually became unavailable to devotees. The search for an alternative seemed futile until finally a parish priest in the Huanchac neighborhood agreed to celebrate a mass. He was censured by the bishop in 2002 for doing so, and there was no mass the following year for want of a venue.

For the annual Gaucho Gil fiesta, a mass is celebrated in the parish church of Mercedes. Gaucho Gil's cross is brought from the shrine to the church for the mass, and afterward a spectacular procession, led by gauchos on horseback, returns the cross to the shrine. Insofar as the Church is concerned, the mass is said for the soul of the deceased person, Antonio Gil, not for a folk saint. Both the current parish priest and his predecessor agree, however, that most devotees do not make this distinction. The Church's participation is viewed more simply as a kind of endorsement. A very small percentage of devotees attend the mass, and before 2000, when the provincial government intervened in the shrine's administration, most devotees were unaware that it was celebrated.

Involvement of the Church is more significant at the Difunta Correa complex, where a church was built beside the shrine. The intent is the usual one—to foster a transfer of devotion from the shrine to the church—but the church remains virtually empty while devotees flock to Difunta Correa. This placing of the church at a folk saint shrine is reminiscent of an evangelical strategy that has been used for millennia. After the conquest of the New World, and during the spread of Christianity in the Roman Empire, churches, crosses, and shrines to saints were situated at the sites of pagan deities. The Catholic buildings were often built over the ruins of pagan temples, which sent the clear message that the site remained sacred but that a new god had been superimposed.

At folk saint shrines today the pagan temple is not destroyed or retrofitted for Catholicism, but rather stands beside the Catholic church. The Church's intent is more a cooptation than a conquest. Devotees, because they are Catholic, welcome the presence—it lends prestige and legitimacy to the shrine—insofar as the priests remain tolerant and respectful of the folk saint.

The Church's inconsistent position on folk saints fosters the confusion and resentment of devotees. A period of tolerance and even collaboration can be followed abruptly by repression, with the about-face owing only to the change of a parish priest, a bishop, or an archbishop. One clergyman will bless folk saint images or celebrate masses, and the next will actively attempt to extirpate the cult. This inconsistency, as one priest explained it to me, owes ultimately to the rift between the teachings of Christ and the Church as a bureaucratic institution. The Church must defend its dogma, but in doing so can stray far afield from the doctrine and the God that authorize it.

Folk saint devotees are explicit in their denigration of shepherds who have lost touch with their flocks. They describe most priests as something like salesmen of sacraments who are oblivious to the spiritual and material needs of their people. Some more educated devotees self-identify as anticlerical and anti-institutional, describing the Church as a human enterprise rather than the one true faith that it claims to be. In the extreme views, such as those of an early channeler of Niño Fidencio, clergymen are agents of the Antichrist: "The Popes of Rome, the Archbishops, Bishops, and Priests are all in a celestial jail, because they have falsified the scripture of God, Our Father."[68]

Devotees also commonly view priests as obsolete, as unnecessary and troublesome intermediaries who are struggling to maintain the illusion of their importance. One morning at the Niño Compadrito shrine a woman related stories concerning the image of Christ that had appeared in a tree in Izcuchaca. The Church refused to acknowledge the authenticity of the Lord of Phuchu Orcco, as this image is known, to the great dismay of devotees. Before she got to her conclusion, which relegated priests to obsolescence, the woman narrated a story that expressed a common urge for just reconciliation. A priest intended to chop down the tree in Izcuchaca, but then became gravely ill, understood the error of his ways, and said a mass before the Lord of Phuchu Orcco. Having brought this priest back into the fold—channeled him back to the folk devotion—the woman concluded that Christ was revealing himself in towns and rural areas, outside of the churches, because he wants to be in direct contact with the people.

No matter what priests do, their actions are interpreted to the benefit of folk saint devotions. If a priest is accommodating and participatory, then devotees celebrate the endorsement while more or less ignoring the priest's attempts to purify their Catholicism. The willing priest also raises the expectation that the folk saint will eventually be canonized. If a priest is tolerant and neutral, condoning folk devotion without getting involved, then this is interpreted as tacit approval. And if a priest is actively opposed to folk devotion, militantly seeking to repress or extirpate it, then the cult unites in solidarity against this common enemy, entrenches to defend its faith, and adheres all the more radically to its prohibited convictions. The more folk saints are rejected by the Church, the more they are embraced as the private property of devotees and as inalienable aspects of folk culture. Church attacks also dignify a cult with the backhanded compliment of being worthy of such attention.

Defiance is indeed an important attribute of folk saints and their cults. Like Christ himself, such folk saints as Gaucho Gil, Niño Fidencio, and San La Muerte gain prominence in part because they rise up against or compensate for corrupt institutions. Their devotees, likewise, have chosen faiths that defy Church authority. This, for many, is a great part of the appeal, because defiance contributes to the restitution of meaning and pride.

Ignacio, whose home shrine in Resistencia is filled with images of San La Muerte and other saints, describes the Church as an institution that has gotten lost in theological disputes rather than fulfilling its responsibility to Catholics. Hundreds of people seek Ignacio's counsel each week, and this booming business requires that people take numbers, as at a deli counter, to keep track of their turns. Ignacio views his work as partial compensation for the Church's failures; if priests were doing their job, he wouldn't have his. "I'm a rebel," Ignacio says, and he likes to "accumulate devotions" that are unapproved by the Church.

Despite that, however, Ignacio dresses in the likeness of a Catholic priest as he draws on the curative powers of San La Muerte. His home shrine includes countless images of canonized saints—even a poster of the pope— along with the museumlike accumulation of folk saints.

This ambiguity underscores the essential paradox of folk saint devotions: no matter how rejecting or critical devotees may be of the Church, their devotions are entirely dependent on Catholicism, from its conception of the supernatural to the powers exercised by the very priests who are devalued, despised, or displaced. The best example is San La Muerte, whose image is powerless without a priest's blessing. The José Dolores shrine in San Juan, built in the early 1960s, is remarkably similar to a Catholic chapel, with an altar, pews, and stained-glass windows representing Christ and St. Joseph (José) with the Christ Child. The caretakers of the shrine take liters of water to mass for blessing, then pour this holy water into a font so that devotees can sign themselves with the cross—as in church—upon entering.

Almost all aspects of devotion—prayers, novenas, processions, the organization of chapels and altars, the masses said for folk saints, the uses of holy water, the ubiquitous presence of Christ and canonized-saint imagery, the similarity of folk saints to canonized prototypes, and even the idea of intercession—are derived from Catholicism. Folk saint devotions are dependent upon the very institution that they subvert. They are not restricted by dogma or subordinate to institutional authorities, so they borrow at will to produce alternative concepts of sanctity that at once appeal to and challenge Catholicism.

San La Muerte

In the remote Esteros de Iberá, about 150 years ago, there lived a
shaman who was famous for healing. He also cared for lepers who
were abandoned in a prison, bringing them water and easing their
sufferings, but he never caught their disease. Some say he was a
Franciscan friar or a Jesuit who stayed behind after the expulsion.
The shaman often repaired to a tree beside the water, squatting, in
order to meditate and restore his powers. His great charity and love
of his neighbor were interrupted, however, when Catholic priests
returned to the region to resume control. One day, when the shaman
was entering a village to tend to someone sick, the priests had
him arrested and imprisoned with the lepers. The shaman accepted
this unjust punishment without resistance. He refused to eat and
remained standing, wasting away, and supporting himself with a
long walking stick that looked like an upside-down L. No one knew
of his death until much later. They discovered him standing in his
black tunic, supported by his stick. He had withered away to a
skeleton.

There once was a king who was famous for his exemplary administration of justice. After his death he rose to heaven, and in recognition of his just reign on earth, God assigned him the greatest
responsibility. He was given a throne before which infinite candles
burned, one for each life on earth. The long candles represented
lives that still had a lot of time, and the candles that were almost
completely burned represented lives that were about to end. The just
king was charged with the task of returning to earth to gather the
souls of those whose candles had gone out. He also watched over
people who were still entitled to life, protecting them until their

candles burned down. He thus became God's delegate in the just oversight of life and death. For this reason San La Muerte is sometimes called *San Justo* (the Just Saint, or Saint Justice) and *Señor de la Buena Muerte* (Lord of Good Death).

San La Muerte is known by many names, among them:

San La Muerte (Saint Death)
San de la Muerte (Saint of Death)
Señor la Muerte (Lord Death)
Señor de la Muerte (Lord of Death; this is sometimes
    compounded with San Justo)
Señor de la Buena Muerte (Lord of Good Death, this is some-
    times compounded with San Justo)
San Justo (the Just Saint, or Saint Justice)
Pirucho (Skinny, from Guaraní)
Flaquito (Skinny, from Spanish)
Santito (Little Saint, owing to the tiny amulet)
San Esqueleto (Saint Skeleton, used primarily in Paraguay)

Centuries of contact between Guaraní natives and European immigrants has produced a unique culture in northeastern Argentina, one in which folk saints are part of everyday life. San La Muerte (St. Death) emerged in this context. From origins in colonial magical practices he evolved into a folk saint with thousands of devotees, especially in the provinces of Corrientes, Misiones, and Chaco. The original rural base of the cult has expanded, via migration, to encompass Buenos Aires, where images of San La Muerte are prominently displayed in the windows of downtown religious shops.

San La Muerte is believed to have emerged in Corrientes and is associated with that province, but the principal sites of devotion today are in and around the cities of Resistencia (Chaco) and Posadas (Misiones). The deathly image of San La Muerte relates him to San Esqueleto (St. Skeleton) in Paraguay and to Santísima Muerte (Most Holy Death) in Mexico, although the latter—a variation of the Virgin Mary—has an entirely different identity.

All of these images are indebted to the medieval Dance of Death and to the widely disseminated personification of death as the Grim Reaper. (The Grim Reaper is a skeleton who carries a scythe to harvest lives.) They also relate more broadly to imagery associated with the Day of the Dead, particularly in Mexico; to the Andean veneration of skulls and bones; to the iconography of Christ's crucifixion; to imagery in Catholic Holy Week rituals, such as the representations of death used by Penitentes; and to the death imagery used in such magical and esoteric practices as witchcraft and tarot.

San La Muerte was originally used as an amulet to injure or kill one's enemies. The absolute, inescapable power of death was concentrated into this tiny, skeletal figure and then released by rituals that sent out a curse. Uses of San La Muerte for black magic gradually became secondary as personified death evolved from an amulet into a saint. Of the many folk saints in northeastern Argentina, San La Muerte is regarded as the most powerful. The saint, like the amulet, can be used for cursing one's enemies, but today most devotees request the usual miracles concerning health, work, love, and family. The power of death is thereby redirected and deployed to positive ends.

Despite San La Muerte's mostly positive uses, the negative associations persist in his deathly appearance, the carving of his image in human bone, and the long historical association with black arts. Most nondevotees regard San La Muerte as fearsome and diabolical, and they become uncomfortable at the mere mention of his name.

Devotees, on the other hand, favorably view even the wrath that San La Muerte brings down upon their enemies. One might anticipate an exception in Pelusa—a shrine owner in Posadas who advocates a charitable San La Muerte—but she too condones proactive supernatural bodyguarding as a countermeasure against adversity. San La Muerte "will take care of your enemies," Pelusa wrote, because "he is an overprotective saint." If any sort of danger approaches "he will defend you with his scythe and cover you with his cape."

Even the weapon he wields to cut down the enemy is perceived as defensive: "Make your scythe like a shield against all people who come at me and my family." Self-defense and attack fuse into a single operation. San La Muerte, addressed in prayer as a "protecting angel," can also take the offensive. Pelusa's grandmother kept her San La Muerte in a tiny coffin, and whoever messed with her—she would say—would wind up lying there beside him. "If God and San La Muerte are with us," Pelusa preaches, "who will be against us?"[1]

The protective power of death extends into the belief that San La Muerte makes one invulnerable to lethal weapons. This use of the amulet is particularly prevalent among criminals, police, and—much less now than in the past—gauchos prone to knife duels. A 1917 book on folklore in Misiones typically described San La Muerte as "excellent against bullets and knives." That defensive excellence again extends into the offensive: One should take San La Muerte only to the most serious fights, because the death of one's enemy is certain. The preferred material for carving a body-saving San La Muerte amulet is a bullet dug out of a dead body. This preference reiterates the dominant motif: death is transformed into a protector of life.[2]

In addition to San La Muerte's work as a protector and as a generalist, he has also developed a specialization for the recovery of lost and stolen objects. A 1950 report from Corrientes was unequivocal: "He is the best advocate for finding things that are lost." In the village of Itá Ibaté, in Corrientes province, I met a man who once lost a pistol while riding horseback in the country. He himself was a nondevotee, but a friend took San La Muerte for a ride and the pistol was recovered in short order. Others hang San La Muerte upside down by a twisted cord (the same is done with St. Anthony). When the image stops spinning, it faces the lost or stolen object. The favor can be repaid pursuant to these poetics of inversion by burning a candle upside down in thanks.[3]

Others believe that the recovery of an object requires putting the saint *en penitencia* (a state of punishment). "In order to find a lost object you bury 'death' (a little iron saint) at the threshold of the door and light him a candle threatening not to unbury him until the lost object is found." Some bury the saint in dirt piled on the altar, or make him face the wall, until any miracle request is granted. Poroto, a devotee in Goya, requests a miracle and then buries San La Muerte for three days while awaiting the response. Images of the crouching San La Muerte are often carved with a flattened top, so that the saint can be stood on his head until a miracle is granted.[4]

In devotion to a miraculous skull in Tilcara, similarly, an eye socket was covered if the skull let a week pass without granting a miracle. After another week the other socket was covered, and if a third passed the skull was turned to face the wall. Elsewhere in northern Argentina, the folk saint Santo Pilato is tied up with string and is not released until he grants a request. Many devotees regard such treatment of saints—particularly San La Muerte—as ill-advised and counterproductive. How, they ask, can one show such disrespect to a powerful saint with a reputation for vengeance?

Sometimes the return of a stolen object is coerced precisely through this fear that San La Muerte inspires. A devotee who is a victim of theft recruits San La Muerte's assistance and spreads the word that he has done so. Common knowledge holds that the thief is dead meat unless amends are made, so the stolen object tends to find its way back home. The recovery is realized through the medium of fear because the devotee, the thief, and the community all share the belief (even if only to hedge the bet) that San La Muerte defends his devotees. Similarly, those who have a San La Muerte inserted under their skin or tattooed on their bodies can boast invulnerability and command respect because others are reluctant to risk the challenge.

In short, the reputation for being powerful, vengeful, and jealous makes San La Muerte a saint to be feared. Even people who are comfortable with the devotion and close to devotees keep their distance from San La Muerte himself. One man attending a San La Muerte fiesta in Resistencia spoke for many when he explained that he was a afraid to request miracles for fear of reprisals. "I'm irresponsible," he said, and he therefore feared that he might neglect to fulfill his end of the bargain—the promises made when requesting miracles—and end up with more punishment than reward from San La Muerte. A woman argued along these same lines, then added that the burden was too heavy: "it's like a priesthood, and the truth is if I wanted that I would have become a nun."[5]

The general consensus is that the devotion must be taken very seriously, because San La Muerte gives but also takes away. Miracles that are not duly thanked result in their reversal—a restoration of the premiracle condition— plus interest: your crops don't grow, someone in your family dies, your house burns down. San La Muerte is a dangerous weapon of self-defense that injures those who cannot use it properly. You can shoot yourself in the foot. And the consequences are all the more severe if one disrespects the saint intentionally.

Traditional devotion to San La Muerte was semisecret, owing to two related factors. The first was public perception: San La Muerte's associations with black magic made upstanding citizens reluctant to acknowledge devotion. An implicit policy of "don't ask, don't tell" fostered a relative secrecy. The second factor was the belief that San La Muerte loses or refuses his powers if he is not kept out of public view. (The losing implies an amulet itself charged with power, and the refusing a saint in heaven.) This belief was held particularly in relation to the cursing of enemies, which was effective only when the rituals were done secretly.

Together these two factors slowed the growth of the cult's external expressions, such as fiestas, processions, and chapels. San La Muerte was to some degree an open secret, however—everyone knew of the devotion, if not exactly who adhered to it—and benign uses, such as finding lost objects, were more acceptable than those that did harm. Leaking the secret could also contribute to the saint's efficacy, as in the case of the stolen goods returned to their rightful owner.

Today the devotion to San La Muerte is surprisingly public. It is now common for domestic shrines to host open-house annual fiestas that are sometimes promoted by local media. These events typically include religious exercises, such as group prayer and processions; a constant flow of devotees to San La Muerte's altar; and festivities (at which devotees and nondevotees freely intermix) with food, music, and dance. The once underground image of San La Muerte is mass produced, widely displayed, publicly sold, and situated amid canonized saints. A roadside chapel to San La Muerte is open to pass-ersby. Folk songs, press coverage, and general visibility help to destigmatize San La Muerte and to ease his cult into the mainstream.

The shrines of many serious devotees strike a balance between public and private. In Posadas, Pelusa and Isabelino open their chapel and host events for a one-week period in August, but their San La Muerte is inaccessible to outsiders for the rest of the year. Ramón in Resistencia likewise accommo-dates his San La Muerte on a public altar during the fiesta that he hosts annually, but the image is otherwise kept in his bedroom. Devotion to San La Muerte combines public and private, solitude and spectacle, in accord with the needs, beliefs, and disposition of each devotee. If private rituals and domestic shrines are still the rule, then the stigma of the past is clearly eroding as San La Muerte gains visibility and acceptance.

The devotion is also growing rapidly because of association with Gaucho Gil, who is believed to have been a devotee of San La Muerte. The relation is clearly hierarchical, with San La Muerte above, but Gaucho Gil's popularity is flowing upward. Gil's shrine in Mercedes is visited by hundreds of thousands of devotees. The prominent display of San La Muerte beside Gaucho Gil on the sales stands in Mercedes enhances San La Muerte's acceptability and the transition from the one folk saint to the other. Gaucho Gil's cult is well in-stitutionalized and favorably regarded, and some of this legitimacy accrues to San La Muerte by proximity, osmosis, and association.

Many devotional crossovers occur between San La Muerte and Gaucho Gil, but there is more traffic in one direction than the other. San La Muerte devotees readily accept or at least acknowledge Gaucho Gil, but many Gaucho Gil devotees want nothing to do with San La Muerte. Matías, who lives and owns a shop at the Gaucho Gil shrine, is an exception. He sells San La Muerte images along with those of Gaucho Gil, he is tattooed with San La Muerte, he has an altar to San La Muerte in the back room of his shop, and he is building a public chapel to San La Muerte in his hometown, about an hour from Mercedes. His devotion began one stormy night, Matías relates, when San La Muerte appeared at the Gaucho Gil shrine. It was about 2 o'clock in the morning. A young woman from Buenos Aires, on her first visit to the shrine, was the first to see the apparition. She pointed, speechless, and five others turned to witnessed the events.

San La Muerte was about 7 feet tall, and his face was covered with the hood of the black, monklike frock that he was wearing. He threw the scythe back and forth between his hands. The witnesses fell to their knees and prayed. They were transfixed by San La Muerte's presence and unable to take their eyes off of him. Matías eventually approached and asked if San La

Muerte needed anything, but there was no response. The vision lasted six hours, until 8 in the morning. Matías and the others were sitting on a sturdy log bench that suddenly snapped when San La Muerte took his leave. Matías later requested a miracle, and it was granted; that is when he got the tattoo. Everyone in his family is likewise tattooed with San La Muerte, and his cousin's entire back is covered with the image.

The identity of San La Muerte is still in formation. There is no fixed myth as there is, for example, in the devotion to Gaucho Gil or Difunta Correa. Multiple myths compete for primacy as they advocate quite different origins. They also appear to be evolving rapidly, so that many of those that were common in the 1960s and 1970 have already fallen out of circulation. Sometimes a detail is preserved and transferred from a disappearing myth to an emerging one, even though the narrative changes completely. The candles that represent lives in Myth 2, for example, were a prominent feature of earlier versions but have been adapted to suit this newer narrative. Similarly, many of the older versions emphasized San La Muerte as a curandero who received the power to heal from Christ. In the more recent myths, the role of San La Muerte as a curandero is still central but Christ has disappeared from the narrative.[6]

Variations on all themes are multiple. In a version from Posadas, San La Muerte was a king committed to charitable deeds and defense of the poor. His mission ended when powerful outsiders entered his lands and arrested him. They chained him to his throne until he starved to death and was reduced to nothing but a skeleton. In more prominent versions, San La Muerte is imprisoned with lepers, standing (Myth 1), and the throne appears only in the alternative, heavenly narrative (Myth 2). This Posadas version provides a composite, a hybrid, while at once making an appeal to the seated image of San La Muerte that was once popular.[7]

In other variations, a 1969 version from Resistencia agrees with current accounts that San La Muerte was condemned to prison and starved to emaciation, but it differs in that he was later released for subsequent adventures. In a version of Myth 2 from Corrientes, God distributed responsibilities and jurisdictions to the various saints. He appointed one of them Señor de la Muerte (Lord of Death), but this saint objected, saying that no one would love him if he were responsible for ending people's lives.[8]

Two curanderos, one in Goya and one in Resistencia, related that San La Muerte is the fourth horseman of the Apocalypse—Death—as described in Revelation 6:8. In the version from Goya, the Virgin Mary, San La Muerte, and a few saints are combating the legions of evil. They have no arms or armor against their well-armed adversaries, but San La Muerte's troops nevertheless win the battle by creating illusions—raising dust, for example, that gives the impression of an approaching army—to bluff their way to victory. In these wars and in the slaying of devotees' enemies with his scythe, San La Muerte ("the protecting angel") recalls the Old Testament "angel of death" or "destroying angel" whose heavenly might and wrath are brought to the battlefield.[9]

In the cases of most folk saints, particularly those for whom there is no photographic portrait, a life story precedes the icon that eventually puts a face on the biography. San La Muerte, however, was a carved amulet before he was a folk saint, so the process occurred in reverse: a life story was invented to suit the image. Because the images of San La Muerte are multiple, with one quite different from the next, they each inspired separate myths consonant with the respective images from which they were derived.

Variation and evolution are also fostered by the ways in which the myths are related. Some devotees simply repeat, some repeat but introduce errors, some elaborate, some invent freely, and some synthesize different myths or the parts of them with which they are familiar. Myth 1 is a noteworthy hybrid because it consolidates the two traditional figures of San La Muerte—one squatting and the other standing with the scythe—and provides an explanation for how the latter became a skeleton. It also provides a visual complement for the scythe (the walking stick in the form of an inverted L) and integrates the most important themes: healing, the selfless care of rejected and marginal people, the defiance of evil authority by a principled folk hero, and the intermingling of Guaraní and Catholic traditions.

As San La Muerte myths circulated widely they resulted in a new generation of images. The original, hand-carved amulets inspired myths that, in turn, inspired revised images to represent the new protagonists. The images and the myths regenerate one another, and the changing identity of San La Muerte evolves through these dynamics.

This interaction is particularly apparent in the development of San La Muerte as a Jesuit or Franciscan—devotees often use the term *monje* (monk)—in lieu of the Guaraní shaman with which he is also associated. San La Muerte as a robed monk is indebted visually to the dark, hooded cloak associated with the Grim Reaper, and to the black cape that often wraps San La Muerte images displayed on altars. When Myth 1 took the leap of linking the indigenous shaman with a Jesuit or Franciscan, the shaman—at one time more prominent in the myth—dissolved into a syncretic composite as the hooded monk became predominant. A 1963 study registers a "San La Muerte with the appearance of a monk," and the current mass-produced images of San La Muerte conform almost exclusively to this monkish identity. Even the apparition reported by Matías reveals a San La Muerte true to this form.[10]

This traditional image of San La Muerte, from Corrientes, was carved in the wood known as palo santo.

As this image gains critical mass, it gently pressures other alternatives into conformance. The skeleton comes to seem inappropriately naked and is dressed up to suit the myth. Ramón has always kept the bony body of his San La Muerte unadorned, but others advised that proper care required a black cape. Ramón finally acquiesced and put a cape on his image, but soon afterward San La Muerte appeared to him in a dream. "How am I supposed to help you," San La Muerte asked, "if you have me all tied up?" Ramón removed the cape that he had tied around San La Muerte's neck and has not dressed up the image since.

The malleability of San La Muerte's identity allows for highly personalized adaptations. Pirucha, a curandera in Goya, is always concerned that the authorities will sanction her for the illegal practice of medicine. (A 1950 report from the same region notes that the law requires arrest for the illicit practice

of medicine but also that the policemen themselves use the services of curanderos.) When Pirucha told her version of San La Muerte's story, the version with the lepers, she repeated for emphasis that San La Muerte was
imprisoned because he was a curandero. This coincided precisely with her
own fear, and she enhanced the affinity between it and the myth by retrieving
San La Muerte from the distant past and making him a more recent gaucho
pursued by the police. Pirucha also stressed that illegitimate charges were
brought against San La Muerte for his charitable deeds, as they were likewise
against Gaucho Gil. Anyone else who does unacceptable good deeds, like her, is
also subject to the same harassment. Pirucha's myth of San La Muerte provides
a model for her own aspirations as a curandera, but it also serves as a cautionary
tale, an assessment of risk, and a pardon in advance for the unjust charges that
she anticipates.[11]

Pelusa, the owner of a shrine in Posadas, is yet more emphatic in her
devotion to a customized San La Muerte. Rather than the diabolical, evildoing
amulet of occult tradition, she has conceived of a Christlike San La Muerte
who inspires ever deeper commitment to her personal priorities: love of one's
neighbor and charity. Pelusa describes San La Muerte as the "protector of the
sick, the distressed, and the abandoned," who "did not eat so he could give
food to the lepers." She and her husband seek out others in need, including a
woman with AIDS and her children. Just as San La Muerte was immune to
the contagions of lepers, so Pelusa and Isabelino are protected because their
mission puts charity first. In 2005, they began providing for dozens of foster
children. San La Muerte grants them miracles—health, economic stability—
and they repay him by helping others. For them, the deathly saint inspires
reaffirmation of life.[12]

The centrality of charity in Pelusa's conception of San La Muerte extends to
the symbolic interpretation of offerings. Pelusa explains that alcoholic drinks
are offered in commemoration of the aguardiente that indigenous people gave
to San La Muerte in thanks for his care and cures. Bread is also offered, she
adds, because San La Muerte shared his bread with the poor, and devotees
should follow his example.

Pelusa preaches to her followers that being a San La Muerte devotee
consists above all in love of one's neighbor and good deeds. This inspira-
tional discourse is reinforced by a revision, a moralistic redirection, of San La
Muerte's diabolical identity and the harmful purposes that it has served.
People who use San La Muerte for evil, Pelusa wrote, "usually suffer the same
pains that they cause their victims," but "those of us who know how and are
able to do good" are repaid in goodness. Thus, she concludes, "do no harm to
your neighbor, because it is the same as doing harm to yourself."[13]

Pelusa presides over an annual San La Muerte fiesta in Posadas, the capital of Misiones Province.

From Amulet to Folk Saint

San La Muerte is a complex and enigmatic object of devotion, functioning at once as a *payé* (an amulet that itself contains magical power) and as a saint (a soul in heaven interceding on behalf of devotees). These distinctions are far from absolute, however, and even in mainstream Catholicism they tend to intermingle. A particular statue of a canonized saint, for example, may in itself be regarded as miraculous, together with the saint in heaven that it represents. For practical purposes, the wooden image on earth and the saint on high become indistinguishable components of a single composite. San La Muerte epitomizes this conflation—he is always at once both amulet and saint. San La Muerte makes portable and personal a supernatural power similar to that of the miraculous statues in the churches. The empowered object in this world is backed up by an empowered person in the next.

In northeastern Argentina, where San La Muerte emerged, amulets have widespread use. The word *payé* originally referred to a person who had healing or supernatural powers, like the shaman in some San La Muerte myths. Today the word is used more broadly to denote amulets that embody such powers. Payés are made in many forms and for multiple purposes relating to health, invulnerability, and social relations, among others uses. San La Muerte is one payé among many, but it is one of the few that is also a saint. Other payés that represent canonized and folk saints include San Marco, San Alejo, Santa Librada, Santo Pilato, and San Son (an adaptation of the biblical Samson). Each of these borrows from Christian supernatural powers but nevertheless remains essentially magical. San La Muerte is the only payé to have evolved from original magical use into an object of widespread religious devotion.

Payés were once made ritually by specialists initiated into the mysteries of amulet production. Loosened norms eventually resulted in a free-for-all. In a 1940 report from Corrientes, payés are described as "amulets that each person makes according to his taste, for lack of any determined model or material." Another document from the same region reported in 1950 that locals "have a payé for everything"—luck, love, gambling, courage, and protection from injury or illness. Chamamé lyrics relate that a timid young man held tight to the payé in his pocket at a dance, for luck and for the courage to approach young ladies. "The payé is carried, if not under the skin of its owner then hanging around the neck toward the side of the heart: the first is permanent and the second is temporary." Others mention payés tied to a belt, worn as a bracelet, or pocketed together in a pouch. The payés that are "under the skin" are surgically incorporated into the body that they protect. This practice was common with San La Muerte.[14]

The material of traditonal payés varied in accord with the amulet's specific function. Feathers are often mentioned. A "friendship payé" consisted of a silver coin submerged in the font of holy water at the entrance of churches, so that all who dipped in their fingers would become friends. San Son, known for his strength, is usually made out of the horn of a bull, but tiger bone gives unprecedented power. Many payés, like San La Muerte, were made to protect one from violence. Those who have a San Marco "fear nothing" because "bullets can't enter them, lightning doesn't strike them, and not even the sharpest knife" can pierce them. Another report describes generic payés for invulnerability: "A payé is used against bullets and knives, made of the white cloth draped on the crosses in cemeteries." A 1921 report expanded on the idea, providing a context for San La Muerte:

There are payés made of the bones of the dead, preferably children, others of the white and narrow cloth that is draped on the crosses of the cemetery or on indicated roads designating the place of a sudden death, a murder, etc. This payé is called Curuzú Yeguá [Adorned Cross] and is highly recommended against bullet wounds. Payés are also made of laurel root, giving it human form, and they serve to indicate the direction in which lost things can be found.... Another famous payé is San Son, made with the tip of a bull's horn to give power to whoever carries it. San La Muerte is the payé made of lead on Good Friday and that is used against bullets and knives.[15]

Lead is actually one of the many materials out of which images of San La Muerte were carved. When lead is used, as mentioned earlier, the preferred raw material is a bullet that has been extracted from the body that it killed. Pirucha adds that the bullet has to be removed before the victim dies. Others say that any bullet can be used. When San La Muerte is carved from wood, many devotees say that only certain woods—such as palo santo and wood from a cemetery cross—are acceptable.

Human bone, however, is widely considered the best material for carving San La Muerte. As one devotee explained, "if the representation is a skeleton, there's nothing better to make it with than the bone of a human skeleton." A 1975 study observed that San La Muerte is usually carved in wood, but that the few carved in bone are more powerful. This is also the common belief today. The custodian of a San La Muerte shrine in Resistencia was emphatic on the point. He repeated a few times, as though citing statistics from a scientific study, that a San La Muerte made of bone is "40% to 50% more powerful" than others.[16]

The preferred bones are those of infants who were baptized before they died. This assures the purity of the raw material, because these babies were cleansed of original sin and died before committing any sin of their own. Finger bones are the most desirable, and some say the pinky is best. Human bones are difficult to acquire. Cautious devotees, including Elmo in Posadas, are reluctant to leave that acquisition to others, lest they wind up with a San La Muerte carved in pig or cow. To assure the authenticity of their preferred material they go to the cemetery to get a bone for themselves, then deliver it to the carver. One man from Corrientes explained that he would wait until his father died, then have a San La Muerte carved from one of Dad's bones. Aquiles, who carves San La Muerte in the Corrientes prison, gets his bones from medical students. He offered the inside view that infant bones are

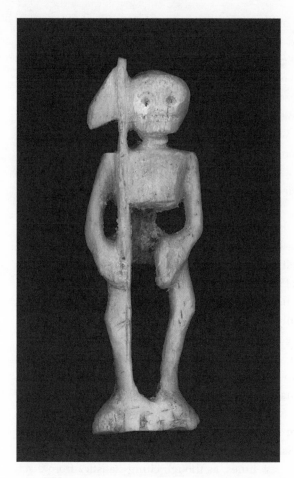

San La Muerte, carved in
human bone.

best for spiritual reasons concerning purity and innocence, but also because
they are not as brittle as other bones and thus are easier to carve without
breaking.[17]

A San La Muerte made of human bone acquires even greater power if it is
carved by a prisoner or Indian. The preference for indigenous carvers is partially derived from a general exaltation of Guaraní culture and, more specifically, from associations of the Guaraní with the origin of San La Muerte.
Ramón, the son of bicultural Paraguayans, opens his annual fiesta by giving
thanks to San La Muerte in the Guaraní language. When I asked him why, he
explained that speaking in Guaraní is the most intimate means of communicating with San La Muerte. He added that he can best express his deep feelings
in Guaraní, particularly in times of need. For others, who are perhaps further from Guaraní culture, there is a certain exoticism attached to anything

indigenous. Indian carvers authenticate San La Muerte—reconnect him to his roots—while at once imbuing amulets with the mystique of shamanism.

The preference for imprisoned carvers is partially indebted to the myth of San La Muerte's death in prison. San La Muerte also has a strong following among criminals and inmates. They request success in crime, pardon or leniency in court, protection in prison, and speedy release (after which the cycle repeats). Many are attracted by San La Muerte's macho image, which they display in prominent tattoos or carry under their skin. The family that owns one of the oldest San La Muerte shrines, in the Chaco town of Barranqueras, expressed dismay that criminals came to their shrine in order to more successfully engage in theft and violence. This unease underscores the adaptability of folk saints to diverse purposes, often quite incompatible. Pelusa's San La Muerte, for example, is diametrically opposed to this protector of criminals.

The prestige of inmate carvers has made the prison in Corrientes a pilgrimage destination, even to the degree of being dramatized in a 1972 movie, *In Search of San La Muerte.* When I arrived for the first time at the Corrientes prison, in 2001, there was a slouch with a machine gun standing at the door. His stomach looked as if it had been pressurized with a pump, then partially deflated. I hoped that he would turn me away, so that I would have made my good-faith effort without getting raped or knifed, but instead I stated my business—San La Muerte—and he allowed me to pass with startling nonchalance. The guards are accustomed to devotees coming to purchase images of San La Muerte, and they make access easy because they take a cut of the profits.

I waited in a dank visiting room with sweaty walls until Aquiles came down a few minutes later. He was soft-spoken and seemed reserved, almost withdrawing. Aquiles explained that carvers come and go to the tune of their sentences, and that currently he was the only carver in the prison. He was sentenced to life for murder, and while in the throes of a suicidal depression he was befriended by an older inmate—now paroled—who carved San La Muerte. The friend set Aquiles on the path as a carver, and Aquiles advanced by trial and error. Carving the tiny image is difficult, he explained, particularly because the bone breaks easily. Other inmates try but fail.

Aquiles was familiar with San La Muerte prior to his incarceration. He once had the amulet, a wooden one, but burned it. That's when things started going badly for him. Initially he carved San La Muerte without devotion, simply as a means to make money. As time went on, however, "doors began opening," as he put it, and life in prison got better. Aquiles was not sure if the improvements were a result of San La Muerte's intercession or of his good behavior, which the authorities have recognized, but with growing faith he presumed that San La Muerte was protecting him.

When I returned to visit Aquiles in 2003 there was no one at the front door, so I pushed open the unlocked iron bars and let myself in. A guard inside asked the purpose of my visit; I replied that I was there to visit Aquiles. Rather than showing me to the improvised visiting room, as they had on my first visit, he directed me through a set of bars into the main yard of the prison. A couple of inmates looked at me, then at each other, as though to say, "Who's this guy?"

I stood against a wall looking goofy until a group of guards, hanging around on tired chairs, invited me to join them. They sent an inmate to a soccer game elsewhere in the yard to tell Aquiles that I was waiting. One guard asked what I had in the bag—I had a camera and tape recorder—and told me that they were prohibited in the prison. I missed the cue of this understated introduction to negotiations and excused myself to lock the camera and tape recorder in the trunk of my car. Aquiles showed up soon after I returned and, to my (compounding) surprise, led me away from the safe haven of the guards and through a labyrinth of buildings to his quarters.

He lived in a private room rather than a cell. The door was a curtain, and the room was appointed with a television, stereo, personal items decorating the walls, a small altar, and several large San La Muerte statues that he had

Aquiles carves images of San La Muerte while serving a life sentence for homicide in the Corrientes prison.

carved. The room and its luxuries were among the privileges that Aquiles had acquired thanks to some combination of San La Muerte and his good behavior. He was also allowed a daily three-hour leave from the prison to study computer science, and he was hopeful that parole was imminent.

Aquiles explained that he is in frequent contact, by cell phone, with devotees who are in need. He does rituals by their request, but mostly spends hours counseling and simply lending an ear: "I feel as though this is my calling." Upon release from prison, he intends to establish a San La Muerte shrine in Corrientes. I had noticed earlier that Aquiles is also active in the discussion group of a San La Muerte Web site, where he announces the availability of his carvings.

At the end of our conversation I mentioned that the guards forbade entrance with my camera and tape recorder. Aquiles, with a shocked look yielding to an expression that suggested, "We can take care of that," got up and headed for the curtain. He called in an older inmate to watch over me, left to talk with one of the guards, and returned with the news that for 100 pesos I could bring in whatever I wanted. I negotiated the bribe down to 50 and paid the guard, who smuggled the camera in under his coat. It was already too late for the tape recorder.

There is a certain mystique, an exoticism, in acquiring a San La Muerte from a prisoner (as from a Guaraní) rather than buying it off a rack in a shop or a table at a fiesta. Even supply and demand increases the value and, with it, the power of a rare, newly carved images from the source as opposed to a machine-made replica from a box. The pilgrimage to the prison, the foreboding ambience, and acquisition of the amulet from the carver in person all enhance the esoteric value. Much the same holds true with Indian carvers: an image of molded plaster cannot compete with a bone carved by a shaman-like Guaraní with genetic links to tradition.

No San La Muerte amulet has power in itself, however, until it is blessed by a Catholic priest. This procedure is often referred to as a baptism, in part because holy water was sometimes used to give traditional amulets their magical charge. Some devotees still use holy water to baptize their San La Muerte, but a priest's blessing is nevertheless the most common form of activating the amulet. Priests are unwilling to bless images of the pagan San La Muerte, of course, so their unwitting collusion must be recruited on the sly. Some devotees hide San La Muerte behind the image of a canonized saint, or inside a hollowed-out candle, and thus acquire the blessing. Others say that the amulet must be taken to mass at seven different churches on seven Fridays to receive its charge during the general blessings. Still others say nine churches and nine Fridays, or that repeated visits to the same church are fine on any day of the week. In all cases, the blessing is a catalyst that initiates the amulet's power.

The required activation of San La Muerte with a priest's blessing under-scores the essentially syncretic nature of this devotion. On the one hand, like all folk saint devotions, San La Muerte is a protest against institutional Ca-tholicism, an alternative and anti-institutional route to miraculous power. On the other hand, however, it is dependent upon the very institution that it evades. The Catholic supernatural is borrowed—stolen—and adapted to uses that are unapproved, even illegal. Catholicism is bent to the will of devotees. It is broken away from its source and used to other purposes. The blessing is all the more potent because it is forbidden, and because it consolidates the su-pernatural powers of folk and institutional Catholicism. At the same time, the priest's blessing helps distance San La Muerte devotion from its association with evil, and reaffirms the Catholic identity of the devotees.

In recent years, the cult to San La Muerte appears to have become more self-sufficient and less dependent upon institutional Catholicism. Priests' blessings are still the norm, but many devotees also charge their images on the altar of a San La Muerte reputed to be extraordinarily powerful. This is done either in addition to or in lieu of a priest's blessing. The charging in this case occurs through contact and proximity, usually with one of the old, bone San La Muerte images on a domestic altar that is accessible to the public. These images have often been in families for generations, and their antique and Guaraní-associated origins afford them a special value impossible to acquire through new purchases.

Pirucha, the curandera in Goya, explained that a San La Muerte amulet can be charged by leaving it for thirty days beside the "true" image on her altar. The "true" is telling, because it implies an authenticity lacking in the manufactured images that most devotees buy today. Similarly, at an annual San La Muerte fiesta in Posadas, attending devotees leave their images—usually mass-produced—on the altar of Pelusa's San La Muerte, which is antique and made of bone. The altar is in the form of a stairway, with San La Muerte at the top, and the higher levels are available on a first-come, first-served basis. Serious de-votees arrive early in order to have their amulet placed closer to Pelusa's San La Muerte, closer to the power that they are absorbing.

In many cases, such as this last one, the intent is to recharge an image rather than to acquire its initial activation. Images lose their power, par-ticularly if frequent demands are made of them. They can be revitalized by offerings—food, drink—and by rest, but sometimes an extra jolt is needed. Some devotees say that the San La Muerte amulets that are inserted under the skin are eventually exhausted of power because they have to work constantly without rest.

The surgical insertion of San La Muerte amulets is, like payé use generally, part of a broader practice. The traditional amulet known as a *contra* (literally "against," as in protection against bullets, knives, and other causes of death) establishes the context. These amulets—like San La Muerte—are inserted under the skin to protect one from all bodily harm. They come in multiple types, including even injected holy water from the shrine of the Virgin of Itatí. A 1921 report from Misiones Province provides a recipe for making oneself invulnerable: "Have a little crucifix made from a piece of church bell—it should be completed on three Fridays—and then have it inserted under the skin near the heart." Many say that San La Muerte should be inserted in the same location, between the heart and the left shoulder. Some advise that the hand or forearm is better, and others say that the amulet can be inserted wherever one wishes. The practice is disappearing and being replaced largely by tattoos. It still occurs, however, and sometimes in improvised ways. At the San La Muerte shrine in Empedrado, a man cut himself open in front of the altar and inserted San La Muerte into the flesh of his chest.[18]

Both contras generally and San La Muerte specifically are usually removed when death is imminent. The amulet's purpose is precisely to prevent the body from dying, so prolonged suffering results if the amulet is not removed when death is unavoidable. After the gaucho folk saint Francisco López was caught by police and left for dead, nearly decapitated, his moans were heard by a passing local. López asked him to remove the "relic"—San La Muerte—that he had under his skin, so that he could die in peace.[19]

The same is told of Pato Piola, a notorious criminal in the Chaco. He seemed invincible and evaded police for years thanks to the San La Muerte under his skin, but when he was fatally wounded, in 1962, the amulet was removed so that he would not suffer unnecessarily. Isidro Velázquez, an outlaw who became a folk saint, had a St. Catherine amulet under his skin and would not die, although riddled with bullets, until the police removed it. A hitchhiking policeman whom I picked up at a control point outside of Apóstoles, in Misiones Province, had the idea that a San La Muerte amulet had to be inserted and removed by the same curandera. If the curandera dies, or is otherwise unavailable when one is moribund, then an excruciating death is guaranteed. "You can be totally destroyed but San La Muerte won't let you die."

Tradition holds that many other outlaws, including Gaucho Gil, were protected by San La Muerte amulets. That is why they were invincible. A common story in Corrientes features a magically invulnerable outlaw mounting his horse with a leap and galloping to safety while the bullets of the frustrated police whiz by him. Even today, some policemen believe that bullets will not enter the bodies of criminals who are protected by San La Muerte. Similar stories of invulnerability are told of the prisoners tattooed with San La Muerte.

Surgically inserted amulets are also used for purposes that are not criminal. Many lifetime devotees have an amulet inserted in order to consecrate themselves completely to San La Muerte. Pelusa says that upon receiving the amulet one's body becomes a temple of San La Muerte. Another devotee compared this corporal union to nuns becoming brides of Christ. The procedure, which is painful, is also described as a sacrifice and demonstration of faith. Pelusa had at least one amulet inserted, and she also has a pictorial image of San La Muerte—like a tattoo, but beneath the skin—over her heart. She and Isabelino agree that an amulet must be removed before death, and they go one step further by adding that it must be placed in a tiny coffin and buried together with the deceased person, on the left side of the body. If a tattoo is used rather than an amulet, then the skin must be cut off and rolled up for similar burial.[20]

Others acknowledge the validity of inserted amulets and tattoos, but prefer to carry San La Muerte "in their spirit." At the same time, tattoos are gaining prominence for purposes other than those that inserted amulets serve, notably as expressions of thanks for miracles. One man had a large San La Muerte tattooed on his back after his daughter was cured miraculously of leukemia. Another devotee did the same when San La Muerte resolved his infertility and granted him and his wife the miracle of two children.

The insertion of San La Muerte under the skin, the carving in bone, and the ritual charging of amulets by priests all indicate magical use of an image that in itself embodies supernatural power. The payé, "despite its preservation of the indigenous name, is more similar to the practices of European sorcery and witchcraft than to those of indigenous shamanism." It also has a great affinity with approved Catholic practices. Medieval amulets of protection included bone relics of saints, which were believed to be more powerful when purchased from a priest. Relics also had curative properties and sometimes could heal an ailment simply by being touched to the ailing body part.[21]

Catholicism permits the veneration of relics, and many of the most important medieval and early modern churches, such as Santiago de Compostela in Spain, were established on the remains of a saint. Technically the miraculous power does not reside in the relic itself, but this nuance is lost in common practice. Bones provide tangible contact with the dead and make

Catholicism, the Jesuits permitted similar food offerings to the saints in churches. For the celebration of Corpus Christi, "the Guaraní continued to hang dead and live birds and other live animals on the tabernacles of the altars they constructed on the four corners of the main plazas in the missions." Catholic imagery was displayed together with these offerings, as were other items that included "carved figures of people."[26]

The Guaraní veneration of bones interacted with Catholic imagery of death as the missions went about their daily business of conversion. Death had been personified in fourteenth-century Europe, and subsequently its skeletal figure was prominent in baroque art, literature, religious theater, church and tomb imagery, and popular imagination. Monks and friars gave sermons on the imminence of death, often in cemeteries, after which actors in skeletal costumes appeared for the spectacle known as the Dance of Death. Death took by the hand those who were doomed and had with them, as it were, their last dance, which was out of this world.[27]

Medieval images and attitudes that today may seem morbid and macabre "testify to a true familiarity with death," which resulted from the decimation of populations during the Black Death. Entire villages fell at once to the plague, with corpses lining the streets, and penitents flagellated themselves to appease the God who had sent the terrible epidemic. "Let us remove death's strangeness and practice it instead," Montaigne advised. "Let us grow accustomed to it, having no thought in mind as often as that of death." In baroque Spain, too, "death is so common and ordinary, and everyday we see so many go from this world to the next, that it truly seems that we have lost the fear of death." Despite the rhetoric of familiarity, however, death engenders fear, including dread of judgment, and the Church exploited this fear for evangelical purposes. An "evangelism of fear" also accompanied the conquest of the New World.[28]

In Spanish American missions, churches, convents, and monasteries, the prominence of deathlike iconography (the crucifixion is the paradigm) was complemented by representation of death itself. A wooden image of death was probably used in processions from the San Agustín church in Lima; several images of the skeletal Grim Reaper are in Andean churches—particularly those for indigenous worship—between Cuzco and Potosí; and the anonymous 1739 painting La muerte in the Church of Caquiaviri (La Paz, Bolivia) features twin images of death. One shoots the saved with arrows made of lily branches, and the other shoots the damned with arrows of fire. Apocalyptic frescoes painted on the interior walls of San Diego de Pitiquito (a Franciscan church in Mexico) include a large skeleton accompanied by a motto alluding to the scales of justice that determine the soul's destiny.[29]

In the Jesuit missions, the publication of many books included, in 1705, a translation of Juan Eusebio Nieremberg's *De la diferencia entre lo temporal y eterno*. Among the engravings in the book was one of a triumphant personified death, holding a sickle (a variation on the scythe) in one hand and an hourglass in the other. Death as a skeleton also appears in another image, which was likewise copied from a European original.[30]

These engravings document the presence of the Grim Reaper in the missions, but more important in folk culture were theatrical productions staged by the Jesuits for the Guaranís' religious instruction. The performances often included Christ's resurrection, with props of skulls and bones and with the Grim Reaper in the supporting cast for dramatization of Christ's triumph over death. Such performances contributed to fixing the personified image of death within a religious context.

Almost all of the artists in Jesuit missions were Guaranís who were trained by Europeans. These indigenous carvers of saints thought of their work more religiously than artistically: "Image-makers quite literally believed that they were making saints and gods." This observations is particularly suggestive in the context of San La Muerte, whose traditional carvers were likewise creating, not representing, a supernatural power. For the Guaraní mission artists, "The reality of things was not expressed by imitating their visual appearance, as in European art, but by capturing their essence." The imagery, including the image of death personified, was adopted from European traditions and then invested with this "essence." The carvings transcend mere representation and become empowered in themselves, like amulets.[31]

Religious ideas and carvings intermixed with magical practices in the Guaraní-Christian culture that evolved over time. The emergence of a precursor to San La Muerte specifically is documented in the records of criminal charges, for witchcraft, that were brought against converted Guaranís in the eighteenth century. The prosecutors itemized the contents of a medicine bundle owned by the defendant Silberio Caté, which included tiny figures "of a doll, of a Soul, of Death, and of St. Joseph." Such figures date back at least to 1734. Their probable use was magical homicide, for which San La Muerte is still used today. (In the seventeenth century, Ruiz de Montoya mentioned "magicians" who were dedicated to homicide, but without specific mention of a deathlike amulet.)[32]

Of the three images that are identified in the document, one represents death and the other two (the soul and St. Joseph) allude to it. Death imagery is also stressed in the descriptions of Caté's magical arsenal: "the figure of death made of wood"; "a statue of death"; "a wooden figure in the form of death and another of a soul that has been tied to a St. Joseph." Another passage specifies that the figure of the soul was tied to St. Joseph's back, and that this composite was together in a wolf-leather pouch with the death figure. All of these images, like the tradition images of San La Muerte, were a few inches tall.[33]

Many saints are associated with death. St. Martha protects the dying from the devil, St. Anne is invoked for a peaceful death, and St. Barbara protects against sudden death and consoles those in agony. The principal saint for the moribund is nevertheless St. Joseph, because he died attended by Christ and the Virgin. Joseph, often known as the patron of good death, was favored by the Jesuits, and his cult was actively promoted in the missions. He was also the saint listed by name most frequently in the art inventories made when the Jesuits were expelled, which indicates that his image was prominent in the mission churches.[34]

Joseph's patronage of good and peaceful death is likewise attributed to San La Muerte, one of whose alternate names is *Señor de la Buena Muerte* (Lord of Good Death). As explained in a 1950 report from Corrientes Province, San La Muerte "has infinite devotees because he helps with a 'good death,' freeing the sick from unnecessary sufferings." In this sense San La Muerte is also reminiscent of the fusion of the Christ Child and indigenous myths in the Peruvian Niño Nakaq, who has a knife in his belt and uses it to expedite the death (and thus minimize the suffering) of people with incurable ill-nesses. When the powers of St. Joseph and San La Muerte are redirected to evil purposes, then their association with death is used to kill enemies rather than to alleviate the sufferings of devotees. The adjective "good" drops out.[35]

The eighteenth-century trial document thus records the existence of a tiny image of death that precedes what today is known as San La Muerte. This magical object evolved in the context of religious, social, cultural, and eco-nomic disorientation following the expulsion of the Jesuits. San La Muerte is the result of dynamic, transformative interactions between the indigenous beliefs and practices that survived forced conversion, and the European be-liefs, practices, and imagery that were superimposed.

The Guaraní were in a precarious situation after the expulsion of the Jesuits, and some turned to cattle rustling and theft for survival. The cacique of the mission of Santa Ana, Eugenio Mbacaro, explained in a letter to officials in Buenos Aires that "our women and children suffer such hunger that many leave the town to look for their sustenance, primarily in Corrientes and Ytaití, and if they return, they are cruelly punished; this is the reason why many are afraid of being punished, and they do not return, and they wander dispersed wherever their misfortune may lead them." In another correspondence, eight caciques reported that when the hungry asked for food, they were given instead twenty-five lashes by order of the local authorities. The identity of folk saints—such as San La Muerte, Gaucho Gil, and the many noble bandits—is formed under such circumstances, and it is no wonder that they are conceived as anti-institutional protectors of dispossessed people who have no recourse within the system.[36]

The squatting figure of San La Muerte has the strongest claim to a Guaraní origin, because it closely resembles the fetal position in which many indigenous groups buried their dead. Squatting human skeletons, with elbows resting on their knees and hands under the chin, were found at the Pecos Pueblo in New Mexico; and Incan burials, as seen for example in Cuzco's Museo Inka, are similarly postured, with their hands on the cheeks. As described by a Jesuit in 1618, the corpses are "seated, the knees next to the mouth, and the hands on the cheeks." Guaraní customs were similar: the dead were buried in a fetal position with the knees and head upward. The position of the body, the boniness, and the hands on cheeks, chin, or temples all relate these burials to the squatting image of San La Muerte.[37]

Also contributing to conception of the squatting image (or else attributed to it in retrospect) is the idea that Guaraní shamans crouched under riverside trees to fast and await visions. At least one colonial source describes Guaraní shamans seated (but not necessarily squatting) under a willow tree during such a fast and vision quest. This same image is incorporated into some San La Muerte narratives, which have a shaman beside a river fasting for so long that he becomes a skeleton. In a variation on the theme—as in Myth 1—the shaman is replaced by or intermingles with a Jesuit or Franciscan.[38]

The image of San La Muerte seated in a chair appears to have emerged at the other end of the spectrum, where Catholic influence is predominant. This image was frequently mentioned some thirty or forty years ago, but today it has virtually disappeared. I have only seen one San La Muerte in this form, seated with the head resting on a hand. As described in a 1976 study, San La Muerte is usually represented "seated, because the folk-saint carvers imagined him in the well known posture of the 'Lord of Humility and Patience.'" The seated San La Muerte holds a scythe, which is an adaptation of the walking stick often held by Christ in these images. At least one myth makes explicit this connection between the scythe and the walking stick.[39]

Sculptures of the Lord of Humility and Patience, which were carved by Guaraní craftsmen in the missions, represent an exhausted, defeated Christ in the period between his flagellation and his crucifixion. He has a wounded, pensive countenance, is resigned to his death, and rests his weary head on a hand (in a variation, his tied hands are on his lap). In some regions of Spanish America this same image is known as *Cristo el Justo Juez* (Christ the Just

Judge) or *Cristo de la Justicia* (Christ of Justice), and one of San La Muerte's alternate names is San Justo (the Just Saint, or St. Justice). San La Muerte is also called *San Paciencia* or *Señor de la Paciencia* (St. Patience or Lord of Patience). Some devotees do not distinguish between San La Muerte and the Lord of Humility and Patience. For Pirucha in Goya, conversely, the Christ image has nothing to do with this representation of San La Muerte. He is seated, Pirucha explains, because that is how his body was discovered in the lepers prison. "It is the last image we have of him."[40]

The image of San La Muerte that is by far most popular today is a standing skeleton with a scythe. This form—almost an advocation—is generally believed to be the most powerful San La Muerte. The image is clearly indebted to death personified as the Grim Reaper, who likewise carries a scythe and often wears a dark, hooded cloak. Myths pursue this relation by narrating the guardianship over life and death that Christ assigned to San La Muerte. San La Muerte protects life, but when one's time is up he releases the soul with his scythe and provides safe passage to heaven. These responsibilities again link San La Muerte with the skeletons in the Dance of Death and other morality plays that were staged by Jesuits and Guaranís in the missions.

In sixteenth-century literature, as in versions of the San La Muerte myth, personified death is subordinate to Christ. He is an instrument of divine design, not an independent player who exercises his own will. San La Muerte measures time with burning candles rather than with the hourglass often held by the Grim Reaper, but both images convey the idea that you die when your time is up. There is nothing arbitrary about life's end in death; your time on earth is predetermined. In early medieval Christianity, parents lit three candles, a name written on each, and gave to their child the name on the candle that burned the longest.[41]

In some versions, however, San La Muerte defies the will of God by making his own decisions concerning life and death. One has Christ grant a poor man the power to heal, so that the man could earn a living. If the patient's time was up, Christ explained, this would be indicated by a candle going out at the foot of the bed. These patients were not to be treated. One such patient was a millionaire, however, and the healer did not want to lose the fortune that he anticipated by restoring the man to health. The healer switched the extinguishing candle at the millionaire's feet with another so that he could proceed with a treatment. Christ, angered by the insubordination, retaliated in kind by switching the healer's candle with that of the millionaire. "Since then the one who switched the candle is called San La Muerte."[42]

The owner of a religious shop in San Ignacio related along these lines that San La Muerte was expelled from heaven (like Lucifer) for wanting more power than God had granted him. Those on earth who want to be more than they are, she continued, thus make requests to San La Muerte. Another attendant at a religious store, this one in south Texas, explained that the Mexican Santísima Muerte was an angel assigned by God to guide the dead into the next world. One image represents a pietà with the Virgin replaced by Santísima Muerte, holding a skeleton: "She is showing him to God to see what the fate of his soul will be."

The gathering of souls is also reminiscent of St. Michael the Archangel, whose identity as an otherwordly courier was derived from the pagan Mercury. In the sixteenth and seventeenth centuries, St. Michael served for dying people a triple role as protector, conductor, and advocate. He was appointed judge in matters concerning death, and he carries a pair of scales (like that of the allegorical Justice) that weigh the soul against its sins.

Michael had a certain importance among the Jesuits, as suggested even by the name, San Miguel, of one of the important missions. He appears also to have had a role in conversion of the natives. A document written in Guaraní around 1753 says, "The very God Our Lord sent St. Michael from heaven to our grandparents." The author, Miguel Guaiho, states that God gave lands to his poor ancestors, and then St. Miguel, the Holy Archangel, appeared to "make our ancestors know God's will." Michael instructed them to seek out the Jesuits and to construct a cross in order to achieve "eternal well-being." Michael also appeared to a converted Guaraní and frightened off the devil who was trying to capture his soul. Many Guaraní mission images depict St. Michael the Archangel in his classic pose of slaying the devil.[43]

St. Michael appears on some San La Muerte altars, including that of the curandera Pirucha in Goya, but the two are more strongly linked through their common association with justice. The idea of justice that is suggested by Michael's scales and is explicit in Christ's title as the Just Judge is also evident in San La Muerte's identity. Many devotees explain that "San La Muerte" is a nickname for the saint whose full name is San Justo, El Señor de la Buena Muerte (St. Justice, The Lord of Good Death). This title is directly related to Myth 2, in which a just king becomes God's appointee for administering death.

San Justo merits the name because he comes for one precisely at the moment that destiny has scheduled, not before or after—the just moment, or just the right moment. One devotee explained that he waits if you still have some life left in you but acts if you are fatally injured or ill, so that you avoid unnecessary suffering. One thus has "a good death, the right death" and is happy to leave this world for the next. Such just allotment also characterizes the miracles he concedes. San La Muerte does not make you win the lottery, but always assures that one has "just enough, because he is just." Pelusa suggests the same when she advises, "Ask for what is just, and it will be granted."[44]

Justice is also served by death's function as an equalizer, a neutralizer of this-worldly hierarchies and inequities. Death is for everyone, regardless of individual attributes or privileges, and afterward all skeletons look more or less the same. In one San La Muerte myth a poor man sets out in search of a godfather for his son. His primary criterion is that the person be just. After he discards the possibilities of St. Peter, St. John, and the devil, Death offers to be the child's godfather. The man will find no one more just, Death explains, because when the time comes Death takes people whether they are young or old, rich or poor, men or women, good or evil, happy or sad.[45]

Justice is similarly emphasized through San La Muerte as an equalizer in many versions of myths from the 1960s and 1970s. These ideas are identical to a prominent strain in the sixteenth- and seventeenth-century Spanish discourse on death. As explained by Fray Luis de Rebolledo, "although men may be different during life, some tall and others short, some rich and others poor, some nobles and others villains, in death they are all the same." Equality in death neutralizes the inequality of life. Many early modern works of art have titles like "Death Interrupts a Pastoral Idyll" and "Death Attacks the High and Mighty."[46]

The "Good Death" of San La Muerte's full name—San Justo, El Señor de la Buena Muerte—leads rather directly back to Christ, particularly the crucified advocation known as *El Señor de la Buena Muerte* (The Lord of Good Death). Ignacio in Resistencia related that San La Muerte is also known as the *Cristo desencarnado* (fleshless Christ), and a religious store attendant in San Juan similarly explained that San La Muerte is the skeleton of Christ. In a document from the 1970s, a devotee referred to her San La Muerte as "the crucified one," and another myth establishes San La Muerte as an advocation of Christ. A prayer addressed to San La Muerte, similarly, applies (confused) biblical details to him: "You were mocked, flagellated with thorns, died and were buried," but then "with your ten commandments you triumphantly crushed your enemy, the devil." One informant explained that San La Muerte died and resurrected from the dead. When the anthropologist asked her if she was referring to Jesus Christ, however, she replied, "No, they are two different things."[47]

In summary, then, San La Muerte probably began as a witchcraft amulet used for magical homicide; evolved more generally into an amulet used in black magic, but also to protect the body from harm; and then, in turn, became a payé with generalized functions, including a specialty in the recovery of lost and stolen objects. From these origins as an amulet, San La Muerte gradually evolved into saint. Myths of origin began to circulate, the sacred fabrication of the image in specified materials became less important, the devotion went public, and religious practices displaced occult rituals. As each new stage of evolution emerges, however, those that precede it remain active. Some propagate the saint and others adhere to the payé, most mix and match, and the saint itself—like miraculous statues in churches—reserves the right to representation that is miraculous in itself. Thus magic and religion happily intermix, along with Catholic and syncretic antecedents.

At the Shrines

The specific date of San La Muerte's fiesta varies, although it is always in August. At some shrines, particularly those in Posadas, the fiesta is celebrated on August 13; at others, notably in Resistencia, on August 15. The date in Empedrado is August 20. Pelusa advocates a weeklong commemoration from August 13 to August 20 because this was the week that San La Muerte starved to death in prison. Ramón relates that the date was fixed in Resistencia decades ago by an end run around the law. Permits were required for religious fiestas, but officials refused to grant them for celebration of San La Muerte. Cecilia, the now deceased owner of an important shrine in the region, requested a permit for the feast day of the Virgin of the Assumption, August 15, and under that cover hosted her San La Muerte fiesta. This was done with the collusion of a police official who was a San La Muerte devotee.

Just as the date varies, so too does the form of celebration. Regional traditions are what is constant. Folk song and dance (*chamamé* and *bailantas*), gaucho dress, and grilled beef (*asado*) are the prominent accompaniments to San La Muerte devotion, as are the colors black and red. At the fiesta hosted by Ramón, song and dance are the centerpieces of the event and in themselves constitute offerings to San La Muerte. Several chamamé groups attend Ramón's fiesta, each with a song written for the saint. (This is consonant with a tradition of chamamés to folk saints. A 1949 collection titled *Cancionero Guaraní* ["Guaraní Song Book"] includes a song to San La Muerte.) The lyrics are sometimes customized to the occasion, with reference to Ramón and his fiesta. Each group serenades the saint by playing its song before San La Muerte's altar; then the party begins.[48]

Ramón opens the event with a brief greeting in Spanish and the mentioned prayer to San La Muerte in Guaraní. He then reserves the first few dances for couples in traditional dress; thereafter the dance floor is open to all.

Folk devotion is inseparable from tradition music, dance, dress, and food. This fiesta celebrates San La Muerte's feast day in Resistencia.

The musicians make frequent reference to San La Muerte during their performances, and they repeatedly say that the applause following each song is really for him. The links between the folk culture and the folk devotion are reinforced constantly.

In Posadas, which is further from the epicenter of chamamé culture, the performances are more diverse. When I attended the festival in 2003, chamamé and traditional dance were an important presence, but they were accompanied by mariachi, rock, folk, moonwalking, and belly-dancing performances. The facial expressions of more traditional people at the fiesta indicated their surprise—in some cases tending toward objection, in others toward awe—at these innovations. Some of the performances were repaying miracles, but the music at this fiesta nevertheless seemed to function more as entertainment than as an essential and integral aspect of devotion, as it was at Ramón's fiesta. All of the nontraditional performers were young, which gave the event the feel of a talent show.

Similarly, in Empedrado, the music and dance are the entertainment dimension of a more comprehensive devotional and social occasion. Long lines form for visits to the altar, and the most anticipated event—here as at some of the Resistencia shrines—is the procession of San La Muerte. Devotees take turns carrying the small litter on which San La Muerte is carried for a round trip (he visits a local Virgin) up Route 12. A long procession follows with its fabulous spectacle of red flags, itself backed up by a parade of trucks unable to pass.

Each San La Muerte shrine has its own feel, norms, history, and fiesta style, but the draw is generally an old San La Muerte image believed to be exceptionally powerful. A son of the shrine owner in Empedrado explained that his grandfather found their carved image of San La Muerte while working for a lumber-cutting operation in the country. No one knew what the image was, and the grandfather stored it away in a trunk. It was forgotten there for some time, but one day San La Muerte made some noise because he wanted to get out. Everyone thought the noise was made by a rat, but when they opened up the trunk they found nothing, not even turds. That's when they realized that the image was making the noise.

An old Indian woman explained that the image was San La Muerte and that it was very powerful. The grandfather built San La Muerte an altar, and devotion spread through the grandfather's use of San La Muerte to help locals find lost and stolen livestock. They would bring him a piece of a candle, and he would burn it on San La Muerte's altar. The way that the candle burned revealed the critical information regarding the animal—if it was lost or stolen, dead or alive, and where it could be found. As devotion gradually grew, a small chapel to San La Muerte was built at the family's home. It was considerably enlarged around 2002. Devotion has boomed in recent years, particularly after a television program on San La Muerte was broadcast on the Infinito channel. The shrine's relative proximity to Buenos Aires has also made it a popular choice for devotees from the capital.

The demographics at Empedrado are quite different from those at other shrines. San La Muerte generally attracts local folks and families deeply rooted in gaucho tradition. In Empedrado this base audience is very much present, but it is complemented by an urban contingent and by more (or more visible) "delinquents," as they are described locally. This mixed group is partially the result of the shrine's location and high profile. Other San La Muerte shrines are at private homes and are generally unidentified; one must know where they are and enter private property to gain access. The Empedrado shrine, conversely, is in plain view on a national route, and it is closer to the capital than other shrines. San La Muerte is announced in huge letters, and the chapel is open to anyone who wishes to enter. The urban audience is also cultivated by the family's promotion of the fiesta. One of the brothers, who lives in Buenos Aires, charters buses and sells tickets to facilitate attendance and raise the comfort level of first-time visitors. They arrive wearing name tags provided by the tour, and many buy a San La Muerte T-shirt.

These aspects of the Empedrado shrine's operation give many locals the impression that the shrine is a commercial venture. San La Muerte fiestas are generally free—even the food—because the saint (meaning donations made to the saint) sponsors them. In Empedrado, however, almost everything is sold. Large numbers of visitors, including those transported on the buses, are stranded at the shrine and purchase the food and drink sold out of kiosks by the owners. San La Muerte paraphernalia and other items are also offered for sale by concessionaires. The owners explain that the proceeds offset the costs of the fiesta, but some devotees regard the sales as profiteering.

The situation in Posadas is quite different. Pelusa and Isabelino, who host the fiesta at their domestic shrine, do so at considerable expense to themselves and they derive no material gain from the cult. In a neighborhood where many others live in shacks made of scrap wood, Pelusa and Isabelino own an attractive, well-maintained, air-conditioned house surrounded by a high security fence. The quality furnishings include a stereo and—unusual for the area—computer, and they own at least one recent-model car. Pelusa and Isabelino relate that they have experienced poverty and hunger, and now that they enjoy economic stability, which they attribute to San La Muerte, they are eager to share their good fortune. The poor people who attend their annual fiesta are treated as "special guests," Pelusa explains, because they are not treated kindly elsewhere.

Each year the street in front of their home is closed for the two-day celebration that they host in the name of San La Muerte. The events include a free dinner, open to whoever wishes to attend, during which hundred of pounds of grilled beef and side dishes are distributed. Every nine years, an alternative menu, locro—a kind of stew—is served. Hundreds of gallons of locro cook over firewood all morning, and locals line up with pots and buckets until the supply is depleted. (The grilled beef is an eat-in meal—integrated into the fiesta—but the locro is takeout and served in the early afternoon.) In exchange for their generosity, Pelusa and Isabelino ask participants only for "love of one's neighbor, faith in San La Muerte, and hope for the future." I noticed that very few of the people who came for the food—most were nondevotees—made any effort to give thanks.

The fiesta actually begins the night before, at midnight on August 12, when the chapel is ceremoniously opened for its annual week of public access. Mariachis approach to serenade the saint as Pelusa unlocks the chapel door. She has structured the devotion (like the altar in her chapel) hierarchically, and she enforces protocols for those who wish to begin or advance their devotion. Newcomers must be present at the August 12 opening for their first

Locro, a kind of stew, is distributed to the poor during the San La Muerte fiesta in Posadas.

rite of passage. Pelusa has hidden wallet-size images of San La Muerte around the altar, and the newcomers must find them to be admitted to the devotion. They approach the altar one at a time, visibly shaken. The crowd of already initiated devotees chants "One, two, three," and the newcomer has an instant to find one of the hidden images. During my visit in 2003, none of the four people who tried was successful. They walked off looking dejected, heartbroken. Even this door was closed to them.

Those who are successful may begin their devotion with a San La Muerte in the form of one of these wallet images or prayer cards (known in Spanish as *estampitas*). This must be blessed in seven churches. In subsequent years they return to the shrine on August 12, at midnight, to leave their image on the altar of Pelusa's San La Muerte, where it remains until midnight on August 19. After a significant period as a neophyte (Isabelino says nine years), those who meet Pelusa's approval graduate from the prayer card to a plaster

On the outside: Nondevotees watch the performances during a San La Muerte fiesta in Posadas.

statue of San La Muerte. Another nine years of dutiful devotion entitles one to a San La Muerte made of human bone. The devotees wear these bone images around their necks, usually in a locket. Pelusa sometimes carves them—she has done about eight to date—beside the chapel on Good Fridays. Carvers, she explains, must fast for three days and avoid sexual relations before they work.

The fiesta proper begins on the night of August 13. I was stuck by how clearly the crowd was divided into two groups, which were separated by the high iron fence between them. On the inside were the inner circle of devotees and invited musicians and dancers. They together constituted a small percentage of the crowd. On the outside of the fence were the masses, most of whom were not devotees. They had come for the entertainment and the party, as earlier some had come for the food. Those outside the fence who were devotees formed a line and were permitted entrance, a few at a time, to visit the chapel. They prayed, paid their respects, made their requests, and gave thanks for miracles received. Some left offerings for San La Muerte—bottles of wine or liquor, a braid of hair, the clothes of a saved baby—and then they went on their way.

Gaucho Gil

Antonio Gil was born around 1847 in the province of Corrientes. Civil war was raging in the region, and around 1875, Gil was forcibly recruited by Colonel Juan de la Cruz Zalazar into a gaucho militia. Gil deserted shortly after because he was unwilling to kill his fellow gauchos. Some say that an angel had advised the desertion during a vision, or that the Guaraní god Ñandeyara appeared to Gil in a dream. Afterward, Gil lived by necessity outside the law, on the run, stealing from the rich to give to the poor and always evading the authorities. He was handsome, noble, and invincible, and his penetrating gaze was hypnotic.

On January 6, possibly in 1878, Gil was attending a party for the feast of St. Baltasar. He was betrayed by a friend and captured. He surrendered peacefully, without any resistance. A police escort was ordered to transport him to Goya for sentencing, but en route, just outside of Mercedes, the sergeant in charge decided to execute Gil. This was done under the pretext of an attempted escape. Gil was hung upside down from an espinillo tree and his head was cut off with his own knife, which he offered for this purpose.

"This is an injustice," Gil told the sergeant just before the execution. "You are spilling innocent blood." Gil also said that the sergeant's son was gravely ill but that Gil would intercede in heaven to save the boy's life.

When the police arrived in Goya, they discovered that Gil had been pardoned and would have been freed had they not executed him. The sergeant went home to find, as Gil had prophesied, that his son was on the verge of death. He implored Gil's help and forgiveness, the miracle was granted, and the moribund son recovered. In gratitude the sergeant returned to the site of the execution, and in the ground reddened with Gil's blood, he erected a cross made of ñandubay wood. Thus began the devotion.

The typical story of gaucho sainthood is as political as it is religious. A rebellious figure, often a civil war deserter, is forced to the margins of society and survives through his courage and ingenuity. He commits crimes of necessity rather than greed, and he is welcomed as a benefactor among impoverished people who harbor or help him. He obeys a higher moral standard, kills only in self-defense or just revenge, protects and cares for the poor, inspires locals with his feats, and, although clearly the underdog, outnumbered and outgunned, he evades and mocks his people's feared oppressors. When the gaucho is finally apprehended, often as a result of betrayal, he becomes the victim of a gruesome execution. His death is always perceived as the authorities' unjust abuse of power. Out of this injustice, the gaucho saint is born. The unsaintly life, when later it is known or referenced at all, is lauded for its justifiable, even saintly defiance of the corrupt and exploitative ruling class. Otherwise only the sacrificial death is remembered.

Antonio Mamerto Gil Núñez, known as Gaucho Gil, is without a doubt the most prominent of the many gaucho folk saints in Argentina. His principal shrine, at the site of his death just outside the town of Mercedes in Corrientes Province, attracts hundreds of thousands of devotees, and these numbers are redoubled by devotion at a multitude of domestic shrines throughout Argentina. Gil, like most of the gaucho saints, was a *bandolero* (bandit). These outlaws roamed in bands on the fringes of society, always hiding from the law. They made their living on the run by rustling cattle and robbing landowners. Gil and other bandit leaders were legendary—strong, brave, handsome, noble, bold, charismatic—and they were revered for their heroic attributes by their followers and the public alike. Only the privileged class despised them.[1]

Gaucho Gil emerged in the context of the bloody civil wars that polarized Argentina in the nineteenth century. These were times of fragmentation, anarchy, and indiscriminate violence, with militias prone to abusing the defenseless population. Young men were conscripted into the troops of one side or the other. In many folk saint devotions these wars are represented as struggles caused by the conflicting interests of the landed elite but fought by poor people who have no choice and nothing to gain. The term *gaucho alzado*, which is often applied to outlaw folk saints, designates those who defied landowners by refusing to participate in local struggles.

Gaucho Gil's desertion, like that of many others, was in protest against killing "brothers"—meaning the rural poor, who, like him, were exploited for war and profit—to advance the political and economic ambitions of one politician or another. This same theme turns up in Difunta Correa's story when her husband resists recruitment: "Why this impious struggle among brothers?"

A similar scenario also provides the context for José Hernández's famous epic poem "Martín Fierro," written in the 1870s. The protagonist, very much like Gaucho Gil, is a poor gaucho who deserts the military and becomes an outlaw.[2]

Desertion and the other crimes of gaucho folk saints are in effect correctional protests against a social order that is itself perceived to be criminal. Traits associated with the ruling class, such as cruelty and greed, are also corrected as gaucho saints recuperate the traditional values of honor, bravery, solidarity, and defense of local culture from encroachment and domination. Theft is part of the greater struggle against a distressingly misordered world. It is an act of civil disobedience, an adjustment to the political and economic inequities that disadvantage common people.

When asked about the life of Gaucho Gil, even devotees who know little or nothing can readily produce the phrase, "He stole from the rich to give to the poor." The same is said about many gaucho saints, and some have charitable attributes registered in their nicknames. Juan Batista Bairoletto (in various spellings) was "the Robin Hood of the pampas" in the 1920s. José Dolores in San Juan is the "Protector of the Poor."

These are the champions of underclass people, the vanguard of a never-realized liberation that gains symbolic expression and compensation through the escapades of outlaw avengers. The context is always one of oppression and exploitation, of impunity for the wealthy and injustice for the poor who dare to oppose their own subjugation. Gaucho heroes and saints are the rebel reaction to this injustice. They epitomize defiance. They are the manifestation, the radicalization, of the popular will for equality, dignity, and a fair chance to survive economically. They do what others only dream.

Devotees who are familiar with the myths of outlaw saints acknowledge their crimes ("he stole from the rich") and pardon them ("to give to the poor") in the same breath. The illegal law legalizes crime. It is also common to dismiss the crimes completely: the gaucho was falsely accused or was punished in error, which makes the bloody execution all the more horrible.

The most prominent version of Gaucho Gil's myth explains that he was killed by authorities while en route to a court in Goya, where a pardon was awaiting him. (Such killings were commonly done under the pretext of attempted escape, and the heads of victims were delivered as proof of capture.) Other variations stress scapegoating. In a 1950 version from Corrientes, Gaucho Gil is a handsome man of "good behavior" but was "opposed to the authorities." In their haste to make an arrest the police apprehended Gil— implicated only by his attitude of defiance—and he was "executed in error." When the actual criminal was later arrested, the responsible sergeant realized his error, returned to the site of the killing, and prayed for forgiveness. Thus began the devotion.[3]

The romantic idealism that characterizes gaucho saints is largely attributed in retrospect. Bandits paid well for protection, and those who harbored them may have done so more as a means of economic survival than as an expression of true solidarity or political commitment. Fear also factored into the equation: bandits were both generous and dangerous. Take your pick. It made good sense for poor and powerless people to remain in the bandits' good graces. The support that gaucho bandits received was probably the result of hero worship combined in various degrees with practical self-interest. The bandit's generosity was also practical: a cow is big, and rustlers live on the run, so leftovers were shared with locals.

The balance tipped toward the heroic, and then toward folk sanctity, when the crimes of outlaws were overwhelmed by excessively violent punishments. The criminality of the punishment is so great that the crime—stealing to survive—is readily pardoned. The poor people who witness the executions, like devotees later, identify with the victims. Empathy and sorrow cleanse all affronts. Whatever self-interest—fear or food—once conditioned the support of outlaws now dissipates beneath the shock of the kill and the pressure of the myth. The slate is wiped clean for everyone. When new generations hear of the gaucho, as hero or as saint, they learn and retell only the romanticized version.

A 1921 report from Chaco is characteristic in its interrelations of crime, punishment, and sainthood. According to the report, the gaucho saint Francisco López was tortured and killed after being falsely accused of stealing a chicken. As a consequence of the execution he became "the idol adored by common people." The veneration of López results from the dissymmetry between the crime and the punishment. False accusation redoubles the injustice and, consequently, the attribution of martyrdom.[4]

Anecdotes of outlaw escapades often stress how the underdog hero, by virtue of sheer ingenuity, outsmarts the enemies of the people. Isidro Velázquez, one of the last romantic bandits, once ate at the home of a man who was on the verge of losing everything. Foreclosure was imminent because the man was unable to make a payment on his house and land. Velázquez asked how much the man owed, and at the end of the meal he left the 2,500 pesos necessary for the payment. When the authorities arrived the next day with the foreclosure papers, the man paid up and was saved. Velázquez, hiding in wait on the authorities' return route, ambushed them and recuperated his investment, plus interest. Other Velázquez tactics, such as wearing his sandals backward to lead the police in the wrong direction, likewise testify to his ingenuity.[5]

In many cases the folk saint's ingenuity and daring are backed up by supernatural powers. Police were surprised when their bullets entered Velázquez's body and that of his partner, Vicente Gauna, because these outlaws were believed to be magically invincible. It is also said that Velázquez could stop people in their tracks with his "paralyzing gaze," and chamamé lyrics attribute this same power to Gaucho Gil. Gil's invincibility was indebted to the San La Muerte amulet inserted under his skin, which protected his body from all harm. Devotees accordingly clarify that Gaucho Gil was not caught by the police; he surrendered. And even then his life could not be taken until, at his request, the San La Muerte amulet was removed. The hero retains invulnerability and control even during his demise. The point is driven home in Gaucho Gil narratives when he offers his own knife for the execution.[6]

The Cross

In the early Middle Ages, as pagan worship made a gradual transition to Christianity, crosses appeared at former pagan shrines, at crossroads, on property lines, and beside certain rocks and trees. Legend held that sites marked by the cross were populated by spirits, and that rites, prayers, and offerings at the cross would placate these spirits and solicit their powers. Crosses were attributed mysterious and diverse powers. They frighten off the devil, they bring fecundity in agriculture and childbirth, and they protect the community from natural disasters. These were crosses without the image of Christ, and they were venerated in themselves, for their magical power, and not as commemorations of Christ's crucifixion (that came later).

The crosses of early Christianity thus marked sites of folk devotion, where pagan beliefs and Christianity intermingled. Rituals were conducted at the crosses by magicians, fortune-tellers, and other self-appointed intermediaries. Promises were made, candles (sometimes blessed by priests) were lit, food offerings were left, and sorcery was practiced. Early medieval crosses were also situated on roads and hilltops to guide travelers, and to protect them from the dangers that they encountered on their journeys. These crosses thus served two purposes simultaneously, one practical and the other supernatural.[7]

In Argentina, the cross had an auspicious debut in 1588 during the founding of the city of Corrientes. Rebelling Guaranís tried to burn down the huge cross that had been raised by colonists, but the cross resisted their best efforts. The *Cruz del Milagro* (Cross of the Miracle), as it is known, became an object of devotion in itself—not as a representation—very much like the medieval crosses. Its reproductions were enshrined on home altars.

The wood of other crosses, particularly cemetery crosses (along with the white cloths draped over them), have for centuries been used for making amulets. Even the crosses that are worn around necks today are often attributed magical powers that are activated by touching and fondling. Catholics similarly sign themselves with the cross for protection and luck on dangerous roads, as planes take off, during soccer games, or before an interview or date. In many regions of Spanish America the cross has the power to dispel all sorts of evil (although it doesn't appear to be effective against presidents and dictators), and many crosses—such as the Mystical Crosses in Sucre, Bolivia—perform miracles.

Argentine crosses also mark the spots where deaths have occurred—often on the road—even when the bodies are removed for burial in cemeteries. These crosses, like the medieval roadside crosses, have both practical and supernatural purposes. They are place markers and reminders of tragic deaths, but they are also loaded symbols that consolidate the horror and sorrow of death with the otherworldly powers that it makes accessible. The cross, like the death that it marks, is a point of contact, a link between this world and the next. No sooner is a cross put down than someone prays before it. Travelers interrupt their trips to pay respects to the dead, often leaving an offering—candles, coins, food—as a means of beseeching a safe and trouble-free journey. These stops at roadside crosses are jointly inspired by veneration of the dead and the living needs of passersby. They are to a certain degree a practical religious obligation, a prudent inconvenience for the maintenance of well-being, a kind of insurance.

Crosses have also served as sites for the indirect distribution of alms. As explained in reports from the 1940s and 1950s, people in need may take the offerings that are left at crosses, provided that they pray for the salvation of the dead person's soul. This practice increases the visits to the cross, which in turn attracts the attention of others. If someone takes an offering without praying, or if there is a great disproportion between the prayers offered and what is taken in exchange, then the dead person exacts revenge.[8]

A 1940 report from Mercedes, where the Gaucho Gil shrine is located, establishes a direct connection between these practices at death-site crosses and the emergence of devotion to Gaucho Gil. At the cross raised where Gil was killed, passersby left offerings of cash, cigarettes, and food. "In order to take any of the offerings found there, they must say a prayer for salvation of the soul who suffers for sins committed during life. Thus, the people of this town and the residents of that rural area offer their faith and their admiration to the soul and the cross of Gil. They pray in their manner to favor the salvation of a soul that in this isolated region did not have anyone to pray for it. In this way that cross, so miraculous for the people, became popular and famous."[9]

Reports such as this one, particularly in the broader context of cross offerings generally, provide a historical origin for devotion to Gaucho Gil that competes with the mythic accounts. In the myths, Gil's tragic death purges all sin and sends him directly to heaven. The miracles therefore begin immediately—even via Gil's squirting blood during the killing itself—and ignite devotion spontaneously.

The process is much slower, more evolutionary, in the quoted report. Devotion to Gaucho Gil begins with the customary prayer and circulation of offerings at the site of a tragic death. At the start, and even as late as the quoted passage from 1940, people kneeled at Gil's cross to pray for him—"for salvation of the soul who suffers for sins committed during life"—and not to him. Gil is not yet in heaven and accordingly lacks the capacity to perform miracles. The purpose of the prayer is precisely to help work off sin so that Gil's soul will eventually enter heaven. The original favors received by those who pray at the cross are limited to whatever offerings they take in exchange. And when miracles are reported, they are first attributed to the cross, not to Gil.

At some point, however, all of the praying paid off, and Gaucho Gil entered paradise. There, close to God, he began to reciprocate prayers with miracles. As the news of miracles circulated, praying for Gil gradually yielded to praying to him: the folk saint was born. Typical rituals at a death-marking cross were transformed into a folk saint devotions because miracles altered the agenda.

The close association of "the soul and the cross of Gil" is the essence of this emerging devotion. It provides an approved Catholic entry even for priests, who see in the affinity of Gil and the cross an opportunity for corrective evangelization. For lay Catholics, too, "the religious cult has an acceptable explanation when it develops around a cross." The same is true in devotions to other gaucho folk saints, such as Francisco López and Gaucho Lega, who are likewise closely associated with crosses.[10]

The site of Gaucho Gil's shrine was originally know as *la Cruz de Gil*, *la Cruz Gil*, or, in Guaraní, *Curuzú Gil* (Gil's Cross or, literally, Gil Cross). Many devotees still refer to it by these names today. "Gil Cross" suggest almost a hyphen between its two components, as though they form a single compound. This composite is first evidenced in the frequent use of the site name, *Cruz Gil*, to refer to Gaucho Gil himself. The fusion of Gil and the cross then becomes visually explicit in the now standardized iconography.

Gil stands in front of the cross—or, more accurately, is attached to it at his back—with his head proudly uplifted rather than bowed in agony like that of the crucified Christ. The overall impression is one of confidence and strength. This is more a resurrection than a crucifixion. Gil's right hand holds *boleadoras* (bolas), a symbol of gaucho culture. If earlier in this devotion the cross was prominent and the quasi-anonymous Gil—with an identity only as a victim—was secondary, now the cross is a backdrop that showcases the triumphant Gil in the foreground.

Despite the implications of such iconography, devotees have little to say on the similarity of Gaucho Gil and Christ. Even with prompting they come up short. It seems almost as though the bare cross must remain Christless, with Gil first buried beneath it and then resurrected before it, without the complication of a third-party God. Gil and Christ nevertheless hold significant attributes in common, among them brotherly love, pacifism, charity, defiance of authority, obedience to a higher moral standard, and defense of outcasts and the poor. They both are arrested as a result of betrayal, passively accept their unjust punishment, pardon and miraculously heal their executioners, and suffer sacrificial deaths. These similarities, though not specifically recognized or articulated by devotees, are integral to the myths that they create and to the attraction that Gil exerts in their culture. The Christlike attributes build a familiar and appealing hero for devotees who bring their Catholicism to folk devotion.

Sacrifice, Martyrdom, and Injustice

The first Christians to become saints—and they were folk saints long before they were canonized—were the martyrs killed by the Romans. Martyrdom continues to generate folk saints, but today they die not for the faith but rather for causes, such as justice and economic survival, that bind them to their communities. These social and political causes gain religious value retrospectively. Because Gaucho Gil is killed unjustly, a kind of purgatory on earth, he enters heaven directly and there, close to God, brokers miracles. The power to perform miracles is directly indebted to the tragic death. This world and the next intermingle in the interpretation of his slaying, in the transformation of the victim into a saint, and in the relation of miracles to the circumstances around his demise (poverty and oppression, for example). In the absence of an unjust killing, there is no Gaucho Gil. A 1973 news article captured the idea precisely: "It is not that faith makes martyrs, but rather that martyrs make faith."[11]

Gil's happy life is interrupted by a cruel and sudden death, but in other cases, such as that of José Dolores, the death merely crowns a suffered life.

The purge that wins heaven is thereby comprehensive: life is purgatory and violent death is a sprint at the finish. "Your life has been a martyrdom / Your death has been another," relate song lyrics about José Dolores. "You have suffered so many miseries / That you will be a Saint," because owing to all of this purging agony "God has pardoned / Your sins."[12]

The causal relation between suffering and sainthood is similarly explicit among Gaucho Gil devotees. When I asked one if Gaucho Gil's death and miraculous power were related, the response came back on target: "Yes, because he was innocent and they killed him." Martyrdom thus begins to yield to sacrifice: spilled blood washes away sin. A photocopied prayer that is distributed at a shrine in San Roque explains why Gaucho Gil is miraculous: "divine Justice / gave you this privilege / pardoning your sins / because of your redeemed blood." Christ's sacrifice pardons the sins of others, but Gil's sacrifice pardons his own sins. The benefit, however, is for others. The Gil of folk narratives typically relates: "When my innocent spilled blood reaches God, I will return transformed into favors for my people"; or again, "My spilled blood will return in favors for my people."

The theme of miraculous sacrifice is literalized when Gil's squirting blood cures the crippled hand of one of his executioners. The same detail is found in myths of Francisco López, and it is similar to medieval legends concerning the soldier Loginus, who stabbed the crucified Christ in the side. Loginus's dimming vision was miraculously restored when blood ran down the shaft of his spear and into his eye.

In a 1950 report from Corrientes, Gaucho Gil requests his own execution, offering his knife for this purpose, in order to embark on a higher mission: "I want you to kill me here so that I can serve my fellow countrymen." The same Christlike mission is alluded to in chamamé lyrics, "You offered yourself to the Redeemer / in order to alleviate suffering." These examples make explicit the self-sacrifice that is only suggested elsewhere. Gil offers himself to the Redeemer—delivers himself for sacrifice, like that Redeemer—in order to redeem his people. In this perspective he is a second Christ, a regional Christ, who continues vicarious suffering for the salvation of others. The nature of salvation has changed, however: Christ's sacrifice saves the soul, but Gil's affords the entirely this-worldly benefit of miracles for everyday life.[13]

The ultimate cause of Gaucho Gil's death, if one follows the chain of events backward, is his military desertion. As explained in versions of the myth, an angel, or else the Guaraní deity Ñandeyara (Christianized, with the requisite white beard and luminescent aura), appeared to Gil, advising him to desert rather than spill the blood of his fellow gauchos. When Gil related his intended desertion and its reasons to other recruits, he was mocked as a coward but nevertheless stood by his convictions. He became a fugitive and was finally captured and executed as a consequence of this pacifism; his innocent blood was spilled because he refused to spill innocent blood. His sacrifice in this case literally saves others: had he killed "enemy" gauchos he would not have been killed. Gil's death also makes him a martyr to a moral principle–thou shall not kill, particularly not one's brother–in defiance of corrupt values that are forcibly imposed.

In short, killings that are viewed as sacrificial martyrdom make their gaucho victims miraculous. Many evolve into Christlike figures who are bound to the salvation—the this-worldly salvation—of their communities. A gaucho saint's death is a tragic accentuation, a hyperbole, of his people's slow death by poverty, marginality, and exploitation. The defeat is reversed after death, however, because the execution itself—the spilling of innocent blood—transforms the victim into a saint. Through unjust suffering the community gains an advocate who alleviates unjust suffering. The gaucho saint's death is thereby turned against its perpetrators, because the killing ultimately benefits both the victim and his community. Defeat in this world becomes victory in the next: there is full vindication. The struggle continues through miracles. And the folk saint's community, earlier the recipient of stolen goods, now receives the help supernaturally.

Among the many folk saints who conform to this prototype is Olegario Alvarez, known as Gaucho Lega, who was born around 1865 in Corrientes Province. He eventually became a police sergeant, killed a criminal in self-defense while on duty, was sentenced to prison for homicide, and fled to avoid incarceration. Thus, at least in myth, Gaucho Lega was a just man forced out of society by an injustice. He then formed a group of bandits which included Aparicio Altamirano, who also became a folk saint.

When the police finally caught up with the group, around 1908, Gaucho Lega was killed along with several others. The brutalized bodies were brought back to town for public display, partly as evidence of police efficacy and partly to deter other outlaws. The gruesome spectacle had unexpected side effects, because the horror, shock, and empathy it elicited transformed the police's trophy into the public's martyr. Gaucho Lega became another "authentic symbol of the sacrificed gaucho and victim of justice." A wreath of red roses and carnations on his tomb included a message that expressed the general sentiment: "Damn the bad government that persecutes the good gaucho."[14]

The Velázquez brothers Claudio (1929–1963) and Isidro (1928–1967) provided a twentieth-century revival of romanticized banditry through populist tactics and deft evasion of the authorities. After Claudio was shot to death by police (he was not wearing the red poncho consecrated to St. Catherine that protected him), Isidro joined up with Vicente Gauna (1942–1967) for more escapades. Isidro Velázquez and Vicente Gauna, both also deserters, went on a crime spree of robbery and homicide until they were killed by the police. The two were hiding among the Toba and planning a bank robbery when they were denounced by a teacher and a mailman.

An outburst of spontaneous devotion followed the deaths of Velázquez and Gauna. The police were baffled by public resentment against them for having eliminated two notorious criminals. To impede devotion the authorities cut down the tree where Velázquez had died, censored folk songs celebrating the bandits, and prohibited the offering of flowers or candles at the tombs. Thirty years later a guard was still posted in the cemetery to enforce the prohibition of devotion. Today the tombs of Velázquez and Gauna are nevertheless the site of a minor devotion in the Chaco town of Machagai. As a folk song put it, Velázquez and Gauna are "two entombed dreams."[15]

The Argentine tradition of martyred Robin Hood–type outlaws continues today, but it has migrated from the provinces to the capital. (In Venezuela there are similar urban devotions, including the folk saint Machera, who was the leader of a criminal gang until killed by police in Mérida in 1977, at the age of 22.) Víctor Manuel "Frente" Vital, a teenage thief from the San Francisco shantytown in the San Fernando district of Buenos Aires, became a folk saint after he was killed by the police in 1999. Frente had a reputation for giving away stolen goods and money, in part because his mother, a uniformed security guard in a supermarket, disapproved of his criminal activity. The mothers of Frente's accomplices encouraged, or at least condoned, their lives of crime, because the income helped to maintain their families, but Frente's mother would not allow stolen money or goods in the home. Frente's generosity found outlets for the surplus. His friends reported that everyone "either ate, drank, or got high with something Frente gave them."[16]

Frente's most famous caper was the hijacking of a truck from La Serenísima dairy company. Cases of yogurt, kefir, and cheese were loaded onto horse-drawn carts and distributed to the residents of his shantytown. Some of the cases were also delivered to thieves incarcerated in nearby prisons. Everyone feasted on foods that otherwise they could never afford. "Although he was a thief, he always had an incredible heart," said one of his girlfriends. "He watched the kids eating yogurt, opened a kefir for himself, and said, 'this is life.'"

Like earlier outlaws, Frente had many places to hide because locals were grateful for his generosity. He and an accomplice were in one of these homes, crouching under a table, when the police caught up with them. A sergeant kicked the table over with his boot and aimed his pistol. "Don't shoot, we surrender," Frente screamed; then he crossed his hands over his face, as though to protect himself, as the sergeant shot four times and killed him. One of the bullets pierced a hand before it lodged in his head. Frente was seventeen years old.

In Frente's case, as in hundreds of others, youths suspected of delinquency are eliminated by summary execution. Through this informal policy, known as *gatillo fácil* (literally "easy trigger"), the police function almost as a death squad to cleanse society of undesirable elements. More than five hundred complaints have been filed in Buenos Aires concerning gatillo-fácil killings, but usually the grievances have little effect. The families and communities of these dead teens regard them as victims of a system that permits murder with impunity of unconvicted petty thieves. In Frente's case, the outrage immediately after the killing was so great that shantytown residents pelted the police with stones. Mothers kicked officers and spat in their faces, two policemen were wounded, special forces were dispatched to the scene, and the situation escalated toward a riot until Frente's mother asked the crowd to disperse, fearing that the police would open fire. The residents of the shantytown later mounted such a scandal that the officer responsible for the murder was eventually imprisoned.

Frente Vital became a folk saint for residents of the impoverished district of Buenos Aires where he lived. Many families displayed a photograph of Frente in the unlikely, angelic pose of receiving communion. He was particularly popular among young thieves who visited his tomb-shrine and commended themselves to his care before committing their crimes. Frente's face was prominently displayed on their T-shirts as they smoked joints in a circle around his tomb, leaving the roach for him. If things went badly and they were shot at by police, Frente sent the bullets off course or, that failing, made sure that the wounds were not fatal.[17]

A variation on the theme of criminal folk saints is provided by Pedro Perlaitá, whose devotion is based in the Corrientes town of Empedrado. According to a 1940 report, Perlaitá was a soldier in the late nineteenth century. He was ordered back to the barracks by an arrogant young lieutenant, whose boastfulness defamed Perlaitá's honor in the presence of a woman. Perlaitá disobeyed the order, a fight ensued, and Perlaitá was wounded by the lieutenant's sword. He was subsequently imprisoned for insubordination, which gave him plenty of time to plot his revenge.

Upon release from prison Perlaitá murdered the lieutenant—"I have come to avenge the affront that defiled my honor as a soldier"—and then turned himself in to the general, resigning his fate to the disposition of the court. Perlaitá was sentenced to death. The public was shocked. The sympathetic crowds attending the execution saw Perlaitá refuse the blindfold, wave goodbye, and die after prolonged suffering, because the firing squad bullets were badly aimed. He was finally put out of his misery by a shot to the head from a lieutenant's pistol. The witness viewed this brutal and incompetent spectacle as a "barbarous outrage." Perlaitá had only defended his dignity, they argued, with honorable rather than criminal intent, and did so openly and honestly. He was nevertheless "executed by inflexible military law" and as a result became "a martyr transformed into a miraculous saint."[18]

Similar circumstances resulted in devotion to Juan Soldado (Juan Castillo Morales) in Tijuana, Mexico, not far from the border. Juan Soldado (the name means "Soldier Juan") was a poor soldier killed in 1938 after being arrested for the rape and murder of a girl. As in Gaucho Gil's case, he was killed under the pretext that he was attempting to escape custody. The pretense in Juan Soldado's case was particularly specious, because the "escape" was staged publicly—in a cemetery—and the firing squad on hand ordered Juan Soldado to run prior to shooting him.

Tradition holds that Juan Soldado was innocent of the crimes for which he was executed. His death is one of the many occasioned by the sleazy machinations of superiors. Most devotees maintain that Juan Soldado was framed by the officer who had actually committed the rape and murder. Others give a more Christlike, self-sacrificial spin to the story, explaining that Juan Soldado, though innocent, purposefully accepted the blame for someone else's crimes. Women walking past the site where he was slain were surprised by a voice—Juan Soldado's—that explained with otherworldly resonance, "I am innocent. I sacrificed myself for the sake of another." Today Juan Soldado continues to perform miracles in Tijuana, where he is also a patron of immigrants attempting the perilous crossing of the U.S-Mexico border.[19]

In Peru, similarly, innocence is maintained and devotion is instigated when an execution seems unjust. The folk saint Ubilberto Vásquez Bautista, a poor campesino from Cajamarca, was accused in 1966 of raping and killing an eleven-year-old girl who tended sheep. When Ubilberto's underwear were discovered, stained with blood, he first said that they belonged to his brother, then that the blood was from a pig, and finally that he had relations with his girlfriend—who was eight months pregnant—while she was menstruating.

To create enough doubt to avoid the death penalty, Ubilberto's attorney had the idea of trying to divert responsibility for the crime to one of Ubilberto's brothers. "Without intending it, I contributed to the creation of the myth," the attorney said later, meaning the myth of Ubilberto's innocence. That myth was reinforced by Ubilberto's model conduct as a prisoner, which led other inmates to believe that he was innocent. His conversion to the Adventist Church likewise created the impression of a pious man wrongfully condemned. Ubilberto, who never admitted guilt, was executed in September 1970. "God gave him the power to do miracles," explained a fellow inmate, because Ubilberto was executed unjustly.[20]

In Arequipa, there is active devotion to Víctor Apaza Quispe, who was born in the Miraflores district in 1932. Apaza led a vagrant life supported by odd jobs after fleeing his abusive father. In a variant version that he related to inmates, he was sold by his father into farm labor. Apaza married in 1953, continued a life of transient jobs and petty crime, drank heavily, and physically abused his wife and daughter until he finally abandoned the home. When he returned ten years later, the marriage was beyond repair. In January 1969, Apaza dreamed that his wife was unfaithful to him. He went to the location revealed in the dream and saw the shadowy figure of a man escaping. His wife, also there, was not as fortunate. Apaza beat her to death with a rock.[21]

It was later revealed that the crime was premeditated and carefully planned. Apaza originally denied responsibility but confessed his guilt once the evidence mounted against him. Later, during appeals for clemency, he again declared his innocence. He was convicted partially on the evidence of his two daughters, who wittingly or unwittingly offered testimony that supported the death penalty. Apaza did not understand the sentence until his lawyer translated it for him into Quechua. He hugged his lawyer, the two of them crying, and then collapsed into his chair.[22]

People in the courtroom were shocked by the death sentence. The rarity of the event—this would be the first execution in Arequipa—resulted in extensive press coverage. Apaza suddenly gained a celebrity derived less from his crime than from the punishment. The press represented him as a poor, simple man and a good Christian. According to Apaza's defense attorney, "the very foundation of society was shaken" when the public learned that Apaza had been sentenced to death. Horror and indignation were aroused because the imminent execution was "an unjust action of human justice." Divine justice would make amends.[23]

Apaza faced the firing squad in prison on September 17, 1971. (The drama is intensified in some folkloric versions by locating the execution in Arequipa's main plaza.) Arequipa's residents were outraged, even traumatized, and some fifteen hundred attended Apaza's funeral. They organized themselves into squads, taking turns to carry the coffin.

Apaza had been in prison for two years before he was executed. Like Ubilberto Vásquez Bautista in Cajamarca, he became a model prisoner and something of a populist. Fellow inmates described Apaza as a good, hardworking, honest man. In 1971, the 531 men incarcerated with him sent a letter to the court petitioning clemency, in part because Apaza had proven himself to be "an honorable man and dedicated to his work." The prison chaplain, a Jesuit, found Apaza to be pious and God-fearing, and the warden thought he was a "completely good" man. Later, retrospective press accounts described Apaza and Ubilberto together as "innocent men crushed by the Kafkaesque and labyrinthine cruelties of the administration of justice in Peru."[24]

The devotees with whom I spoke in Arequipa knew little about Apaza. Even the official *rezador*, a man who prays for tips at the shrine, did not have the story clear. Many devotees had a vague idea that Apaza had been executed under circumstances that suggested injustice, however, and the key word offered by all was "innocent." Some believed that the true killer confessed the crime after Apaza was executed.

When I asked devotees how they knew that Apaza was innocent, one woman astonished me with her answer: "because a sinner cannot work miracles." I later encountered this same response in other devotions. Once a folk saint's fame for miracles is accepted as true, then this truth—this evidence— revises backward to create the conditions necessary for the production of miracles. Miracles make Apaza's apparent guilt impossible, so the verdict is reversed. Innocence causes miracles, and miracles cause innocence. Miracles occur within the circularity defined by these parameters.

Apaza is miraculous, like all folk saints of this prototype, because "he died innocent and is beside Our Lord." "You were shot, you suffered," people said when they requested the first miracles, because these misfortunes qualified Apaza for sainthood.[25]

The same is true of Emilo (or Emile) Dubois, a flamboyant criminal and adventurer originally from France, who robbed and murdered several prominent businessmen in Valparaíso, Chile. He was captured, pleaded innocent, and was sentenced to death in 1907. Dubois declined a priest's offer of confession, saying "You should be taking the judge's confession, not mine. The judge who ordered my murder. Go inspire his repentance." At the time of his execution Dubois refused the blindfold and faced the firing squad calmly, smoking a cigarette. He reiterated his innocence to the crowd of witnesses. By combination of unflinching composure before death and an execution perceived as unjust, Dubois became a folk saint.[26]

The most extreme case of a criminal elevated to folk sainthood is perhaps José (or Jorge) del Carmen Valenzuela Torres, known as the Jackal of Nahueltoro. Valenzuela, a Chilean, murdered a widowed mother and her five children. His repentance in prison was so great, however, that his execution in 1963 was regarded as cruel and excessive. Valenzuela was no longer the Jackal of Nahueltoro, so it seemed that the authorities executed the wrong man.

At the Shrines

The province of Corrientes in northeastern Argentina is a region rich in devotion to folk saints. The cemeteries of even the smallest towns often boast one or more miraculous souls, and their decorated graves attest to effective intercession in heaven and to the gratitude of local beneficiaries. The walls of Gaucho Gil's shrine in Mercedes are covered with some fifty thousand plaques giving thanks for miracles. The site is frequented throughout the year, but on and around the day of the fiesta, January 8, it is transformed into a carnival of devotion. Locals arrive by car and on foot, bicycle, and horseback. Others come by the carload and busload from afar and from abroad—Paraguay, Uruguay, Brazil, Chile, and even the United States and Europe. The total attendance at the fiestas is well in excess of a hundred thousand people. Buses (more than six hundred in 2004) and cars line the highway for miles in each direction.

Conspicuous upon approach to the Gaucho Gil shrine is the flash and flurry of color from the flags, banners, ribbons, and clothes that boast the bright red associated with this devotion. A swarming movement of devotees converges upon the tomb, some dressed in full gaucho regalia. Hundreds of candles are burning. Vendors hawk religious images, food, souvenirs, and bootlegged brand-name anything. The whole conglomeration is held together by the heat. Boom boxes compete with live chamamé; asado smoke intermingles with clouds of grease rising from fried empanadas; and the smell of rain, then the rain itself, cleanses the stench of camped-out humans and overrun, improvised bathrooms. Everyone is happy. Devotion is the centerpiece, but the fiesta is also a festival of food and drink, of fun with old and new friends. Here, once a year, devotees escape from the dreary toil of economic survival to recharge their will, their joy, and their hope.

The color red has many meanings. For some devotees it represents blood and sacrifice, specifically Gil's spilled blood. One reporter referred to the intense spectacle of redness accordingly, "as if the stain that Gil's blood made when he died came back a century later." Also suggestive, but not mentioned by devotees, are the broader uses of the color red for luck and protection. In Buenos Aires, for example, many people put red ribbons on the rearview mirror of their car to protect them from envy. The red-ribbon bracelets that are tied on babies' wrists in many parts of Spanish America serve the similar function of warding off the evil eye of envious onlookers.[27]

More critical to Gaucho Gil devotion is the political affiliation designated by the color red. The color-coded struggle between the Federales (red) and the Unitarios (blue) during the nineteenth century was repeated in Corrientes

A roadside Gaucho Gil shrine in Vaqueros, Salta Province.

nalia. Advocates of the site—the vendors—explained when I visited in 2003 that the bones of Gaucho Gil may be in Mercedes, but the Tree of Faith is the only site where Gil's image has appeared, and twice. They envision this shrine as a major center of Gaucho Gil devotion, and, owing in part to the many migrants from Corrientes to Buenos Aires, it appears to be well on its way.

The principal shrine in Mercedes has enjoyed relatively peaceable relations with the Catholic Church. Our Lady of Mercy, the parish church, cautiously participates in the annual fiesta by celebrating a mass for Gaucho Gil's soul. The cross from the Gaucho Gil shrine is brought to the church, mass is said in the early morning, and afterward a spectacular procession, known as the *caravana*, returns the newly blessed cross to the shrine. As the caravan departs from the church, the gauchos on horseback who take the lead are joined by a growing contingent of pedestrians, bicycles, and cars, all displaying red flags. The caravan establishes a symbolic link between the shrine and the Church, a

Gaucho Gil at the "Tree of Faith" shrine in Buenos Aires. Gil's image miraculously appeared on the back of the cross pictured here.

reminder that the devotees are Catholic, but the fiesta begins in earnest, with chamamé and dance and folk rituals, when the cross is resituated at the shrine. As soon as they leave the formal and restrictive environs of the church, devotees make clear that the faith belongs to them, that they express it in their manner, and that Gaucho Gil is integral to their culture.

Despite the Church's ambivalence and occasional objection to Gaucho Gil devotion, the growth of the cult is largely indebted to a priest, Father Julián Zini, who for many years was the parish priest of Mercedes. Zini was trained in the doctrines of the Second Vatican Council (Vatican II) and the subsequent meetings of bishops, particularly those in Medellín and Puebla, that applied the reforms to Latin America. He believes that folk devotions are the expression of a profound faith integral to everyday life, and that they should be accepted, even celebrated, as they are gradually guided toward orthodox practices. As Zini puts it in the language of Vatican II, the priest's responsibility is to assume, purify, and complete the religious instincts of his people.

Father Julián Zini.

During my conversations with Zini he repeatedly stressed the long view, particularly the Guaraní origins of local culture and the negative conse- quences of forced conversion. Catholicism was imposed following the Span- ish conquest, but the religious instruction of the Guaraní was rudimentary and unfinished. This resulted in the perpetuation of indigenous religious and magical beliefs, which intermixed with Catholicism to produce, evolving over centuries, the syncretic religion that is common in the region today. The dogmatic, post-conquest prohibition of one religion as another was imposed by force seems hardly Christlike, of course, particularly since the errors of the semiconverted Guaraní were often expressions of the faith as they understood it rather than manifestations of ill will.

Today, Zini argues, the mistake of colonial missionaries is repeated when intolerant priests discount the validity of local culture, prohibit folk expres- sions of faith, and impose Church dogma from above. Folk saint devotees, like the converted Guaraní, are professing their Catholicism in a way that makes the best sense to them. Prohibition today, as in colonial times, results only in tacit obedience to priests while people secretly do as they please. Pressure from above may force folk devotions underground, or to the margins, but the devotions never disappear.

Zini explained the point using the analogy of a tree: One can cut it down but the roots remain, and new sprouts soon shoot up somewhere else. (It was for this reason that colonial missionaries were so fond of the phrase "extir- pation of idolatry," which literally means pulling it out by the roots.) Folk devotion is the religious expression of a culture, and as such it takes multiple forms, evades repression by constantly creating new objects of devotion, and even imbues its resilience with religious and cultural meanings.

Evangelization should therefore appeal to "the Christian memory of our peoples," Zini says, borrowing from a passage that emerged at the bishops' meeting in Puebla. He calls for what the Church refers to as inculturation: rather than assimilating diverse cultures to Catholicism, Catholicism should be assimilated to diverse cultures. The priest's task in this perspective is to recognize the value and validity of syncretic folk culture while guiding devotees' strong faith toward approved beliefs and practices. The verb *encausar* (to channel) is used by Zini and many other priests to describe this process. Rather than quashing folk devotions, they should be gently persuaded to flow in the right direction. A priest must be with his people continually, earning their trust and guiding their intense religious expression. Otherwise, for better or worse, the faith takes its own direction.

Zini describes the crowds converging on the Gaucho Gil shrine as "sheep without a shepherd." He quotes the passage from Mark 6:34, then narrates the scene, recounting how Christ stayed with the people and fed them what they had—two fish and five loaves—by transforming it into a feast for five thousand. That scene epitomizes Zini's mandate: the shepherd must be with his flock, the priest with his people, and perform the miracle from what they have to offer, from who they are, rather than from what the priest imposes. Folk devotion is a natural, unguided expression of faith that needs a shepherd—a pastor—to guide it toward the Church.[29]

Zini is a local hero among many Catholics in Corrientes, in part because his appreciation of folk culture has made parishioners feel that they can belong to the Church without abandoning their traditional beliefs and cultural identity. As a shepherd who remains close to his flock, Zini conducted fieldwork on folk beliefs in rural Corrientes, wrote popular chamamé lyrics celebrating Gaucho Gil, and has been considerably involved in the enhancement of the Mercedes shrine as a site of religious devotion. Zini believes that the January 8 mass for Gaucho Gil should be celebrated at the shrine itself, rather than in the Mercedes church. "The shepherd is telling the sheep to come to him," he explains, "instead of caring for his flock." The purpose of mass at the shrine should not be to impose Church dogma, but rather to continue the priest's constant work of assuming, purifying, and completing.

When I pressed Zini on the point, suggesting that mass at the shrine might give the impression that the Church endorsed public cult to Gaucho Gil, he conceded that this was true. Many priests are indeed opposed to what they regard as Zini's inappropriate encouragement of unauthorized devotions. They see his efforts as counterproductive, because they give the impression that the Church condones folk saint devotion, thus contributing to growth of the cult, but have little success in channeling the faith toward orthodox practices. Zini is quite aware of these objections and responds that the example of Jesus, not conservative Church bureaucracy, mandates what must be done. He wants to put the biblical precedent and the principles of Medellín and Puebla into practice, but he recognizes that his position is polemical and that he is in the minority: "Only a few nuts like me believe in this stuff."

Zini seemed less nuts in January 2005, when Ricardo Faifer, the bishop of Goya, accompanied him to the Gaucho Gil fiesta. This was the first time in the history of Gaucho Gil devotion that a member of the Church hierarchy made an appearance at the shrine. Faifer clarified that his presence in no way implied official recognition of Gaucho Gil by the Church, but also that he respected people's faith in Gil, who is "a deceased brother close to God." Faifer had come, at Zini's urging, to make a gesture of peace and to demonstrate the Church's interest in "channeling the religious faith" of devotees toward approved devotions.[30]

Devotees were delighted by the bishop's visit. For decades they had been marginalized by nonacceptance, and they now felt reincorporated into their Church. The specific purpose of the bishop's visit, however, was a nuance easily overlooked or dismissed by devotees. None or few will cross over to approved devotions, and many will interpret the bishop's presence as a suggestion of formal Church recognition or even as an indication that Gaucho Gil will eventually be canonized. The message of peace is perhaps what was best communicated. Devotion to Gaucho Gil will continue as usual, but now with the pressure of disapproval somewhat alleviated.

Faifer's visit to the shrine, which was described in the press as "historic," illustrates the degree to which local Church policy can fluctuate depending upon who is in charge. Indeed, the joy of Gaucho Gil devotees was the outrage of conservative Catholics, who were perplexed by the bishop's seeming endorsement of this pagan devotion. Some members of the Church hierarchy also found the bishop's visit scandalous and received it with a strong, negative response.

Faifer assumed the bishopric in late 2002, replacing the conservative, German-born Luis Teodorico Stöckler, who had been in the position since 1985. Under Stöckler's direction, the Goya diocese (which includes Mercedes) took a conservative turn. This was consistent with a more general retreat in Latin America from the liberal reforms initiated at the Medellín and Puebla conferences. Stöckler was himself preceded by Alberto Devoto, who was the first bishop of Goya (the dioceses was established in 1961).

Just prior to Stöckler's appointment as bishop, in 1984, Devoto circulated an internal document to give priests guidance on the issue of Gaucho Gil. The content and tone are more or less similar to those of Faifer's recent statements. "Antonio Gil is not considered neither a Saint nor a Beato by ecclesiastical authority; he is a deceased person, about whom practically nothing else is known." The clergy should "have a respectful, courteous, and cordial attitude" toward devotees, but at once be "critical, patient, firm, and constant." Priests may accept requests to celebrate mass for Gil's soul, but should "avoid the repetition of Gil's name from the pulpit, so as not to contribute to the growth of his cult." They also must "refuse the blessing of anything that could contribute to confusing this deceased person with a saint," such as statuettes and prayer cards. In the language of Vatican II and in conformance with the ideas of Zini, the 1984 document also stated that "It is the church's role to assume this massive movement of popular religion, assuming, purifying, and completing the existing values, without legitimating, sanctifying, or canonizing Antonio Gil and his tomb."[31]

In 1992, now during the bishopric of Stöckler, a pastoral letter to parishioners addressed the issue of Gaucho Gil. According to the current parish priest, Father Luis María Adis, this letter was delivered door to door in Mercedes. Its diplomatic tone conveyed a message of low tolerance. The phenomenon of Gaucho Gil is "confusing our people," because

Antonio Gil, whose existence is probable, is neither a beato nor a saint. Accordingly, the place of his eternal rest must not be called a 'Sanctuary,' and the day of his death is not a Patron [Saint] Feast. Antonio Gil is a deceased person, for whom we may pray. One can also direct prayer to God himself, asking for his help through this deceased person, in the event that Our Lord wishes to recognize his merits.

In its tightrope walk on theological nuance, Stöckler's letter thus acquiesces to the petition of miracles (putting God back in charge) and objects only to the public cult and to the erroneous belief that Gil is a saint.[32]

By 2001 the tone had changed. On January 7, a day before the annual Gaucho Gil fiesta, Stöckler gave a radio address during which he offered some of the common arguments used to deter folk devotions. The public cult to Gaucho Gil undermines the possibility of his canonization, Stöckler explained. And people who attend the Gaucho Gil fiesta are led astray by false prophets, are exploited commercially, and are exposed to influences (drugs, alcohol, and possibly prostitution) that "facilitate impurity." Many occurrences at the shrine "are deviations that are repugnant to any healthy mind." The true road to salvation is through the Ten Commandments and the sacraments, Stöckler advised, and everything that does not lead to "the holiness of life" comes not from God but from "sinful men or the very devil." Rather than resorting to Gaucho Gil in times of sickness and need, Catholics should "redouble their humble prayer, ask God for help, and invoke the saints who intercede for us, especially the Mother of Our Lord."[33]

The development of this progressively hard line ended when Stöckler was transferred to another Argentine diocese, in Quilmes, which occasioned the appointment of Faifer. Stöckler's position is at odds with that of Zini or Faifer, but what all hold in common is dismay with the lamentable state of the shrine. Devotion to Gaucho Gil has grown exponentially in the past twenty years, and with it the Mercedes shrine has expanded in haphazard conglomeration. The problems are multiple, but the most egregious are the development of a shantytown around the shrine and the encroachment of informal commercial interests on the site of devotion.

The improvised dwellings that surround the shrine, the people who live in them, and the unattractive aspects of daily life in poverty (cooking, laundry, naked kids) have made the shrine unattractive to locals. Mercedes residents used to frequent the shrine for birthdays, weekend cookouts, and general recreation ("because we don't have a beach," the administrator explained), but today most avoid the area because they regard it as unappealing or even dangerous.

Annual visits well in excess of a hundred thousands make the Gaucho Gil shrine an extraordinary commercial opportunity. Unlike the smaller folk saint shrines in the region, where almost everything is free, at the Gaucho Gil shrine everything is sold. In addition to the permanent religious-article stands and the improvised restaurants, which are open all year, there are countless concession stands (on rented spaces) during the fiesta. The shantytown was established gradually as vendors of religious articles stayed on at the shrine to set up permanent shops. Today the shrine is overwhelmed by these sales stands, which encroach on the devotional space and make the shrine appear less a religious sanctuary than an impoverished emporium. During my visit in 2003, Gil's cross itself was barely accessible.

The negative impression is further aggravated by the many ambulant vendors at the shrine. As cars pull up, swarms of vendors, mostly children, descend upon and surround them, hawking Gaucho Gil wares. Devotees are disconcerted because "they are turning faith into business," and one cannot pray "without having to chase away ten vendors at a time." Over the years a few priests have attempted to establish an undisturbed devotional space at the shrine, but the commercial encroachments have nevertheless prevailed. Zini and Faifer again advocated the restoration of a devotional space during their visit in 2005.[34]

The issue has become complex and political, and what ultimately occurs will depend more on the courts than on the advocacy of clergy. In the late 1980s, Gaucho Gil devotees from Mercedes formed a not-for-profit organization know as the *Comisión del Centro Recreativo para los Devotos del Gaucho Gil* (Commission of the Recreational Center for the Devotees of Gaucho Gil). This commission was responsible for the growth and care of the shrine, including the receipt and administration of donations made by devotees. Some modest social-service functions were established—such as the lending of donated wedding dresses, crutches, and wheelchairs—but mismanagement and certain procedural irregularities resulted in the intervention of this commission by government authorities, which have now assumed control of the Gaucho Gil shrine.

As explained to me by the new administrator, who was appointed by the governor, the intervention was the result of the commission's failure to fulfill statutory requirements, such as the routine filing of reports and the periodic change of leadership. The same president had been in charge, for example, since the inception of the commission. In addition to these irregularities itemized by the administrator, residents of Mercedes hold as common knowledge that for years the commission's leaders embezzled the shrine's considerable income. Other profiteering schemes are likewise suggested, but illegitimate exploitation of the shrine (at least by private interests) ended with the government intervention.

The commission's nonconformance with statutes provided grounds for governmental intervention, but the new administration's highest priority is to dislodge the shantytown that is undermining the shrine's appeal. The idea, as the administrator put it, is to "improve the image" so that locals and visitors will frequent the site in greater numbers. The shantytown is a squatter settlement and as such has no legal right to the property that it occupies. The administrator is also quick to point out that the residents and vendors pay neither rent nor taxes, and that they steal water and power by tapping into pipes and wires.

In March 2003, shortly after his appointment, the administrator issued an expulsion order to force the residents of the shrine from the shantytown. The legal foundation of the order was the shantytown's encroachment on the right-of-way of National Route 123. Somehow (miraculously, some said), the order was blocked by a judge, and a legal battle ensued. The administrator had the water and power to the shrine interrupted, and the equally efficacious vendors implemented countermeasures. There is general support in Mercedes for renovation of the shrine, but in mid-2005, the situation still remained unresolved.

The effort to eliminate the shantytown is part of a more comprehensive plan to develop the site. Although the government intervention is technically temporary, architectural drawings of an envisioned Gaucho Gil shrine indicate an access road that leads to an extensive complex. An undisturbed devotional space is complemented by a range of nearby goods and services. All commerce would be resituated to a center behind the shrine, on twenty-two hectares that were donated several years ago. Business would be normalized, and those selling in the booths at the new location would pay rent, utilities, and taxes. The administration's clear intent is to recuperate a site of local patrimony, but also to enhance the region's economic growth by developing the shrine as a destination for religious tourism.

Residents of the shantytown see the matter quite differently. During my most recent visit to the shrine, in August 2003, they were distressed by the situation and anxious to have their version on the record. The agitated, activist disposition of the people facing eviction contrasted sharply with the smug, mildly arrogant calm of the administrator. The residents and vendors felt as though their homes (some have lived there for more than fifteen years) and livelihood were being unjustly expropriated by the government. They have been accused of commercializing the devotion, they say, but the government has plans for a "shopping center" (as they call it) that is far more commercial than their wildest ambitions.

The administrator assures that space in this retail center would be reserved for the current vendors at the shrine, but they are not interested. Some explained that the rent, utilities, taxes, increased competition, and cost of living elsewhere (after eviction) would make the business unviable. Currently the vendors at the shrine compete only with one another and with the official store inside the museum. The museum store has a certain advantage, owing to the belief that the Gaucho Gil images bought there are more miraculous. A sign in the museum store also announces (truly or falsely) that its statuettes are blessed by a priest.

The residents of the shantytown are fighting the government as best they can, and in the meantime are counting on the support of sympathetic devotees. One donated a generator to restore electrical service. Another donated a car as part of a fund-raising effort toward the purchase of a parcel of land, the drilling of a well, and the restoration of water service.

The informal economy perseveres despite government oppression, in the same way that folk devotion perseveres despite Church oppression. The struggle between the shantytown and the authorities expresses in legal, political, and economic registers what folk devotions express religiously. The underclass's challenge, counterclaim, defiance, ingenuity, and resilience face off with the institutions that overpower them. In one case, land rights, water, and power are borrowed or stolen, and in the other, aspects of Catholicism are borrowed. The deformations that are viewed from the outside—shantytown, heterodoxy—are from the inside natural expressions of everyday life and local culture.

These struggles in Mercedes are quite similar to those that occurred at the Difunta Correa shrine beginning in the 1970s, when it too was growing out of its folk roots and toward increasing institutionalization. A huge income from donations made Difunta Correa's shrine, like Gaucho Gil's, an easy mark for embezzlement. Administration of the shrine eventually passed to the provincial government of San Juan. The government's intent is to develop the Difunta Correa shrine as a center of religious tourism in order to enhance the province's economic growth. A successful government intervention in Mercedes will likely result in a similar destiny for Gaucho Gil. When devotions go public, however, the passionate faith of core devotees is easily overwhelmed by the casual faith of day-trippers and tour groups. That's when the roots of the cut-down tree shoot up a new sprout somewhere else.

Sarita Colonia

Sarita Colonia, a poor girl from Huaraz, migrated to Lima around 1930 in search of a better life. She worked odd jobs—cleaning houses, selling fish, waiting tables—to support herself and her impoverished family. Sarita was kind, innocent, beautiful, and generous. Her own circumstances were difficult, but despite them she shared the little that she earned with others who had even greater need.

In 1940, when Sarita was twenty-six years old, she was accosted by police or soldiers who intended to rape her. Sarita forfeited her life in order to preserve her virginity. Some say that she threw herself into the ocean or off a bridge to escape the rapists. Others say that God lifted her up into heaven. Her body was found later and was buried in the common grave of the cemetery in Callao, where she had lived. Those who prayed at the common grave soon reported Sarita's miracles and her fame spread throughout the country.

The most prominent Peruvian folk saint, Sarita Colonia, was born in the poor Belén neighborhood of Huaraz on March 1, 1914. Sarita was the first child of Rosalía Zambrano and Amadeo Colonia Flores, a carpenter. Around 1922, she migrated with her family to Lima, where her father sought employment. She and her sister Esther attended a Catholic boarding school, Santa Teresita del Niño Jesús, which was run by French nuns. Some four years later Sarita's mother became seriously ill and the family returned to Huaraz. Sarita was thus obliged to leave the convent school and, according to her family members, abandon her aspirations to become a nun. The mother died four months after the return to Huaraz, and Sarita, by then twelve, inherited the domestic and childrearing responsibilities.

The family's financial outlook, already grim, was further burdened by the addition of more children through the father's remarriage, and by the father's subsequent illness; according to Sarita's brother, he suffered from aphasia. When Sarita was around fifteen, she took a job in a bakery to help support the family. Continuing struggle for economic survival was Sarita's only future in Huaraz, so she resolved to return to Lima. She migrated sometime between 1930 and 1933, when she was sixteen to twenty years old. Sarita thus became part of a huge wave of migration from the provinces to the capital that had begun in 1919. She migrated with the hope of building a life for herself and of better supporting her family.

Sarita's father and her brother Hipólito accompanied her on the difficult journey by horse or mule to Casma, where the new Panamerican Highway made the remaining leg to Lima less arduous. In Casma they shared a table with an Italian family also traveling to Lima, and this chance encounter resulted in employment for Sarita as a live-in maid and nanny. The arrangement lasted nearly three years, until Sarita's desire for greater independence inspired her to move in with an aunt who lived in Callao, the port city adjacent to Lima. Sarita worked in the aunt's fish stand in the market, then sold fish on her own. The income was insufficient, however, so she soon tried selling clothing and then working in cafés and dairies. Her continuing struggle for economic survival was aggravated by the death of her stepmother in Huaraz, after which Sarita's father sent the remaining children, except two of the boys, to live under Sarita's care in Callao. Sarita also sent money to Huaraz to help support the father and siblings there. Among the daughters who came to Callao were Esther and Rosa, who now care for Sarita's shrine.[1]

Esther returned home one afternoon in December 1940, to find Sarita gravely ill. Sarita was taken to the Bellavista hospital and died there the next day, on December 20, 1940, at the age of 26. Her death certificate cites malaria as the cause of death, but her survivors, particularly her brother Hipólito, have rigorously contended that Sarita died of an overdose of castor oil. Many people ingested castor oil periodically to cleanse the body of impurities, and some say the soul was cleansed too. Even the word for laxative in Spanish, *purgante*, which is related etymologically to "purge" and "purgatory," suggests such a comprehensive cleansing. Esther maintains that Sarita used castor oil frequently as part of a more comprehensive quest for purity. The two competing causes of death—malaria and castor oil—may be reconcilable if Sarita ingested the laxative, perhaps in excess, as a home-remedy response to malaria symptoms. What is certain is that later myths displaced the tragicomic death by laxative and the banal death by malaria with a demise more conducive to Sarita's grandeur as a folk saint.[2]

Innocence and strength: the standard iconography of Sarita Colonia.

Sarita's poverty afforded her burial only in the common grave of Callao's Baquíjano cemetery. Her father placed a wooden cross on the grave to identify her remains. Family, friends, and neighbors frequented the grave, as did beneficiaries of the food and clothing that Sarita distributed to those poorer even than herself. The grateful lit candles and left flowers, and when onlookers asked why Sarita received so many visits, the response, as the brother has it, was: "Because she was a girl whose purity of soul is very close to God, and because she does impossible miracles." Among the first recipients of the miracles was Sarita's sister Esther, who on the night before a liver operation was cured after prayer to Sarita.[3]

Also conducive to the growth of devotion to Sarita was the very nature of the common grave itself. When people came to visit their loved ones who were buried without markers or headstones, they tended to leave flowers at the only identifiable spot, which was Sarita's cross. Many knelt to pray there. This conglomeration of flowers and gathering of praying people at one place in the cemetery—which is so typical in folk saint devotions—fostered the impression that Sarita was miraculous. Some of those kneeling at the cross to pray for their dead loved ones took the opportunity to say a prayer to Sarita. Others came especially for this purpose. Miracles were granted, news of them circulated, and Sarita's status as a folk saint gradually was established.[4]

A similar phenomenon seems to have occurred at the tomb of Ubilberto Vásquez Bautista, a folk saint from Cajamarca who was sentenced to execution after a murder conviction. No one visited or cared for Ubilberto's tomb, so a few people took pity and began to frequent the site. They prayed and lit candles not to request miracles, but rather to implore the salvation of Ubilberto's soul. Others mistook this kindness for devotion, however, and began to pray to (not for) Ubilberto with the hope of miraculous solutions to their problems. Folk saint identities are similarly forged when pity for someone who has endured a tragic death inspires exceptional prayer at a cross, or, in criminal cases such as Ubilberto's, when the extra prayer effort required for a soul's salvation yields gradually to petitions for miracles.[5]

The common grave in Callao's cemetery also produced two minor folk saints, the Soldadito Desconocido (Unknown Soldier) and Sor María (Sister Maria). Both of these devotions dissipated when the common grave was excavated to build new pavilions aboveground. Devotion to Sarita was salvaged and solidified, however, because her family appeared on the day of excavation to retrieve her remains (as best they could determine). The bones were gathered in a wooden box and reburied nearby. Long lines of devotees soon formed. This provisional grave served as the site of devotion until around 1983, when the mausoleum-shrine that currently stands was built with donations from devotees.

Sarita's cult has always been broad based, encompassing devotees from diverse social groups. Stevedores, who worked at the nearby port of Callao, were an important constituent in the early years. In the 1940s and 1950s, Sarita attracted devotees from criminal and ostracized groups. Such outsiders as thieves, prostitutes, and homosexuals found in this informal devotion a saint more accommodating than any at church. The attraction may have been enhanced by the belief that Sarita cared for marginal groups during her lifetime. She visited "the most dangerous neighborhoods of Callao" to provide moral guidance, according to Esther, and others add that Sarita "helped delinquents a lot."[6]

At the same time, and continuing until around 1961, a new wave of migration more than tripled the population of Lima. Most of these poor campesinos, like those newly arriving today, settled in the shantytowns that surround the capital. With the encouragement of dictator General Juan Velasco Alvarado, hundreds of thousands of migrants arrived in more waves in the late 1960s and particularly in the 1970s. Political violence later combined with poverty as a motivator of migration after 1982, when the Sendero Luminoso insurgency and the heavy-handed government response caused massive flight to Lima and other coastal cities. Today, Lima's population approaches eight million inhabitants, most of them poor migrants like Sarita.

Devotion to Sarita Colonia grew in tandem with Lima, particularly in the 1960s and 1970s. Sarita has particular appeal to internal migrants who negotiate their precarious lives in an inhospitable urban environment. The explosion of her popularity coincided with the migrants' increasing social and cultural assertion as they made a place for themselves, however humble, in society. Their emerging identity as an urban population with rural roots was forged, in part, through counter-rejection of institutions that disadvantaged them or abandoned them to corruption and dysfunction. Adopting Sarita as their unacceptable saint was part of a greater package of mutual unacceptability. The activist politics of shantytowns, the boom of the informal economy, and the failure of these to redeem migrants from destitution and poverty all provide a context for devotion to Sarita.[7]

Sarita's life story is attractive to Andean migrants because it so closely resembles their own. Like her, they are born in poverty in the highlands, migrate to Lima seeking a better life, and find little opportunity for advancement. The theme of migration has extended most recently into the adoption of Sarita Colonia as a patron of illegal immigrants—from many countries—into the United States. As they sneak across the U.S.-Mexico border, some carry Sarita's image "in their underwear, which makes them invisible or conceals them with fog." Sarita protects their passage, then helps them with their resettlement and job search.[8]

As she worked to support her family in Huaraz and, later, in Lima, "Sarita was not ashamed to do any kind of work, however modest or humbling." Her brother describes her as poor but proud, generous, and committed. She chose the common grave so that even in death she would be together with the poor people to whom she was dedicated. "I'm leaving as I came," Sarita says, "without taking anything from this life." Poverty is embraced and thematized. It acquires positive values and religious meanings. It is the bond that unites Sarita with her devotees. Song lyrics refer to her as "patron of the poor" and ask her to bless "all poor people of the world." A prostitute began her narrative of Sarita by saying, "She was a poor girl and her parents were poor, just like us." St. Martin de Porres is "the saint for the poorest people," Sarita used to say, and this is precisely the role that she came to assume for her own devotees.[9]

New devotee groups in the 1960s and 1970s included bus, truck, and taxi drivers; ambulant vendors and others outside of the formal economy, among them the unemployed; and domestic workers. By the 1980s, and continuing into the present, Sarita's cult encompassed diverse groups from all social classes, but with a clear majority among the poor.[10]

The myth known by each devotee often reflects his or her own condition, and details from Sarita's life are likewise customized to suit the saintly profile to individual preference. Domestic workers, for example, explain that Sarita was abused (as they are) when she worked as a maid. A thief relates that Sarita was accused of theft while working "in the houses of rich people." A prostitute stresses that Sarita was beautiful and pure, and (varying from the more common failed attempt) was raped by soldiers and died as a result. "As punishment, some soldiers are now bow-legged and it's hard for them to walk." A stevedore has Sarita escape to the ocean: "She took the veil off her head, put it on the water, sat on it, and disappeared among the waves and clouds, on her veil." The next day she appeared on the pier more beautiful than ever, distributing roses from a basket. In each of these cases, the narrative is adapted to the personal interest and situation of the devotee telling the story. A stronger personal connection is thereby established—lo nuestro (what is ours) becomes lo mío (what is mine)—and this intimacy increases the sense of protective patronage and the probability of miracles.[11]

Sarita Colonia has also developed a reputation as the patron saint of thieves and prisoners. In Lima and in distant provincial cities, nondevotees define Sarita almost exclusively in reference to these two groups. Some thieves commend themselves to Sarita before committing their crimes and then thank her afterward for their success. Local legends relate that the police stake out Sarita's shrine with the hope of ambushing the criminals likely to appear there. On at least one occasion, in 1994, the legend had a basis in fact: bank robbers who visited Sarita before a planned assault on two banks were surprised at the shrine by police. A shootout ensued, after which some of the criminals were arrested.[12]

If, as in this case, miraculous evasion of the police is unsuccessful, then Sarita follows through by protecting her devotees in prison. Many inmates are tattooed with Sarita's image, their families visit the shrine to petition freedom, Callao's prison itself is informally called "Sarita Colonia," and an image of Sarita that was made by prisoners is prominently displayed near her tomb. Folk saints elsewhere are also patrons of inmates and advocates of their freedom, including San La Muerte in Argentina and José Crisel Somoza, known as Montenegro, in Venezuela.

Press accounts generally depict Sarita Colonia's devotees as a collection of undesirables. Criminals, prostitutes, and transvestites are the usual suspects. Such individuals (some of whom, such as transvestites, tend to stand out visually) do indeed constitute a percentage of Sarita's cult, but my impression after several visits to the shrine is that the majority of people devoted to Sarita are little different than other poor people in Lima. They seem to be a cross-section of what one might encounter on the streets of the city's less affluent neighborhoods. I met extended families, a lot of mothers and grandmothers, housewives, unemployed and underemployed people hoping for a break, honest fathers worn down by work and looking for more, packs of happy children, and, in short, old and new residents of a city that had long since run out of opportunities.

In recent years devotion to Sarita seems to be waning, or at least changing. Though attendance at the annual fiestas is still high, it seems considerably lower than it was in the 1970s and 1980s. A 1978 article notes that two thousand people visited Sarita's shrine daily. Today, visits to the shrine are more occasional than constant or multitudinous. Devotion to Sarita Colonia in Lima is nevertheless second only to the Church–authorized Christ advocation known as the Lord of Miracles.[13]

Another index of change is the status of Sarita Colonia among taxi and bus drivers, which were once an important constituent of her cult. In the 1980s almost all city buses and taxis had Sarita Colonia's image hanging from their rearview mirrors, but today her image has given way to that of the Lord of Miracles. The same pattern of preferential devotion to local Christs (or Virgins) seems to hold in other regions: the Lord of Luren in Ica, the Lord of Earthquakes in Cuzco.

The shift from Sarita to a Christ advocation is partially indebted to a change in the nature of the taxi business. When Sarita Colonia's cult was growing in the 1970s and 1980s, taxi drivers were fewer and were dedicated by choice to this profession. Today, however, many unemployed or underemployed people become taxi drivers with the hope of making a living. Levels of class, background, education, and profession thus intermix behind the wheels of taxis. Most drivers readily volunteer (it inspires good pity tips) their hard-luck story: "I'm an engineer" or "I'm a lawyer" or "I used to teach."

Inside Sarita Colonia's shrine in Callao.

I even encountered a desperate, middle-class housewife driving a collective taxi—her car—between Lima and the Miraflores suburb in an apparent state of anxious fear. Thus the working-class, uneducated taxi driver once devoted to Sarita Colonia has been displaced, or overrun, by diverse others who are perhaps more attracted to mainstream religion or to no religion at all.

The change in the nature of taxi drivers could not account for Sarita's absence elsewhere, however, so amid the bumps and rattles and ecstatic dilapidation of Lima buses, I inquired. The bus drivers never seemed to know why Sarita's image was no longer used on rearview mirrors. Their remarks ("It's easier to get the Lord of Miracles") vaguely supported my impression that the choice was governed more by fad than by conviction. The strong preference for the Lord of Miracles in the fashionable format of a printed CD was also suggestive in this regard.

Taxi drivers were more informative. When I first talked with them in the 1980s, the Sarita image hanging from the mirror was complemented by at least a basic knowledge of her story. In 2003, however, many taxi drivers knew nothing but Sarita Colonia's name, and a few younger ones had never heard of her. The overwhelming majority had the same impression of Sarita as other nondevotees: she was the patron saint of thieves. Some explained that the few taxi drivers who displayed Sarita's image did so to advise thieves that their taxi was protected and not to be robbed. Another redirected this idea to explain that Sarita's image is bad for business, because of her strong association with thieves. When people see an image of Sarita hanging from the rearview mirror, they assume that the driver himself is a thief and refuse to get in the taxi.

Sarita Colonia evolved as a protector from sudden death—notably in traffic accidents—by virtue of her own sudden death. Her youthful life fore-closed by tragedy returns in sainthood as miraculous oversight. Taxi, bus, and truck drivers are the natural audiences for folk saint protection on the road, but the services are available to anyone who travels. Sarita's protection of drivers is still in evidence—I saw in Cuzco, for example, a tour bus with "Sarita Colonia" written in giant letters across the top of the windshield—but is not nearly so common as it was twenty years ago. Today, Sarita is more of a generalist backed up by the lingering historical resonance of her fame as a patron of drivers.

A billboard on the Panamerican Highway south of Lima, near Chicha, shows a windshield from the inside, with Sarita's image hanging from the rearview mirror. The advertisement is for an insurance company, and the text reads: "No one can save you from reckless driving." The billboard advocates road safety, but also creates demand for its this-worldly protection product by facetiously pointing out the unreliability of heavenly protection, or at least Sarita's. The choice of Sarita is prudent because it appeals to local cul-ture (even those who can afford insurance are charmed from a distance by Sarita) while at once avoiding the blasphemy of underestimating a canonized saint.

The Official Story

There is a notable difference between the Sarita Colonia packaged and propagated by her family and the Sarita Colonia who appears in myths. The family's version of Sarita is more a hagiography than a biography. Its focus is on heroic virtue, exemplary deeds, and religious calling, which is to say on the attributes of canonized (as opposed to folk) saints. As her brother explains it, Sarita was a pure girl of humble origins whose religious calling was revealed in her early years by apparitions of Christ and the Virgin. Sarita had been chosen, and as a child she was transfixed before religious images, encouraged others to be saintly, and obliged her father to pray with her to the crucified Christ, to St. Rose of Lima, and to St. Martin de Porres. As summarized in a biographical sketch distributed by Sarita's family, "From a very young age she felt a clear and evident religious vocation and God's divine calling, which were actively expressed in her eagerness to protect the poor, the invalid, the sick, the old, and children, and in her concern for teaching prayer as a means to receive God's blessing."[14]

Sarita's religious inclinations were stimulated in the convent school, and she would have become a nun had her family not returned to Huaraz because of the mother's illness. Even in life outside of the convent she remained a virgin until her death. Charity was her priority, and when she worked for a bakery, "the bread was not only sold for the benefit of her family; a lot of it was reserved to give to the poor, the needy, children, and old people." Even when Sarita was struggling in Lima for her own economic survival, "she never forgot about her brothers, the poor, to whom she had made a commitment for the love of Christ." Esther describes Sarita as an angelic soul—all goodness and generosity with no capacity for evil.[15]

Sarita's religious calling was reconfirmed during a near-death experience in her early teens. She had lost her balance and fell into the fast flow of a canal while doing the family laundry. A gruesome death was imminent as she was washed away toward the jaws of a hydraulic mill, but just then a powerful hand lifted her by the hair from the water. Sarita's savior "was tall, with a very white tunic, with a beard and blonde hair." He had a striking face with "big and beautiful eyes" that cast a "penetrating and piercing gaze." This godly man repeated what Sarita had heard in earlier apparitions: "You are my favorite, predestined daughter. You have much to do for your brothers, the dispossessed and the disinherited of the Earth."[16]

The marvels of this hagiographic Sarita include miracles that she performed during her lifetime as a prelude to the thousands that would follow after death. Sarita miraculously reversed the irreversible brain injury that had disabled her father. She also saved her younger sister Rosa from an incurable illness and, in a miracle reminiscent of St. Rose of Lima, saved her step-mother from an attacking bull. Some of the miracles are specious (the step-mother, for example, was inside the house, cooking in the kitchen, when the bull attacked), but her brother Hipólito nevertheless describes each as "an in-disputable and real miracle." Hipólito himself was the beneficiary of a later indisputable and real miracle: Sarita sent firemen to rescue him from an elevator stuck between floors during a blackout.[17]

In contrast to this hagiographic profile, the Sarita of folk devotion is more the victim of a tragic life and death than she is an exemplar of heroic virtue.

Two attributes from the hagiography—virginity and charity—do, however, carry over into the conceptions of Sarita that are widely held by devotees. Virginity is the essential precondition of the attempted-rape myths, and dying to preserve it links Sarita to a long tradition of female saints.

Ideas about Sarita's charity, and her goodness generally, are substantially indebted to her face. The single photograph upon which all iconography is based depicts a sweet, angelic girl "with eyes that radiate love." The image emanates a warmth and kindness that complement and seem to verify the virtuous Sarita propagated by her siblings. "She had a face that was not for this world," Esther says, a heavenly face.[18]

This portrait of goodness contributes to—and illustrates—belief in Sarita's charity. Devotees who are more familiar with the official story relate that Sarita "helped poor people since she was little," despite her own desperate situation. Poverty makes Sarita one with her community, but she is an exceptional one who somehow transforms her own destitution into generosity toward others. The devotees who distribute food and gifts at the shrine make Sarita an offering in kind. They act in her image. They express gratitude by imitating her charity and generosity.[19]

With these two concessions—virginity and charity—to the official story, folklore diverges from the family's version to construct a Sarita of its own. The details of her life are relatively unimportant as the emphasis falls heavily on tragic death. A few devotees, particularly those closest to Sarita's family, describe an early death by laxative or by illness (the disease varies—malaria, bronchitis, meningitis, pneumonia). One woman related that Sarita died of an illness contracted upon leaving the convent, as though her purity could not survive the contaminated world. In all of these cases, the death is tragic not so much in its form as in its timing.

The great majority of devotees, however, relate that Sarita died during an attempted rape. They know little more than this detail. They relate it in innumerable versions, but most hold in common that Sarita was trapped by rapists and escaped (even into death) to protect her virginity. In one version Sarita throws herself into the ocean but does not sink. This miracle frightens off the attackers, and her corpse is discovered the next day at the site of the attempted crime. In another, a group of soldiers chase Sarita with the intention of raping her, but at the Puente del Ejército (Army Bridge) she magically disappears. Her corpse is discovered the following day, beneath the bridge. "God did not want her touched; he preferred to take her away." Others likewise stress divine intervention, including rapture: "God lifted her to heaven so that they wouldn't harm her." Another hand-of-God intercession, this one more poetic, spares Sarita an imminent rape by "two tall black men" who have her cornered. Her savior is a venerable old man who is holding a cane that emanates "light like the rays of the sun." Sarita thanks him, and he replies by counseling her to continue her charitable work and to teach people kindness, love, and peace.[20]

All of these narratives are variations on the preservation of Sarita's virginity. Death is preferable to rape. When Sarita is overpowered and in jeopardy, God intervenes to protect her virginity and bring her purity to heaven, where it belongs.

Some versions of the myth nevertheless allow the rape to occur before Sarita dies or escapes. The virginity in these cases is irretrievably lost, but that serves to make Sarita's death doubly tragic. Virginity is forfeited, but its saint-inducing value is compensated by stressing stolen youth (including stolen virginity) and horrible death. All of these attributes are conducive to folk sainthood, so mix-and-match versions trade off virginity and tragedy in accord with personal preference. The crime in some versions is robbery rather than rape—virginity is preserved—but in others robbery and rape come together.

Recent myths take a different direction by downplaying or dismissing the rape and stressing political themes. Abusive government has always been implicit in Sarita myths, notably in police and soldiers as representatives of rapacious authorities, but these newer versions make it explicit. I have never heard these versions related directly by devotees, however, so their sources remain unclear.

An eleven-hour television miniseries on Sarita Colonia, broadcast in Lima in 2002, offered six versions of her death. The official castor-oil overdose is one of them, embellished now by an apparition of Sarita's mother to lead her away to heaven. The other five versions have no historical basis and provide variations on tragic death. Sarita is distributing used clothing to the poor when she is murdered—shot twice in the head—during an attempted robbery, and she rises to heaven before the eyes of her assailants. Sarita, a virgin, is on a beach when three fishermen attempt to rape her. She walks into the ocean to preserve her purity, and her body—perfectly preserved, as though it were alive—is discovered three days later. (In traditional hagiography, the incorruptible flesh is a perquisite of virginity.) Sarita's death is ordered by the dictatorship, which regards her as part of a seditious movement because of her dedication to the poor. The usual victim of crimes (rape, robbery) is replaced here by a victim of political violence. Sarita is cornered by three men who attempt to rape her, but upon closer look they discover that she has no genitals, so they kill her with a knife. Sarita is distributing clothes to the poor when some policemen harass her, telling her she must respect authority. "You're not authority, you're a disgrace," she replies defiantly and then walks away. The police run after her but cannot catch up, even though she is only walking, so they shoot her in the back instead.

In their respective ways, these five versions of tragic death represent Sarita's goodness, purity, and charity against the backdrop of an evil world that, in two of the narratives, is directly connected to abusive authorities. Sarita is traditionally the victim of police and soldiers (and, by extension, of the government they represent), but in these two television versions she stands up to them rather than graciously folding into her death.

Sarita thus begins to emerge more clearly as a symbol of resistance to corrupt and repressive authority. She is an allegory of the marginalized, defenseless people who feel raped and robbed, who forge a bond with a saint shot in the back and locked down in a state of siege, a saint made in their image. Sarita is the patron of prisoners in the broadest sense of the term—prisoners of dictatorship, of poverty, of oppression, of exploitation. A sculpture recently exhibited in Lima features Sarita herself as a political prisoner. She wears a striped prison jumpsuit (reminiscent of the one worn by Sendero Luminoso leader Abimael Guzmán when he was displayed in a cage for the press) and is surrounded by armed soldiers.

The story of Sarita's disappearing genitalia was first published in 1984 by the Peruvian magazine *Caretas*. The remarkable detail that distinguishes this version—Sarita's miraculously vaginaless body—has made it an appealing choice for the media. The missing genitalia attest symbolically to absolute purity, to an unbroken hymen doubled over, to being twice "sealed to God." Sexuality is not an option because both the desire and the equipment are absent. Sarita is as asexual as an angel.[21]

The story is reminiscent of the attempted rape of an Italian beata, the Blessed Colomba da Rieti. Three men first tried to ply Colomba with gifts, then took out their knives and threatened to kill her if she did not comply with their desires. When Colomba was stripped by her would-be rapists, however, their passions were cooled by the hair shirt, the iron belt punishing her hips, and the studded iron chains crossing her breasts. The sight of these instruments of penance and the scars of whiplashes on her body sent the two younger rapists running off frightened and desireless. The third, an older man, fell to his knees. Sarita does not usually escape so easily, but her story shares with Colomba's an attempted rape foiled by God's greater designs for his virgins.[22]

A similar motif is expressed in stories concerning saintly men who have phallic deficiencies. Niño Fidencio, who was also a virgin, reportedly had the genitals of a prepubescent. The young Casimir, a late-fifteenth-century Polish saint, contracted an illness that could be cured only by sexual intercourse. His parents placed a beautiful virgin in his bed, but Casimir refused to embrace her because he preferred death to this sinful cure. Later, when his corpse was prepared for burial, his parents discovered that he had the undeveloped penis of a child.[23]

Sarita Colonia's disappearing genitals are also suggestive in consideration of the transvestites or transgenders who are attracted to her cult. These men who wish to be women, who wish their genitals would disappear, have in Sarita an ideal patron. It is unclear how many of them are familiar with this version of the story, but the coincidence is nevertheless compelling. The shock of the would-be rapists upon seeing Sarita's missing genitals likewise seems the complement, the flip side, of the surprise that customers of these transvestites (some work as prostitutes) might experience when the drawers are dropped.[24]

A Saintly Prototype

Sarita Colonia's story of death before defilement is as old as Christianity itself. The beautiful Saint Margaret of Antioch (legendary, date unknown), also known as Marina, was watching over a flock when her graces caught the eye of a lustful Roman prefect. When Margaret could not be persuaded to succumb to his amorous designs, the Roman denounced her as a Christian and she was brought to trial. Margaret refused to renounce her faith, as she had refused to relinquish her purity, and she was tortured by various means and then beheaded. She went to her maker, however, as a virgin.

Very much the same story is told of St. Agatha, who was martyred in Sicily around 250. Agatha refused the advances of a libidinous consular official, then managed to preserve her virginity while serving her sentence in a brothel. The frustrated official ordered that her breast be tortured and then amputated, but throughout the ordeal Agatha persevered in her faith and in her chastity. Also similar is the story of the third-century St. Agnes, who rejected the love of a governor's son because she considered herself a Bride of Christ. The governor and his son wooed and Agnes refused; she was executed but took her happy virginity to the grave.

In Ireland, St. Dymphna was murdered by her father for refusing his advances; he turned to her as a replacement spouse after his wife (her mother) died. The legendary St. Liberata (also known as Wilgefortis and Uncumber) found herself in a fix when her vow of virginity conflicted with her father's plans to marry her to the king of Sicily. Liberata prayed, God granted her wish to grow a beard to ward off the king, and the angry father, in retaliation, had her crucified. And St. Ursula, as *The Golden Legend* has it, chose death in lieu of the prince of the Huns, who wished to take her for his bride. Her death in chastity came after the slaughter of the eleven thousand virgins accompanying her.

Around 311, when she believed she would be raped by the soldiers who had arrived to arrest her for being Christian, Pelagia of Antioch excused herself under the pretext of changing her clothes and then jumped out an upper-story window or—according to versions closest to the story of Sarita—off the roof and into the ocean. Similar to Pelagia, and Sarita, was St. Solange, born near Bourges, France, in the ninth century. Solange was a young shepherdess who had made a vow of chastity and was murdered during an attempted rape, in this case by the son of the count of Poitiers.

More recently, St. Maria Goretti was born in Corinaldo, Ancona, Italy, in 1890 into the poor family of a farmworker. The father died of malaria in Maria's childhood, leaving the mother desperate to feed the six children. In 1902, when she was not yet twelve, Maria was attacked in an attempted rape by an eighteen-year-old neighbor. During her resistance, which included the argument that she would rather die than submit to this sin, the assailant stabbed her fourteen times.

Maria survived the attack and lived some twenty hours in the hospital, which gave her time enough to forgive her attacker. From heaven she later appeared to him in prison and gave him flowers. This offering of peace and purity inspired his repentance, his conversion, his testimony in her cause for beatification and, in 1950, his attendance at her canonization ceremony. Maria's mother also attended, being the first mother to witness her own child's canonization. In Maria Goretti's 1947 bull of beatification, Pope Pius XII observed that God "has given to the young girls of our cruel and degraded world a model and protector" who "sanctified the opening of our century with her innocent blood." Maria became the youngest saint in the canon.[25]

The Blessed Antonia Mesina (who bears a physical resemblance to Sarita), was born in Sardinia in 1919, died defending her purity in 1935, and was beatified in 1987. She left elementary school to take over domestic and maternal obligations after her mother fell ill from a heart ailment. Her narrative, like Sarita's in the official version, emphasizes her renunciation of pleasures and her self-sacrifice to the family's needs. At the age of sixteen, while returning home from wood gathering, Antonia was attacked by a young man who intended to rape her. She fought back so desperately—preferring death to loss of her virginity—that she was finally beaten to death with a rock.

These canonized saints and beatas from the earliest years of Christianity to the twentieth century establish a prototype of sanctity in which Sarita—the Sarita created by folklore—fits perfectly. In all of these cases, as in the dominant Sarita myths, virginity is preserved at the expense of a young woman's life. The life is forfeited, often happily, because virginity and its reward, heaven, are far more highly valued. Sanctity emerges from the tragedy of spilling "innocent blood," as Pius XII put it, but the preserved virginity guarantees the purity of the sacrifice. Thus these victims are doubly worthy of devotion: once because of their heroic defense of virginity, which extends into a broader defense of ideals in a corrupt world; and again because of their tragic death, which in all cases is enhanced by youth and beauty and in some by martyrdom.

The nature of the perpetrators likewise contributes to the sanctity of the victims and to the implied message of the narratives. The police and soldiers who assault Sarita are complemented in the summarized hagiographies by a prefect, a consular official, a governor's son, a prince, the son of a count, and more soldiers. All of these corrupt officials abuse positions of power for their own sexual gratification, while they at once represent the greater apparatus of government abuse and corruption. The coercive modus operandi, presumably effective against the majority of their victims (whose lives never get recorded), fails in these narratives because the perpetrators confront women of moral strength and conviction that will not be violated. The lives of these exceptional women are taken, often after gory trials of torture, but they hold their integrity, beliefs, and identity in reserve. The narratives, particularly the earlier ones, stress this double agenda: to persevere against all odds not only in one's virginity, but also in one's religious convictions.

Some of Sarita's narratives from the miniseries have the same motif, save that the religious convictions of the earlier cases have been replaced by implied or explicit political convictions. Margaret, Agatha, Agnes, and Pelagia are killed because they will not renounce Christianity or acknowledge pagan authority; Sarita is killed because she will not renounce her commitment to the poor or acknowledge police and military authority. The double agenda (sexual and political) of the hagiographic accounts splits in the miniseries narratives: death results either from the preservation of virginity or else from insubordination to authorities. The two agendas are implicitly reunited in the most popular myth circulated among devotees, in which the attempted rape of Sarita is perpetrated by police or soldiers.

Even when the perpetrators are not associated with government, such as the imposing fathers of Dymphna and Liberata or the men who assault Maria Goretti and Antonia Mesina, they represent forces that overpower women and coerce their subjugation. The refusal to acquiesce always results in death, but this death—a chosen death—is seen as an indirect defeat of overpowering forces. The victim's will is done, not the perpetrator's, so that control of death is reserved along with virginity. Like the executions of outlaw and criminal folk saints, the murders of these virgins are represented as victories because they result in sainthood and miracles for the community.

When Sarita's perpetrators are not police or soldiers they tend to be black or dark-skinned men (*negros, morenos, zambos*) who contrast with Sarita's lily-white innocence and purity. This racist scenario, with the white beauty defiled by the black beast, is particularly suggestive because most of Sarita's devotees are more the color of the rapists than of the snow-white saint. A similar paradox characterizes Niño Compadrito devotion in Cuzco, where many indigenous and mestizo devotees prefer a blond and blue-eyed effigy. Devotee commentary on such points is minimal, but I would conjecture that these representations express internalized racial biases concerning purity, beauty, criminality, and good and evil. As the myth forms and the roles are assigned, everyone knows how the villain is supposed to look.

Virginity and purity are irretrievably lost after rape, but the tragic violation of youth and innocence provide an alternate route to sainthood. The shock, pity, empathy, and sorrow of devotees intermingle with the purgatory-on-earth experience of the victim to generate an emerging saint. María Soledad, Almita Sivila, and Pedrito Sangüeso, among other folk saints, all conform to this model. Details of their tragic deaths, such as the mutilation of the women's corpses and the rape of six-year-old Pedrito, accentuate the horror and, with it, the passion of devotion and the predisposition to miraculousness. The shock of the kill is particularly strong when rape itself is the form of murder. One devotee envisioned such a death for Sarita: she was so young and small when she was raped that she died as a consequence.

This was precisely the fate of another Peruvian folk saint, from Ica. Julia Rosa Muñante Milos, known as Rosita de Pachacutec, seems almost a hybrid of Sarita Colonia and St. Rose of Lima. With Sarita (whose image is painted on a wall at Rosita's shrine) she shares youthful innocence and charity abruptly ended by a tragic death associated with rape; and with St. Rose she shares a precocious, mystical attraction to the Christ child; a passion for gardening; food and fasting motifs; and, again, a charitable concern for the poor. Rose imagery is prominent in the iconography of all three. There are also direct interrelations of St. Rose and Sarita, notably in the biography written by Sarita's brother.

Rosita de Pachacutec's mother was orphaned at the age of four and, after a brief period of abandonment and homelessness on the street, was taken in by a convent. She lived a nunlike life, including penitential exercises, until she was twenty, at which time she married and had children. Rosita was the last. The mother's life, as she described it to me and as it is represented in a folk hagiography distributed at the shrine, was one of severe poverty. She worked endlessly to support hungry children, who likewise worked to contribute to the family's survival. When she delivered Rosita, the mother explained as illustration of her hardships, she did so at home and alone. She lifted her newborn daughter from a pool of blood, cut the umbilical cord, and passed out, hemorrhaging. Her children later discovered her and screamed for help in the street. The mother regained consciousness in the hospital.

Rosita manifested at an early age the religious fervor with which her mother had imbued her. The refrain of Rosita's early childhood—"Mommy, mommy, I want you to bring me a Christ child"—is proudly repeated by Rosita's mother, who adds in despair that the request had to be denied repeatedly. The mother explained to Rosita that the family's meager income was needed for food, but Rosita responded that she would go without eating, that she preferred the Christ child to food. The mother finally agreed and prepared the family for a fast so that the doll could be purchased. That's when the miracle occurred: after buying a doll of the infant Christ, there was somehow money left over for food. The same cycle was repeated later when Rosita requested cloth to make vestments for her Christ child.

Food is a central theme in the life story of Rosita de Pachacutec. In this detail from a mural at the shrine near Ica, Rosita miraculously fills the pot to feed her famished siblings.

Rosita's weary mother was surprised one day after work by her three-year-old daughter splitting a log to make a cross. Rosita also had a rose garden, and first on her agenda each morning was to adorn her Christ child with its most beautiful flower. She rarely showed up at mealtime, because the aroma of her roses was enough nutrition to sustain her, and instead she withdrew to silence and solitude with her doll. When she did accompany the family at the table, she merely moved her food around her plate until she finally offered it to her siblings. Many of these scenes correspond in significant detail to the hagiography of St. Rose of Lima.

It is not surprising, given the emphasis on food, that one of the living Rosita's principal miracles concerns the feeding of her hungry family. It occurred on another evening when there was nothing to eat and all of the children were crying. Rosita went into the kitchen and somehow, out of nothing, miraculously filled the pot with an excess of hot, cooked food, though the ashes in the hearth remained cool. This provision and replenishment of food was repeated in miracles after Rosita's death. Rosita also contributed to the family sustenance more practically by selling vegetables from her garden and, in the afternoons, selling bread for a local baker. Her first earnings from the bakery sales were set aside for devotional candles.

Praying before Sarita Colonia's image inside the shrine in Callao.

As the youngest child, Rosita was left at home alone while the other family members were at work. On January 5, 1974, she was raped at knifepoint by a man about forty years old. Upon return from work the mother found Rosita agonizing in bed, her legs and genitals covered in blood, as though the story of Rosita's birth were in some way prophetic. Rosita died in a hospital five days later. On that same day her garden died, and for a year afterward the house was filled with the fragrance of roses. When Rosita's mother asked a priest about this miraculous occurrence, he explained that it was the odor of sanctity. Funeral flowers that touched Rosita's tomb later cured incurable illnesses.[26]

At the Shrine

On a typical visit to Sarita Colonia's shrine a devotee prays before Sarita's image, which is housed in a case with a glass front, and again at her tomb. Candles are then lit in a section of the shrine reserved for this purpose. Most devotees buy their candles at the shrine, where they are sold in mixed groups of four. The candles are color-coded for health (white), happiness (yellow), work (green), and love (red). I have never seen a black candle at Sarita's shrine, although some say that the same purpose—cursing others—can be served by tying a red ribbon around other candles.

The four candles are generally burned together, suggesting a blanket petition that covers all needs. There are exceptions—I saw one man return the three colors and asked for all white candles—but my impression generally was that visits to Sarita's tomb were more to renew a lifelong relation than to request specific miracles. Many devotees attending Sarita's fiestas confirmed this: they had come to pay tribute, to renew their mutual commitment with Sarita, and to give thanks because they still had their health or a job. Sarita is the patron of her devotees, and they visit her in love and gratitude as she watches over all aspects of their lives. This generalized patronage is registered in the text of many plaques at the shrine: "protect me always," "thank you for your permanent blessing," and "thank you for taking care of us always."

Touching is the rule inside the shrine, and some devotees also cleanse themselves by wetting their faces and hair with the irrigation water that flows through the flowers on Sarita's tomb. Flowers themselves are a crucial aspect of this devotion. Roses adorn the foreground of Sarita Colonia iconography, and most devotees arrive at the shrine with mixed bouquets that they purchase at the entrance to the cemetery. Sarita's tomb is soon covered with vases full of these bouquets, and during the fiestas the shrine itself seems to fill with flowers as the excess is displaced to wherever there is room.

Flowers are also given to devotees during the shrine's day-to-day operations. Some request them, some are repeat visitors treated preferentially, some receive the flowers as a bonus after making a purchase, and some are happily surprised. The flowers are supernaturally charged because they have been in prolonged contact with the tomb. Their distribution serves the dual purposes of clearing the way for new bouquets and of making Sarita's power portable. It is also consonant with the spirit of gift-giving that is characteristic of this devotion. Flowers come and go in constant circulation. Those that leave the shrine adorn home altars and are used for cleansing, healing, and protection. (Rosita de Pachacutec's devotees put flower petals from her shrine in their baths.) Sarita's sisters also distribute smaller, semidried purple flowers, which are carried in a pocket or purse for good luck. Portable luck and protection are also available through the Sarita amulets sold at the shrine.

The water from the flowers is also taken by some devotees, for the purpose of rubbing or sprinkling it—like holy water—on their cars, businesses, and ailing body parts. Others drink the water. A prostitute used water from Sarita's tomb to ritually cleanse her room of evil spirits belonging to previous clients who have died.[27]

The flowers and the water from Sarita's tomb are also used in healing rituals at the shrine. The remedies of one curandera included mouthfuls of "Sarita's holy water" sprayed over the body of her patients. Sarita's sisters, particularly Esther, are attributed a certain power and prestige by virtue of their relation to Sarita, and this is used at the shrine to multiple purposes. Adjacent to the tomb, and beside the burning candles, Esther does ritual cleansings using Sarita-charged water and flower petals. Cleansings are sometimes done with candles instead, which are then lit to send up a petition. This doubly efficacious ritual is similar to one from the Andes. The impurities absorbed by the candle burn away with the same offering (the candle) that petitions a cure.[28]

Perhaps the most distinguishing feature of devotion to Sarita Colonia is its emphasis on communal sharing. In other devotions thanks are given, for example, through physical sacrifice (walking on one's knees to a shrine) or symbolic ex votos (braids, models of homes), but at Sarita's shrine gratitude is expressed more practically. In commemoration of Sarita as patron of the poor, devotees arrive at the biannual fiestas with gifts that they distribute among the crowd. Sarita gave and gives, so her grateful devotees do the same. Her commitment to the poor helping the poor continues amid the ranks of her cult. The offering, in effect, passes from one needy devotee to another through the mediation of the needless Sarita.

Devotees select the particular gift that they will distribute in accord with their means and inclinations. Food and drink—meals, cakes, sodas, sandwiches, fruits—are the most common. Some devotees distribute images of Sarita. A man who was well known and treated deferentially arrived at a Sarita fiesta with a huge box of gifts. He delivered it directly to Esther, paying homage to her in the process, and she reciprocated by ritually cleansing him with candles. The two then distributed the gifts together.

Devotees more typically distribute the gifts on their own. New distributions are always readily identifiable, because they incite stampedes of devotees competing for supplies that are quickly depleted. At times the clamoring for free food divides the cult along class lines. As some people push and shove quite naturally to get the freebies, others are offended by the lack of manners and decorum. One woman asked rhetorically how people could act that way just to get a free soda. For others, however, many of them children, the soda and the piece of cake were worth whatever had to be done. One mother asked if I was going to finish the soda that someone had given me. Her son's big eyes and hopeful half-smile looked up, awaiting my response, until I handed it over.

The charitable giving at other fiestas, such as the San La Muerte fiesta in Posadas, is far more substantial than it is at Sarita's shrine. In the Argentine case, however, the giving is partially subsidized by offerings to the saint. It is also an expression of individual generosity, a philanthropic gesture made by devotees of greater means toward others in financial crisis. The structure is vertical—from the saint and the shrine owners to others. At Sarita's shrine, conversely, the giving is entirely horizontal, from devotee to devotee. The poor feed the poor, however modestly. This charity is not sponsored or subsidized by the shrine. It is random and small-scale. And it is a generalized practice of devotional culture—a form of offering—rather than an independent expression of goodwill.

A sense of community is also suggested by devotees' reference to one another as "brother" and "sister." The same tendency toward solidarity is evident in some messages posted on a Sarita Colonia Web site. One devotee wrote, for example, "I need your prayers so that together we can achieve the miracle that Sergio and Maria can conceive a baby." The petition to Sarita is strengthened because the community pulls together—like a union—for an individual cause. The gift is prayer.

The Church has formally and publicly disapproved of devotion to Sarita Colonia, but nevertheless the Baquíjano cemetery priest shows up dutifully at the biannual fiestas. I witnessed two of his participations, one at the March fiesta (commemorating Sarita's birth) and the other at the December fiesta (commemorating her death). At the March fiesta the priest offered only a brief *responso* (prayer for the dead). He did so outside the shrine, standing before

Sarita's tile image on the wall, with Esther beside him. Devotees seemed largely indifferent to the priest's March appearance. Rather than gathering around him to bow their heads or to pray along, they preferred to remain on the long line to enter the shrine, to converse in groups, or to charge toward the new distributions of food.

At the December fiesta the same priest presented a liturgical act (mass without celebration of the Eucharist), now through a microphone and to a large crowd. People participated as though they were in church, saying their lines in response to the priest's. Many looked pious, with their heads bowed and hands clasped. The ambiguity of the priest's presence at the fiesta was redoubled by his homily, which discouraged devotion to Sarita. On the one hand he said "mass," as devotees call it, before Sarita's shrine and during her fiesta, and on the other he reminded devotees that their cult was inappropriate.

No one seemed troubled by that mixed message. What was important to devotees was that the priest showed up. Despite the ambiguities and any explicit disapproval, the priest's presence enhances the fiesta with Catholic supernatural powers. When the holy water came out it caused a reaction

An ambiguous message: A Catholic priest offers services during Sarita Colonia fiestas at the same time that he makes clear his disapproval of the devotion.

similar to the stampedes for food. A spectacular hedge of flowers appeared overhead as bouquets were raised for the blessing. The priest then found himself in the absurd position of having to aim his sprinkles very carefully to avoid the Sarita images also raised by devotees.

Priests justify their presence at folk saint shrines, and their masses for folk saints in churches, by explaining that these liturgies are available to any deceased Catholic. This particular priest, however, seemed uncomfortable with his role at the fiesta. He was visibly troubled by my camera, and after his liturgical act, as he hastened away without even cursory cordiality to devotees, he dismissed me (following after him at a trot) and my questions with a wave of his hand. Unlike many other priests, who openly shared their ideas on folk devotions, this one rudely turned his back and walked off. I was left with the impression that he had no idea how to reconcile his presence at the shrine with his disdain for the devotion. He seemed cold and un-Christian even to devotees, as though he were bothered by attending their pagan gathering but was duty bound (he is the cemetery chaplain) to make an appearance.

The Church commonly accuses folk devotions of being commercial deceptions that exploit the desperation of gullible masses. The bishop of Callao followed suit: he saw "signs of fraud" at Sarita Colonia's shrine. "Behind this cult there is a business, an interest in making profit, and this should be controlled by the authorities." There is no doubt that at least four or five people, including Sarita's two sisters, make a living of sorts at the shrine. Almost everyone who enters buys candles (four for one *sol*—about 30 cents; a cheap meal costs 2 or 3 *soles*), and some also buy prayer cards or other Sarita paraphernalia. These items are available elsewhere, but the idea that they are sold inside the shrine greatly enhances their appeal. Sarita's sister Rosa rubs candles on the tomb to give their miraculousness a boost.[29]

The attendants and vendors at the shrine are sensitive to the insinuations of commercialism. They always gave me permission to shoot photographs freely, with a single exception: the sales displays—small arrangements of images, candles, and amulets—were forbidden. Business at Sarita's shrine on a day-to-day basis is nevertheless discreet and unimposing. If someone wants something, it is there; if not, there is no obligation or pressure. I have seen exceptions only twice, both at the end of 2003, when candles and images were hawked as one barely crossed the threshold, sometimes with an insistent pitch.

In the earlier years at Sarita's shrine, a "sale" was never made. The purchaser would say, "I will give you the gift of such-and-such an amount of money," and the vendor would reply, "And I would like to give you the gift of this image of Sarita." Exchanges were made in this way because the image of

Sarita Colonia's proud sisters, Esther (left) and Rosa, wanted to pose holding the family photograph and the biography of Sarita written by their brother.

Sarita is priceless, and because the community forges its bonds through mutual sharing.[30]

This courteous commerce also suggests sales as a consequence, rather than a motivator, of the devotion. Were profit the intent, the vendors could far better exploit the large crowds gathered for the fiestas. Currently, sales inside the shrine are supplemented only by one or two tables outside during the fiestas. These stands offer only images of Sarita that no one seems to buy. Sarita's shrine is more commercial than any other folk saint site that I have seen in Peru, but the commerce is virtually nonexistent in comparison to the emporia and profiteering that surround the folk saint devotions to Niño Fidencio, Gaucho Gil, and Difunta Correa, or—in Lima itself—the Catholic devotion to the Lord of Miracles.

Sarita's fiestas are also less festive, and less spectacular, than these others. In many devotions music, dance, food, drink, and grand processions are the rule, but at Sarita's shrine the event is modest, calmer, and devotion oriented. (The same is true, to an even greater degree, at the shrine of Niño Compadrito in Cuzco.) In addition to the "mass" and a Mariachi serenade that sometimes occurs, Sarita's fiesta consists of visiting the shrine, giving and receiving the mentioned gifts, and visiting with friends and family. The line to enter the shrine is long, so much of the devotees' time, perhaps most, is spent waiting. Some leave immediately after their visit with Sarita. Others hang around to talk, maybe keeping an eye out—particularly the kids—for the arrival of new food offerings.

Difunta Correa

Deolinda Correa was born in La Majadita, in San Juan province, in the early years of the nineteenth century. She was married to Baudilio Bustos in her early twenties and the couple had a son. Around 1841, Bustos was conscripted into the troops of Facundo Quiroga, despite his resistance due to illness, perhaps pneumonia. Some say instead that Bustos was imprisoned by enemy forces, and taken away in chains toward La Rioja.

Deolinda could not bear the thought that her husband—sick or captive—was suffering without her care. She entered the desert with her infant son in her arms, following behind the troops on foot. The trail was soon lost, however, and Deolinda wandered under the merciless sun. She eventually ran out of water, collapsed in exhaustion, and died of thirst and exposure. Some livestock drivers found her shortly after and buried her body at the site, in Vallecito. Her son survived by nursing at the breast of his dead mother.

Bad luck struck Flavio Zevallos as he was driving a herd of cattle across the desert. A violent storm frightened the herd and it stampeded in all directions. Zevallos's frantic search seemed futile—the cattle were nowhere to be found and he feared that everything was lost. That's when he happened upon Difunta Correa's grave. He pleaded for her help in recovering the cattle and promised to build a chapel in exchange for the miracle. When Zevallos resumed his search the following morning, he was astounded to discover his herd happily reunited and grazing in a canyon. Some of the cattle probably lifted their heads to look at him stupidly, chewing. "Not a single one was missing," marveled Rolando, his grandson, as he related this frequently told story. The herd made it safely to the market in Chile, where it brought a good price, and the grateful Zevallos remembered his promise. Adobes and water were carted to Difunta Correa's grave from nearby Caucete, and what today is a sprawling complex—a town in itself—thus had its humble beginnings around 1890.[1]

The miracle granted to Zevallos is widely considered the first performed by Difunta Correa (excepting the miraculous breastfeeding that saved her son). It stimulated devotion among *arrieros* (livestock drivers) and other travelers, who, like their folk saint, faced the perils of exposure on the desert.

Difunta Correa's miracles are on record earlier, however, beginning in 1865. A text from that date notes that "travelers have complete faith in her miracles and invoke her in their tribulations, and when passing by they never fail to say some prayer or deposit a silver coin in the collection box." The same source observes that many murders and robberies had been perpetrated at this site in Vallecito, known as Las Peñas, because outcroppings of rock on both sides of the road provided cover for thieves who ambushed travelers. The place was so notorious for crime that housewives, infuriated when shopkeepers tried to overcharge them, would say, "Don't be a crook, and if you want to steal, go to Las Peñas." The fortuitous location of Difunta Correa's grave at La Peñas afforded protection to travelers precisely where it was most needed. Difunta Correa protects one on the road, even—especially—at the place where danger is the greatest. One can travel now in peace.[2]

There was probably no more than a cross (with an attached collection box) at the grave, but there appears to have been substantial devotion. Church records document several masses said for Difunta Correa in the Caucete parish as early 1883.[3] A stone plaque of gratitude from June 1895 thanks the "charitable soul of Difunta Correa," presumably for a miracle. It was probably removed from the ruins of the old church at Villa Independencia, a town near Caucete, after the earthquake in 1944. Others say that the stone, which resembles a headstone, was originally in the cemetery of Caucete. (The text of the stone includes "q.e.p.d.," which is the Spanish equivalent of "R.I.P.," meaning rest in peace.) The stone was affixed in the 1960s to the altar of the Catholic church built at the Difunta Correa shrine, but a bishop ordered its removal around 2001. It is currently displayed near the rear door of the church.

Devotion to Difunta Correa was well established at the end of the nineteenth century and continued to grow at a steady pace. Reports from 1921, including the following one from Caucete, suggest the degree to which it competed with formal Catholicism among locals: "They have greater devotion and faith in her than in the very saints of the Catholic religion, and instead of making promises to these they make them to Difunta Correa because she is more miraculous." The shrine itself had evolved from a cross to a chapel, perhaps the one attributed to Zevallos: "a small room with an altar in front and on it a collection box with a lock, where all those who make promises or pass by there have to leave money." The obligation of passersby to stop and make an offering, which is more generally expected at the sites of any accidental death, accelerated the growth—and the funding—of this devotion. Then, as today, visits are inspired, or even required, by the belief that troubles or dangers will plague the travels of those who fail to stop and pay their respects.[4]

Another 1921 report from San Juan Province illustrates this obligation by relating the trials of an old man who passed Difunta Correa's tomb with his herd and neglected to make an offering. The man lost some of his cattle, went back to the tomb and left money (the value of candles) as an offering, and then recovered what he had lost and reached his destination without further difficulty. Such cautionary tales reinforce the obligation to stop and make an offering, along with the underlying belief that Difunta Correa punishes those who fail to comply.[5]

The same holds true for the many satellite shrines (with their collection boxes) to Difunta Correa that were built along the roadways. Livestock drivers traveled over broad expanses, thereby disseminating the good news of miracles far from Difunta Correa's original grave site at Vallecito. Shrines began appearing along the roadways as miracles proliferated in new areas, and, again, "all traveling livestock drivers who pass by on those roads have the obligation to deposit a coin, no matter how small." The roadside shrines to Difunta Correa that one sees along Argentine routes today have their antecedents in this diffusion of the devotion by livestock drivers.

Strong devotion among truck drivers later made a second contribution—now national—to dissemination and growth of the cult. Truckers spread the news far more efficiently than their precursors as they take to the highways with Difunta Correa's name or "Visit Difunta Correa" displayed prominently on their trucks. The nineteenth-century belief in Difunta Correa's protection of all travelers has likewise been modernized to encompass anyone who travels by car. Difunta Correa's ill-fated journey is reversed into a safe journey for devotees. The provision of having to stop and pay respects is still current, but is perhaps interpreted more loosely now than it was in the past. Few passersby stop at the roadside shrines, and the shrines themselves—far fewer now than in previous decades—are also on the decline. The main shrine in Vallecito has a drive-through road that loops in and out as a bypass, which

A roadside Difunta Correa shrine between Salta and Cachi. Tires, car parts, and water bottles are traditional offerings.

allows devotees to fulfill their obligation on the run, often without making a full stop. This is a popular option with truck drivers—they slow down for a look and maybe sign themselves with the cross, then get back to work.

The obligation of passersby to stop and make an offering (even if only a prayer) also helped to establish the widely held belief that Difunta Correa is *muy cobradora*. The idea is that she makes you pay up, that she demands what is due to her. This belief is the flip side of the corresponding idea that Difunta Correa is *muy pagadora*, meaning that she delivers on her end of the bargain. These concepts are particularly used in reference to the spiritual contract made when requesting a miracle: each party is bound by a reciprocal responsibility, and Difunta Correa, always true to the letter, punishes those in default. The terms chosen to describe the arrangement, *cobrar* (to charge) and *pagar* (to pay), suggest the degree to which relations with saints are based on this-worldly protocols of exchange. Devotees frequently make comments such as, "If you make a promise to Difunta Correa, you have to pay up," meaning deliver on your promise if she grants the miracle. "Difunta Correa is *muy cobradora*, and you're in trouble if you don't fulfill your promise—something bad will happen to you."

These beliefs gain all kinds of expression in the everyday lives of devotees. A medical doctor once went with his family to the Difunta Correa shrine in order to *pagar una manda* (fulfill the promise made when requesting a miracle, with the implication of paying for or paying back). When the doctor had fulfilled his responsibility and was ready to leave, his car wouldn't start. It appeared, after checking, that nothing was wrong with the engine, but the car remained stubbornly out of service. Just then an old man came out of nowhere and asked if they had taken anything from the shrine. The doctor replied that they had not, but his adolescent son confessed that he had taken a medal. The father instructed the son to put the medal back where he had found it, which the boy did, and the car started without a problem. The old man then provided the moral: "Difunta Correa is *muy cobradora.*" You can't get away with anything.

Difunta Correa's protection of travelers extends figuratively into all endeavors, even life itself as a journey. Her tragically foreclosed journey—and life—made her the saint who guides others through peril and on to their destinations. She does not resolve problems magically, but rather provides assistance and protection "on the difficult roads of life," as it is worded in a prayer. Devotees explain that Difunta Correa gives you the strength "to get wherever you are going," but you have to get there on your own. She helps those who help themselves. The miracles collaborate with effort. Difunta Correa fortifies the strength, will, and resolve of devotees. Her suffering becomes their alleviation, her failed journey their happy achievement of their goals, and her hunger and thirst their plenitude.

The Difunta Correa shrine has grown into a huge complex, with several devotional chapels, a museum, retail arcades, a small hotel, many restaurants, a Catholic church, administrative and support buildings, a police station, a health center, and a post office. Expansion of the shrine and the town that has grown around it were boosted by the arrival of the railroad around 1908, and then again by the paving of the national route on which Vallecito is located. A haphazard and impoverished conglomeration resulted—a shantytown like the one at the Gaucho Gil shrine today—and inspired the formation, in 1948, of the Vallecito Cemetery Foundation.

This foundation was established to receive and manage offerings (including significant donations of cash and valuables) and, in general, to oversee public uses of the shrine. The bylaws provided that the minister of public works serve as president (by 1972 the director of tourism had assumed this position) and that the parish priest of Caucete serve as vice president. The intent was to invest donations in the maintenance and development of the shrine. The sums were considerable: a 1969 news article referred to income of 20 million pesos a year, and one in 1982 mentions 220 pounds of gold that had accumulated, in addition to significant cash reserves. Noteworthy progress was not made at the shrine until 1963, however, when Father Ricardo Baez Laspiur became actively involved in the foundation. The Difunta Correa complex was transformed by the vision and initiative of this Catholic priest. The foundation's first priority was infrastructure—electricity, water, telephone—and this was followed by such developments as the retail center and hotel. The shop and restaurant owners at the Difunta Correa shrine organized into an association in 1973.

Baez Laspiur explained that as a priest he had the obligation to work with all aspects of his people and their culture. Until 1959 the Church had ignored or rejected the Difunta Correa shrine, and it was "entirely pagan," as he put it, when he began his work. Under the influence of Vatican II, and like Father Julián Zini at the Gaucho Gil shrine, he regarded folk saint devotion as an authentic expression of faith. It was incumbent on him to steer the positive aspects of this "spiritual center" toward mainstream Catholicism. Perhaps his most daring move toward that end was the construction of a Catholic church at the Difunta Correa complex, in 1966. Earlier, upon arrival, he celebrated a collective wedding of some thirty couples who were living out of wedlock, and he baptized their children.

Progress at the Difunta Correa shrine was disrupted by the 1976 coup, after which the "dirty war" began in Argentina. Baez Laspiur and the other board members were displaced when the government of San Juan found "irregularities" in the shrine's management and took control of the Vallecito Cemetery Foundation. The Church also took a conservative turn, and the tolerance of the Baez Laspiur years yielded to outspoken condemnation of Difunta Correa devotion as heretical. Baez Laspiur, who died in March 2005, was less dogmatic. When I asked him about Difunta Correa's standardized iconography, which is sometimes attributed to him, he responded that Difunta Correa is not a canonized saint and therefore her image cannot be made or blessed. Then he added a long "however . . ."

It appears that business at the complex continued more or less as usual during the dictatorship. The president of the merchant's association observed that attendance was down during those years (1976–1983) because many presumed that the shrine had been closed, and others may have been intimidated by the dictatorship's prohibition of unorthodox devotions. At the same time, however, several full-page ads were published in San Juan's *Diario del Cuyo* in the 1970s and 1980s, itemizing the construction projects that aspired to transform the site into a national tourist center. News articles from the same years also make frequent reference to the need for development of infrastructure in order to attract and accommodate visitors. Toward the end of the dictatorship, in February 8, 1982, an article in the same newspaper had the headline, "Difunta Correa Can Be a Major Tourist Center," and beneath it, "That Is Why It Is Necessary to Support the Projects of the Residents and Businessmen at the Sanctuary." Another 1982 article added that the Difunta Correa shrine was "the greatest tourist attraction in the province."

While site development was continuing, however, a conservative counterforce was attempting to eradicate Difunta Correa devotion. On March 24, 1982, the military governor in the nearby province of San Luis issued a decree prohibiting roadside shrines to Difunta Correa and ordering their demolition. "The cult to Difunta Correa lacks historical foundation" and is not "duly inscribed in the National Register of Religions," the decree said. The governor gave thirty days to remove the roadside shrines, after which the task would be assigned to security forces.[6]

The bishop of San Luis enthusiastically received the decree and reinforced it with a message from the Church. He reiterated that Difunta Correa was only legendary and prohibited Catholic devotion. The bishop supported his argument by referencing a Church document that had been issued in 1974, when (according to official estimates) some two hundred thousand people visited Difunta Correa's shrine for Holy Week. Devotion to Difunta Correa had caused "serious abuses" of the faith, the bishop continued, and these were detrimental to "public order" and the decency of Catholics. He added that the roadside shrines "have turned modern roads into garbage dumps."[7]

In 2002, the Vallecito Cemetery Foundation was dissolved permanently and direction of the Difunta Correa complex was transferred to a division of the San Juan provincial government. The Difunta Correa Administration, as the new management is known, has a clear priority: to develop and promote the shrine as a major site of religious tourism. (The shrine also provides an important venue for distribution of artisan products of the region, such as wine and crafts.) Opposition to folk devotion has thus yielded to the higher priority of steering faith in Difunta Correa toward San Juan's economic growth. The tolerance of the shrine is the result of a change in politics, but also in perception. What was regarded earlier as deviant Catholicism is now regarded as an opportunity for development.

The Miraculous Breast

Devotees generally know little about Difunta Correa's life, but almost all can relate that after death she breastfed her infant son. This post-mortem feat suggests an eternal motherhood, a love beyond death that Difunta Correa

The miraculous breast is represented in the standard iconography of Difunta Correa.

extends now to devotees. Even after fatal dehydration her body transformed the absence of water into a plenitude of milk. With her help, therefore, one can—even out of nothing, out of one's personal and economic exhaustion—acquire the means and stamina to carry on in a world as inhospitable as a desert. Just as the infant son drew life from the dead body of his mother, so devotees survive on the nourishment that Difunta Correa provides for her spiritual children. She is quintessentially maternal and, like the Virgin Mary, almost a deification of maternity. In their plaques and prayers, devotees repeatedly refer to her as "mother of those who suffer," "mother of those who cry," and "protector of the helpless who suffer and cry."

Difunta Correa's life-giving and life-saving breast is preceded by a long tradition of maternal goddesses who date back to Paleolithic times. Like Difunta Correa and maternal protagonists in folklore internationally, these deified mothers provide succor that nurtures, saves, and soothes. Through the medium of this most basic of foods—milk—the attributes of the goddess are transferred to (usually ailing) humans in thin streams of purifying whiteness. Goddesses transcendentalize the female body's miraculous capacity to sustain the life that it produces. Milk as the essence of maternity is transformed into a supernatural substance that nourishes both body and soul.[8]

The Egyptian mother goddess Isis, who was associated with milk-giving cows, breast-fed the pharaohs who were ascending to the throne. Nursing at her breast confirmed their legitimacy, attested to their divinity, and granted them immortality. In Greek mythology, the Milky Way was created when Hera's breast squirted into the heavens. It was believed that this goddess's milk transferred her immortality to whoever nursed at her breast. Zeus, who wanted immortality for his son Hercules (who was born of a mortal), placed the boy at Hera's breast while she was sleeping. The startled Hera awakened and withdrew her breast—lucky Hercules got down a gulp beforehand—and the squirting milk created the stars. The story, sometimes attributed to the Roman Juno, was later represented on several canvases, including Tintoretto's famous *The Origin of the Milky Way* (circa 1508). A Christianized version told in Argentina has the Milky Way created when the Christ Child, nursing at the Virgin's breast in heaven, inadvertently bit the nipple. The Virgin pulled away in response, and thus the stars were created.[9]

Lactation and nursing are also central to the Roman legend of Romulus and Remus. These infant twins were abandoned beside the Tiber, but their lives were saved by a she-wolf that suckled them. Romulus and Remus became associated with the founding of Rome—even today the city is represented by their nursing at the wolf—and early Romans were thought to be their descendants. The legend also registers the enduring belief that attributes and character traits (such as Hera's immortality) are transmitted through breast-feeding. Because Romulus and Remus drank the milk of a predatory animal, they and their descendants were imbued with military skills conducive to empire.

Another legend, the Roman Charity, is a moral tale of reversed maternity. A mother was sentenced to starve to death in prison, and her adult daughter, unable to smuggle in food, offered her breast instead. The mother survived by nursing at the breast of her daughter. The surprising consequence was the mother's release from prison in honor of her daughter's "pious affection." A temple to filial love was built on the site. Later, in Renaissance versions, the mother in the legend was replaced by the father, who likewise survives on his daughter's milk.[10]

Charity itself, as an allegorical virtue, is also depicted as a lactating mother. The advocation of Mary known as the Virgin of Charity is an adaptation of this pagan motif. The Virgin Mary is of course more broadly associated with breast-feeding, as illustrated by the innumerable paintings in which the Christ Child appears at her breast. There is, however, a remarkable difference between Mary's role and those of Isis and Hera. The mythological goddesses nurse mortals into divinity, but Mary, a mortal, nurses a god (Christ) into humanity. In the pre-Christian myths the maternal milk is an induction to immortality; in the Christian myth it is an induction to mortality. Immortality is then restored, for humanity as a whole, by the mortal Christ's death on the cross.

In more figurative and symbolic representations, the Virgin's breast milk refreshes, nourishes, and transfers divine graces. There are several examples in Madrid's El Prado Museum. Pedro Machuca's *The Virgin and the Souls in Purgatory* features the Virgin squirting milk from one breast while the infant Christ squirts it from the other. This shower relieves the souls burning in Purgatory. (Nut, the Egyptian sky goddess, also made a rainfall of her milk.) Some adult male saints, notably St. Bernard, are likewise blessed with the graces of the Virgin's lactation as jets of it stream from afar into their mouths.[11]

The cult of the Virgin's milk was extensive in late medieval Europe. Emphasis on the Virgin's maternal attributes freely intermingled with representations of the Church itself as a nursing mother. Clement of Alexandria (died before 215) and many others had made the connection earlier: "And calling her children to her, she [the Church] nurses them with holy milk," by which he meant the Word of God. The visionary writings of the medieval mystic Mechthild von Magdeburg have Mary explaining that "my breasts began to fill with the pure, unspoiled milk of true, tender mercy, and I suckled the prophets and sages, before God was born. Later on during my childhood, I suckled Jesus, and during my youth I suckled God's Bride, holy Christianity." The culmination of such ideas came in 1964, when Mary's maternal supremacy was dogmatized in a new title: "Mother of the Church."[12]

Thus in this symbolic web of interrelations, Mary and the Church are together represented maternally, offering their love, care, protection, and spiritual nourishment to all Catholics. The breast and its milk have gone far beyond their literal meanings to become symbols of maternal care generally, now both corporal and spiritual. It is precisely this otherworldly, comprehensive nurturing of body and soul that makes Difunta Correa (like the Virgin Mary) an attractive or even necessary addition to patriarchal religion. The most basic act of maternal sustenance, breast-feeding, retains the focus while at once it is transcendentalized and made miraculous. The male gods, who lack the capacity for maternal nurturing, are supplemented and to some degree displaced by these quasi-divine females.

A sixteenth-century indigenous myth from the same region as Difunta Correa redirects the theme of supernatural maternity by endowing a father with breast milk. The man's wife had died during childbirth in the desert, so in desperation he put the infant to his own chest. The infant sucked futilely at the first nipple, but the other one gave milk in abundance.[13]

There are countless Catholic texts and images that treat breast-feeding themes, but one is particularly relevant in the context of Difunta Correa's miraculous breast. This medieval legend relates that a governor and his wife were unable to have a child until they beseeched the help of Mary Magdalene. Their idols had failed them, but Christ granted their wish, and the happy wife became pregnant with a son. The governor, intrigued by the new faith, decided to make a pilgrimage to Rome in order to meet St. Peter and verify what Magdalene had preached about Christ. His pregnant wife insisted on accompanying him. The rough seas caused her great torment, she died during childbirth, and, because there was no one else aboard who could breast-feed, the newborn was doomed to certain death.

The governor carried his wife's corpse ashore with the intention of burying it. The hardness of the ground made that impossible, however, so he lay his wife to rest on a rock, placed the child between her breasts, draped a cloak over them, and resumed his pilgrimage to Rome. When the governor returned two years later, he was shocked to discover that the child was quite alive, playing on the beach. The child, also shocked, for he had never before seen a man, ran for cover under the cloak on his mother's incorruptible body. The governor followed him, "and found the handsome child feeding at his mother's breast," even though the mother was dead. The child had fed at her breast for two years. Mary Magdalene then compounded the miracle by bringing this long-dead wife and mother back to life.[14]

This remarkable antecedent to Difunta Correa's story emphasizes the survival of the child and eventual resurrection of the mother as rewards for the governor's conversion. The breast is miraculous because the faith is strong. In some versions of Difunta Correa's story, similarly, right behavior of a different sort earns heavenly reward. When Difunta Correa, lost on the desert, realized that her death was imminent, she prayed that God would save her child. The miracle was granted because God recognized that the death of this exemplary wife and mother was a consequence of her love and fidelity. (In the Roman Charity, conversely, the mother is spared due to the extraordinary love and fidelity of the daughter.) The implicit intent of these morality tales is to provide incentive for exemplary behavior: if your faith is strong enough, or if you are a wife and mother beyond the call of duty, then you too will merit miracles.

Difunta Correa's story provides a role model, particularly for mothers who are struggling for the survival of their own children. They seek otherworldly help (as did Difunta Correa) because their this-worldly resources are exhausted. This quest for alleviation—almost a surrender—can come back to them unexpectedly as an enhanced burden, however, because their insufficiency is quietly implied by measure against their saint. In patriarchal interpretations, the stress falls heavily on imitating Difunta Correa's self-sacrifice: "The mother gives up even her life so the child can live."[15]

This idea has little to do with the history or even the myth—Difunta Correa dies of thirst and exhaustion, not to save her child—but the message of motherhood unto death is nevertheless conveyed to female devotees. It is received almost as a mandate, particularly in the context of traditional, exalted motherhood, be it religious (the Virgin), political (the Mothers of the Plaza de Mayo), or politicoreligious (Evita Perón, as both a first lady and a folk saint). All of these highly symbolic figures express motherhood through the suffered dedication of their lives to their literal or figurative children.

Abnegate motherhood also evoke *marianismo* (the female complement of *machismo*), which prescribes behavioral norms extrapolated from ideas about the Virgin Mary. Faithfulness, suffered love, self-sacrifice for husband and family, and chastity (excepting the pleasureless necessities of reproduction) are the highly prized attributes of such women. Difunta Correa's pursuit of her husband and postmortem care of her son are easily accommodated within (or born of) Marian ideals. The idea of Difunta Correa as an idealized wife and mother was actively propagated beginning in the 1960s by the priest-led, male committee that developed the shrine. Today, women tend to stress the maternal qualities of Difunta Correa, while men, particularly older men, stress her fidelity and the sacrifice that she made for her husband.

A recent, widely circulated book is the best example of the male view, meaning Difunta Correa's virtuous preference of death to infidelity. The book offers an alternative version of Difunta Correa's story, one that displaces the focus by advocating an escape from imminent adultery as the reason for travel and, ultimately, the cause of death. Rather than leaving home to care for her sick (or imprisoned) husband, the Difunta Correa of this version flees into the desert to avoid the sexual designs of corrupt authorities. Unscrupulous men were exerting their powers to coerce her submission, but she risked—and suffered—a tragic death rather than succumbing to adultery. In an article written for a brochure distributed to thousands at the shrine, the same author concluded that Difunta Correa "had the courage and dignity to fulfill her obligation to love and fidelity until death."[16]

Precisely the opposite argument is made in a 1946 report from San Juan. In this version it is the shame of a sexual transgression that drives Difunta Correa into the desert: "This woman was forced to leave her home due to a grave mistake." The fruit of the mistake, a boy, was born during her wanderings. Desperate and dying of thirst, Difunta Correa tried to dig for water, failed, and finally collapsed of exhaustion. The following day her corpse and her child were found by chance. The sadness of her death was compounded by the cruelty of unknowing: had she dug another couple of feet, she would have hit water and survived. A chapel was built, with the belief that Difunta Correa "must be miraculous because she lost her life in search of what is indispensable in order to live: water." Thus saintliness emerges not from exemplary performance as a wife and mother but rather from tragedy, pity, and deprivation of life's most fundamental need. The sin of Difunta Correa's transgression is forgiven because the penance of her death purges it. Self-sacrifice is never mentioned or implied.[17]

With the exception of idiosyncratic version such as this one, myths and spin tend to stress Difunta Correa's marianismo as a legacy for her female devotees. Like the Virgin Mary herself, Difunta Correa, "is the emblem of the common woman, the housewife, as is our wife, our mother, or our daughter, and through her humility she left us her example and her teaching." Otherworldly exemplars are at once ordinary and extraordinary. They are like other women, so other women can be like them, but at the same time they are capable of supernatural feats (virgin birth, postmortem breast-feeding) beyond the reach of other women.[18]

Perhaps this is because ordinary women like Difunta Correa are made extraordinary in retrospect by myth. Difunta Correa's miraculous breast is unquestionably her most important attribute. It defines and distinguishes her. It is the basis for her maternal identity, for her Marian appeal, for her subsequent miracles and, to a great degree, for her sainthood itself. In the earliest known versions of Difunta Correa's story, however, the breast-feeding miracle is entirely absent.

The folklore reports from 1921 sometimes mention a child at the breast or protected by the breasts, and one has a child sucking at the breast, but there is no reference to miraculous nourishment from the mother's dead body. When the child in these versions clings to the breast, the sense is one of pathetic desperation alleviated only by chance when passersby come to the rescue. In many versions there is no child at all—Difunta Correa dies alone on the desert. Tragic death, rather than the miraculous breast, is what stimulates devotion; the breast-feeding embellishment later enhances the appeal. "The tragic death of this woman" attracted "the compassion and love of everyone who knew her story."[19]

By the 1940s, however, the child's miraculous survival at the breast began to enter the myth. Some versions are still decidedly nonmiraculous, like those that preceded them, and at least one culminates in the death of mother and son together. Another version has the narrative structure in place, but the miracle won't happen: the child "nursed futilely" at the dead body until saved by a passing hunter. In other versions, however, the miracle occurs explicitly, as it does today: the child is saved by feeding at the breast of the dead mother.[20]

It therefore appears that the miraculous breast entered the story some-time between 1920 and 1940, about a century after Difunta Correa died. (These dates are flexible, and there remains the possibility of exceptions that are currently unknown.) Once it entered the myth, the attribute of the mi-raculous breast gradually gained prominence to become the essential feature of Difunta Correa's identity. Today the miraculous-breast version of the myth has superseded all others. It is also the basis for the standardized iconography.

Earlier versions are sometimes insistent, however, and can intermingle at random with the dominant version. A 1987 issue of *Difunta Correa*—once the shrine's official publication—offered four versions of the story in a kind of fragmented medley. One includes the miraculous breast, one suggests it, one has the child sucking futilely at the dry breast, and one has God bless the dead Difunta Correa's breast so that her child could nurse and be saved. The version that was printed on the back cover of the magazine's earlier issues, from the 1970s, has the child nursing at the body of his dead mother.[21]

Iconography, too, can be ambiguous. The image of Difunta Correa that is now unrivaled is probably based on the foreground of the painting *Fiebre amarillo en Buenos Aires* (*Yellow Fever in Buenos Aires*). The original painting is by José Manuel Blanes; a copy by Ignacio Cavicchia was donated in 1949 to the Sarmiento museum in San Juan. The child in the painting holds the breast of the dead mother but is not actually breast-feeding. The same is true of the image printed on the back cover of each issue of the magazine *Difunta Correa*: the infant is at the breast but not nursing, despite text to the contrary. The large statues of Difunta Correa at the shrine today and the countless replicas that are sold in the shops conform to the miraculous version: they all clearly depict the child nursing at the dead mother's breast. The dead mother and living son of the yellow-fever painting represent the despair of an orphan; their adaptation to Difunta Correa devotion represents the postmortem sur-vival of maternity.[22]

Difunta Correa's miraculous breast is the collective creation of a devo-tional culture. It is an ambitious revision of the tragic death, an afterthought that emerges almost of necessity to create a saint worthy of her miracles. This mythic precedent was projected backward to underwrite past miracles and to facilitate those to come. By virtue of her miraculous breast Difunta Correa transcended the ranks of countless tragic-death saints and was elevated to the goddesslike status of glorified maternity. One might say that a mother god-dess was born from her son's miraculous survival. The original inaugural miracle, doomed to the banality of finding lost livestock, was superseded—or preceded now—by this new feat misplaced tardily in the chronology. The miraculous breast recast Difunta Correa in the likeness of the Virgin who saves and soothes with her milk. It brought the prototype home to San Juan. And it reinforced the dream of an ideal wife and mother—to be her or to have her—that many cannot achieve without a miracle.

At the Shrine

Penance is more prominent, or at least more visible, at Difunta Correa's shrine than it is at others in Argentina. Countless pilgrims make the thirty-eight-mile overnight hike from San Juan to Vallecito on foot—or even bare foot—to commemorate Difunta Correa's arduous journey. Others join the pilgrimage en route from Caucete, at twenty-one miles, and often entire families negotiate the distance, weather, and darkness together. These pilgrims follow in Difunta Correa's footsteps, in effect, through the suffering and then on to the miracle.

This sacrifice or "via crucis" (literally "way of the cross") is most prominent during Holy Week. The pilgrims arrive on Good Friday to commemorate the day when Christ carried his cross and was crucified. Some approach the shrine on their knees or crawling on their backs, even without shirts, in order to suffer like their God and their saint. One group on the road advanced in a threesome, the first sweeping the way clear with a broom, the second crawling on his back, and the third holding up a towel to shade the penitent. Similar penance is done daily on the stairway to the hilltop shrine. One young girl climbed the steps in a serpentine shimmy on her back, while balancing her offering—a bottle of water—above her chest. Others hold someone's hand as they climb on their knees, or go it alone and break down with emotion upon arrival, hugging the statue of Difunta Correa.

As in the Mexican devotion to Niño Fidencio, which is also openly penitential, the purpose of such sacrifice is to fulfill a promise made when requesting a miracle (*pagar una manda*) or to make an extraordinary gesture in advance. The sacrifice, like ex votos, is a public announcement of a personal devotional commitment; privacy has yielded to community. Devotees who witness such penance guarantee its validity—the spectacle is dependent upon its audience—and also receive its implicit message. The miracles are so good, the spectacle suggests, that these pains are merely symbolic. One penitent establishes a precedent for the next. If you need something badly enough, give this a try.

Some marvel at the penitents' faith, stamina, and conviction, but others view these sacrifices as inappropriate. Father Baez Laspiur did not approve of them. He regarded crawling on the road or walking up the stairs on one's knees as showy, even hypocritical displays that were no substitute for the more meaningful sacrifice of living a good Christian life. People sin as they please throughout the year, Baez Laspiur commented, then hope to atone with one day of pain rather than mending their ways. Baez Laspiur did not mention that this atonement occurs at Difunta Correa's shrine rather than at church, but that point is also significant. If devotees are settling accounts with God at all, it is only through Difunta Correa. Atonement, or at least the confessional-booth type, might also be beside the point, because this penance occurs within the economy of miracle request and repayment. The penance is less an atonement than a payoff for miracles or an on-account installment for patronage.

In his effort to redirect devotees to an approved devotion, Baez Laspiur propagated the Virgin of Carmen as the preferred alternative to Difunta Correa. The church that was built beside the shrine is consecrated to this Virgin. When I asked Baez Laspiur why the Virgin of Carmen in particular was selected, he explained that she is the patron of the dead (some say of the souls in purgatory). Devotees add that she is also the patron of Vallecito (where the shrine is located), and many make a direct connection between the Virgin of Carmen and Difunta Correa. They relate, for example, that Difunta Correa was wearing an image of this Virgin when she set out on her journey, or that she commended herself to the Virgin of Carmen at the moment of death and consequently her son was saved.

Baez Laspiur situated the Virgin of Carmen church very close to the shrine of Difunta Correa, "who is considered an exemplary wife and mother." The proximity of the church and the shrine is indebted to this similarity— hierarchical to be sure—of the one exemplary mother and the other. The closeness of the physical structures and of the two mothers' identities hopes to suggest the ease with which devotees can switch from the unapproved to the approved devotion. The likeness of Difunta Correa and the Virgin Mary fosters a gradual transition.

Documents published by the shrine similarly intend to channel devotion toward the Virgin. A "Prayer to Difunta Correa" that I found in the shrine's warehouse, in a box of leftovers, begins as its title implies but then streams into the "Hail Mary" with which it concludes. Other Difunta Correa prayers likewise end by hailing Mary. The unauthorized devotion is thus presented as a prelude (in the same way that the shrine precedes the Virgin of Carmen chapel appended to it) that streams seamlessly into the authorized devotion. You begin with one devotion and end with the other. That occurs mostly in theory. For devotees, the two prayers are natural complements that mutually enhance one another. Abandonment of Difunta Correa is hardly on the agenda, so the "Hail Mary" strengthens the folk saint with high-ranking reinforcements.

In *Difunta Correa* magazine (and also in regional news), there was a clearly disproportionate presence of the Virgin of Carmen church, of the Virgin of Carmen herself, and of Catholic (rather than folk saint) events held at the Difunta Correa complex. The magazine offered ample Christian instruction, celebration of regional culture, and profiling of local people, but Difunta Correa's presence was kept to a minimum. The prominence of formal Catholicism in the magazine gave the impression of its prominence at the shrine, but in fact it was—and still is—of secondary or minor importance. Devotees make the pilgrimage to Vallecito to visit Difunta Correa, not the Virgin of Carmen. And they read about the Virgin (or look at the pictures) in *Difunta Correa*, not in a parochial publication.

Overrepresentation intends, again, to urge a transition, but it may ultimately be counterproductive. Baez Laspiur's promotion of the Virgin is open to the interpretation of committed devotees whose conclusions probably precede his arguments. The priest envisions a flow of devotion from Difunta Correa to the Virgin, but devotees are more inclined to the counterflow. Close association with the Virgin is an unbelievable resource for anyone seeking legitimation of a folk saint associated with maternity. And canonization seems all the more likely if the similarity between Difunta Correa and the mother of God is propagated by the Church.

A more specific effort to encourage devotion to the Virgin of Carmen was made by promoting use of her scapular. A brochure on the topic, which was distributed at the shrine, described the meaning and virtues of the scapular, but also clarified that a scapular does not provide magical protection, nor does it release one from responsibility to "the exigencies of Christian life." (The last point, reminiscent of Baez Laspiur's objection to showy penance, perhaps indicates a priority of his catechizing.) This simple brochure thus offers a triple dose of Catholic instruction: Difunta Correa devotees are redirected toward the Virgin of Carmen, are deterred from amuletlike magical use of a Catholic artifact, and are advised that the scapular (like the showy penance) is not a substitute for being a good Catholic. The ambitious intent is to change not only the object but also the manner of devotion.

The spiritual contract, by which devotee and saint are bound to mutual obligations, has developed uniquely at Difunta Correa's shrine. In most other devotions, if not all of them, the terms of the contract are left entirely to one's discretion. Devotees often promise an offering that has a relation in nature or magnitude to the miracle that they are requesting. The greater the miracle, the greater the promise and payback. In Difunta Correa devotion, however, the administration of the Vallecito complex has played an active role in defining the offerings that repay miracles. The practicality of this guidance has contributed to growth of the shrine, but also to growth away from its folk roots.

A 1972 article in the magazine *Difunta Correa* summarized the rules of the game. It is permissible to ask Difunta Correa for miracles and to make promises to thank her, but one may not condition the request—I will give you this only if you give me that—as though it were a trade or bribe. (This nuanced distinction is perhaps unclear to many devotees.) The fulfillment of the promise may entail sacrifice, but not to the degree that one is harmed physically or economically.

Because God and Difunta Correa need nothing, however, the article suggested replacing superfluous gifts and sacrifices with practical offerings, "things that are useful to our poor brothers: clothing, construction materials for the school in Vallecito," and so on. The shrine thus functions as an informal social-service agency. Offerings flow through Difunta Correa to those who need them, and her miracles have a ripple effect—a pay-it-forward effect—because the beneficiaries of miracles in turn help others. Love of one's neighbor is the offering most conducive to miracles, so "Let's promise to love our brothers more and to work toward their happiness."[23]

The Vallecito Cemetery Foundation nevertheless stressed its preference for offerings that support development of the complex. The call is still for donations that are utilitarian rather than symbolic, but they are invested more in the shrine than in the community. One billboard from the 1970s read: "Instead of candles, bring us iron, cement, bricks. Instead of flowers, water! Let's change our promises. Don't be afraid!" The tangible results included a new retail gallery, and ads in *Los Andes* and other San Juan dailies in December 1971 appeared under the banner "Visit Difunta Correa," followed by: "Where the donations of devotees become works of progress."[24]

Offerings today have the yet more practical and urgent purpose of meeting the payroll. As explained by the current administrator, the 2001 law that transferred ownership of the Difunta Correa complex to the government provided no funds for support services. The staff of at least thirty employees is therefore supported entirely by devotee offerings. The governmental administration, like the foundation that preceded it, also encourages practical offerings that help to develop the complex as a tourist destination.

Bottles of water, which pay homage to Difunta Correa's death by thirst, have traditionally been a prominent offering at both the principal and the roadside shrines. Water is particularly significant at the Vallecito complex, which is located on the desert and has no well. The bottles offered by devotees were poured into a cistern and provided the drinking water for visitors and the community. The shrine and the saint have the same need; water is doubly efficacious. The symbolic offering is at once practical, and the collective endeavor to irrigate the shrine of a saint who died of thirst made Vallecito an "oasis of faith."[25]

As the complex grew, and after a failed initiative to construct an aqueduct, the administration began importing water from Caucete. More than five hundred gallons are trucked in daily for the shrine and surrounding community. The urgent need was thereby satisfied, and water-bottle offerings declined accordingly, despite their symbolic value. In 2004, however, the preferred offering came full circle when a drought left the complex in need of—and again requesting—water. Thus, to a certain degree, the tradition of water-bottle offerings is conditioned by the exigencies of circumstances that are less religious than practical.

More than a half million Argentines visit the Difunta Correa complex annually. It is impossible to determine what percentage of these are devotees as opposed to tourists, but in the end the distinction may be academic. The tourists are predominantly Catholics who choose to spend their limited time

Bottles of water offered to Difunta Correa at a shrine near Charata, Chaco Province.

and money at a folk-saint shrine rather than at a Catholic or secular destination. Their tourism facilitates familiarity, and even those who come to the
Difunta Correa complex for recreational purposes, or out of curiosity, are
exposed to a new religious option. They are moved by the passionate devotion,
the peaceful ambience, and the visual evidence of miracles everywhere. Many
of those who come first as tourists return as devotees in times of crisis.

Recreational visits to the shrine are also traditional—which is to say not
only a result of marketing—and in the past were integral to devotion. As
explained in a 1951 report from San Juan province, strong devotion to Difunta
Correa was sometimes expressed by "family picnics" that combined fulfilling
promises with having a good time. Spending the day with the saint can in
itself be a means of giving thanks or maintaining good relations.[26]

People from all walks of life intermix at the Difunta Correa complex. One
sees rich and educated professionals along with simple and impoverished
campesinos, but the overall impression is of middle-class people. Perhaps that
impression owes to the dilution of a lower-class devotional base among bus-
loads of more affluent tourists. Many buses arrive from the nearby city of
Mendoza on outings organized by travel agencies. In recent decades, and
particularly since direction of the shrine was assumed by the government, the
promotion of tourism has been ambitious. The Difunta Correa administration
actively promotes events for Holy Week, Worker's Day, the National Truckers'
Festival, and the patron-saint day of the Virgin of Carmen. An annual event
known as the *Cabalgata de la Fe* (which translates roughly to a horseback
parade or procession for the faith, or of faith) is also hosted by the shrine.

The very roster of these events evidences the interrelation—or one might
say the conglomeration—of Catholicism, tourism, professional conventions,
and folk saint devotion. Holy Week is the most conspicuous example of orthodoxy tested by the pressures of economic interests. The last days of Holy
Week are the most important Catholic holidays in Spanish America, but tens
of thousands of Catholics choose to visit Difunta Correa, not church, on Good
Friday. The administration is sensitive to this delicate issue, but is caught in
the predicament of balancing Catholic tradition against fiscal realities and the
opportunity for profit.

Rhetoric helps to maintain appearances. In a message on the rear cover of
a Holy Week program, the San Juan government noted that the Difunta
Correa administration strives to "channel the people's Faith." It remains
unclear how that is done, but in any case this assertion is contradicted by the
explicit policy and concerted effort to increase attendance at the shrine. A true
effort to channel the people's faith toward Catholicism would require decreasing attendance. In fact, a decrease has occurred on its own, which must be

viewed positively by orthodox Catholicism and negatively by business interests. Holy Week has traditionally attracted the largest crowds, but in recent years the numbers appear to have declined to a fraction of the 100,000 or 200,000 people reported in previous decades.

The official marketing brochure today refers to the Difunta Correa complex in carefully chosen words as a "Sanctuary of Faith," but also as a "Center of Tourist Attraction." Eventually "theme park" may be more appropriate words. Progress in development of the complex has been slowed by a lack of funds since the economic crash of 2001 interrupted the flow of cash offerings from devotees. A newspaper article in 2004 used the headline "Promises, Yes; Donations, No" to indicate that thousands visited the shrine to make or fulfill promises to Difunta Correa, but precious few made cash contributions. The middle-class façade may gradually crack under this strain of economic hardship.

Secular events and folk devotion intermingle when nonreligious gatherings are held at the Difunta Correa complex. The National Truckers' Festival, which since 1992 has been promoted by the private and then government administrations of the shrine, is attended by some fifteen thousand people each year. The event is essentially a professional gathering, but it doubles as a religious fiesta in homage to Difunta Correa as a patron saint of truck drivers. It also offers the opportunity for prayer and expressions of gratitude for another safe year on the road under Difunta Correa's protection. Workers' Day, a national secular holiday, likewise becomes religious when devotees opt to celebrate it at the shrine. They thank Difunta Correa for their continued employment or, in its absence, beseech her help in finding new work.

Attendance at other events may be decreasing, but the Cabalgata de la Fe had a record increase in 2005, with some 2,700 participants. This April event entails a horseback procession from San Juan to Difunta Correa's shrine, followed by a festival of music and dance. It is hosted by the Difunta Correa complex but organized by the San Juan Gaucho Confederation in cooperation with the Argentine Gaucho Federation. The intent of the organizers, which was made explicit in the various welcoming speeches, is to develop a spectacular and high-profile event of interest to tourists nationally. Significant press attention was attracted by the dignitaries who saddled up for the 2005 ride, including the governor and vice governor of San Juan and the Argentine minister of the interior. Difunta Correa tended to fall to the background, however, providing more a folk-culture than a folk-religion context. As the folk saint yields, and as the event moves toward the mainstream in pursuit of audience, the field is cleared for reassertion of the Church. In 2005, for the first time in the Cabalgata's sixteen-year history, a priest ceremoniously blessed the procession before it left San Juan en route to the Difunta Correa complex.

Perhaps Difunta Correa's most outstanding miracle is the transformation of an inhospitable, waterless, practically useless patch of desert into new promise for San Juan's economic development. Who could have imagined that a woman who died of thirst in the middle of nowhere would draw hundreds of thousands of tourists?

Devotion perseveres at the Difunta Correa complex despite the festivals and the tour buses that occasionally overrun it. Even when the gift galleries and picnic tables are full, one can readily discern a core group committed to deep and sincere devotion. This occurs primarily at the complex's principal shrine, which is located at the top of a hill and accessed by two covered stairways. Another primary site of devotion, known as Chapel 1, claims to house Difunta Correa's remains, but devotees nevertheless prefer the hilltop shrine. Excavation decades ago proved that Difunta Correa's remains are not actually located in Chapel 1, but a sign continues to advertise falsely. (Baez Laspiur believes that Difunta Correa was buried in Villa Independencia, which was the closest cemetery to the site of her death.)

The hilltop shrine features a life-size Difunta Correa in the standard iconography, reposed with the infant nursing at her breast. This grotto and an adjacent room are filled with ex votos—primarily photographs—and Catholic images. Devotees wait in line to enter the shrine, then stand deeply moved before the statue. They sign themselves with the cross, pray, and touch the image, particularly at the miraculous breasts, and then move on to make room for others. All sorts of miracles are requested of Difunta Correa, but petitions relating to economic survival have become predominant since devaluation of the peso in 2001.

The hillsides sloping downward from the grotto are covered with small-scale models of the homes and businesses that were acquired through Difunta Correa's intercession. Many of these replicas are elaborate works of craftsmanship. I have never seen this type of ex voto—representations in miniature—as a standardized offering at another folk saint shrine in Argentina, but they are offered at some shrines in Venezuela. The models are also reminiscent of the smaller miniatures used in devotion to a mythological figure, Ekeko (*Iqiqu* in Aymara, "god of abundance"), on the Andean altiplano. During an occasion known as Alacitas, miniature houses, foods, cars, tools, home appliances, and plane tickets, among many other items, are bought and sold. The idea is that the miniature item, combined with the powers of Ekeko, will lead one to acquiring what it represents. A similar use of miniatures occurs

A few of the countless models offered to Difunta Correa in thanks for the homes and businesses acquired through her intercession.

during the Peruvian fiesta for the Lord of Qoyllur Rit'i. In the Andean cases the miniatures anticipate the miracle; at the Difunta Correa shrine they acknowledge it.[27]

Just outside of the grotto is a huge outcropping of rock, blackened with soot, around which innumerable candles burn. A pond of melted wax gradually flows down a channel into a collection vat at the bottom of the hill. Many devotees offer their candles and then linger at the hilltop. They describe the feeling there as one of profound tranquility, using phrases such as "a very special inner peace." Devotees visit Difunta Correa's shrine as though it were a church, as one employee put it, and they find there a churchlike regenerative quietude.

There appears to be little interest in the Virgin of Carmen chapel. It was once used more frequently by devotee families that wished to celebrate their baptisms and weddings there. The Catholic church at the Difunta Correa complex gave them a legitimate means to extend their folk devotion into the sacraments. Difunta Correa was the draw; the church provided the priest and the rituals. This is no longer permitted—only local parishioners may use the church for such purposes—so the church's uses today are limited to Sunday mass and the blessing of cars afterward.

Another backflow in the channeling of devotion toward orthodoxy is suggested by the twenty-some plaques that are affixed to the pews in the Virgin of Carmen church. These thank Difunta Correa for miracles, not the Virgin or canonized saints. When I expressed my surprise to Baez Laspiur, he replied only that he had no problem with Difunta Correa plaques in the church. The devotees who made this choice—to post their thanks to Difunta Correa in the Catholic church rather than at the adjacent folk saint shrine—seem to challenge their preference for the church with the very act by which they express it. Perhaps their intent is to bring Difunta Correa inside the church, where they believe she rightfully belongs. The most probable explanation is the simplest one: the plaques in the chapel seemed a good idea to devotees who are not particularly interested in the distinction between canonized and uncanonized saints. They value both their Catholicism and their folk devotion, and opportunities to integrate one with the other are always welcome.

The stark emptiness of the church, with bare stone walls and only a single small statue (of the Virgin of Carmen), stands in striking contrast to the overabundance of images, statues, photos, plaques, and stuff of all sorts in the several chapels to Difunta Correa. This contrast provides a visual testament to institutional control, design, and reserve as opposed to the freedom of folk devotion's chaotic improvisation. The relation of scarcity to abundance also holds true for visitors. Though the grounds are full and a steady flow of devotees visit Difunta Correa, the Catholic church remains virtually empty.

Niño Fidencio

Niño Fidencio began to acquire a reputation in the 1920s for his remarkable ability to heal the sick and injured. In 1927 he had a vision, during which Jesus Christ called him to the sacred service of relieving suffering. As the miracles grew and the word spread, thousands of pilgrims journeyed to Espinazo to be healed by Fidencio. Even the president of Mexico visited him, and the pope sent Fidencio a commendation in recognition of his outstanding service. Doctors and priests were jealous, however, because Fidencio's successes were their failures. In 1938, when Fidencio was almost forty, he went into a three-day trance during which his body seemed lifeless. Doctors eager to be rid of Fidencio declared him dead and slit his throat under the pretext of doing an autopsy. Fidencio prophesied that his spirit would be channeled after his death, and today his mission continues through mediums.

José Fidencio Síntora Constantino, known as Niño Fidencio, was born in the village of Iramuco, in the state of Guanajuato, Mexico, in 1898. Tradition holds that his family was large and poor; that as a young boy he worked for a couple of years on a plantation in the Yucatan; and that subsequently, after return to Guanajuato, he served as an altar boy in the local church. Fidencio also worked as a kitchen helper for a wealthier local family, the López de la Fuentes. He had befriended one of the family's sons, Enrique, as a schoolboy, and this lasting relationship would be decisive in his later life.

Fidencio was always somewhat unusual, even odd, and it is said that Enrique López de la Fuente defended him when he was ridiculed and tormented by other boys. This protective relationship evolved into one that was decidedly paternal—Fidencio eventually called López de la Fuente *papá* (Dad)—even though López de la Fuente was only about two years older than Fidencio. The whereabouts of the two are unclear for a period of years, but it appears that when López de la Fuente left Guanajuato, he may have taken Fidencio with him or called for him later. It is certain, in any case, that the two were together in the village of Espinazo, in the state of Nuevo León, in the early 1920s. López de la Fuente had found work there as the administrator of a huge hacienda owned by a German, Teodoro Von Wernich. It was in Espinazo that Niño Fidencio established his fame as a curandero, and he remained there until his death in 1938.[1]

Niño Fidencio was preceded by other curanderos in the region, but none of these rival his stature as a folk saint. Pedro Rojas (known as Tatita) was popular in the 1860s, as was Teresa Urrea (known as the Saint or Niña of Cabora) twenty-five years later. Also in northeastern Mexico, in Nuevo León, was Niño Juanito, who attracted multitudes between 1911 and 1914 (when he was three to six years old) because his saliva and urine effected cures. Don Pedrito Jaramillo was a Mexican curandero who migrated to south Texas— near what is now Falfurrias in Brooks County—around 1881 and died there in 1907. His mission, like Fidencio's, continues from heaven today, sometimes through mediums who channel his spirit.[2]

The Mexican Revolution (1910–1920) and its aftermath provided the context for the emergence and success of Niño Fidencio's work in Espinazo. Some say that López de la Fuente fought in the troops of Pancho Villa from 1913 to 1916, that he met Von Wernich during the war, and that Von Wernich was a friend of the revolutionary Francisco Madero. What is certain is that years of death, destruction, chaos, danger, and dislocation resulted in extreme poverty and in massive migration. Hundreds of thousands of Mexicans fled to the United States with the hope of finding social and economic stability. Those who remained at home suffered great privations and sought relief wherever they could find it. This context of crisis, instability, and necessity was ideal for the reception of Niño Fidencio, both as a curandero and as a messianic figure.

The conflict shifted to a political and, ultimately, armed struggle between the Catholic Church and the Mexican government for the ten years following the revolution. The constitution of 1917 substantially curtailed the power and privileges of the Church. Secular education was mandated, the rights of the clergy were severely restricted, Church property was nationalized, and the clergy was forbidden to criticize the government in any manner. Plutarco Elías Calles, president from 1924 to 1928, enforced these provisions with a vengeance. The "Calles Law," as 1926 anticlerical legislation came to be known, advanced the government's anti-Catholic agenda and specified rigorous punishments for violation of the constitutional provisions. In retaliation, clergymen

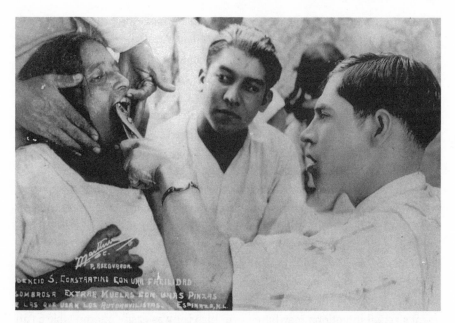

Niño Fidencio's faith healing and folk remedies were complemented by informal surgeries, such as the tooth extraction depicted in this historical photograph.

released that faith, catalyzed it, put it to work. Religious beliefs combined with Fidencio's folk-medical professionalism to make a comprehensive positive impression, spiritual and material, that predisposed patients to heal.

Fidencio was aware of his resemblance—his imitation—of Christ but was always clear on hierarchy: he was Christ's servant and no more. Much of what Fidencio did and said were nevertheless conducive to his followers' belief that God was in some sense among them. It was believed that Fidencio stole away to the Cerro de la Campana in the early morning hours to converse with Christ and the Virgin. He was fond of posing for photographic portraits; one shows him carrying a cross. The image known as the "El Niño Guadalupano," in which Fidencio fuses with the iconography of the Virgin of Guadalupe and of the Sacred Heart, is based on another photograph for which Fidencio posed. Imaginations were also stirred by Fidencio's annual performance as Christ during Holy Week reenactments of the Passion. Fidencio eventually became known as "the Christ of Espinazo," and many devotees, even today, believe that he was a reincarnation of Jesus Christ.

Tradition holds that Fidencio healed Von Wernich of a bullet wound, a fistula, or some lifelong ailment (the accounts vary), after which Von Wernich vowed to announce Fidencio's special powers to the world. Von Wernich used his political connections to make a public-relations contribution to Niño Fidencio's career, including at least one newspaper announcement. Press exposure generally was decisive in solidifying Fidencio's reputation. He freely gave interviews, encouraged photographs, and generally healed in public view before crowds of marveled witnesses.[4]

Regional fame as a curandero was transformed into national fame as a miracle worker by several news articles published in Mexico City in 1928 and 1929. The articles described miracles (the blind see, the lame walk), lauded Fidencio as a saintly man selflessly dedicated to healing, and reported that a shantytown housing thousands of health-seeking pilgrims had grown around Espinazo. The spectacle of healing and its sensational media representation redoubled Fidencio's visibility and credibility, which in turn increased the crowds converging upon Espinazo.

Fidencio received an unimaginable boost in February 1928, when he was paid a visit by Plutarco Elías Calles, the president of Mexico. The event was particularly significant given Calles's anti-Catholic politics. Whatever the president's actual intentions may have been, his visit was easily interpretable as an endorsement of Fidencio's folk religion—or at least folk-religious healing—as an alternative to the institutional Catholicism that the Calles Law sought to curtail. The post-1926 religious vacuum made room for Fidencio as a genuine, saintlike miracle worker who had no political or economic ambitions, no counterclaim to power, and no opposition to the Calles government.

Espinazo was on an active railroad line at the time, and Calles's presidential train made a stop while passing through on a political tour. The president was accompanied by other politicians, including the governor of Nuevo León and the mayor of nearby Mina. According to tradition, Fidencio treated Calles for a skin ailment by covering his body in honey and then swathing it with bandage or cloth. Fidencio, busy with other patients in the interim, apparently forgot about the president and had to be reminded to complete the treatment. Calles is said to have been dressed in one of Fidencio's white tunics, waiting patiently, but photographs were prohibited. Fidencio's popularity soared after the presidential visit, and by March 1928 there were some thirty thousand people camped out in Espinazo.[5]

Niño Fidencio's success thus resulted from the combination of multiple factors: a postwar context of instability and need; a spiritual vacuum created by Calles's anti-Catholic legislation and the Church's strike in response; Fidencio's talents as a healer, enhanced by saintlike asceticism and selfless dedication; the spiritist doctrine introduced by Von Wernich; the mystical experience that solidified Fidencio's conviction to his calling; the extensive press coverage and consequent national visibility; and the lucky strike of the president's visit, which redoubled Fidencio's prestige and fostered the impression of authenticity. By 1930 the media blitz was over and most of the shantytown residents had moved on, but newcomers continued to arrive in a steady flow. Fidencio's national fame as a healer, which was firmly established in 1928, continued until his death ten years later.

Visibility had a downside, however, insofar as it attracted the attention of potential enemies. A newspaper noted in February 1928, when Niño Fidencio's health services were booming, that drugstores and medical doctors in northern Mexico were suffering the financial consequences of displacement of the sick to Espinazo. A year later, on February 18, 1929, the state of Nuevo León initiated legal proceedings against Niño Fidencio for the illegal practice of medicine. For the remainder of his life he was almost constantly under attack by officials of public health and medicine, and he was arrested twice. The Church also became more aggressively opposed to Fidencio during the last years of his life.[6]

Most often, however, Fidencio was simply dismissed by his adversaries. A medical doctor who conducted an incognito fact-finding visit to Espinazo in 1930 concluded that Fidencio "suffers without knowing it from a mental illness that consists of believing he is enlightened and responsible for alleviating the pain of those who suffer." Had Niño Fidencio profited from his healing, the consequences might have been different. The honesty and selflessness with which he tended to his mission (though others around him may have profited) made him a less viable target. Unless their interests were directly threatened, critics could simply disregard Fidencio as a harmless oddball exalted by credulous masses. Other curanderos who emerged in Fidencio's wake fared differently. Two who healed in Torreón, apparently not for free, were hauled off to prison as "swindlers who exploit poor people."[7]

The Catholic Church's objection came not from Fidencio's incursions into unauthorized medicine, but rather from trespass on clerical privilege. There was no church or priest in Espinazo, and Fidencio happily filled the void by administering baptism, confirmation, confession, communion, marriage, and last rites. According to his brother, Fidencio preached that "any of you can baptize a child as long as you do it in the name of God." (Teresa Urrea also preached that priests were not needed for such sacraments as baptism and marriage.) In 1936, the archbishop of Monterrey sent a delegation to Espinazo to request that Fidencio stop administering the sacraments. Fidencio apparently agreed, but then continued business more or less as usual.[8]

The version of this visit that is related by devotees is characteristic in its counterclaim to religious prerogative, and in its implication that the Church has been superseded by folk saints who are sent by God directly to his people.

A priest was dispatched to Espinazo to investigate, devotees relate, and Fidencio openly admitted that he performed the sacraments. When the priest asked by what authority, Fidencio pressed softened candle wax to the roof of his mouth, waited until it hardened, and gave it to the priest, saying, "On His authority." The crucified Christ was molded in the wax. Devotees similarly relate that after Fidencio's death the image of Christ was found inside his chest, and that the Virgin of Guadalupe was stamped into his heart. It is also commonly believed that the pope sent a letter of commendation to Fidencio in recognition of the holy work done in Espinazo.

Other stories circulate concerning the opposition and—at times—hostility of doctors toward Fidencio. The most explicit allege assassination. As patients were flocking to Espinazo rather than to medical clinics, envious doctors sent assassins to eliminate the competition. The plans were foiled supernaturally, however, because the clairvoyant Fidencio foresaw the danger, or the guns were aimed but would not fire, or the ingested poison had no effect. The murderous doctors are ultimately successful, however, at least in the most widely circulated of these assassination legends, and some versions implicate López de la Fuente (or his wife) as an accomplice.

The belief that Fidencio was murdered by medical professionals is derived largely from a historical photograph of Fidencio's corpse. Two people in surgical masks appear to be opening Fidencio's throat, probably for an embalming procedure. Devotees argue that Fidencio was not yet dead, or entirely so, when this occurred. Some say that he was in a three-day trance—either to recharge his powers or to spiritually visit distant patients in need of his care—and others say that he had died but was planning to resurrect on the third day. López de la Fuente (or in some versions his wife) hastily ordered the embalmment, and the doctors eagerly complied. Warm, fresh blood—that of a living person—squirted out of the wound when Fidencio's throat was slit. Fidencio thus died under the knife of envious doctors who took advantage of his vulnerability during a spiritist absence. Formal medicine returned with a vengeance to eliminate the folk alternative that had challenged it.

The themes of spiritism are prominent in a version of the death related by Alberto, who channels Niño Fidencio in Edinburg, Texas. Fidencio never left Espinazo physically but on occasion traveled spiritually—that is why he was seen in several places during his lifetime. His body seemed dead during the deep trances necessary for spiritual flight, but he was nevertheless quite alive. On one occasion Fidencio informed Consuelo Villareal (the wife of López de la Fuente, and thus Fidencio's foster mother) that his spirit would travel for three days. Consuelo should not be concerned by his lifeless body, he said, because his spirit would reinhabit it upon return.

When Consuelo discovered what appeared to be a corpse, however, she disregarded Fidencio's forewarning and called for doctors. They confirmed that Fidencio was dead, perhaps because they were happy to get rid of him. Fidencio's throat was slit to drain the body fluids, at which time his startled eyes opened wide as he turned toward Consuelo, saying, "Mama, what are you doing? Didn't I tell you not to do anything?" Fidencio added that he had not yet completed him mission, then closed his eyes and died. The precious spilled blood was collected as a relic by devotees, and the doctors who slit Fidencio's throat died shortly after.

The exact medical cause of death is unknown, although Alberto's observation that Fidencio "worked himself to death" probably holds a measure of truth. Fidencio worked tirelessly, sometimes two or three days at a time without sleep, and was probably undernourished as well. An illness (many say pernicious anemia) began to debilitate him in 1935, and he is clearly bloated in photographs from the last years. Some devotees relate that what appears to be bloat caused by disease is actually a swelling with the Holy Spirit. Fidencio died on October 19, 1938, shortly before his fortieth birthday. After the embalmment it was too late for resurrection of the body, but Fidencio vowed to continue his interrupted mission in spirit.

Channeling

Spiritist beliefs were as essential to Niño Fidencio's life as they were to his death. The mystical experience under the pepper tree empowered Fidencio; he was recharged and guided by communication with Christ, the Virgin, and other spirits; and Fidencio's healing miracles themselves were manifestations of the spirit of Christ working through him. The presence of God during healing was symbolically suggested by Fidencio's use of a hand—the form of a hand—that he found in a mesquite tree. He called it the *Mano poderosa* (Powerful Hand), saying that it was the hand of God. The spiritist implications are multiple because the Powerful Hand, a religious image of great popularity in Mexico, has saints (Joseph, the Virgin, and her parents) positioned, like puppets, on the fingertips, with the infant Christ on the thumb. The hand also reveals a nail wound from the Crucifixion. When Fidencio's own hands bring this Powerful Hand down upon his ailing patients, they are jolted by a potent composite of otherworldly forces. In this perspective, Niño Fidencio—who will later be channeled by others—was himself a channel of otherworldly powers that flowed through him and into his patients. He was, as he often explained, God's instrument.

The belief that Fidencio left his body and flew off to cure distant others (sometimes sailors at sea) is likewise essentially spiritist. Today, now as a postmortem spirit, Fidencio continues these visits from heaven. Sick and injured people report surprise appearance by Fidencio in their homes and hospital rooms—even during surgery—and are cured miraculously by his presence or touch. Some were unfamiliar with Fidencio, and when later they discover the identity of their savior they become devotees for life.

One woman, suffering from complications after heart-valve surgery, found herself repeatedly on the brink of death. She had to be readmitted to the hospital every few months until finally, she reported, "Niño Fidencio operated on me and removed the valve and now I live normally without suffering." Countless others relate that Fidencio communicates with them in dreams, visions, and voices, sometimes as a doctor, in order to reveal or administer the necessary remedy.[9]

Toward the end of his life Fidencio advised his trusted followers that after death he would continue to heal through mediums. He dictated revelations to guide those who would continue the mission in his name, and other mandates were later revealed through a medium in Espinazo. One of Fidencio's concerns as death approached was that impostors might compete with authentic mediums, "because only a special few will truly deliver my message." His brother added that Fidencio frequently remarked, "After my death there will be many Niño Fidencios, but remember that there is only one." The one Fidencio would be channeled by many mediums, but they would be his instruments, not his replacements, and only a few would be genuine.[10]

During channeling, as explained by a prominent devotee, "it is not the person who talks, acts, or heals, but rather it is Fidencio's spirit that in those moments takes over the medium's body to effect cures." This is suggested by the words used for a medium in Fidencio devotion—*cajita* (literally "little box") and *materia* (literally "matter"). Both terms imply a containing or embodying of a spirit and power not their own. Mediums, like mystics, empty themselves, disappear to themselves, and are filled with supernatural presence. God's miraculous power transfers to Fidencio's spirit, which inhabits the possessed mediums. The spirit can be channeled, even simultaneously, by many mediums, but it is always inherent to one and the same Fidencio. Devotees explain that conversations begun with Fidencio through one medium can later be picked up where they left off through another.[11]

Fidencio's spirit began communicating to and through mediums about two years before his death. Some say that seven of Fidencio's close associates were mediums during his lifetime, but the two most mentioned are Damiana Martínez and Víctor Zapata. Following Fidencio's death Zapata became the

A medium and devotee at Niño Fidencio's shrine in Espinazo.

revisador, meaning the one who evaluated mediums to assure their authenticity and their conformance to Fidencio's mandates. The revelations that had been dictated by Fidencio, which were transcribed and are known today as the *escrituras* (writings), served as the criteria for Zapata's assessments of authenticity and propriety. After Zapata's death the oversight of mediums was assumed by his daughter, known as Panita (and also as Ciprianita).[12]

This monitoring of emerging Fidencio channels, although well intentioned, carried the potential for dissent and division. It established a self-appointed (or Fidencio-appointed) elite with the power to ostracize others. It was based on criteria, some acquired through unsubstantiated revelation, that had not been collectively ratified by those who were being judged, and that in any case were open to interpretation. And it was at odds with the freedom of folk devotion, which generally resists imposed dogma and, when it cannot, customizes it to individual advantage.

This potential for divisiveness, along with multiple other causes, including personalities, resulted in a rift and rival factions. On the one side stands Panita, who through her father's closeness to Fidencio, his early channeling of Fidencio's spirit, and his doctrinal basis in Fidencio's revelations inherited a spiritual claim to authenticity and prevalence. On the other side is Fabiola, of the López de la Fuente family. Her father was Fidencio's foster father, which afforded her a familial claim. Because both factions are verified by the channeled spirit of Fidencio, both can claim authenticity with no measure of falsity other than the adversary's counterclaim. Fidencio, like the bible, can be used to support any side of a dispute. When the authorization comes through a channeled spirit, the medium and the message can intermingle.

The divide got wider when Fabiola and her now-deceased husband, Heliodoro, formalized their faction into a church. The Iglesia Fidencista Cristiana (Fidencist Christian Church) was recognized by the Mexican government in June 1993. Normalization of spiritist practices began much earlier, with the couple's founding of the Center for Fidencist Cultural and Spiritual Studies in March 1978. These institution-oriented contenders in effect out-dogmatized the dogmatists by codifying spiritism and making specific demands on devotees, including required authorization and training to become a medium. The church was established precisely to control Fidencio devotion and channeling, with the goal of preventing such abuses of the faith as fanaticism, fraud, and profiteering. Those who initiated and adhere to this branch of Fidencio devotion seek to establish their primacy. The church aspires to a monopoly on all mediums' claims to legitimacy.[13]

In the simple view, then, the road forked, with one branch taking an institutional turn and the other remaining closer to its roots in folk devotion. That neat arrangement is complicated by subsequent rival factions (including an important one in Texas), subdivisions within groups, a potential power vacuum as the elderly leading figures pass away, and the fact that devotees are less interested in who owns Fidencio's legacy than in visiting their medium and getting well. One might as well refer to a thousand factions of independent groups (known as missions) that form around mediums and go about their business without formal accountability to anyone.

When I met with Alberto, a medium in Texas, my ignorance of spiritist cults was almost absolute. The South American devotions that I had studied did not involve the channeling of spirits, and I had only a vague knowledge of the practice. When people talk to Niño Fidencio, Alberto explained, "they have a conversation the way you and I are having a conversation right now." I was still thinking through that when he asked, "Do you want to meet him?" The "meet," in particular, caught my attention, because the "him," Fidencio, had been dead since 1938.

What would I say to someone dead? We entered Alberto's ritual space through a small door with *Consultorio Espiritual del Niño Fidencio* (Spiritual Office of Niño Fidencio) hand-painted in blue letters. The business hours followed: 10:00 a.m. to 5:00 p.m., seven days a week. The room was filled with religious imagery, a giant powwow drum, and the coolness, rattle, and groan of an old air conditioner. Alberto covered his clothes with a white tunic and sat beside one of those images of Jesus that seems to follow you with its eyes. I was settling into the idea of talking with a spirit when Alberto began breathing deeply, then yawning, and told me that Fidencio was on his way. There was a sense of urgency for us to finish whatever we were saying because Alberto's conscious presence would soon be displaced by Fidencio's spirit. A moment later Alberto's face, body posture, and movements changed, and he began speaking in a high voice. Niño Fidencio entered with a litany of otherworldly blessings, and when he paused I introduced myself. I figured that Fidencio was probably not interested in the details of my career or had otherworldly access to that information, so I spared him my résumé and kept the introduction brief. We had a good exchange for about fifteen minutes—mostly my questions followed by his answers—and at the end I asked Fidencio what was most important to include in my book.

"The light of Our Lord God," he replied. Fidencio then clarified that my work should benefit my fellow humans and bring the blessing of God upon them. That is what was most important: to spread the grace of God for the

Alberto channeling the spirit of Niño Fidencio in Edinburg, Texas.

benefit of humanity. I was too shocked at the time to be amazed, but I later realized the perfection of this answer. Fidencio also asked what other saints were included in the book, but he didn't seem to know any of them in heaven. He said that he admired me for taking on this important project, wished me good luck, gave me his blessing, and then took his leave praying the "Our Father."

Albert came back to himself and placed a towel over his head as he recovered from the intensity of the experience. Mediums have no memory of what occurs during channeling, so in response to Alberto's questions I recounted the conversation that I had with Fidencio. Alberto describes channeling as a wonderful feeling but also as draining, particularly when one channels for long periods. His services are in relatively high demand—he sometimes sees a hundred people per week—and he ends the day exhausted after channeling for hours.

Some visit Alberto specifically as a channel to Niño Fidencio, but others come because Alberto is a curandero in his own right. As a curandero he heals, advises, and consoles without channeling Fidencio's spirit. This is done through prayer, counseling, spiritual cleansings, massage, and traditional medicine, much the same as Fidencio had done in Espinazo. Many visits to Alberto concern the healing of body and mind, but others run the gamut of human problems. Alberto regards some issues—like jealous anxiety that a boyfriend or girlfriend may be cheating—unworthy of otherworldly involvement: "I'm not going to bother the spirit of Niño for something unimportant."

Niño Fidencio is one of many spirits who are channeled in the border region. Others include Don Pedrito Jaramillo, Pancho Villa, Indian spirits of various origins (including the last Aztec emperor, Cuauhtémoc), and Niña Aurora. In borderland spiritism, as in the spiritist cults of Venezuela, new spirits are continually integrated into the repertoire of options. Channeling implies a vertical chain of communication—with God at the top and the miracle-seeking devotee at the bottom—and even the spirits themselves are often arranged hierarchically. Miraculous power originates with God, is brokered in heaven by a saint-spirit, and then channels down through a medium to the devotee in need. There are thus two intermediaries situated between the devotee and God, one on earth (the medium) and one in heaven (the folk saint). Once possessed, the medium loses his or her own personality traits and assumes those of the spirit being channeled.

Niño Fidencio mediums are overtaken by his boyish voice and, sometimes, by the playful behavior that was characteristic during his lifetime. Fidencio's childlike disposition, lack of facial hair, and unchanged voice all gave the impression of a prepubescent: "He lives like a child, he talks like a child," explained a 1928 newspaper article. The work-oriented side of Fidencio was complemented by a theatrical, even histrionic, inclination. He loved to pose, dress up in costumes, act in theater, sing melodramatically, and imitate others in caricature. Another dimension of his childlike demeanor was expressed in his dependence on López de la Fuente, who provided a kind of parental supervision.[14]

Fidencio is also reputed to have had underdeveloped genitals, like those of a prepubescent boy. He always maintained that he was a "virgin like Christ," and he believed that loss of virginity would result in the loss of his healing powers. The boyish asexuality could also tend toward a bending of gender roles. Fidencio had effeminate gestures and manners; chose to use his mother's surname (rather than the father's, which is the custom in Spanish America); sang in a falsetto female voice; and sometimes disguised himself as a woman to flee incognito for rest and reprieve. He also tended toward social roles and employments more typical of women at the time, such as cooking, cleaning, washing clothes, caring for children, and delivering babies. Some of the children for whom Fidencio cared called him *mamá* (mom) without his objection and perhaps at his encouragement.[15]

Any affronts to machismo or suspicions of homosexuality must be pardoned or dismissed to maintain the type of dignity that is conducive to sainthood. Once that is done, however, Fidencio's atypical masculinity made him a natural for the title "niño," which literally means "boy" but implies a saintly person of childlike purity. Though others have to earn this title, God sent Fidencio to the world as a niño forever, in body and soul. The person, physically and psychologically, was congruent with the mission, and the boyishness channels through to the medium. Fidencio's unmanliness, virginity, and even underdeveloped genitalia are all interpretable as evidence of his inherent saintliness. Oddity can be the most important attribute of those who work miracles against the odds.

Other channeled spirits likewise manifest themselves as they were in life, even in their flaws and limitations. Visits with Niño Fidencio must be in Spanish (sometimes through interpreters) because he does not speak other languages. Niño Perdido does not speak at all—he went to eternity before he learned how to talk so the mediums who channel him make prearticulate noises. Those who are possessed by Niña Aurora, who also died young, are overtaken by a childlike silliness. Pancho Villa's mediums talk in the crude manner of a soldier and, because Villa had the reputation of being a womanizer, they tend to grope the women in the room, even when the mediums themselves are female. When Pancho Villa came in spirit to his birthday party near San Luis Potosí in Mexico, the national anthem was sung, the people in attendance—primarily women—began marching in place, roll call was taken, and then the gathering proceeded with its business of miraculous cures.[16]

In the Venezuelan spirit cults, similarly, the behavior of the possessed medium conforms to stereotyped characteristics. Those possessed by Indian warriors act "very macho," drinking aguardiente, smoking cigars, and wailing in loud voices. They also dress for the part in "Indian" costumes—feather headdresses, bows and arrows—which are derived not from indigenous Venezuelans but rather from reruns of American Westerns. A medium privileged to be possessed by María Lionza herself, who is at the summit of this spirit hierarchy, exhibits the grace of a princess: "She speaks in a sweet voice and behaves like a refined lady."[17]

The assumption of a channeled spirit's identity was particularly significant in another experience that I had at the home of Alberto and his wife, Lydia, in Texas. Lydia channels spirits different from those that are channeled by Alberto, among them Niño Perdido. I had just visited Niño Perdido's shrine in La Coste (in Medina County, Texas), so Lydia graciously offered to channel Niño Perdido so I could meet him. Alberto prayed a rhythmic litany, then picked up what was at hand—the remote control to the television—and banged the wall three times to call the spirits. Lydia fell into a trance and began gesturing, then making prearticulate sounds in a high-pitched voice. Because Niño Perdido cannot communicate with words, Alberto asked him, through Lydia, to get Niño Jesús de Praga (an advocation of the Christ child) to serve as an interpreter.

I thus conversed with Niño Perdido through Lydia and, in turn, through Niño Jesús de Praga, who mediated. Lydia's voice, demeanor, and discourse changed depending upon which of the spirits she was channeling. The channel switched as the occasion warranted between Niño Perdido and Niño Jesús de Praga.

Alberto had learned the unknown story of Niño Perdido during previous conversations, through Lydia, with Niño Jesús de Praga, who had found Niño Perdido's dead body under a tree in Mexico. He explained to Alberto how it got there.

Long ago, a man and his wife lived in a remote mountainous region. The man drank heavily, neglected his infant child, and abused his wife. One day he came home drunk and beat his wife nearly to death. He left her on the floor, bleeding, and she eventually died. The baby crawled out of the house, then fell off the porch, rolled down the hill, and landed under a large tree. The baby was weakened by crying, hunger, and the cold nights. He finally died. God sent Niño Jesús de Praga to retrieve his spirit, and the two boys have been together ever since.

When Alberto asked if Niño Perdido was a patron saint, the response was affirmative: he is the patron of soldiers and their families. "When people pray for their family members off to war," Alberto explained, "they hear the voice of a child, the voice of a child crying." That's Niño Perdido, he continued, who protects soldiers. "It is ironic that a baby would be the patron saint of such an enormous mission."

An ensemble of supporting factors contributes to the success of mediums and curanderos. Ambience, ritual, attire, gestures, voice, imagery, and demeanor all send signals that enhance the probability of cure. Miracles are predisposed by the white tunics and priestly robes; the otherworldly inflections; the holy lands and sacred places filled with saints, candlelight, and offerings attesting to previous miracles; and the gravity, confidence, conviction, knowledge, and dedication that good mediums convey. Rituals and prayer add structure, rhythm, familiarity, otherworldly discourse, and hypnotic repetition that are conducive to supernatural experiences. Eyes communicate emotions, gesturing hands send religious signals, and the mysterious absence of mediums to themselves verifies the presence of channeled spirits.

Alberto once grasped my head with both of his strong, warm, heavy hands. One, cupped on my forehead, pressed backward while the other, grasping the back of my neck, pulled forward. The sensation was one of being enveloped within a power that those hands released but did not own. One can imagine how much more powerful that experience is for believers who deliver themselves to the care of mediums—of Fidencio—with absolute faith in the healing force flowing into their bodies. What happens when the faith in those hands comes into contact with the hands themselves?

A curandero's reputation also makes a substantial contribution to the faith of the patient and, consequently, to the success of the cure. In this regard Niño Fidencio is reminiscent of high-profile curanderos elsewhere in Spanish America. Pancho Sierra (1831–1891), a wealthy rancher in the Buenos Aires province of Argentina, was a charitable, patriarchal figure for the many poor families who lived in the vicinity of his El Porvenir ranch. Photographs from the period depict him in the image of a prophet, with a long white beard and a sagelike demeanor consonant with his fame as a spiritist and curandero. Multitudes seeking well-being flocked to his ranch in the same way that they had to Espinazo for Niño Fidencio. He became known as the *médico del agua fría*, meaning the curandero who uses cold water, because his patients were healed by drinking water saturated with the power of spirits. Pancho Sierra, like Fidencio, was clairvoyant: he knew patients' maladies before being told and could see through lies and deceptions. Again like Fidencio, he was accused of practicing medicine without a license, was followed by many authentic and fraudulent imitators, and after death was channeled by mediums who continued to heal with his powers.

One of Pancho Sierra's patients, a wealthy woman named María Salomé Loredo y Otaola, became a nationally famous curandera known as Madre María. In 1881 she had become gravely ill and doctors were unable to help her. Madre María visited Pancho Sierra "without faith and without hope." The unexpected cure changed her life forever. After her second husband's death she moved to Buenos Aires and dedicated herself to charity. She became known as "the lady of the black cloak," owing to the outfit in which she circulated among the poor to give away her wealth. From these humble beginnings, Madre María became famous as a healer and her mission grew, like Fidencio's, into the eventual formation of a state-recognized church. Her followers believe that Madre María "has formed a new religion, more modern, more healthy, and easier to understand and practice" than Catholicism, but nevertheless "based on the Doctrine of Jesus Christ."[18]

Spiritist beliefs and practices are also similar in the devotions of Madre María and Niño Fidencio. Some believe that the spirit of Pancho Sierra worked through Madre María in the same way that Fidencio possessed his early followers. Her own preaching on reincarnation described earth as hell populated by a circulation of spirits returning for tours of duty until their perfection and purification earn heaven. Madre María is closer to Fidencio by virtue of her inner circle of followers (in this case referred to as "apostles"), her writing of guiding doctrine at the end of her life (which included the apocalyptic prophesy that the world would end in 2000), and her problems with the law concerning the practice of medicine without a license. She died in October 1928 and today remains, like Fidencio, the spiritual guide of devotees.

Crises and near-death or rebirth experiences are often decisive in the formation of curanderos. Niño Fidencio was in a state of breakdown when he had his vision; Madre María's life was transformed after she was saved from a fatal illness; Don Pedrito Jaramillo got his calling after burying his nose in mud for three days to alleviate pain; and Teresa Urrea emerged from a thirteen-day cataleptic state with the power to heal miraculously. People attending Teresa's wake were startled when she sat up among the candles. The reborn Teresa then began her career as a curandera, tending primarily to poor Indians, and thousands flocked to Cabora seeking her care.[19]

In Argentina, similarly, at the far reaches of Corrientes Province in a place called Itatí Rincón, there lived a girl who came to be known as "Juanita, the Savior of the World." After suffering a seizure at age sixteen, Juanita was thought to be dead. Her body was shrouded and laid out on a table for the wake, but then suddenly Juanita sat up and said, "Don't cry, mom—I've resurrected because God has sent me to save the world."

Juanita then dressed like a virgin, acted like a saint, fasted, and was attended by two female sacristans. Pilgrims made the journey to see her, offering money and jewels. Devotees wore on their arms, around their necks, or over their hearts a long band boasting, "Juanita, the Savior of the World." Devotion was strongest during Holy Week. Juanita's face was covered on Holy Thursday and then, after she suffered Christ's Passion in her own flesh, her face was dramatically revealed on Holy Saturday. Juanita also made excursions on a horse carriage, surrounded by flowers and followed by a procession of devotees, as she ventured out to heal the sick and the wounded.

The salvation of the world was interrupted by the police. Juanita was arrested, ordered to stop pretending to be a saint, and forced to break her fast by eating "a good bowl of stew." The police also obliged her to stop dressing like a virgin, "because she wasn't one." Juanita eventually died of tuberculosis, at the age of twenty-five. Her devotees, like Fidencio's, anticipated her resurrection, leaving a hole in the grave so she could climb out. When she stayed in the grave instead, however, the devotion died along with her.[20]

A historical photograph of Juanita, the Savior of the World. Her covered face was revealed on Holy Saturday.

At the Shrine

Niño Fidencio's presence is everywhere in Espinazo. One sees him in the faces and gestures of the mediums channeling his spirit; in the photographs, prayer cards, and framed images that fill sales booths lining the streets; in the huge statues near his tomb; on the standards that identify groups of pilgrims; and in the pennants that flutter overhead throughout the town. Fidencio is the topic of conversation, the image on the T-shirt, the mural on the wall, and the reason for being there. Song lyrics pay homage to his wonderworking through scratchy loudspeakers nailed to the power poles. And when a homily is given by a leading figure, such as Panita, Niño Fidencio speaks through her mouth.

Devotees arrive in organized groups, known as missions, that are led by a medium. In general, a mission forms around a local medium who channels Fidencio, and then this group makes the pilgrimage together to Espinazo. The journey begins at any of the hundreds of Fidencio shrines (known as *tronos*, literally "thrones") in Mexico or the United States, particularly in the border region. Most pilgrimages coincide with the biannual Fidencio fiestas in March and October. The March fiesta celebrates the saint's day of Fidencio's namesake, St. Joseph (March 19), and the October fiesta encompasses the dates of Fidencio's birth (October 17) and death (October 19). Each independent mission has its own manner of organization, dress, and public presentation. The styles range from simple and humble to quite elaborate. Colorful shawls, scarves, and hats are common, as are white dresses and robes. Homage is also paid to Niño Fidencio by troupes that perform *matachines* (a traditional dance, with accompanying drums) in neoindigenous costume, and by *cabalgatas* (horseback processions).

Arriving missions first visit the sacred pepper tree, where Fidencio received his calling. The pepper tree is at the entrance to Espinazo, near the train tracks that once transported droves of devotees but today serve only the occasional freight train. Devotees circle the pepper tree three times, counterclockwise, giving thanks for having made their pilgrimage safely. The pepper tree is one of the most active religious sites in Espinazo, and mediums channeling Fidencio's spirit frequently conduct healing rituals there. In previous decades, the pepper tree was endangered by amulet-seekers who broke off pieces of bark, but today the tree is protected by a fence.

Fidencio's tomb is uphill from the pepper tree, and the route between these two sacred sites is often referred to as the Road of Penance. Many devotees make their sacrifice en route to the tomb in order to *pagar una manda* (fulfill the promise made when requesting a miracle) or to make an advance

On the "Road of Penance" under the weight of the cross.

payment toward a miracle that they plan to request. The arduous journey to isolated Espinazo is itself a sacrifice, but it is redoubled on this penitential road by carrying crosses, crawling on backs or knees, and rolling in the dirt.

Missions accompany the one or few devotees who do penance on the way to the tomb. It is common to see a circle of devotees holding hands, with a couple of others in the center, rolling uphill in the dirt. The feeling all around is solidarity. The mission supports the devotees who are making their sacrifice, and the medium, possessed by Niño Fidencio, provides the spiritual power to help complete the penance. As I observed one suffering woman rolling in the dirt, it occurred to me that this sacrifice was a startling metaphor of many devotees' lives: a gritty, uphill struggle that only a miracle could alleviate.

Niño Fidencio's tomb is located in a room of the López de la Fuente home. Healing rituals, matachines performances, mission gatherings, and visits by individual devotees occur at the tomb throughout the day. Devotees touch and kiss the tomb, pray while kneeling over it, and drink the purifying water stored in a fishbowl on top of it. The water is imbued with the spirit of Fidencio, and by ingesting it one receives Fidencio's medicine and blessing. Devotees make additional contact by placing a foot over Fidencio's footprint, which is under glass beside the tomb. This contact of the foot and the print also implies following in Fidencio's footsteps.

Rolling uphill to Niño Fidencio's tomb in Espinazo.

The mood at the tomb is intensely spiritual. In the course of an hour one might witness penitents rolling in on the floor, accompanied by their colorful missions; possessed mediums conducting healing rituals; rhythmic oral prayer; kneeling devotees surrounding the tomb on four sides; and all of this suddenly interrupted by the approach, then thundering entry, of a matachines troupe in full percussion.

There are several rooms adjacent to the tomb, including galleries of ex votos, the living area of the López de la Fuente family, a shop selling Fidencio paraphernalia, and a large room with a stage that doubles as an altar. During Fidencio's lifetime this room, known as the *foro* (literally "forum," here denoting an informal auditorium), was used for religious events, theatrical productions and other entertainments, and the collective healing of large groups. Some of these uses are still current, and they are complemented now by masses of the Fidencist Christian Church.

A crucified Christ provides a prominent backdrop to these masses, but there is no image of Niño Fidencio on the altar. A large statue of Fidencio is situated instead to one side of the room, looking toward the altar, as though he were watching celebration of the mass. All of the ministers whom I saw were women, and young girls participated formally in the mass by bringing water, flowers, incense, and oil to the altar. Each of these offerings has a symbolic significance, some in allusion to biblical scenes. Christ washing the feet of his disciples, for example, provides the antecedent for feet-washing during the mass. The Last Supper is also imitated through the ritual sharing of bread, which is done in lieu of the transubstantiation of the Eucharist that is essential to Catholic mass. The ministers, who are not necessarily mediums of Fidencio's spirit, offer four sacraments: baptism, confirmation, marriage, and extreme unction (last rites). There is no confession; one appeals directly to God without intermediaries. Devotees may simultaneously belong to the Fidencist Christian Church and the Catholic Church.

The mass that I witnessed in Espinazo was solemnly celebrated by its ministers, but there appeared to be few devotees who were interested. The great majority preferred to remain in prayer at the tomb, to watch the matachines performances in the adjacent courtyard, or to continue with whatever they were doing. The door of the López de la Fuente residence opens into the auditorium, so the mass competed on that side with a television on high volume and on the other with the matachines drums in the courtyard. People came and went, dogs roamed around, the melodramatic music of a soap opera intermingled with polyrhymic percussion, and in the middle feet were washed. The overall impression was surreal, but the reality was an institution asserting itself in a context that was decidedly folk.

The *charquito*, a pool of muddy waters, is another prominent devotional site in Espinazo. Mediums, devotees, and sometimes entire missions enter the pool to conduct healing rituals. The medium channels Fidencio's spirit, then incorporates the water into cures, as Fidencio once did at the Charco Azul. Mediums generally dunk devotees into the pool, then conduct the rituals while the mud covers their bodies. Other devotees enter the pool alone to seek well-being by application of the mud. Some simply hang around in the water, as though the charquito were a public pool or bath, thereby extending their contact with its curative properties.

Near Espinazo there are other sacred sites associated with Fidencio that today are visited by pilgrims. Outstanding are the Cerro de la Campana, where Fidencio communicated with spirits and conducted mass healings, and the Dicha de La Santa Cruz, where two corrals once contained lepers and the insane as they awaited their turns for sessions with Fidencio.

Devotion to Niño Fidencio has become sufficiently large and disperse to accommodate a range of conflicting views. A mission from California, for example, related in dismay that a Texan medium had channeled Niño Fidencio so he could appear on a radio talk show. There is more substantive debate on the relation of Niño Fidencio and Jesus Christ. Some regard Fidencio as Christ's reincarnation; others say that Fidencio was not Christ himself but was

A medium channels Fidencio's spirit for healing rituals in the charquito.

Christlike in his love, charity, humility, and sacrifice. The Fidencist Christian Church is particularly adamant on this point: Fidencio was an exemplary imitator of Christ, but to think anything more is a "great error of ignorance and knowledge." One high-ranking official of this church nevertheless explained to me that Niño Fidencio was probably an incarnation of the Holy Spirit, because Christ had already been incarnated. The formal view of the Fidencista church is more judicious: Fidencio was the "thirteenth apostle" of Christ. Other devotees fall in according to their personal dispositions, but whether Fidencio is Christ, the Holy Spirit, or an imitator of Christ, he is attributed godlike, messianic, and miraculous powers. One prayer card features the Holy Trinity and the Holy Family presenting Niño Fidencio to the world.[21]

Devotees are also vocal about the transformation of Espinazo into a commercial emporium during the fiestas. When Niño Fidencio was alive, he allowed at least one man to reproduce and sell his image. This was done not for Fidencio's own profit, but rather to help the man work his way out of poverty. During the fiestas today, the streets are literally lined with stands that sell mostly religious imagery but also carry anything else one might need. There are several informal restaurants as well, and many homeowners rent rooms at inflated prices.

My own impression is that the commerce is unfortunate, because it imbues the town with the feel of a carnival rather than a religious event. One might argue, however, that mainstream Catholic events are carnivalesque, so why should folk devotions be held to a higher standard? No one is obliged to buy the luxury items ("luxury" in the strict sense, meaning not required for devotion) that are offered at the stands. I witnessed little interest in the vendors, but that little interest, which at times may be greater, is apparently sufficient to keep them returning. In the spirit of Fidencio's consent to image sales one might regard the commerce positively, because at least someone gets to make a living. Rental of the concession sites also provides the municipality with a needed and welcome source of income.

Mexican psychology students on a field trip to Espinazo expressed their concern that the mediums, like the vendors, were also at the fiestas to make a profit. The consensus was that the mediums were insincere exploiters of faith who took advantage of credulous devotees. This condemnation is perhaps too comprehensive. Mediums and curanderos, because they are people, come in all varieties. Some are fakes and profiteers. These are identified easily enough by the financial conditions that they place on healing. Others who are more honest and genuine fall in along the spectrum from mediocre to outstanding, with the majority—if professions generally establish the rule—tending toward left of center. Those few who are outstanding are deeply, selflessly, and effectively dedicated to their profession, and their absolute sincerity is beyond question.[22]

The real problem emerges if one does not believe that spirits are actually channeled, or that folk and faith healing are truly efficacious. By this measure all mediums and curanderos could be regarded as fakes. But might not an atheist say the same of all priests, or a Christian Scientist of all medical doctors? Are scholars and scientists inauthentic or dishonest because their premises are later proven false?

Even if their practices are scientifically unviable, the honest curanderos, the ones who do not unduly profit and who do have a positive effect on their clients, must be regarded as authentic within their cultures and in the terms by which they self-define. The cure may not come exactly from the egg rubbed over the body, the secret potion, or the massage with rose petals, but a cure is nevertheless effected. Patients go home pleased by the results. A positive, informal service is provided where formal resources are inaccessible or unsuccessful. Repeat customers wait in line, and the successes of curanderos (even if others regard these as "successes") are widely recognized.

Channeling is more complicated. Frauds may pantomime a spirit and improvise on a script, but the authentic mediums are not acting. They channel (or "channel") something. If the claimed source of their discourse, spirits, turns out to be false, they are nevertheless absent to themselves and bespoken by a discourse that is not properly theirs. The source may be in their own minds—a trance-accessed corner of human psychology—but it is beyond conscious volition. This discourse takes hold of them and speaks through them. If it is not spiritual, then this is the discourse of a religious culture assimilated so deeply that it speaks for itself—it knows what to say—when the conscious mind shuts down and yields. This phenomenon is analogous to a dream populated by multiple, complex characters (spirits), all born of one's experience but now independent, differentiated, dialogical, and beyond one's conscious control.

Perhaps a better analogy is the writing and delivery of speeches. When a president delivers a speech written by a speechwriter, the content is attributed to the president, not to the speechwriter. Imagine that a president is scheduled to deliver such a written speech but dies suddenly before the occasion. The speechwriter (who, we'll assume, is also a spokesperson) delivers the speech instead, but attributes its content to the dead president. "This is what the president would say," the spokesperson thinks. "This is what the president *does* say; I know because I write it. I am saying it now for him, in his absence." The discourse of the one intermingles with the discourse of the other until finally they are indistinguishable. Attribution becomes impossible, even moot. And what the president says, what the speechwriter says for the president, is largely conditioned by the protocols of presidential discourse and by what the audience needs to hear.

Niño Compadrito

A rich Spanish viceroy married a woman from Cuzco and had a son whose name was Mario. The viceroy was an evil man who cruelly mistreated his subjects. When Mario was around thirteen he was kidnapped by people who wanted revenge against his father. They took Mario to the jungle and rubbed him with magical herbs that shrank his body. He long suffered this torture until he finally died. Mario's shrunken skeleton was later discovered beside a creek and was passed down from generation to generation. The skeleton, which became known as Niño Compadrito, began to perform miracles. It also began to grow and to reveal its true identity to devotees. Over the years Niño Compadrito was embellished with teeth, hair, eyes, and eyelashes in response to requests he made in dream revelations.

At a chapel a few blocks from the tourist district in Cuzco, candles burn before a tiny skeleton. Devotees say it is the skeleton of a child; some press accounts call it a fetus; and the former archbishop, in an attempt to quash the cult, alleged that the skeleton was from a monkey. Niño Compadrito, as this adored skeleton is known, is dressed like a saint, crowned, and housed in a chapel adjacent to the private home of its owners. The effigy is protected in an *urna* (a wooden display case with a glass front) at the elevated center of its altar, and it is surrounded by flowers, offerings, and images of Catholic saints. Devotees arrive at random, particularly on Tuesdays and Fridays, and gain access to the yard where the chapel is located by ringing a doorbell at an unmarked entrance.

One has to know where the shrine is in order to find it; I asked around. A man pointed to a blue door. As I approached, trying to look less gringo, the door suddenly opened before I rang. Clara was as startled as I was. For a moment we just looked at each other across the threshold. Then Clara said that Niño Compadrito must have been expecting me.

Clara is the wife of Juan. He inherited the effigy from his mother, María Belén, who cared for it from the late 1950s until her death in 1989. No one knows exactly where Niño Compadrito came from, and myth freely intermingles with evolving recollection as the supposed origins are told and retold.

In his less mythopoetic moments, Juan relates that his grandmother, Isabel, traded a gilded-framed portrait of the Virgin of Carmen (patron of the dead) for Niño Compadrito around 1950. This story—which is suggestive in its exchange of an authorized Catholic image for an object of folk devotion—also comes in other versions. Juan later told me, for example, that the skeleton was given to his grandmother around 1943 by old people who no longer wanted it. María Belén similarly explained that a dying woman gave the skeleton to her mother, but nothing else was known about the skeleton's origin. Juan's oldest son, Yuri, offered a related version: a woman entrusted the

Niño Compadrito. The eyes, eyelashes, teeth, and hair were added following dream revelations.

skeleton to the temporary care of Isabel but died before she could retrieve it. Isabel attempted to return the skeleton to the woman's heirs, but because they did not want it—"What are we going to do with a skeleton?"—it remained in Juan's family. Juan, his son, and María Belén all agree that the woman who died was never asked about the origins of the skeleton, so beyond the scant details already summarized (some of which, already, are elaborations), all stories concerning Niño Compadrito are necessarily folkloric.

Most devotees are unaware of and indifferent to the possible origins of Niño Compadrito. Like the adepts of other folk devotions, they are content with knowing only that he is "very miraculous." When fragmentary ideas of origin are related, they tend to emphasize a tragic death: he was "practically a martyr" because of the beating and abuse he suffered while alive; he died in a car accident; he was a shepherd boy sent to shop in Cuzco and was run over by a car. All of these inventions fill the void of unknown origin by working backward from the effect (Niño Compadrito works miracles) to the causes (suffering, tragic death) that should precede it.

One prominent version that circulates among those who are more informed has Niño Compadrito as the son of a viceroy (or on occasion as the viceroy himself) who suffered a very painful death. Rosa, an inner-circle devotee, related similarly that Niño Compadrito was the son of a rich king. Everyone wanted the king's remains to be buried and venerated in the church, Rosa explained, but the king preferred to be outside of the church, among common people. That's why Niño Compadrito, very much his father's son, showed up one night outside the home of Juan's ancestors: to seek an altar for himself outside of the church. The family saw his bony figure through a window.

Juan, the current owner and caretaker of Niño Compadrito.

Niño Compadrito's preference for veneration outside of the church underscores the devotees' own preference for folk rather than formal Catholicism. (The same preference is registered by trading the Virgin of Carmen for the skeleton.) I heard many accounts of the viceroy story, all brief and fragmentary, but they all included the principal motifs of sociopolitical status (viceroy, king, wealth) and suffering. In Peru, and more so in colonial Peru, class implies race, and devotees identify Niño Compadrito as creole (white, of Spanish heritage) or mestizo (mixed race, of white and indigenous heritage), but never as indigenous. Juan bounced back and forth between creole and mestizo, as though they were interchangeable, while relating Niño Compadrito's story on different occasions. A racial preference also seems to be suggested by the blue glass eyes that embellish Niño Compadrito's skull and by the current initiative to replace the dark-hair wig with a blond one.

When I pressed devotees regarding the blue eyes, however, race seemed to be the least of their concerns. There was a consistent preference for Caucasian features, but it was bound to culturally inherent (and inherited) biases concerning beauty and desirability rather than to the racial hierarchy from which these are derived. No one mentioned race. Race and its consequent, obvious inequities seemed to be taken for granted, like bad weather or any other given beyond one's control. Jorge, a mestizo lawyer devoted to Niño Compadrito, explained that the blue eyes are more visible and attractive than dark eyes, and that many images of the Christ child likewise have blue or green eyes. Juan's response was similar: the devotee responsible for this embellishment "liked blue eyes, not black, eyes that are visible and stand out more." My questions regarding the blond wig received similar responses ("blond hair is more striking"), and some devotees relate that Niño Compadrito appears with blond hair in their dreams.

Nothing like a complete narrative of Niño Compadrito emerged until one morning in March 2003, when Juan confided a story that astounded me. He related that Japanese scholars had recently done a scientific study of Niño Compadrito. They scraped a bone sample from one leg, did an analysis on scientific equipment, and determined that Niño Compadrito lived during the colonial era, sometime between 1700 and 1750. The analysis further revealed that Niño Compadrito had died between the ages of twelve and fourteen, and that he had been kidnapped, taken to the jungle, and suffered a slow, excruciating death by shrinking, in the same way that heads are shrunk.

It is impossible, of course, for bone analysis to reveal such narrative detail, and skull size is not actually reduced during head-shrinking rituals. I suspected that no scientific study had ever been done. I knew, however, that a Japanese scholar, Takahiro Kato, had been researching Niño Compadrito for years. It seemed likely that Kato's work provided a basis for Juan's story. If bone samples were analyzed Kato surely would have been involved, or at least informed, so I wrote to him to eliminate any doubt.

Kato confirmed my suspicion: nothing resembling bone analysis had been done. I therefore understood that Juan's narrative was purely folkloric, and I recognized its desire to establish a body of retroactive facts—a scientific backfill for the missing history—that would re-create a Niño Compadrito worthy of his owner's ideals. The visits of the Japanese scholar to the shrine, reinforced by the association of Japan with technology and science, provided a medium to fix the dates, the age, and the fatal sufferings.

Niño Compadrito's identity is generally revealed in dreams, but in Juan's version scientific scholarship is the medium of revelation. The death by shrinking is an ingenious condensation that provides the requisite tragic death together with an explanation for the size—perhaps too small to be human—of Niño Compadrito's skull and bones. I credited the shrinking to Juan's personal innovation and thought it may have been partially derived from the herbal odor that, according to Yuri, the bones once emitted. Yuri thought this odor to be the residuals of herbs used in mummifying the effigy; others associate magical herbs with shrinking.

Months later, however, a devotee named Silvia, a newcomer from Puno with no knowledge of Juan's story, responded to my inquiry concerning size with similar ideas. Silvia first recognized that a boy of thirteen would have a skull much larger than that of Niño Compadrito; she then suggested that the skull had been shrunken with herbs. This is perhaps a devotee's only option: the boy was a teen, the skeleton is too small, therefore the skeleton was shrunken. Silvia further conjectured that the body had probably been burned and, upon reassembly, the bones were somehow compressed.

What was missing in Juan's narrative was the link to viceroyalty that was commonly made by other devotees, including Clara. In December 2003, I again asked Juan about the origin of Niño Compadrito. He had apparently forgotten the account he gave some months earlier and now offered an expanded version.

About four years ago, Juan related, a Japanese scholar came to Cuzco looking for something to study. Things weren't going well for him until he happened to sit beside a devotee, a professor, on a bus. The Japanese scholar expressed his woe—he couldn't find anything to study—but the professor reassured him and promised to introduce him to Niño Compadrito. Sometime earlier, Juan had told the professor that Niño Compadrito didn't have a life story, so the professor suggested that the Japanese scholar research and write it. Once the scholar met Niño Compadrito, he would surely be interested in the project.

Thus Juan and the Japanese scholar were introduced at the shrine. The scholar began his studies, returned a month later to report that everything was going well, and said, "Since Niño Compadrito doesn't have a life story, let's do an analysis." The scholar brought scientific instruments, everyone prayed and asked for Niño Compadrito's forgiveness, and then Juan undressed the effigy. Bone was scraped off three different parts of the skeleton.

The analysis revealed that Niño Compadrito lived between 1700 and 1750, that he was ten or twelve at the time of his death, and that his father was a Spaniard, a viceroy, who was married to a *Cusqueña* (indigenous woman from Cuzco). The viceroy was an evil man who abused his subjects cruelly, and Niño Compadrito was abducted out of revenge. Niño Compadrito was taken to the jungle and died a horrible death as he was shrunken alive with herbal rubs and potions. Subsequently the shrunken skeleton passed from family to family until it came to Juan's grandmother and then finally to him.

Thus the expanded version establishes the historical time frame and age of Niño Compadrito, integrates the common belief that he was the son of a viceroy, clarifies the ambiguous mestizo ethnicity (creole father, indigenous mother), accounts for the too-small skeleton, confirms the tragic death, and provides a scientific-historical basis for Niño Compadrito's origin. Niño Compadrito is directly associated with wealth and power by birth, but the moral of the tale—the son dies for the sins of the father—distances him from symbols of detested authority and, further, makes him the sacrifice, the penance, the victim of his father's cruel government. A measure of *lo nuestro* (what is ours, one of us) is retained by providing Niño Compadrito with the mother from Cuzco. And Juan tellingly appears as a character in his own story—a character in need, precisely, of a story for the anonymous skeleton in his care.

The idea of death-by-shrinking is particularly interesting in relation to the widespread belief that Niño Compadrito is growing. If the tragic death resulted in size reduction, then life-in-death reverses that shrinking with growth. The effigy's growth is a process of restitution or recuperation. Juan first mentioned it to me in the context of a growth in devotion after Niño Compadrito passed from his grandmother to his mother and was brought to his current altar. When mother and son tried to dress Niño Compadrito in one of his old outfits, they discovered that the leggings were about an inch too short. Niño Compadrito's growth has also necessitated that the *urna* be replaced for larger sizes some three times. When I asked why, what made Niño

Compadrito grow, Juan made the connection: "As devotion grew, Niño grew too." He added that growth was the result of the many prayers and masses offered to Niño Compadrito, as though these constituted a kind of spiritual nourishment that fed the saintly bones' defiance of death. Vitality is also suggested by the related belief that Niño Compadrito's skull is growing hair.

The growth of a religious image is unusual but not unique—in Pisac, a child-shaped rock found in an irrigation ditch began to grow inside the local church. In the town of Itá Ibaté, Argentina, I was introduced to a growing statue of St. Anthony. Growth also relates to the larger complex of living attributes manifested by saint statues that bleed, cry, gaze, move, and talk. In Andean contexts it echoes the myth of Inkarrí, in which a decapitated head grows a new body.

Growing also implies growing up: some devotees explain that Niño Compadrito once liked offerings appropriate to childhood—toys and candy, for example—but now prefers pisco, anisette, cologne, cigarettes, and miniature casinos (he likes to gamble). For others, Niño Compadrito retains the infant age congruent with his size, despite belief in skeletal growth and the teen saint advocated by myths. One woman visited the shrine with her brother, who was holding his infant daughter. The breast-feeding mother was not present and the hungry baby would not stop crying, so the woman put the girl to her own breast to feed it. When she looked down a moment later, she told me, "It wasn't my niece, it was Niño Compadrito who was breast-feeding."[1]

Other myths of Niño Compadrito's origin seem to be modern, urban adaptations of traditional rural beliefs. One story that has enjoyed some popularity since its debut in a 1987 magazine article carries the echo of *apus* (mountain gods or spirits) that manifest themselves as children or the Christ child. In this version Isabel, grandmother of Juan, got lost as a child in Tambomachay, outside of Cuzco. Her desperation was alleviated when beside a creek she happened upon a boy, younger than herself, who guided her home. Isabel's parents offered to accompany the boy on the return trip because night was falling, but the boy declined, saying that he knew the way well. A month later Isabel and her parents returned to Tambomachay to try to locate the girl's mysterious protector. Beside the creek they found only his small skeleton, which they took home and kept for many years until Isabel passed it on to her daughter, María Belén.[2]

A similarly mysterious and precocious boy is also the protagonist of a story that Juan tells about an apparition of Niño Compadrito. In 2002 a detective had gone with policemen to a location near San Jerónimo, where they expected to surprise thieves. The detective was left alone, isolated, when the police ran off searching for the criminals. It was late in the day; night would soon fall. The detective was getting nervous and prayed: "Niño Compadrito, you have to help me. I'm all alone."

Soon after he heard a whistle and saw a boy in the distance, gathering flowers. The detective approached the boy and asked what he was doing there, and the boy responded that he had come for firewood. "Where are you going to get wood?" the detective asked, "There's nothing here, and everything is wet." The boy explained that he would climb a tree to cut wood. In response to other questions he related that his name was Mario and that he lived nearby with his family. The detective wanted to give the boy a gift but had nothing with him, so he wished the boy well and told him to be careful not to fall. After a few steps the detective turned around and saw that the boy was already in the tree. After a few more steps he checked on the boy again. By the third look the boy had already fallen. When the detective ran back to the tree there was no sign of the boy anywhere—he had disappeared. That is when the detective realized that it was Niño Compadrito.

Stories similar to this tale of apparition are frequently told in Cuzco, where many people believe that apus assume the form of children. One man related, for example, that near his home on the outskirts of Cuzco a boy in traditional campesino dress plays with local children but disappears if adults approach. Such apu children often accompany young pastors as they tend their flocks in isolated regions. Another man related that he visited a cur-andero to seek relief from a pain in his side. He was taken into a dark room, an apu arrived in spirit, and when the apu touched the man, to cure the malady, he felt on his skin the small hand of a child. In this case, as in many others, the apu also spoke through the medium with the high-pitched voice of a child (much like Niño Fidencio in Mexico). Apu Ausangate, the most powerful in the region around Cuzco, has the reputation of appearing as a child with blond hair and light skin, wearing white clothes and riding a white horse.[3]

Apus who manifest themselves as children are mischievous and playful, as are the syncretic advocations of the Christ child that are influenced by Andean traditions. Niño Manuelito, the Christ-child advocation most popular in the Cuzco region, escapes from churches to play with local children (thereby tearing and dirtying the finery of his clothing), steals bread to feed orphans, helps pastors tend to their flocks, runs off to visit or court saints in nearby parishes, and, in some cases, must be tied or chained down to prevent his naughty adventures.[4]

Perhaps the most notorious syncretic Christ child relevant to Niño Com-padrito is the Christ of Qoyllur Rit'i, venerated in Ocongate. In 1780 an indigenous boy, Mariano, was sent by his father to tend a flock of sheep in a remote location called Sinak'ara. Mariano made friends with a mestizo boy (white in some versions) of about his own age, who kept him company and provided his daily bead. The two boys danced and played and, despite Mariano's insufficient care, the flock prospered. When the father learned that Mariano had company, he went to investigate and upon arrival happily discovered that his sheep were thriving. He asked Mariano about the friend, but Mariano knew little more than the boy's name: Manuel.

The father rewarded Mariano's good work with new clothes, and Mariano, remembering his partner, asked that Manuel be given the same. They took a sample cutting of cloth from Manuel's clothes (because mestizo and indigenous dress are different), but the father couldn't find the cloth in Ocongate. His search led him to Cuzco, where he was told that such cloth is used only by bishops and saints.

Mariano was summoned by the bishop to explain the circumstances pertaining to his mysterious friend, and the bishop sent a priest to investigate. As the priest arrived to Sinak'ara, Manuel appeared dressed in a white tunic and radiating light. The rock where Manuel had been seen became a holy place. The people of Ocongate hired an artist to paint the image of the crucified Christ on the rock beside Manuel's apparition, but it was unnecessary because the image appeared there miraculously. In a related legend, Manuel, once discovered, rose onto a tree as though it were a cross and was instantly crucified there. Mariano died of sorrow at his feet.[5]

In Peruvian religious contexts the word *niño* (boy) generally refers to advocations of Christ, such as the Niño del Capín, Niño de la Chutas, Niño Doctorcito, Niño Llorón, and Niño Varayoq, among many others. Niño Compadrito is neither an advocation of the Christ child nor a manifestation of an apu, but he nevertheless holds much in common with the syncretic Niño Manuelito derived from apu traditions.

The similarities between Niño Compadrito and Niño Manuelito include the designation as "Niño"; the white or mestizo race in an indigenous context; the precocious independence; and the playful mischievousness (many use the corresponding Spanish words, *juguetón* and *travieso*, to describe Compadrito, Manuelito, and apu children). Like the threadbare Manuelito of Qoyllur Rit'i, as well as the others who escape from churches and ruin their clothes, Niño Compadrito appears (in dreams) dressed in rags and asks for new clothes, which have become a principal offering. Niño Compadrito also has blue eyes, like some Manuelitos, including the one in Cuzco's church of San Pedro. (In Huancavelica, there is an image known as the Niño de los Ojos Azules, meaning the Christ child with blue eyes.) The reputed wealth of Niño Compadrito's father likewise corresponds to indigenous conceptions of Niño Manuelito, whose name in Quechua, *Qapaqpa Churin*, means son of a rich person.

The white clothes associated with apu and Manuelito apparitions are—according to Juan—likewise a favorite of Niño Compadrito. The effigy's underclothing, against the sacred bones, is always white. Until it was replaced by a crown, Niño Compadrito also wore the traditional indigenous cap with ear coverings, very much like the image of Niño Manuelito that is displayed on the wall of the shrine. The playful escapes that are characteristic of apu children and Manuelitos are not shared explicitly by Niño Compadrito, but he does get out and about (as in the Tambomachay and San Jerónimo stories) and sometimes does so at night. When Niño Compadrito was in the custody of Juan's grandmother, he used to steal away to play on the courtyard well, holding a lantern as he circled its rim.

The toy offerings made to Niño Compadrito likewise conform to Niño Manuelito devotion. In Cuzco's La Merced church a much-venerated Niño Manuelito is displayed inside a glass case that is filled at the bottom with toys. These offerings are primarily from mothers grateful for miracles concerning their children. Niño Compadrito is similarly surrounded by toys and also has a strong devotion among mothers. The petitions include ("above all," in a 1983 account) safe pregnancy and healthy childbirth, but also requests for the success of children in their education and professions.[6]

An interesting variation on the theme of toy offerings emerged recently in Izcuchaca, about an hour from Cuzco, where an image of the crucified Christ appeared in a tree in 2001. The Lord of Phuchu Orcco, as he is known, expresses himself through shapes formed by melted candle wax. The wax reveals religious imagery—the face of Christ, a dove, the Sacred Heart—but also the toys that the Lord would like as offerings. The face of this adult Christ is disintegrating as the bark on which it appeared separates and falls from the tree. The shrine owner explains, however, that the purpose of this shedding is to reveal the face of the Christ child beneath the bark.

That still undisclosed revelation provides an explanation for this adult Christ's taste for toys. It also reverses the narrative order in the story of the Lord of Qoyllur Rit'i. In Ocongate the child becomes the man as Manuelito is suddenly transformed into the crucified Christ, whereas in Izcuchaca the man peels away to reveal the child. There are no such radical transformations in Niño Compadrito's story, but there is a sense of age change as Niño Compadrito grows and grows up, and as myths metamorphose the infant-size effigy into a teenage boy.

In addition to the similarities he shares with apu children and Manuelitos, Niño Compadrito also holds much in common with other traditions

The Lord of Phuchu Orcco. As the face peels off, the Christ child beneath is revealed.

concerning childhood. Infants who die after baptism but still in sin-free purity are known in much of Spanish America as *angelitos* (little angels). It is believed that these children go straight to heaven, and consequently their deaths are occasion for celebration rather than mourning. Angelitos can intercede effectively on behalf of people back on earth because their purity gets them close to God. They are the essence of the religious conception of *niño*, the maximal expression of childlike innocence as an agency of intercession. In Cuzco, infants are generally associated with good luck, and it is not uncommon to see a baby's shoe hanging as an amulet in a car.

Despite an appearance that strikes some as diabolical, many devotees consider Niño Compadrito to be an angelito and address him as such in letters of petition and gratitude. One devotee explained characteristically that Niño Compadrito, having died without sin, reached heaven more quickly and therefore can serve as a messenger to deliver requests for miracles to God. Another added that Niño Compadrito was his preferred saint because he was "a faster way to God" and through him "our requests reach God with more force." When I asked why, he responded that Niño Compadrito died as a child and therefore had a clean soul.

The privileged position close to divinity thus becomes a benefit for people in need who show Niño Compadrito the proper devotion. There is a necessary contradiction between Niño Compadrito as an angelito (miraculous via infant death and innocence) and as a shrunken teen (miraculous via tragic death later), but among devotees such contradictions tend to be compatible because the angelic innocence and the tragic death redouble miraculousness rather than challenging or canceling one another. Yuri further complicated the mix and concretized the angelic ideal by expressing his belief that Niño Compadrito was not of human origin but rather was a "divine apparition," an angel sent by God to help people on earth.

An infant death also afforded rapid reception in heaven for the Argentine folk saint Miguel Angel Gaitán, known as "Miguelito" or the "Angelito of La Rioja." Miguelito died in 1967, shortly before his first birthday. By various means his remains refused to stay in their tomb, so his parents, understanding his desire to be seen, put his remains in a glass-top coffin. Miguelito's tiny, adorned skeleton makes a visual impression similar to that of Niño Compadrito. In both cases the clothes are changed periodically, sometimes to dress the effigies in attire offered by grateful devotees.

The fate is quite different for infants, or even fetuses resulting from miscarriages and abortions, who die before baptism. These become *duendes* (spirits that inhabit a house). Duendes usually result from discarded fetuses and unwanted newborns who are strangled by their mothers or left to die of exposure. These restless souls are believed to cause harm or death to the families that produce them, and they are feared generally by the communities in which they appear. Because Niño Compadrito's certain origin is unknown and his tiny skeleton is said to have been found, many devotees wonder if he was not murdered, abandoned, or aborted by his mother. María Belén's report that the bones "were found on the banks of a river" is particularly suggestive, because some victims of infanticide are buried beside creeks, and duendes are associated with creeks and rivers.[7]

When I asked Juan why masses were said for Niño Compadrito, his first response was "for the salvation of his soul." He then explained that if Niño Compadrito were an abandoned child or fetus, unbaptized, then his soul would need prayers and masses to get him into heaven. This position is also suggested by Niño Compadrito's feast on All Souls Day (November 2, also known as the Day of the Dead), because the theological purpose of this day is to offer prayers and masses for the benefit of souls in purgatory.

Thus Niño Compadrito is situated simultaneously on both sides of paradise: on one side united with God and interceding for miracles, and on the other still outside of heaven and in need of help from friends back on earth. The latter is paradoxical, though, because it calls into question Niño Com-

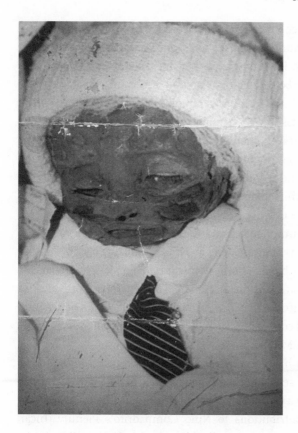

Miguel Angel Gaitán, known as "Miguelito," as displayed at his shrine in Villa Unión, La Rioja Province, Argentina.

padrito's miraculous powers. If Niño Compadrito is not in heaven, not close to God, how does he perform miracles?

Skulls and Bones

One answer to that question is suggested by the powers attributed to human remains in the Andes. Juan is quite proud that Niño Compadrito is the only saint truly made of human bone. Niño Compadrito is the real thing, he explains; all the saints in the churches are nothing but replicas, made of plaster and wood. Even the most venerated image in Cuzco, the Lord of Earthquakes, is only leather. The same point was made by Silvia, the devotee from Puno, who added that the true, bone remains of Niño Compadrito belonged to a real person who once lived among Peruvians, whereas the images in the church are fabricated imports.

Carlos, a devotee and chemical engineer from Cuzco, echoed that idea—locals prefer Niño Compadrito because he is one of them, whereas other saints have foreign origins. He then added that the skeletal form accentuates Niño Compadrito as a symbol of death, as a saint advocating for devotees in the next world. This idea of intercession is contradicted, however, by the pride in the real-bone effigy. If the issue were actually, or always, one of Niño Compadrito's soul interceding in heaven, then the image—a mere visual aid—could be made of Silly Putty with no detriment to miracle. Niño Compadrito devotion and the Andean traditions behind it indicate rather that the bones themselves are charged with magical and miraculous powers.

Carlos underscored the essence of Niño Compadrito when he went on to describe him as an amalgam of Incan and Catholic beliefs. The devotees are Catholic and Catholicism is omnipresent at Niño Compadrito's shrine, but Andean beliefs concerning bones (along with compatible aspects of Catholicism, such as bone relics) are half the attraction. The syncretism provides for double efficiency: Niño Compadrito's real, miraculous bones work on earth in collaboration with his soul conceding miracles from heaven. The same is true of the bone-carved San La Muerte.

Most people in Cuzco have never heard of Niño Compadrito. Those few who have, but have never seen the effigy, believe that Niño Compadrito is a skull or mummy. These two erroneous presumptions index the traditions that have made substantial contributions to Niño Compadrito's identity. Incan mummies, known as *mallquis*, were described by colonial priests as "the bones of their most important ancestors, which they adore as relics" and "the bones or whole bodies of their precursors." Mallquis were treated as though they were alive. They were fed, dressed, consulted, and obeyed; they participated in ritual, governmental, and social acts; they attended dances in their honor and toasted one another. Only the form of their being had changed, and the new form, immortal and imperishable, imbued human transience with the powers of eternity.[8]

The skeletal remains of some infants and children were of particular importance among mallquis. Twins and breach-birth (feet first) children had special religious significance, and "if they die young they are put in pots and kept inside the home as something sacred." Postconquest Andeans tried to hide such babies from priests, so that these children's sacredness in life and death would not be contaminated by baptism. Something of this veneration of children's remains continues today in the community of Qolqa, in Lauramarca. A tea is made from tiny pieces of skin taken from the bones of dead children in the cemetery, and its ingestion, almost a syncretic form of communion, symbolically unites the living with dead children close to God.[9]

The "living dead" quality of Andean mummies is also characteristic of Niño Compadrito and other folk saints. The living and their dead saints alive among them interact in ways regulated by rules of reciprocity. The presence in this world of Niño Compadrito's active remains—they grow, they communicate—suggest an integration of beyond-death power into everyday life. Niño Compadrito and mallquis hold in common their functions of protection, advice, guidance, and the granting of favors. Both are cared for by custodians; are made offerings, including food and drink; are elegantly dressed for ritual purposes; are worthy of absolute respect and deference; and are principles of community cohesion. They provide for their people, they participate in conversations, and they punish those who treat him badly. Mallquis and Niño Compadrito (along with other skeletal saints, such as San La Muerte) are also potentially dangerous, are feared, and are prone to association with diabolical practices. The Church prohibits and persecutes these devotions, but the cults persist, sometimes clandestinely.

Perhaps the most startling aspect of the mallquis was the degree to which their aliveness was taken literally, be it during consultations concerning intimate matters (such as marriages) or at banquets where they shared in the bounty and joy. When Niño Compadrito receives similar treatment it surprises no one but me; devotees take it quite for granted. The owners of the effigy rarely allow it to be removed from its chapel, but exceptions are sometimes made for trusted devotees. One such occasion was Rosa's birthday party. Niño Compadrito was the only invited guest. He was served a piece of cake to celebrate with Rosa her happy day. Clara, who transported and accompanied Niño Compadrito on his outing, perhaps assumed the role of a modern *malquipvillac* (the one who talks to mallquis), as she does at the shrine. Niño Compadrito expresses himself by symbol and suggestion, so Clara helps to interpret the cryptic messages.

Part of Niño Compadrito's mystique is his state of conservation, his seemingly miraculous exemption to decomposition. In medieval and early modern Catholicism, the miraculous preservation of corpses was related to the absence of sin—"Sin is the cause of the body's decay"—and was an important factor in the postmortem assessment of sanctity. The incorruptible flesh, meaning the absence of corporal putrefaction, was evidence of the corresponding absence of sin. The Virgin Mary of the Assumption provided the paradigm: because she was free of Original Sin and sexual contamination, she was freed of decomposition.[10]

Devotees to Niño Compadrito are unlikely to make these associations, but they nevertheless believe themselves to be in a miraculous presence when they stand before this skeleton that defies decomposition. At times the preservation of the bones is accounted for in Andean terms. Yuri says that Niño Compadrito is a mummy, that dried skin holds the bones together, and that the mummification accounts for the absence of skeletal decomposition. (Juan reports, conversely, that there is only a patch of skin on one leg.) Jorge, the lawyer, also compared Niño Compadrito to a mummy, but then explained the crucial difference: the Incan mallquis were preserved by special procedures, but Niño Compadrito's preservation occurred miraculously. Juan also believes that the absence of decomposition is miraculous.

Father Camilo Mora, who once celebrated mass for Niño Compadrito, held a similar opinion. Mora, from Urubamba, had been a priest for forty-seven years when I spoke with him, and he had spent thirty of these years in small villages, with indigenous campesinos. He had no prejudicial opinion concerning Niño Compadrito as a pagan or false devotion, but rather felt that an investigation was necessary to make a determination.

The key issue for Mora was the bones. He believed that Niño Compadrito might be a true saint because as a child he has *huesos duros* (the hard bones characteristic of adults) that, further, have not decomposed. How could the bones have lasted so long, Mora asked, if it is not because of Niño Compadrito's sanctity? This led him, in turn, to wonder if the skeleton was a hoax, if it was not perhaps some imperishable material made to look like bone. That's how Mora arrived at his conclusion: "If it's a real skeleton, then it's miraculous." This miraculous exemption from decomposition, in turn, is the basis, the evidence, for the belief that Niño Compadrito can perform other miracles.

Niño Compadrito is also closely associated with skulls, in part because his skeleton is fully clothed and only the protruding skull (or, more accurately, face) is visible. In the 1960s and early 1970s, when the cult had its strongest rate of growth, the skull lacked the embellishments (eyes, eyelashes, teeth) that it later acquired. It was thus all the more deathlike. Skulls are common in the iconography of Christianity, owing in part to Christ's crucifixion at Golgotha (which means "Place of the Skull") and the subsequent painting of a skull or skulls at the foot of the cross. The attributes of many saints, particularly hermits and penitents, also include skulls, and skulls are prominent as reminders of death in Franciscan churches and monasteries.[11]

Cuzco's ghoulish Franciscan church, where masses to Niño Compadrito were once celebrated, features a prominent St. Francis holding a cross in one hand and a skull in the other. This was the church of preference precisely because the skull held by St. Francis was associated with Niño Compadrito, and some devotees believed that the two were brothers. More recently, Rosa explained to me that Niño Compadrito is very miraculous because he is so close to God. She offered as proof the skull at the foot of the cross in paintings of the Crucifixion: "That's Niño Compadrito."

Ghoulish, grizzly, dead, and deathlike images tend to dominate Spanish American churches, providing a Catholic backdrop for reception of Niño Compadrito. In the Sanctuary of the Lord of Huanca, near Cuzco, a glass case— much like Niño Compadrito's *urna*—exhibits a wounded adult Christ in miniature. This image is approximately the size of Niño Compadrito and is dressed similarly, with only the tiny head (bearded, bloody, emaciated, too small) poking out of the saintly vestments. While looking at this Christ I realized that Niño Compadrito's appearance, which is so alien to my perception, is congruent with the visual culture of everyday religious life in Cuzco. This is what supernatural beings look like: death.

Catholic skull imagery had a welcome reception in the Andes, where it nicely coincided with local traditions. There is a range of traditional beliefs concerning the head and the skull—they fly through the air, the soul is in the head, the skulls of madmen must be crushed—but most common is the belief that skulls protect homes and other buildings. Some prefer the skulls of deceased relatives for this service, but others get favorable results from unidentified skulls found in fields and cemeteries. Particularly effective are skulls that result from drownings and other tragic deaths. Home altars are built for skulls in strategic places to scare off thieves, bad spirits, and other forms of evil. Above or behind the front door is common. If thieves approach, the skull talks to simulate occupancy, barks like a dog, and sometimes manifests itself in ghostly human form to chase off and pursue the fleeing criminals.

The relations with a skull, as with a folk saint, are reciprocal: the skulls (and, by extension, the souls to whom they once belonged) receive the proper ritual care (including prayer, candles, flowers, holy water, food and drink offerings, and the company of saint images), and in reciprocation they fulfill their duties of home protection. When the identity of a skull is unknown, homeowners often give it a name and a history (which are sometimes revealed in dreams), and it is not uncommon to talk to the skull or even to celebrate its birthday. In lieu of a name, or before one is selected or revealed, the nickname "Compadrito" is often used to designate the skull. "Compadrito," which is the affectionate diminutive of *compadre*, implies a relation of ritual kinship, known as *compadrazco* in Spanish, between the skull and its caretaker. The word can also be used to denote close friendship. As one devotee explained, "You have to become compadres with the skull so it will befriend you and take care of you and protect you from harm and robbery."[12]

Juan says much the same of Niño Compadrito: he watches over one as would a compadre. (Some devotees also refer to Niño Compadrito as "father," with similar connotations of paternal care.) Niño Compadrito protects Juan's home and family (and, by extension, all devotees), and Juan understands this protection as reciprocation for the loving care that he provides for the effigy.

Initially Niño Compadrito, like the found skulls, did not have a name or identity. His skull, which was then separated from its body, may have served to protect the home of Juan's grandmother, Isabel. At that time the skeleton had nothing of the folk saint attributes that it has today. As its fame for miracles grew, however, the effigy became known by the generic name "compadrito" (along with other generic qualifiers, such as "santito" and "almita," the affectionate diminutives of "saint" and "soul," respectively), as enshrined skulls do. Around the mid-1970s, when the particulars of Niño Compadrito's biography were gradually being revealed in dreams, Niño Compadrito informed devotees that he preferred to be called by his true name, Mario. This step from anonymity to identity was complemented by other revelations (concerning preferred appearance and offerings, for example) and myths of origin that continue to build—the process is always unfinished—toward a composite identity.[13]

Skulls have also stimulated other Andean devotions. In Huancayo, a skull was found by workers in 1956 during excavation for the construction of a police station. Calavera Panchito, as this miraculous skull is now known, revealed in dreams that before his death he had hoped to become a policeman. In 1986 devotees built a chapel for him across from the police station. On the Peruvian coast, similarly, a miscalculated dynamite blast killed men who were working on the Panamerican Highway. A small chapel was built at the location for Las Calaveritas (the affectionate diminutive for "the skulls"), as these anonymous road construction workers are known. They have a reputation for protecting truck and bus drivers.[14]

In the Argentine Andes, a large cult (in which dreams again play a role) developed around a miraculous skull in Tilcara. In nearby Salta, found skulls are believed to be miraculous. Coin offerings are left in the eye sockets as miracles are requested, and when sufficient money has accumulated a mass is celebrated for the soul corresponding to the skull.[15]

On All Souls Day the Chipaya of Bolivia invite the dead to visit their community. Local authorities get on their knees before skulls in the cemetery's Chapel of the Dead (where the bones of ancestors are kept) to make the invitation, and four skulls are later ceremoniously removed and taken to church, where they are fed. The Chipaya ritually implore the skulls to grant them a good year, after which the skulls are returned to their chapel and lavished with offerings.

The same skulls are also used in interventions following theft. The victim appeals to a shaman, who retrieves a skull from the Chapel of the Dead for a three-day ritual. Offerings are made as the shaman beseeches the skull to plague the thief, forcing the return of the stolen goods. Insomnia and illness induce the thief to make amends, or, that failing, continue as punishment.[16]

Similar beliefs are held more broadly. When Andean skulls are not protecting homes, they venture out on missions to haunt the dreams and disrupt the peace of thieves, until the stolen objects are returned. Campesinos rely on Niño Compadrito for the same purpose. When livestock is stolen, for example, an appeal is made to Niño Compadrito. Juan explains that the stolen livestock have by then already been sold, and the money spent, so the thief shows up at the home of his victim, confesses the crime, and negotiates a way to make amends. A prayer to Argentina's San La Muerte (which is also a skeleton) makes a thief "suffer every minute of his life, he cannot eat, he cannot sleep, he has no peace, no calm," until he returns what was stolen. Many people I talked to in the Calchaquíes Valleys, in northern Argentina, likewise reported that skulls are used to recover lost and stolen objects.[17]

In contrast to these helpful relics, some bones—particularly those associated with *gentiles*, meaning preconquest ancestors—are malevolent. At times the same bones can effect both help and harm, depending on how they are treated. Outside of Puno, near the summit of a mountain known as Marinsa, the bones of gentiles perform miracles for locals. When anthropology students arrived with the intent of studying the site, they were driven off by locals who feared that disruption of the bones would bring a curse upon their homes. Human remains and the malignant ancestor spirits that they carry are referred to in Quechua as *soq'a* or *soq'a machu*, among other names. Contact with these soq'a bones and mummies is dangerous, as is drinking water that flows past them or being struck by the winds that blow down from the regions where they are buried.

The resultant maladies, known as *soqasqa* (many people also use *soq'a* in reference to the maladies), include an often fatal emaciation, crippling contraction or shriveling of limbs (*encogimiento;* literally, "shrinking"), and a drying out of the body. It is almost as though the victims are remade in the image of the offended skeletons and mummies. "Soq'a" is also used figuratively in reference to a skinny (bony) person.

Aymara-speaking Andeans have similar beliefs. Bone spirits live in *chullpas* (pre-Colombian funeral towers), and one who disturbs them can be "grabbed by the gentiles" and get what is known as bone or tomb sickness. In northern Peru, the breathing of dust from old tombs can cause possession by the spirits of the dead. The powders of old or pulverized bones carry otherworldly contagions, and the breathing or drinking of these can be fatal. Witch doctors use these powders to bring harm to their victims.[18]

The cure for soq'a appeals to its cause. A man in Cuzco got soq'a from touching bones that he found in the country, then took the bones to a curandero, who rubbed one over his patient's body as part of the cure. Sometimes, similarly, the bone is scraped, or pieces of skin or cartilage are removed, then boiled and ingested. Others recommend burning the old clothes of saints and eating the ashes, or drinking water from flower vases in church, because the soq'a, being evil, cannot coinhabit one's body with these holy presences. Sometimes there is no cure. Two girls found a mummy in a cave, put manure on its head, and threw rocks to knock it over. Both suffered incurable illnesses and eventually died.[19]

Soq'a remains are not entirely dead—"These dead people are alive"—and at night they become active to engage in various menacing relations with humans. One must show them due respect, provide them care, and make offerings of their preferred food and drink, so that the living and the dead can live together harmoniously. The similarities between soq'a remains and Incan mallquis are striking, but the malignant ancestor spirits carried by the soq'a bones are depicted as more evil, more demanding in their coercion of excessive offerings to appease their malevolence. "These devils want all kinds of fetuses, sweets, and the fat of pigs, guinea pigs, and chickens."[20]

Soq'a spirits often appear in the form of people and are believed to impregnate women. The soq'a myth thus provides a means to avoid the shame and reprisals of illegitimate pregnancies, but the price is high. Children resulting from soq'a pregnancies usually die at birth, so mothers projecting the blame for illegitimate pregnancies to soq'a spirits must conform to the myth by killing their newborns. These victims of infanticide are either burned or buried quickly and secretly, sometimes beside creeks. Abortions are also justified by claiming a soq'a pregnancy.[21]

Some devotees associate soq'a bones and spirits with Niño Compadrito, thereby accentuating the diabolical aspect of the effigy and its uses. The tiny size of the skeleton indeed suggests fetal or newborn remains. The legends regarding burial beside a creek, along with Silvia's conjecture that Niño Compadrito was burned, further resonate with soq'a implications. From another angle, the idea that Niño Compadrito was shrunken is suggestive of the shriveling (encogimiento) caused by contact with soq'a bones. And just as Niño Compadrito rebounds by growing after death, some Andeans likewise believe that soq'a bones are growing.

Against the backdrop of soq'a beliefs, Niño Compadrito's bones can seem the embodiment of a malignant spirit deployable for evil purposes. Unlike soq'a remains, however, these bones do not harm the devotees who make contact with them. They are rather used to redirect malevolent power to one's advantage. Rituals of devotion channel diabolical power toward destructive ends, in the same way that they channel divine power toward constructive ends. And because such destruction is always perceived as retaliatory, as a counteroffensive or act of justice, the evil power can be regarded as a kind of inverted goodness. In the same way that curanderos cure soq'a illness with the very bones that caused it, devotees use the evil power of Niño Compadrito to neutralize evil done to them.

The Black Candles of Justice

Cuzco's market has several stands and stores that sell paraphernalia for witchcraft and folk healing. I feigned ignorance in a few of these to ask questions about Niño Compadrito, and the response was uniformly uncomfortable. The mere mention of the name, and by a gringo, resulted in a strange and sudden silence. When the sparse responses finally came after some persistence, the consensus was that Niño Compadrito was a devil used for evil purposes.

Some devotees, particularly campesinos, share this perception and visit the shrine precisely to request punishment of their enemies. As explained by Yuri, they believe that God sent Catholic saints to the world to help people by doing miracles, and that the devil sent Niño Compadrito to help people by doing evil. The specialty in evil makes Niño Compadrito a unique supernatural asset, because he offers services that canonized saints are unwilling or unable to perform. It also accounts for something of the secrecy that surrounds the cult, in part because evil is unmentionable but also because devotees want to keep their secret weapon from enemies who might redeploy it against them.

The principal days of devotion to Niño Compadrito—Tuesdays and Fridays, instead of the Monday (the day associated with souls) common elsewhere—likewise suggest sinister purposes. Tuesdays and Fridays are considered the days for esoteric and sometimes nefarious or diabolical arts. A candle seller around the corner from the Niño Compadrito shrine explained that Tuesday and Friday were primarily for black candles (used for petitioning harm to others), whereas on other days white and colored candles were lit for such positive purposes as health, work, and love. In devotion to the folk saint Ubilberto Vásquez Bautista in Cajamarca, similarly, most people visit the shrine on Mondays, but those seeking harm to others go on Tuesdays and Fridays. Witchcraft rituals to San La Muerte are also done on Tuesdays and Fridays.

The black art of cursing others (sometimes called *daño*), is done at the Niño Compadrito shrine in the same way that it is done at many others. Black candles are offered to petition harm to an adversary, and they are sometimes burned upside down (the bottom is melted or carved to expose the wick). The name of the person to be cursed can also be carved into the wax of the candle.

The frequent use of black candles at Niño Compadrito's shrine is partially indebted to events that transpired following the Church's persecution of the cult in the late 1970s. In June 1982, the archbishop Luis Vallejos Santoni, who was responsible for the persecution, was killed in an automobile accident near Chuta, in the district of Limatambo. He was heading for the inauguration of a new road built by campesinos when the driver lost control of the car and it fell off a cliff. This death was preceded by that of the archbishop's friend and collaborator, the priest Luis Dalle, who in May 1982 likewise died in an automobile accident.[22]

Devotees interpreted these events as punishments that Niño Compadrito exacted against those who had ruthlessly attacked him. The unnecessarily offensive attitude of the archbishop made his repression of the cult seem a declaration of war. It was he who alleged that Niño Compadrito was nothing but the skeleton of a monkey, and in doing so implied the effigy's unsaintly ugliness. Niño Compadrito advised his devotees to be patient, however, to bear the persecution, because the affront would be avenged from on high. Now the time had come. The reprisals would be in kind. Rumors pursuant to the accident related that the archbishop's face, damaged in the crash, resembled that of Niño Compadrito. Others said that the deformity made him look like a monkey.[23]

The public cult to Niño Compadrito reemerged in 1982, after six years of clandestine devotion, with a notable increase in the use of black candles. By having eliminated his enemies, Niño Compadrito acquired a reputation as an avenger. Devotees who had unsettled scores began to frequent the shrine to seek punishment of their adversaries. Still common today is the belief that Niño Compadrito is a *sancionador* (one who sanctions, a punisher). He brings down his wrath upon those who harm his devotees and upon the devotees themselves if they fail to fulfill the promises made to him. For some devotees, Niño Compadrito is integrated into the pantheon of saints precisely to perform this specialist, black-candle function.

The ambiguous policies of Niño Compadrito's owners also contribute to the use of black candles. María Belén is said to have prohibited black-candle petitions. At the same time, however, she propagated the idea of Niño Compadrito as an avenger, and the heyday of requests for punitive miracles occurred on her watch. According to Yuri, when María Belén died the family found among her belongings a few pierced, black-magic, mummylike dolls accompanied by narratives describing inimical situations and requesting the death of enemies. María Belén had removed these dolls from Niño Compadrito's altar—it is unclear if this occurred because such use was forbidden or because the petitions had already been expedited. Yuri also relates that his mother, Clara, currently removes black candles after the departure of the devotees who light them. I never saw Clara remove a black candle, but I did see her move one from among white candles and situate it on a separate stand with other black candles. Black candles (and their petitions) are segregated from others, but they do not seem to be prohibited.

The family's position regarding the use of black candles depends largely on who is asked and under what circumstances. During a November 2002 news interview, while black candles were burning in force, Juan explained that Niño Compadrito was miraculous for multiple purposes and that the particular request was at the discretion of each individual. This argument put the responsibility on devotees. Yuri explained to me that his father is opposed to the use of black candles and at one time actively discouraged their use, but after years of attempting to restrain the behavior of devotees has assumed a kind of retired acquiescence. Thus Juan's position (in Yuri's view) is less indifference than exhaustion—a resignation to the futility of trying to control all requests.

Niño Compadrito is quite capable of controlling them himself, Juan explained to me. The purpose of black candles is to bring harm upon one's enemies—"so that they have an accident or die"—but Juan was quick to add that Niño Compadrito never grants these miracles. Rather than doing evil, Niño Compadrito responds to such requests by searching for a just solution. He administers justice without resorting to evil.

Niño Compadrito's objection to evil was more dramatically illustrated by a devotee from Cuzco. This man, in a desperate situation of poverty, decided to sell his soul to the devil. He went to Niño Compadrito's altar to make the pact but, much to his astonishment, Niño Compadrito picked him up and threw him across the room, twice. That convinced him: "Niño Compadrito is with God, not the devil." Another devotee, Jorge, left the issue open, but he never offers black candles to Niño Compadrito because it is inappropriate, he said, for a saint to do evil.[24]

Devotees get uncomfortable when one asks about black candles. They almost invariably stress that the purpose of such petitions is to protect devotees from the aggression of others, to neutralize harm by turning back the affronts that evildoers have done to them. Many also clarify that the death of the adversary is not their objective. A man at the shrine told me that the purpose of the black candles was to cause someone's death, but a woman who overheard the conversation took exception. She had just made her petition with black candles and did not wish the death of anyone. What she sought, she said, was "that justice be done, that God does to the person what he deserves."

Another user of black candles added that nothing tragic happened to the people who were doing her harm, but rather, thanks to Niño Compadrito, these people simply disappeared from her life. "He clears all troubles from your path," she said. For her, Niño Compadrito was more a protector than an avenger. Niño Compadrito similarly resolved the situation of a sexually harassed discotheque employee by sending a strange illness that forced her boss from his job.[25]

One common use of black candles by women is to eliminate illegitimate competition in love. Rosa reported that Niño Compadrito had broken up her husband's love affair by sending illness to the girlfriend—blood came out of her nose—and, for good measure, by punishing the husband until he changed his evil ways. When a neighbor insulted Rosa, Niño Compadrito took revenge by sending illnesses to this woman's children. Rosa then clarified that Niño Compadrito's primary concern is justice: he parcels out rewards and punishments in accord with what one deserves. If something unjust is occurring, he resolves the problem to the devotee's advantage because "he doesn't like injustices."

As an example, Rosa related that a judge had been leaning in her ex-husband's favor in a civil suit concerning child support. After an appeal to Niño Compadrito, the judge fell and injured her leg—"it looked like an invisible hand had twisted it"—which resulted in blood clots and other complications. Rosa eventually won the suit, befriended the judge, and went back to Niño Compadrito to petition that the judge's leg be healed.

It is precisely this idea of justice—subjective to be sure—that seems to govern the use of black candles at all folk saint shrines. Just as one rival in war always views the other as the aggressor (as epitomized by "preemptive" war), those who petition harm to enemies always do so defensively. "Do justice for me" is the petition to get even with enemies, and it is particularly resonant in contexts, such as this Peruvian one, in which social justice is scarce, the legal system is corrupt, and poor people are at a decided disadvantage. Many come to the shrine in pursuit of justice, Juan relates, "because there is no justice here in Peru, there just isn't." Thus the miraculous justice administered by Niño Compadrito serves as an alternative to the labyrinths of unjust justice, but also as a weapon of the weak against those who trespass against them. Indeed, according to Juan and other devotees, Niño Compadrito revealed in dreams that he had hoped to become a judge when he was alive. Now "he's like a judge," Juan said, "because he does justice."

. Speaking as a lawyer and as a devotee, Jorge explained that people without resources or recourse arrive at the shrine "looking for 'justice' "—the quotation marks are his—which can at best be symbolic. Carlos, the chemical engineer, added that justice is not always done on earth, so in cases of injustice one must appeal to the superior court of God and his saints. He had done precisely that, making his appeal to Niño Compadrito's administration of divine justice on earth, when he was being forced from a government job for refusing to participate in corruption. Silvia provided a mythic basis for these ideas when she related that Niño Compadrito was burned alive after being falsely accused of theft. A plague decimated the region as punishment for this unjust execution.

The Extirpation of Idolatry

The growth of cults that are based at domestic shrines is dependent upon the personality of the shrine owner. Those who are most successful, often middle-age or older women, have personable characters with varying degrees of strength, pride, willfulness, charity, compassion, and charisma. They establish a warm, welcoming environment for whoever agrees to abide by the (usually minimal) rules. Some station themselves beside the shrine and spend the day there, receiving old and new friends, coaching devotion, and socializing. Devotees arrive in need, sometimes desperate, and these therapeutic listeners offer each the time necessary to console, guide, and reassure. Those who excel can be as helpful as the folk saints themselves, and indeed the line blurs as shrine owners speak in the name of a saint to interpret mysterious revelations. Shrine owners are the principle of cohesion by which the folk saint's gravitational pull is forged into a cult and a community.

From the little I could gather of María Belén, I surmise that she was such a person. The cult certainly grew to its maximal prominence under her tutelage, and she was responsible for establishing Niño Compadrito's saintlike identity and promoting it in Cuzco. (Her mother, Isabel, was not inclined to this devotion.) Yuri relates that people came to the shrine to visit María Belén as much as to venerate Niño Compadrito. They would first pay their respects at the altar, then talk at length with María Belén. In the same way that Niño Compadrito served as a bridge to God, María Belén served as a bridge to Niño Compadrito. She was a magnet and a catalyst, she made the devotee experience meaningful and moving, and she established the theology, imagery, and rituals that facilitated miracles. María Belén interpreted dream revelations, advised on the protocols of devotion, offered personal guidance, and socialized with friends and first-timers who found in the composite experience of the shrine—María Belén and Niño Compadrito—a measure of relief and solace.

Under the tutelage of María Belén the cult began to grow in the mid-1960s; a decade later Niño Compadrito had about a thousand devotees. The trend of growth was abruptly interrupted in September 1976, however, when Archbishop Luis Vallejos Santoni, who had been appointed the year before, began his campaign to eradicate the devotion. Vallejos Santoni, from the coastal city of Callao, had little tolerance for Andean folk Catholicism and took an extirpation-of-idolatry approach reminiscent of post-conquest evangelization. He was intent on purifying the faith in Cuzco and the heretical, paganlike Niño Compadrito made an ideal target. Vallejos Santoni also endorsed a campaign against the Evangelical and Pentecostal churches that were then attracting (and continue to attract) thousands of converts from Catholicism.[26]

Vallejos Santoni issued a degree that forbade Catholic devotion to Niño Compadrito and ordered an immediate end to the cult. Reading of the decree was required in all diocese churches on the Sunday following receipt, and it was also widely publicized by the local media.[27]

The decree's most contentious allegation, that Niño Compadrito was a monkey skeleton, was published in some newspapers as a matter of fact. Cuzco's leading daily ran a front-page headline that read: "Venerated Skull Belonged to a Monkey's Skeleton." The article beneath this banner reiterated the archbishop's prohibition in threatening tones. Devotees, in confusion and dismay, grappled with these allegations, along with other ideas that they attributed to the archbishop: "Niño Compadrito is ugly" and therefore could not be a saint, for example, or "Niño Compadrito is a monkey. He's not a saint, so he must be burned soon." The archbishop's decree also called for a National Institute of Culture investigation to determine the true nature of Niño Compadrito's skeleton, but this was never done. Juan's story of bone analysis by the Japanese scholar is particularly suggestive in the context of this ordered but unrealized study.[28]

The devotees' confusion and crisis resided precisely in the discrepancy between the archbishop's harsh assertions and the miracles that seemed to disprove them. If Niño Compadrito is a monkey, or if his ugliness necessarily excludes him from the host of saints, then how does one account for the miracles? The archbishop's attacks provoked a strong reaction in part because they were incomprehensible. Devotees self-identified as Catholics and felt offended, betrayed by the archbishop—"I think he hates us too"—and by the public antagonism that his degree had instigated. Catholicism in Cuzco is decidedly syncretic—skulls, mountain spirits, Pachamama, saints, and Sunday mass all intermix freely—so why had Niño Compadrito been singled out for persecution? His devotees were being Catholic in the way their culture had taught them. And now the Church, their Church, was turning against them.[29]

The period between the archbishop's proclamation in 1976 and his accidental death in 1982 was one of turmoil for the cult of Niño Compadrito. The owners feared that the effigy would be confiscated and burned (like the mallquis confiscated by colonial extirpators), so it was removed from public view and went underground. Access was restricted to an inner group of trusted devotees. Niño Compadrito was moved from one safe house to another, in conformance with instructions revealed in dreams to María Belén. These hideouts included devotees' residences in Cuzco, and, when the idea circulated that the entire city was unsafe, in the provincial towns of Quillabamba and Sicuani.[30]

Finally, after six months of evasion and flight, Niño Compadrito revealed that his feet were tired, meaning that he was weary of being on the run. Thereafter he was protected at the home of his owners, out of view and out of range even of the police that came looking for him. The public cult practically dissipated during these six years of isolation and inaccessibility, and many people indeed believed that Niño Compadrito had already been burned by the Church. Devotees began requesting visits after the death of Vallejos Santoni, however, and some six months later the clandestine period ended with renewed display of the effigy.[31]

Church authorities in Cuzco today are less militant in their opposition to Niño Compadrito, but even their nonrecognition troubles devotees. A lingering fear—particularly that the effigy may be confiscated and burned—has inspired caution. During the years of repression devotees believed that a competitive jealousy motivated the Church's hostility, that the archbishop's prohibition of Niño Compadrito was an attempt to recuperate the many parishioners who had defected to other devotions. This belief is still common among folk saint devotees today, particularly within the larger cults, and certainly has a measure of truth.

Current devotees offer a wide range of explanations to account for the Church's continuing nonrecognition of Niño Compadrito. One woman thought it was because Niño Compadrito was Jewish. Most devotees, however, conform with Juan's observation that priests simply do not believe that Niño Compadrito is a saint, or that he performs miracles. Many priests also associate Niño Compadrito with witchcraft and superstition because of his reputation for granting black-candle petitions.

Devotees are also baffled by the inconsistency of Church policy. The tolerance of folk saints is subject to pendulous swings depending upon the individual—archbishop, bishop, or parish priest—who is in control. One says yes and another says no: Catholics work with that mixed message to patch together their individual opinions. The intra-Church conflict was clearly in view when Vallejos Santoni censured "unscrupulous" priests "who are tacitly providing incentive for the deviations of the unauthorized cult, disorienting the simple faith of the people." The reference is to priests who at the request of devotees celebrated mass at the Niño Compadrito shrine, or allowed Niño Compadrito to be brought to their churches, and sometimes placed on the altar, during celebration of mass in his name.[32]

This practice resumed after the death of Vallejos Santoni, but not without lingering aftereffects. When priests came to say mass at the shrine, according to Yuri's boyhood memories, Niño Compadrito was brought to the dining room table. The service culminated with devotees standing in turn before Niño Compadrito to pray, then receiving holy communion from the priest. Around 1983, a mass was prevented and the priest sent home by Juan's brother (sometimes depicted as an enemy of the cult), who was employed by the Church and feared reprisals. Masses are no longer said at the shrine, and in recent years the devotees have had difficulty locating priests who are willing to say mass for Niño Compadrito in their churches.

Masses requested in Niño Compadrito's name are typically denied because public cult can be offered only to saints who are canonized by the Vatican. The technicality is bypassed by offering a mass for the dead, for which any deceased Catholic is eligible. Such masses are particularly popular on All Souls Day, which is Niño Compadrito's feast day. When a mass for the dead is denied to Niño Compadrito, devotees circumvent the refusal by requesting a mass in his name Mario (or Niño Mario), who is presumed to be a deceased boy. By this means devotees recruit the collusion of unwitting priests, or of sympathetic priests in need of a pretext. Problems can arise, however, if the devotees arrive with Niño Compadrito for the mass said in Mario's name.

In 2004, the mass for Niño Compadrito's feast day was celebrated in the parish of Mariscal Gamarra, a neighborhood on the outskirts of Cuzco. Niño Compadrito, who is generally transported in taxis by Juan and Clara, arrived very late, some two minutes before the mass concluded. The circumstances in recent years suggest that this tardiness may have been calculated. In 2003 there was no mass celebrated for Niño Compadrito's feast day because a venue could not be found. In the preceding year, Niño Compadrito's mass was said at the Virgin of Fatima chapel in the Huanchac neighborhood of Cuzco. The devotee who arranged it had requested masses and was denied at several other churches before Huanchac's Father Camilo Mora agreed to collaborate. Niño Compadrito was brought to the church by taxi, the mass was reported in the press, Mora was reprimanded by the archbishop, and devotees lost their new venue.

When I interviewed Father Mora in March 2003, he was nervous that our conversation might cause him more problems and asked that it not be recorded. Mora clarified that he only celebrated a mass for a dead soul and did not, as reported in the press, laud the virtues of Niño Compadrito as though he were a saint.[33] He also claimed to have been deceived, because he agreed only to say a mass for a boy named "Mario." Despite that, however, he was amply accommodating to the cult and allowed Niño Compadrito to be placed on the altar during mass.

Unlike Vallejos Santoni, Mora had extensive experience with folk devotions and an empathetic understanding of the Catholics who practiced them. He had spent a long career ministering to mono- and bilingual Quechua-speaking people whose faith, as Mora described it, was simple and prone to spontaneous innovations in response to poverty, hunger, and deep needs seeking fulfillment.

The presence of Niño Compadrito's effigy at mass is integral to a more general and common practice. Religious statuettes, prints, and dolls are taken to church so that they can "hear mass," as many Peruvians put it. An informant explained: "We take images and prints to church so they can hear mass, because if we don't take them to church on holidays they don't get to hear mass. And how would they be if they didn't hear mass?" Outings to mass are part of one's reciprocal obligations. They keep the saint happy and miraculous. At mass the prints and images are charged or recharged with the priest's blessing, holy water, and the sacred ambience generally. Some Catholics also take their home-protecting skulls to mass, so that the skulls continue to perform their duties without manifesting some otherworldly discontent.[34]

The churchgoing Niño Compadrito also recalls the popular practice of taking images of Niño Manuelito to mass. At Christmastime these dolls of the Christ child are borrowed from their domestic Nativity scenes and brought to church. They seem happy hearing mass lined up together near the altar. A priest in Cuzco related to me with a certain frustration that many people drop off and pick up their Niño Manuelito, without staying for the mass themselves. He tries to explain to them that they, not the doll, need to hear the mass, but the advice goes unheeded. Their purpose is to recharge the doll and treat it to the holy experience, and this does not require their presence.

Public opinion concerning Niño Compadrito is quite mixed in Cuzco today. Nondevotees who are aware of the cult are divided between indifference, cautious evasion, mocking dismissal, and vague curiosity that might someday result in a shrine visit. Dismissal and ridicule are often based on the common accusation that the shrine is a business exploiting gullible people. Vallejos Santoni characteristically referred to a collection box and donations for chapel construction as "shameful profit." A shopkeeper in Cuzco more colorfully explained that Niño Compadrito was once the family's pet monkey. When the monkey died, the family had it mummified because they couldn't bear the loss. Now they capitalize on the incredibly lucky fluke that credulous masses think the skeleton performs miracles.[35]

It is true that contributions are aggressively solicited from outsiders (such as the international media) who come to the Niño Compadrito shrine with nondevotional (and commercial) purposes. Among devotees, however, I have witnessed no exploitation. Clara sells candles (for one *sol*, around 30 cents) and photos of Niño Compadrito (for a voluntary contribution), but these goods are kept inside the house, out of view, and are sold only when devotees request them. They are not on display or hawked in any way, as is common at other shrines. Nor have I ever seen a collection box in Niño Compadrito's chapel.

Juan and his family live modestly in an inherited house, although their situation is far better off than that of many Cuzqueños. The family is supported by Juan's meager retirement benefits, by rent from three or four tenants who lease rooms (the house has one external bathroom for all), and by Clara's occasional work as a cook. Doubtless the family derives some benefit from the cult to Niño Compadrito, but among the devotions featured in this book it is clearly the least commercial. Indeed, if profiteering were an objective the doors would be thrown open for the November 2 fiesta, and—as at most other shrines—a range of goods would be available for purchase. Juan's inclinations are precisely in the other direction: to reduce the size of the cult and prohibit nondevotional additions to the fiesta.

Despite the Church's aggressive oppression during the late 1970s and its more tacit disapproval today, devotees persevere both in their folk devotion and in their self-identification as Catholics. When I asked Juan if devotees were Catholic, he proudly showed me the Catholic imagery around the chapel. He, like most devotees, sees no conflict or contradiction in having Niño Compadrito as the centerpiece. Devotees pray to Niño Compadrito using Catholic prayers, and, at least in theory, they are clear on the idea of intercession ("he is the link between God and us"). All of the shrine's embellishments—such as the effigy's saintly robes and crown, the altar ornaments, the candle stands, the kneelers, and even the Santa Claus hat that Niño Compadrito wore for the Christmas holidays—conform to the Catholic cultural precedents in Cuzco's many churches.

Like folk saint devotees throughout Spanish America, however, those who venerate Niño Compadrito are explicit about their disillusion with the Church. They cite the usual reasons: their folk saint devotion results in more miracles, costs less, is consonant with their culture, and is not burdened by the cumbersome oversight of priests. Juan relates that people come to Niño Compadrito because he is "very miraculous," but also because priests have lost their credibility. The Church's accusations are reciprocated when Juan explains that priests "are businessmen, practically" who "charge a fortune" for masses. Niño Compadrito "is good without asking for anything, without saying anything, but priests place conditions on being Catholic." Another devotee, a man from Cuzco, concurred: "Here there is more freedom. You can pray in peace, light candles, cry, without being watched by priests."

A woman who was new to the devotion added candidly that she felt more comfortable and closer to God at Niño Compadrito's shrine than she did in the churches. "The churches are so beautifully adorned that sometimes poor people don't feel comfortable there." Jesus was poor and simple too, she continued, unlike the churches built in his name. He reveals himself in humble, unlikely places (her example was the tree with Christ's face in Izcuchaca) so that he can be among common people in their everyday environment. By these standards, the finery of canonized saints is conducive not to Niño Compadrito's detriment and exclusion, but rather to his benefit and exaltation. It is precisely his stark, unrefined, accommodating image, perhaps even his alleged unsaintly ugliness, that gives Nino Compadrito his appeal.

At the Shrine

Devotion to Niño Compadrito bounced back after the repression and was on the rise again in the mid-1980s. At that time, the cult encompassed, as it does today, a poor and uneducated campesino base complemented by professionals including doctors, nurses, lawyers, politicians, accountants, psychologists, teachers, and engineers. The repression had in some ways strengthened the devotion by giving it visibility, endorsing it unwittingly as a kind of opposition party, and enhancing Niño Compadrito's reputation as an avenger. The post-persecution rebound was also indebted to María Belén, who dedicated herself to building back what had been lost during the years of persecution and hiding. Then, in 1986 (some say 1989), she died.

Following a three-month closure for mourning (again disrupting the continuity and momentum of cult development), the shrine was reopened under Juan's direction. Niño Compadrito was initially displayed in an interim chapel and on an altar in a second-story bedroom. A new chapel, which is still used today, was built in 2001 with the support of devotee donations.

One of these donors, according to Yuri, became the minister of labor under President Alberto Fujimori. He had learned of Niño Compadrito through news reports in Lima, became a devotee, and knew in advance that he would be appointed to the ministry because Niño Compadrito revealed it in a dream. Later, when corruption resulted in Fujimori's flight, this minister escaped reprisals that were suffered by others thanks to Niño Compadrito's protection.

Rosa also donated money, for the cement floor, and the next day a chicken showed up at her door. She asked around, believing one of the neighbors had lost the chicken, but then realized that Niño Compadrito had sent it in thanks. "What one gives him," she told me, "he knows how to reciprocate."

Juan's temperament lacks something of the personable traits that promote the growth of folk devotions, and the same might be said of his wife, Clara. They are cautious, introverted, quiet, protective, and at times unaccommodating. These traits are to some degree a lingering consequence of the years of repression, during which vigilance and discretion saved Niño Compadrito from likely confiscation. Juan clearly prefers a low-profile devotion to one that might again incite a repressive action from the Church. He also became more distrustful of unknown devotees following the burglary of Niño Compadrito's original chapel, which was located closer to the street. A Cuzco-school painting and other valuables were stolen on that occasion, and Juan also relates an attempt to steal the effigy itself.

Under Juan's direction the visits to Niño Compadrito's shrine have assumed a character quite unlike the amenable accommodation offered by María Belén. I was stuck by a certain lack of cordiality at the shrine, a lack of familiarity or community. Excepting the few inner-circle devotees who enjoy closer relations, the visitors did not seem to connect in any significant way with the shrine owners. Most devotees directed themselves to the shrine almost anonymously, barely greeting Juan or Clara (who went about their business) and leaving immediately after a short visit to the chapel. Juan prefers that devotees do not linger, and a sign sometimes on a wall of the chapel announces that "Visits with Niño Compadrito are brief." When I asked Juan what "brief" meant, he replied fifteen minutes.

Juan's hesitant reception of devotees owes in part to the physical location of the chapel, which is more or less at the center of the family's private life. The yard is walled and one must ring to be admitted, which allows for control of access, but once devotees are inside they move through a space ordinarily reserved for family and friends. Juan is reluctant to have large numbers of unfamiliar people walking through his life, and he communicates this implicitly and explicitly. The shrine is owner-oriented rather than user-oriented: it is a home first, opened at the discretion of the family, and Niño Compadrito devotees, including those fulfilling promises to visit, must adapt to this reality.

Juan's preference for a smaller cult was evident on Niño Compadrito's feast day in November 2003. I had just arrived in Cuzco and was expecting an event similar to those on other saint-day fiestas—music, food, crowds—but nothing had been planned. There was no party, no schedule of events, no special decorations or preparations, no extra costs. By midmorning people began arriving in a steady flow, but the volume was a fraction of what I had witnessed at other folk saint shrines. For Juan, however, the numbers were significant. It became clear that he did not want to be overwhelmed by a crowd in the yard between the chapel and his home. New arrivals were made to wait outside of the yard, on the street side of the wall, and were admitted a few at a time as other devotees departed.

Then, quite suddenly, as though the idea had just occurred to him, Juan announced that he wanted to visit his parents in the cemetery (it was the Day of the Dead). He and Clara ushered out the few devotees who were in the chapel and told the others, some of whom had waited more than an hour outside the wall, to return the following day. I was entirely surprised by this move, even by the suggested return "tomorrow" rather than "later," because the sacredness of the feast—the one day of the year singled out to honor the saint—seemed entirely irrelevant to Juan and Clara. Devotees took the dismissal quite seriously, particularly those who feared that they would be unable to fulfill promises made to Niño Compadrito. When the people waiting outside learned that the shrine was closing, their anger flared and some pleaded futilely for entry.

A day that could have fostered devotion, built community, and celebrated the virtues of Niño Compadrito thus resulted instead in the alienation of the small coterie of devotees who had shown up. The only upside that I could discern in the closing of the shrine was accidental: as the supply was reduced, the value of and longing for Niño Compadrito were increased. Restricted access to the effigy also accepted interpretations that were beneficial to the devotees who had gained entry. A group of women who were admitted just before the closing, for example, described this as a miracle granted by Niño Compadrito because he wanted to receive their visit.

Juan, who in this regard is like his mother, is opposed to any sort of fiesta resembling the Catholic saint-day extravaganzas common in the Andes, which generally involve a lot of drinking. "After the mass, the drunken party," Juan laments, and he adds that such events, which incur unaffordable expenses, are more about the food, drink, music, and party than they are about religion.

Juan wants Niño Compadrito's feast to include nothing but devotion: "his masses, his candles, and that's it." This limitation runs counter to cultural expectations, however, and thus frustrates devotees who are accustomed to celebrating saints' days more festively. One devotee, a female lawyer, once brought two bottles of champagne to the shrine, to share with others on Niño Compadrito's feast day. Juan reluctantly allowed her to serve the champagne, but when devotees then began pooling money to buy more alcoholic drinks, Juan put an end to the party.

Thus November 2 at Niño Compadrito's shrine is hardly different from any other day, save that devotees arrive in greater numbers. On a typical day Juan's family, along with the people who rent rooms in the house, tend to their daily business as the occasional devotee comes and goes. Most devotees arrive empty-handed or with candles; some bring flowers or gifts for Niño Compadrito. The protocols of devotion (like the fiesta) are undeveloped, in comparison to those at other folk saint shrines. There is no fixed ritual, no developed iconography, no standardized prayer. One arrives, lights candles, touches the *urna*, and prays in one's own manner—some silently, some aloud, some in tears.

The spiritual contract—miracle granted, promise paid—also seems looser in Niño Compadrito devotion than it does in many others. Devotees may conform to the chronology of making a request and then fulfilling a promise, but often they come simply to pray. Many make courtesy calls to pay their respects and to keep the channels of communication open. Some come in response to dreams.

Offerings are also made in advance of miracle requests in order to establish a relation. One first-time visitor brought flowers for Niño Compadrito "in thanks for the blessing I hope he will give me," as she put it, and another, on her second visit, brought handmade clothes as a gesture, a kind of prelude, before the eventual request that she planned. A young man explained that he had stopped visiting Niño Compadrito because his miracle requests were not granted. He then realized that this was misguided, that he should manifest his faith without tests and hope for the best, so he was there again at the shrine, on his knees.

Some long-term devotees present multiple requests that they reciprocate in installments. Rosa, for example, had a prioritized list: "First, I want my husband to get the police job; second, I want to finish my studies; and third, if Niño Compadrito is willing, I want to go to the United States." To inspire fulfillment of the first request, Rosa had a saintly outfit made for Niño Compadrito in the color of a police uniform. This outfit, along with a police badge that she supplied, were worn by Niño Compadrito for several days

Niñito Compadrito ayudame a q'p∈o una
persona positiva ayudame en mis
estudios y a mi familio, gracias
Papito por Todo lo q' hoces por
mi familio protegelos a que ya
ninguna persona malo se interponga
en su felicidad ayuda a mis hermanitos
en sus estudios y a q' sus
Tengan malas actitudes si no mos
bien a q' sean buenos personas

In this note, written on the back of a school identification card, a young
devotee asks Niño Compadrito for help with her studies and for protection
of her family's happiness. The note stresses positive values—being good people, avoiding bad attitudes—that the devotee desires for herself and her
sisters.

following her petition. Rosa also uses her good relations with Niño Compadrito to help others; she requested food for a hungry family, for example, and
a father's recognition and support of his child. "Let me know specifically what
you would like me to request," Rosa wrote to me by email, "because he listens
to everything I ask of him."

Niño Compadrito's clothes and adornments are changed frequently, often
in response to requests such as Rosa's. Around Christmas 2003, I noticed that
the effigy was adorned with an image of the Virgin of Guadalupe. When I asked
why—supposing there was some significant link—Clara responded that a
devotee had attended a Guadalupe fiesta (December 12) and wanted to put the
image on Niño Compadrito. Such informal reasons as these—the offerings and
desires of devotees—account for the changing appearance and associations of
Niño Compadrito. No one expects greater reason or meaning. Randomness is
the rule. Had the devotee visited the Virgin of Copacabana or the Lord of
Miracles, one of these images would have adorned Niño Compadrito instead.

These examples illustrate how access to Niño Compadrito can be quite
open and relations quite intimate for devotees who are known, dedicated, and
serious. The cult will more than likely continue in this direction of fewer
devotees—an inner circle with no outer ring. After the annual mass in 2004,
which was lightly attended to begin with, a smaller group went to Rosa's house
to pray, sing, and share punch and cookies with Niño Compadrito. Decisions
such as these—a few people gathered elsewhere rather than an open house at
the shrine—condition the future of the devotion.

Juan affords special privileges to devotees who have earned his confidence, but he does so cautiously and not without anxiety. One trusted devotee
asked to have Niño Compadrito spend a night in her home, and Juan agreed
to this extraordinary exception. He and Clara delivered Niño Compadrito to the
home by taxi, assisted the hostess in arranging a temporary altar to properly
accommodate the effigy, stayed for dinner, and then went home. Once in bed,
however, they began to fear that the woman might undress Niño Compadrito to
look at his bones—a privilege that they jealously guard. That's when they heard
the knock at the door. Clara got up to investigate and saw Niño Compadrito's
face, but when they turned on the lights and checked around, Niño Compadrito
was nowhere to be found.

Devotees have contributed not only to Niño Compadrito's dress, but also to
the evolution of the effigy itself. Over the years Niño Compadrito has revealed
in dreams the directives for improvement of his appearance. Interpretation of
these revelations, along with devotee innovation, corroboration, and resistance,
have guided the effigy's gradual transformation. The skeleton is entirely covered with clothing, but the protruding skull has gained a life-in-death quality
by the addition of glass eyes, eyelashes, teeth, and a wig of long, dark hair. A
tooth, inserted in the early 1970s, was the first embellishment. The gradual
refinement of the effigy undid something of the distance between church
saints and Niño Compadrito, but without forfeiting the effigy's real-bone, one-
of-us, and spooky qualities.

In a miracle register a young woman acknowledged her gratitude to Niño
Compadrito, then added, "I had eyes and eyelashes put in because he himself
asked for them." During María Belén's tenure, however, the protocol for
changes to the effigy were not that simple. Devotees related revelations to María
Belén, who considered them, consulted with other devotees, and awaited a
dream of her own to ratify the revelation's authenticity. Sometimes the inner-
circle devotees also had dreams to confirm individual revelations, as was the
case during the discovery of Niño Compadrito's true name, Mario. Once a
revelation from Niño Compadrito had been properly verified, then the news was
announced and the corresponding change was made.[36]

When the devotee first proposed the addition of eyes, and blue eyes
at that, María Belén was disconcerted by the idea of such a major alteration. She consulted with other devotees, who opposed the change, but shortly
after she received a confirming dream revelation. The objections were over-
ruled and the eyes were approved. As Juan reported, Niño Compadrito then
revealed his satisfaction with the eyes: "I am good now—I can see everything."[37]

On another occasion, the authenticity of dream revelations was tested when Niño Compadrito announced that he was married to a devotee. "I am your husband," Niño Compadrito told the woman, but she protested, arguing that she was already married. Niño Compadrito insisted. "I am your husband. You married me, and I am the father of your children," he said, and the woman finally acquiesced. The woman's actual husband was not pleased. His protests were no match for Niño Compadrito, however, who began haunting his dreams. In the wake of these nightmares the husband capitulated, became a devotee, and subsequently was protected during his frequent business travels.

In the meantime, other devotees received the news with reservations, partly because marriage seemed incongruous with Niño Compadrito's identity. Niño Compadrito is growing, these objecting devotees conceded, but nevertheless he is still a child: "How can we believe that he is married?" Only this one devotee had dreamed of the marriage, they argued, and "no one else has confirmed it with a revelation." The revelation must conform to Niño Compadrito's current identity, and, if it does not, then an alteration must be verified by supporting revelations and ratified by consensus.[38]

Today Juan explains that Niño Compadrito is complete, that nothing needs to be added to the effigy. The idea of corporal completion (which is also central to the Andean myth of Inkarrí, and to such image-building devotions as the Lord of Chalhuanca) is important to Juan. He insists that Niño Compadrito's skeleton is perfect in its entirety and unity, not missing a bone, even though at other moments he acknowledges that the effigy was damaged during the 1950 earthquake and depends now on a wooden spine support. The effigy's completion, together with its incorruptible real-bone composition, are regarded as evidence of its authenticity and, consequently, miraculousness.

Niño Compadrito requires nothing new, but Juan believes that the dark wig must be replaced with a blond one. Although Juan is unlikely to make the connections, this change conforms to the precedent of the blond Niño Manuelito (who, like Niño Compadrito, appears in dreams as a blond child) and to cultural biases that privilege Caucasian features and their associations. According to Yuri, some yellow fibers on Niño Compadrito's skull contributed to the idea that "he came from abroad to help us." When a blond wig was brought to the shrine to replace the black one, Juan found the wig to be qualitatively inferior and rejected it as unacceptable. He had no complaint with the color—like the blue eyes, blond "stands out more"—but he required that the devotee provide a wig more or less similar in form and quality to the black one currently in use.

In earlier years a quasi-democratic, collective process sought consensus (but reserved María Belén's veto power) in the gradual construction of Niño

Compadrito's image and identity. The rules were always unwritten and flexible, and the decisions were subject to dream interpretation and the logic at hand, but change was governed by the dynamics of Niño Compadrito's accepted identity, revelations that stimulated additions or adjustments, and community debate. Under Juan's direction the decision-making is less collective—more a privilege he reserves—but alterations, like the blond wig, are nevertheless attributed to devotees, now with the authorizing revelation more in the background. When I asked Juan why the black wig would be replaced with a blond one, he responded simply that a devotee wanted to do it. This same rationale was offered by Clara regarding the Virgin of Guadalupe pinned to Niño Compadrito's clothes. An easygoing informality is suggested, but major change requires Juan's approval. Dream revelations are no longer central, nor are they contingent upon verification or discussion. Juan knows what he wants without revelations, debate, or consensus.

Once Niño Compadrito's image and identity are changed, these changes in turn affect the perceptions of devotees, the nature of dream revelations, and the content of myths. A blond wig would support myths tending toward the conception of a white Niño Compadrito, but only because earlier myths (which in turn are indebted to the blue eyes) predispose acceptance of the wig change. A dynamic interaction keeps the dreams, the myth, and the effigy in mutation, and this in turn affects future interactions, including miracles, between Niño Compadrito and his devotees.[39]

Conclusion

Myths in Formation

The purposes of folk saint myths are multiple: to authenticate and guarantee the saint's miraculousness; to reaffirm claims to sainthood (such as tragic death, healing, charity, and purity); to integrate the saint into local culture; to treat themes, such as poverty and injustice, that are central to the lives of devotees; and to strengthen relations between the saint's life on earth and the postmortem mission accomplished through miracles. Key episodes and attributes are transcendentalized so that from heaven the Robin Hood saints continue to provide for the poor, the curandero saints continue to heal the sick, and the maternal saints continue to nurture and protect.

Most folk saint myths consist of biographical information that mutates as it is told and retold. Emerging myths revise and assimilate historical sources; are enriched with supernatural elements and lessons of morality; and become depositories of local culture, alternative values, and unfulfilled ideals. Folk saint myths, even when definitive versions become fixed, are never static. Their force and vitality reside precisely in their constant re-creation, revision, elaboration, and adaptation. They are made by one group and remade by another, bent to the designs of individual will, lost and found in the corridors of bad memory. Myths are restless and dynamic. They compete with parallel versions of themselves, they are redirected by spin, and they spin off variations under the pressure of new crises, needs, and contexts.

Folk saints are thereby a collective creation for which no one is responsible. The life story meets certain requirements, and then the saint is tailored to the contours of evolving paradigms. Even the essential details of some myths, such as Sarita Colonia's suicide to prevent rape or Difunta Correa's miraculous breast, are nonhistorical inventions—one might say compensations—that are added by devotees to create a saint conducive to their purposes.

When there is no biography, as in the cases of folk saints who are entirely nonhistorical, then the myth is derived from the saint's iconography. The myths of San La Muerte, for example, vary in conformity with his appearance. If he is represented as a standing skeleton holding a scythe, then one life story is inspired; if he is in a squatting, fetal position with his hands on his cheeks, then another story is suggested; and if he is seated, a third story comes to mind. In these cases, mythmaking begins with visual evidence and works backward to establish a saint's life story. The absence of biographical constrictions affords great freedom of invention. One has a look at the icon and invents at will. Entirely different stories thus emerge and follow the courses of their respective evolutions independently, although they are also prone to intermingle. Some versions survive, others disappear. One version often gains supremacy.

Niño Compadrito, who was initially no more than a pile of bones, acquired his story in this retrospective manner. Devotees contemplate the effigy and wonder: "To whom could these miraculous remains belong? Why is the skeleton so small? How did Niño Compadrito die?" The identity is fleshed out, in the same way (but perhaps more earnestly) that colonial friars invented saintly stories upon the chance encounter of human remains. The life story of a corpse washed up on Margarita Island, Venezuela, in 1986 was likewise unknown when it inspired folk devotion among fishermen. In this case, as in Niño Compadrito's, the remains themselves are enough to cohere a cult. The story catches up later.

When a devotee reported that Niño Compadrito requested blue eyes, the cult was divided on the revelation's authenticity. Most devotees have dark skin, hair, and eyes, and a blue-eyed Niño Compadrito violated the critical "one of us" principle of folk devotion. At that time, however, Niño Compadrito's identity as the viceroy's son—as creole (or, in some versions, mestizo)—had not yet been established. One can therefore discern in this debate over eye color the identity in formation of a folk saint whose story was up for grabs. Those in favor of dark eyes advocated the most common option: the congruity of the saint and the community. Those who made the daring leap to blue eyes, conversely, envisioned a messianic Niño Compadrito, a privileged outsider who came with his upper-class looks, connections, and power to help locals.

Thus myth production can work in a forward direction, from biography to myth to the icon that visually represents the myth (as is clear in Difunta Correa's case); or it can work backward, from an icon to a myth that stands in for the biography that is missing (as in the cases of San La Muerte and Niño Compadrito).

A third option is introduced when myths are attributed to spiritual sources. The story of Niño Perdido was related by the channeled spirit of Niño Jesús de Praga, who communicated it through a medium, Lydia, to her husband, Alberto. Alberto received the story in response to his inquiries, then transcribed it. If one considers the three participants in the generation of this myth, to which should it be attributed? Niño Jesús de Praga is the obvious choice of a believer. A nonbeliever would have to argue for composite authorship that encompasses the medium, the interlocutor, and, most important, an assimilated tradition that channels through them.

In all cases, a collective creation is gradually formalized as rumors are consolidated into myths, competing versions work out an arrangement, and a few parallel versions gain prominence. The gradual institution of a version regarded as authentic consolidates the folk saint's identity. Oral tradition then becomes textual as photocopies and booklets distributed at the shrines lend the power of print to definitive versions. Some of these booklets, such as the biography of Sarita Colonia written by her brother, are concerned primarily with correcting the errors that are propagated in oral tradition. When this occurs, a rift can open between more literate devotees who go by the book and others who get their information orally. Print has a certain advantage, but the constancy of oral tradition tends to the erosion of official versions that are regarded as unacceptable or inadequate.

Other textual sources, including print media, mass-produced booklets, prayer cards, and scholarship, also play a significant role in defining the identity of folk saints. Press accounts have a huge impact. While word-of-mouth plods along from person to person, the press reaches thousands simultaneously. News articles are determined by what is interesting to readers, not what is meaningful to devotees, and this conditions how folk saints are represented. Articles about folk saints also tend toward the sensational and are sometimes full of errors, but the mystique of print fosters the presumption of their accuracy. A myth that accrues slowly over decades by word of mouth can thus be challenged suddenly by the rapid diffusion of a representation in the press. New waves of oral tradition are stimulated by press reports, thereby extending the range and longevity of media-based myths both within and outside of devotions.

Perhaps the best example is the story of Sarita Colonia's disappearing genitalia, which was first published in the Peruvian magazine *Caretas*.

Sarita's would-be rapists were confounded when they discovered that she had no vagina. That intriguing detail made the story a popular choice for telling and retelling, orally and in subsequent news articles, which in turn enhanced the exposure that solidified this version's prominence. The idea of the absent genitalia is credited to a devotee, but like many other specifics that individuals relate—Sarita prayed in the cemetery at night, mortified herself in imitation of St. Rose of Lima, drank lots of wine—it appears to be more a personal invention than a conviction held by a substantial community.

What is most significant in the present context is the relation between the source of a myth and the constituencies that hold it to be authentic. When I began my Sarita Colonia research, I expected that the disappearing-genitalia story would be prominent among devotees. I had heard it for years from friends in Lima, mostly professors like myself, which led me to the natural, erroneous conclusion that I would hear it also from devotees. I discovered instead that Sarita Colonia's devotees seem entirely unaware of this version—not a single one mentioned it.

It thus became clear that those who know the *Caretas* version are people who read *Caretas* and similar print media, such as the newspaper *El comercio*, which twice repeated the story. The devotees, on the other hand, are mostly poor migrants to Lima who lack some combination of the money, time, interest, and literacy to access these publications. They get whatever folk saint information they need—and they need very little—by word of mouth, and these versions tend less toward the intriguing poetic detail than toward the reaffirmation of beliefs that are conducive to miracles. A literary version is thus at odds with a practical one. When the literary version does circulate orally, its range is generally restricted to social groups that have little contact with devotees.

Commercial interests also contribute to the establishment and dissemination of a folk saint's identity. Marketing, like publishing, is audience oriented; it produces its goods to suit the demand. Images of San La Muerte were once carved exclusively of human bone, of bullets dug out of murdered bodies, and of approved woods, notably wood cut from cemetery crosses. The forms were sacred and standardized, the carvers were consecrated to San La Muerte, and the purists carved only on Good Friday. Today, however, the images are produced from anything that can be manufactured cheaply. Devotees buy plastic and plaster figurines, tacky oversize statues, and epoxy imitations of human bone studded at the eye with an ersatz ruby. Some of the original postures—such as the squatting figure of San La Muerte—have almost entirely disappeared, and the traditional standing figure has been overwhelmed by monkish novelties competing for shares of the market. This commercial imagery, complemented by mass-market booklets, is contributing to a rapid transformation of San La Muerte's identity. The do-it-yourself booklet and the plastic saint, like the oral texts and hand-carved images that preceded them, interact dialectically to form the saint that is inherited by subsequent generations.

As devotions become commercialized, increasing emphasis is placed on a fixed and printable story, a reproducible and readily identifiable icon, a pageant-like event that attracts thousands, and a shrine with goods and services for visitors. The president of the retail association at the Difunta Correa complex explained that folk saints are not fraudulent inventions of the businessmen who make their living at the shrines. Rather, he clarified, the miracles and devotion precede commerce, which emerges in response as the demand warrants.

Once business and religion were integrated at the Difunta Correa complex, however, and then placed under the direction of provincial tourism authorities, the devotion was changed forever. Difunta Correa is now a vested interest, with dependent third parties serving as publicity and public-relations agents to propagate the faith and, with it, the customer base. Increased attendance is the first priority and tourists are more solvent than devotees. The shrine adapts accordingly, to its audience. Profound and sincere devotion is still prominent at the Difunta Correa shrine, but it occurs now in the ambience of a religious amusement park complete with merry-go-round, gift galleries, restaurants, and picnic areas.

The "folk" aspect of devotions survives these multiple pressures in part because many devotees have little interest in anything but miracles. Even the myths themselves are ultimately of relative insignificance. Folk saints' lives, deaths, and their representations catalyze devotions, but eventually—after decades or centuries have passed—they tend to fade away behind the reputation for miracles. Devotees often have at best a vague knowledge of the life story, and many know nothing at all. (The same is often true regarding canonized saints: devotees know the name and can identify a miraculous image in church, but the saint's biography is beside the point.) The life is superseded by the tragic death, and the tragic death by fame for miracles. When I asked a group of devotees about the life of Sarita Colonia, one responded, "We don't know about her life, only about her miracles." That simple phrase summarizes the situation for tens of thousands.

The lack of knowledge about folk saints is also based on an implicit consensus that the details are unimportant. I asked a devotee, Joyce, who was responsible for the attempted rape of Sarita Colonia. I had hoped that she might expound on the role of police or soldiers, but instead she looked at me

with a confused expression and responded, "Rapists." The tone of the response suggested, "What kind of questions is that?" The specifics that were
of interest to me were quite irrelevant to her. Similarly, when I asked innumerable devotees why rituals were done in a certain manner, the response
was frequently, "That's the custom." No one really knew why. That's just how
it's done. What do you mean, why?

When the life story is better known, a folk saint can become both a miracle
broker and an exemplary human to be imitated. Sarita Colonia's life is unimportant for some devotees, but for others it provides a model, even a mandate, of
charity. These devotees may know nothing other than anecdotes concerning
Sarita's generosity to the poor, but that is sufficient to define their mission. In
other cases, such as that of Niño Fidencio, the availability of greater historical
and biographical information makes a more comprehensive life story possible. Some few devotees conduct research in depth; others have ready access to
whatever they need through extensive oral tradition, mentors, widely circulated
historical photographs, songs, and the many booklets and pamphlets sold at the
shrine. If a majority shows up in happy ignorance only for the miracle, with little
interest beyond the rudiments of the life story, then a minority (substantial in
this devotion) finds in the folk saint's life a model and an ideal.

Such accommodation of individual preference is part of the appeal. Folk
saint devotions can be personalized to suit one's condition, needs, beliefs, and
goals. Because knowledge is partial (in both senses of the term) and no version is fixed, the tailoring can provide custom-made saints for individuals as
well as for groups. San La Muerte is an anonymous amulet for some devotees,
while for others he is a saint of heroic virtue. Pelusa, a shrine owner in
Posadas, found in San La Muerte a Christlike philanthropist who has provided
the model that defines her entire life. San La Muerte cared even for lepers,
without compensation or regard for his own well-being, so Pelusa and her
husband, Isabelino, do much the same in his name. Hungry neighbors, victims of AIDS, and impoverished children have received the graces of San La
Muerte through the charity of these activist devotees.

The devotion is tailored to the saint, but the saint is also tailored to the
devotion. A typed handout produced by Pelusa for distribution at her shrine
well exemplifies how saints are customized. The handout reprints verbatim
one of the four myths—the one emphasizing charitable love—that are included in a mass-produced booklet on San La Muerte. The point is then driven
home by a commentary that Pelusa added in her own words at the conclusion
of the handout: "The people who possess this Saint have the gift of helping
others." Pelusa thereby narrowed the four options to the one that suits (and
helps define) her own charitable disposition, and then enhanced this text to

make the mandate, as she saw it, more emphatic. Those who learn of San La Muerte through Pelusa's mentoring acquire only this single and—for them—definitive version of the story.

Much the same might be said of the booklet that Pelusa wrote on San La Muerte. It provides a certain image of the saint and prescribes certain rituals, just as other booklets, by authors with their own personalized views, restrict the meanings and practices of saints in other manners. Anything goes for most devotees, but for these more rigorous (some would say dogmatic) personalities there is a correct version of the saint's story and a right way of doing things. Pelusa feels a responsibility to the definition and normalization of devotion to San La Muerte. She advocates an orthodox ideal for an unorthodox cult, and many local devotees recognize her authority and accept the correctness and exclusivity of her teachings.

Another shrine owner, Ramón in Resistencia, was exceptional in his determination to avoid such restrictive norms. He had clear preferences and a highly individualized conception of San La Muerte, but he recognized these as personal predilections that were in no way binding on others. Ramón's statements were generally qualified by "in my view" or "that's how I do it" or even "that's what I like to believe." If he advocated anything, it was the understanding that each devotee practices differently and that no single manner—at least not his—can claim correctness or supremacy. "There's nothing special you have to do to become a devotee." Folk saints provide freedom for individuation, Ramón suggested, and devotees desiring more structure can go to church.

My most profound realization during the course of gathering information on folk saints concerned, precisely, how information is gathered. In folk saint devotions everything gets jumbled together, distorted, inverted, manipulated, sidetracked, abused, and misconstrued, because that is how humans think things through when they are responsible to no one but God. Folk devotion is to a certain degree the shared celebration of misreadings and misunderstandings. The process is similar to the way in which mispronounced foreign words become standardized and accepted in the lexicon of the language that receives them. They were once erroneous, now they are correct. Myths are errors that have become correct, or fictions that have established claims to truth.

As the orality of my interviews became textual through transcription, the devotees' exaggerations, fabrications, misperceptions, invented memories, and factual errors began to metamorphose toward something like scholarship. Hearsay graduated to the legitimacy of "sources." The sources are ostensibly valid insofar as they participate in the devotional culture, but that does not mean that they are correct. Nor does it mean that their errors, fabrications, or lies are insignificant. At what point does a scholar, who is subject to tests of accuracy far beyond those of oral tradition, question the interrelations of errors, lies, and myths? At what point does one intervene to correct a source?

These questions haunted me after I conducted interviews in La Higuera, Bolivia, where Che Guevara was executed. Over the years the residents of this village have given paid interviews to so many reporters, filmmakers, and scholars that being interviewed has become a cottage industry. The La Higuera residents with whom I talked seemed eager to repeat their canned speeches and get to the part where the money changed hands. Once they understood that I was looking for something other than the routine recital of what had happened during those fateful days in 1967, then they made an adjustment—as one would pitch a product to a different kind of customer—and began telling me what they thought I wanted to hear. The better the information, they presumed, the better the payment. If I was looking for devotion, there was lots of devotion. If I wanted miracles, they had miracles. Would I like a resurrection from the dead? They fabricated information as best they could, sometimes with emotional facial expressions to strengthen the appearance of their sincerity.

A monument to Che Guevara in La Higuera, Bolivia, where he was killed. The cross and space beneath it for offerings were already at the site when Che's image was installed.

The falsity of the information seemed to me apparent enough, but to test my impressions I sought corroboration from La Higuera residents who were not on the interview circuit and from campesinos of neighboring villages. No one had any idea what I was talking about. Nor was there any material evidence, such as the altars, imagery, or devotional paraphernalia that always accompany folk saint devotions.

My impressions were definitively confirmed when I returned to the nearest town, Vallegrande, and discussed my experiences with the hotel owner. He related that foreign television reporters often return from La Higuera excited by the new information that they have gathered. Some of them show him the interview footage, and, he explained, "It's all lies." Everyone in La Higuera knows that the news media pay well, so residents try to be newsworthy. They say whatever they think may sell. Once these fabrications are cut into a polished broadcast, imbued with studio slick and prestige, they easily masquerade as truths before the huge, passive audiences that consume them. Such errors remain on the record and factual until disproof reaches and convinces those who hold the erroneous ideas.

I had traveled to La Higuera in part because I had read an article that reported significant devotion to Che Guevara. The article's evidence was heavily dependent on the reports of a folklorist from Vallegrande. He related that locals had paid respects to the dead Che in the washroom of the Señor de Malta Hospital, which is true, but he did so in terms that stressed devotion.

> Everyone living in Vallegrande went to see him with deep respect, admiration, and sorrow. Many people cried. There was a woman who said, "Che looks like Christ," and a nun replied, "He doesn't look like him, he is Christ—he died defending poor and humble people, as Christ did." And from that moment the word spread that he was Christ.[1]

When I interviewed this folklorist in 2003, he told me the same story, but the nun's script had mellowed with the years. She now remarked only that the dead Che resembled Christ after the Crucifixion. (There was indeed a physical resemblance, and it made a major contribution to whatever devotion did occur after Che's death.) The folklorist was easily led in the interview that I conducted with him, and I imagined how he and his interlocutors could have arrived at their destination without knowing that they were drifting off course. I found little evidence of devotion to Che in Vallegrande and La Higuera, but I did find this folklorist, who had significant information attributed to community sources. His report, combined with the print articles, the fabrications from La Higuera, and the trace evidence of devotion, could easily have been woven into a convincing, substantiated exposition that nevertheless would have been entirely inaccurate.

Thus untrue information is offered for profit, for sport, and because people believe it is true; it is disseminated by the press and scholarship as though it were true; and it becomes true for significant populations because the presented evidence (or the media that present it) seems convincing in the absence of disproof.

I had another illuminating experience in this regard during conversations with Yuri, whose parents own Niño Compadrito. Yuri is the source of a prominent myth that links Niño Compadrito to a mysterious boy in Tambomachay. One day, as Yuri and I talked in a café on Cuzco's main plaza, he confessed, without any prompting or foreknowledge on my part, that he had fabricated the myth. Yuri, a young boy at the time, was flustered and flattered by the attention of reporters who had approached him for an interview. Something had to be said, he figured, so he made up the story and attributed it to his grandmother. The reporters readily accepted what Yuri told them; like the reporters in La Higuera, they were pleased to acquire something new. The myth was printed in their article and has subsequently been repeated in media and scholarly accounts, as well as by devotees.

Yuri's fabrication is the reality of devotees who do not know or question the source of the myth. When devotees relate this myth to one another, or to reporters and scholars, they are now expressing beliefs integral to their devotion, beliefs exempt from tests of truth. It no longer matters that the source is flawed. All myths are fabrications. Belief authenticates them.

This particular fabrication has endured perhaps for the same reason that Yuri was able to come up with it on short notice. The story rings so true in Cuzco because it resembles (and is indirectly derived from) Andean traditions that are known by everyone. The *apus* (mountain spirits) that manifest themselves as children, including syncretic advocations of the Christ child, readily come to mind, as does the boy Manuel of Qoyllur Rit'i myths. The boy in Yuri's myth also resembles the form assumed by Niño Compadrito in other apparitions. In the end, Yuri offered the reporters more an adaptation than a fabrication. He applied broader folk traditions to the specific case of Niño Compadrito, which is precisely how this devotion gained momentum and definition from the beginning.

Yuri's father, Juan, likewise surprised me with an unexpected innovation. The story was remarkable in content, but also because it was contradicted by the very evidence that Juan presented to substantiate it. Niño Compadrito did not have a life story, Juan explained, so an analysis of bone scrapings was done by a Japanese scholar to determine the skeleton's past. This scientific analysis never actually occurred, however, and in any case the narrative discoveries attributed to it (that Niño Compadrito was the son of a viceroy, for example) are far beyond the range of laboratory science. Niño Compadrito's life story is indebted to Juan rather than to bone analysis, but the fact that Juan's myth is detoured through Japan and substantiated by science is significant.

After relating the story of the bone scraping and how it revealed Niño Compadrito's identity, Juan pardoned himself to get something in the next room. I braced myself for an unpleasant experience—maybe holding a vial or baggy full of bone powder. The baggies always leak. Juan returned instead with an offprint of an article by a Japanese anthropologist, Takahiro Kato, and handed it to me so that I could see the proof for myself. This threw me entirely off balance, because I was quite familiar with the article and knew that it had nothing to do with bone analysis. (The article even gently suggests that the Niño Compadrito remains may not be human.)

I was thus confronted by the paradox of a narrative contradicted by the evidence supplied to corroborate it. I leafed through the article, trying to come up with something to say, while Juan looked on in satisfaction. A couple of guinea pigs were running around on the floor. I wondered how Juan interpreted my goofy smile and lame attempt to conceal my bafflement. He had confided his story and offered supporting proof, and he stood before me totally, happily unaware that the hard-science evidence was as mythological as the narrative that it substantiated. That consonance between the story and the proof, I later realized, was the key: it registered a way of perceiving reality, a means of cognition, a mythopoetic reconciliation of contradictions.

Juan's story and the false evidence that supports it reveal the essence of folk saint mythmaking. The story is a fabrication without being a lie; there is nothing dishonest in its creation. Rather, Juan, like many or most folk saint devotees, lives in a world in which reality, dream, myth, magic, rumor, and imagination freely intermingle. Outside of that world miracles do not happen. Devotees enjoy a happy imprecision that keeps things malleable, that permits an unflinching accommodation of contradiction, and that leaves the exactitude of cold logic at the door. The truth of Juan's story, like the truth of fiction, requires the willing suspension of disbelief. It is a mythic truth in formation, a fiction that becomes history. The truth adapts to the myth.

Juan often maintains that nothing is known about Niño Compadrito's origins, and that the stories told by devotees are pure invention. When he introduces a story of his own, therefore, it must have a greater claim to authenticity than those that are dismissed. It must be substantiated and indisputable. Other devotees invent myths; Juan reports the findings of foreign scientists. The fact that the bone research never occurred, and that the article presented as evidence damages rather than supports Juan's case, are technicalities pushed out of range so that the story can enjoy its truth. Mythmaking will not be confused by facts. Juan's truth is subjective without knowing what "subjective truth" means: it is purely subjective. This subjective truth eventually becomes objective as it dissolves into the collective and leaves its source behind. Folk saint myths do not relate what happened; they construct a mythic reality that is historicized to create what happened retrospectively.

Juan's use of the article as evidence also provides insight into the nature of texts within essentially oral traditions. The document itself, not its content, is what substantiated Juan's claims. He proudly submitted the article into evidence not as a kind of trickery—not with the hope that it would never be read, so that he could pull off a deception—but rather because the fact that it was a scholarly article written by a Japanese scholar was good enough for him. The article is proof in itself. The specifics of its content are beside the point. Texts are imbued with power and authority by virtue of the mystique of their indecipherability. They can say whatever you like.

The standards of evidence in oral tradition are sufficiently informal to make Juan's scientific proof seem exceedingly rigorous. Folk saint myths are substantiated by pushing verification out of range. The common sources, when they are not entirely anonymous, are ancestors or sagelike elders from remote and exotic regions. The accuracy of the source is never questioned. The discourse is always greater than whoever repeats it. Phrases like "people say" or "it is said that" precede much folk saint narrative. The myth is disowned even by the voice that speaks it, while at once its precarious truth is reinforced by attribution to a collective. The vagueness of origin also protects the flexibility of folk traditions, allowing for evolution and adaptation to changing cultural contexts and needs. There is no copyright; you can do with the text what you please. The written word should be less forgiving, but once documents such as the Japanese article assume magical properties, once *it is written* overtakes *what is written*, then the text can support even what it contradicts.

The mother of a Peruvian folk saint, Rosita de Pachacutec, was much like Juan in her unawareness of the discrepancies between what she said and the text that she supplied to support it. At the conclusion of our conversation the mother gave me a shrine-produced booklet on Rosita that—I later realized—provided an account of the events that was less spectacular, less miraculous than her oral version. She gave me the booklet not to contradict herself, of course, but rather to complement and enhance what she had told me. Within and beyond the covers of the booklet, the mother is the primary source of information on Rosita, the authoritative source, the last word. Her memories have been formed and re-formed under the pressure of evolving myths that these same memories themselves substantiate. The myth is derived from the memory that it revises. That is why it gets better with age. The written text of the booklet is fixed, however, and probably needs fixing, because the oral version evolves ever away from it and more deeply into hagiography.

Recurring Themes

Folk saint devotions emerge in varied cultural contexts but nevertheless hold several themes in common. The recurring themes, like the recurring prototypes of the saints themselves, are most suggestive when they emerge independently, without the need for precedent, influence, or imitation. Their unguided and simultaneous expression—their insistence—attest to their necessity in the genesis of folk devotions. I briefly summarize, in conclusion, the themes that are most important.

Politics

Political despair is essential to folk saint devotions. Most devotees are deprived the material befits of capitalism, and their marginal social stations exclude them from the privileges of democracy, such as representation, equality before the law, and a fair chance to survive economically. The Church, too, has failed them, spiritually and politically. Facing what they experience as abandonment, they turn away from institutions toward options outside of the system, options that they invent themselves. They venerate rebels and criminals, outsider heroes who take them into account, and others who represent in the extreme their own sense of victimization. Such folk saints provide reinforcements for a daily struggle not so much against authorities as against the mess that authorities have made of devotees' social reality. In times of great disillusion with governments and with the Church, many devotees explain their folk saint devotion, however strange, by saying, "You have to believe in something."

The implied political content of folk saint myths is diverse, including the summary and judicial execution of innocents, the attempted rape of Sarita Colonia by police or soldiers, the imprisonment of San La Muerte by priests, the murder of Niño Compadrito in revenge for the cruelties of his father (the viceroy), and the legal and clerical harassment of Niño Fidencio and other curanderos. Politics is a more explicit factor in devotion to Pancho Villa, Che Guevara, and, in Peru, Edith Lagos, a cadre of Sendero Luminoso killed in 1982. The Mexican folk saint Teresa Urrea inspired indigenous rebellions with her message of justice, and she and her father were exiled to the United States by the dictator Porfirio Díaz. Some of the later outlaw folk saints in Argentina, such as Bairoletto and Andrés Bazan Frías, had contact with anarchist ideology.[2]

Folk saints also emerge in the context of political struggles that directly affect them despite their own indifference to the causes or reluctance to participate. Difunta Correa and the many gaucho saints, including Gaucho Gil, are inseparably bound to the wars between Federales and Unitarios in Argentina, and the Mexican Revolution and subsequent Cristero Rebellion contributed to the success of Niño Fidencio's mission in Espinazo.

The devotion to María Lionza is permeated with politics, from the Venezuelan flag in the standard iconography to the channeled spirits of independence heroes, notably Simón Bolívar. Other prominent figures in the courts under María Lionza include Negro Primero (Pedro Camejo), who fought with Bolívar in the independence wars; Negro Felipe, a prominent figure in the Cuban struggle for independence; and Negro Miguel, the leader of a sixteenth-century slave rebellion. Some say that María Lionza was the lover of the colonial rebel Lope de Aguirre, who declared war against the king of Spain. Also in Venezuela, the nineteenth-century civil wars produced the folk saint known as the Anima del Padre [José] Magne after this liberal priest was captured and executed in 1862. Conservative politicians also gain folk sainthood. The mestizo general Juan Vicente Gómez, dictator of Venezuela for thirty years in the early twentieth century, is petitioned for freedom from prison.[3]

Folk devotion is a response to corrupt and inept political systems. It is a declaration of preference for outsiders whose otherworldly power can be deployed as a compensatory weapon of the weak. It is a way of being the underdog. "We are fed up" is the implicit discourse of devotees to authorities. "We are a community in miraculous protest because we otherwise cannot survive your failures."

Justice

While her husband was away on a work detail, Mercedes Esquivel, known as La Degolladita, had an affair with an ex-boyfriend. The husband responded to the infidelity by tying her to a tree and cutting off her head. The lover was falsely convicted of the crime and imprisoned, because the court believed that he murdered Mercedes for refusing his sexual advances. Shortly after, however, La Degolladita appeared in his prison cell—she had the form of a white shadow—to reveal where the murder weapon had been hidden. The knife was located, the husband's name was found carved on its handle, the prisoner was released, and justice was served. Thus the devotion to La Degolladita had its auspicious beginning: in the heavenly reversal of human injustice.[4]

The quest for justice is a leitmotif of folk saint narratives. Many depict their protagonists, such as Víctor Apaza or Francisco López, as falsely accused and executed for crimes that they did not commit. Their sainthood is a direct consequence of these injustices. They are framed by corrupt superiors (Juan Soldado), summarily executed by police and soldiers (Gaucho Gil, Frente Vital), or forced outside the law by false allegations (Gaucho Lega). These stories ring true among devotees who live on the margin of society and, often, on the edge of the law. They too feel overpowered by authority and, when they are on the wrong side of an arrest or civil suit, are at a decided disadvantage in courts where verdicts can be bought.

The abuses of criminal justice against a Frente Vital or a Gaucho Gil are extremities that accentuate the more constant, generalized, and inescapable social injustice experienced daily by devotees. In Sarita Colonia's myth the injustice is represented by rape or, more accurately, an attempted rape that Sarita must die to escape. Death is the only way out. Through a kind of death-defying surrender, however, folk saint devotees resign themselves to flawed justice—criminal and social—because they have recourse to higher authorities who bail them out. Human justice is, by definition (because of the "human"), imperfect and doomed eternally to abuses, manipulations, and aberrations. Divine justice, on the other hand, is perfect. It affords devotees a superior court of appeal for miscarriages of human justice.

Folk saints make the necessary corrections and compensations by punishing corrupt or exploitative authorities; by protecting a father who steals a chicken to feed his family; by arranging a not-guilty verdict or release from prison; by haunting a thief until he returns the stolen goods; by disfiguring the lover of one's adulterous husband; and by putting one's adversaries (enemies, judges, competitors, ex-spouses) in harm's way. The line between justice and aggressive hostility is sometimes unclear. When petitions to curse others are made with black candles, they are described both as "doing evil" (when others do it) and as "justice" (when one does it).

The commitment of folk saints to justice is often carried in their myths, titles, and revelations. Niño Fidencio is the *Niño Abogado* (an *abogado* is a lawyer or advocate); Niño Compadrito revealed that he wanted to be a judge; and San La Muerte is known as *San Justo* (the just saint, or St. Justice). In one prominent myth San La Muerte is chosen to oversee life and death because God recognizes his exemplary administration of justice as a king on earth. Christ himself is the *Justo Juez* (Just Judge), and, like the folk saints at his service, he intervenes in earthly affairs to remedy injustices. The Peruvian

Christ child known as Niño de las Chutas, venerated in Oropesa, steals bread from baskets and distributes it among the poor. Such corrective or charitable theft is also central to the identity of Gaucho Gil and the many other folk saints who exact justice through civil disobedience and noble banditry. The are referred to as *justicieros*, which translates as "avengers" but at once indicates their adherence to the principles of justice.[5]

The theme of justice is particularly prominent in the Argentine devotion to María Soledad. In 1990, when María was seventeen, she was raped and murdered by two young men. Afterward they disfigured her face with the hope of impeding her identification. Justice was a prominent theme during investigation and prosecution of the crime, and then later in iconography and devotion, because a cover-up attempted to exonerate the perpetrators, one of whom was the son of a government official. Massive social protest finally resulted in incarceration of the two guilty men. Today, a huge statue holding the scales of justice dominates María Soledad's shrine in Catamarca.

This historical photograph of Niño Fidencio is known as the Niño Abogado. Many images of Fidencio, each emphasizing a different aspect of his identity, are traded among devotees.

Alive in Death

In Spanish America there is significant interaction between the living and the dead, and the aliveness of dead folk saints is a dimension of this more comprehensive phenomenon. Folk saints eat, drink, talk, grow, and bleed. They appear in visions and dreams, they possess the bodies of mediums, and they intervene to protect, guide, avenge, and clear one's path. They also get tired, disappointed, and annoyed, like people. And they get even.

Folk saint narratives are replete with details attesting to life beyond death. Juan Soldado talks from his tomb; Difunta Correa's corpse breastfeeds her child; Miguelito prefers a different sort of casket; Che Guevara's corpse won't close its eyes; and Niño Compadrito's skeleton is growing. When Francisco López was shot by a firing squad, instead of dying he charged forward, grabbed the bayonet of one soldier, and did whatever damage he could before they finally cut off his head. Then "the head jumped and rolled in one direction and another," and witnesses "considered it something like a miracle and like the dead man's protest." When Niño Fidencio's throat was slit by the embalmers, fresh blood—the blood of a living person—squirted out.[6]

All of these examples provide a corporal complement to the life-after-death that is proven spiritually through miracles. The transfer of attributes from the living soul to the dead body has particular longevity when the saint is closely associated with the remains, as in the case of Niño Compadrito.

Dreams

Dreams provide a midway space—half physical, half spiritual—in which supernatural beings, including the souls of dead family members, communicate with the living. Folk saints conform to this practice. San La Muerte is typical: he appears in dreams to give advice and solve problems, but also to inform devotees of the offerings and care he requires. Some devotees make requests to folk saints and then await the response in their dreams. "Make me dream the numbers I should play in the lottery," a devotee wrote to Gaucho Gil.[7]

Entire lives can be affected by dreams and their interpretations. A boy who had been twice rescued from death by Niño Fidencio was pressured by family members to dedicate his life to Fidencio's mission. The father was repeatedly informed in dreams that this was the boy's calling. The boy resisted, however; he had other ideas for his saved life. The matter was settled when Niño Fidencio appeared in a dream to the boy himself. Fidencio, holding a large book, carefully erased the boy's name, thereby releasing him from the obligation.[8]

Dreams are particularly prevalent in the devotion to Niño Compadrito. He appears in dreams for multiple purposes—to reveal future events, to warn of impending dangers, to gives advice or direction in solving problems, to help find lost objects (Juan found his watch, a man found his false teeth lost on the road), to request offerings, and to reveal his identity or mandate changes to his effigy. When a miracle has been granted but the promised offering has not been made, Niño Compadrito appears in dreams to enforce the contract. These anxiety dreams tend to instill fear in their recipients, who often arrive at the shrine anxious to make their payment, appease the saint, and avoid reprisals.

Niño Compadrito most commonly appears in dreams in the skeletal form displayed at the shrine, or else as a boy, with attributes similar to those of Niño Manuelito. He also assumes many other identities. For people with legal problems, he has appeared as a lawyer or judge; for those worthy of a scolding, as a father; for those in need of financial assistance, as a compadre; and for those in need of medical care, as a doctor. Niño Compadrito also appears as a policeman and other authority figures who lay down or enforce the law. All of these forms of apparition are typical of dream revelations in folk Catholicism generally. A devotee of the Lord of Qoyllur Rit'i, for example, explained that "if we dream about police, soldiers, authorities, or condors, we have dreamed about God."[9]

Dream revelations underscore how miracles are rarely instantaneous solutions passively received and are, instead, collaborative efforts between a saint and a devotee. María Catalina, a Venezuelan folk saint, appears by request in the dreams of sick devotees to reveal the remedies for their illnesses. The following morning the devotees visit María Catalina's tomb to make offerings in thanks for the revelation, but they also follow the instructions prescribed in the dream. Folk saints appear in dreams to give legal advice, but one must act on it; business plans, but one must follow them; marital counseling, but one must stop the drinking, womanizing, and wife beating. Miracles are collaborative efforts between the saint's supernatural intervention and the devotee's efficacious action.[10]

Innocence, Purity, and Childhood

Innocence and purity encompass the angelitos who die free of sin and go directly to heaven (such as the various foundling saints); the folk saints who are believed to be innocent of the crimes for which they are executed (such as Gaucho Gil, Juan Soldado, and Ubilberto Vásquez Bautista); and, more broadly, the folk saints whose innocence is recuperated by tragic death that washes away sin with blood. Víctor Apaza scores in all three categories, because his perceived innocence and sin-purging death by firing squad combined with an angelito quality afforded by his confession and communion just before the execution. La Chavela achieved folk sainthood because her entire, suffered life was a penance that purged a secret sin. In San La Muerte devotion, the importance of innocence and purity is indexed by the preference for amulets carved in the bone of sin-free infants.

Chastity and virginity are also crucial attributes of some folk saints. It is important to devotees that Niño Fidencio was a virgin, and Difunta Correa's death is sometimes represented as a defense of fidelity against sexual indiscretions. Sarita Colonia is perhaps the best example, because myth introduces a nonhistorical threat to her purity (the attempted rape) so that the endangered purity can then be preserved by desperate measures (suicide to avoid the rape). Virginity can also be preserved by divine intervention, such as the hand of God that saves Sarita from rape by lifting her virgin body to heaven. María Francia, a folk saint in Caracas, was forced by her parents to marry a man whom she did not love, but on the day of the wedding, in her wedding gown, she was bitten by a snake and died a virgin.

Childhood, particularly in relation to the Spanish concept *niño* (literally boy), is also highly valued in folk devotions. In Mexico and the border region, the word "niño" is almost a title conferred upon or adopted by those who have maintained the saintly attributes—purity, innocence, and sometimes virginity—of childhood. Niño Fidencio's virginity was accompanied by a childish demeanor and prepubescent physical characteristics. "You would see a man," explained a devotee, "but you were looking at a little boy." Many other niños emerged in northeastern Mexico at about the same time as Fidencio, among them Niño Marcialito, Niño Manuelito, and Niño Panchito.[11]

Throughout Spanish America, the word "niño" is readily associated with the Christ child (Niño Cristo). This precedent establishes a more or less distant echo for all other religious uses of the term. In the Andes, the many syncretic advocations of the Christ child, along with the incarnation of mountain spirits in the form of young boys, provide a context for Niño Compadrito. His powers, like those of other folk saints who died young, are partially derived from his stolen youth. Such deaths are tragic but also sanctifying, because purity and innocence are preserved when a life is foreclosed before there is time for sin. The younger the death, the purer the soul. Some devotees refer to Niño Compadrito as an angelito.

Romance, Infidelity, and Sexual Aggression

Love triangles, jealous rage, and rape are prolific producers of folk saints. The female saints in this category are victims: Juana Figueroa was murdered by her jealous husband, and Almita Sivila and María Soledad were raped, murdered, and mutilated for refusing sexual advances. Elvirita Guillén, a fourteen-year-old Chilean orphan, committed suicide after she was drugged and forced into group sex with adults. These victims are defiled—innocence is lost—but they earn heaven, and sainthood, through the purifying ordeal of their deaths. In the exceptional case of María Lionza, female sensuality is deified, untouchable, and therefore can be more explicitly represented without danger of threats to purity.

The male saints in this category are generated in a variety of ways. Some are the aggressors, such as Víctor Apaza, who murdered his wife for a suspected infidelity. Such crimes are forgiven through allegation of innocence after the shock of execution overwhelms them. At least one male folk saint, Pedrito Sangüeso, was a sexual victim; he was raped and murdered when he was six. The irresistibility of romance is a more common route to sainthood. José Dolores, Francisco López, and, in some versions, Gaucho Gil are all caught by authorities and executed as a consequence of their attraction to a woman. They suffer the fatal consequences of their love, and this romantic demise enhances their nobility. Difunta Correa's myth, which is essentially a romance, develops a similar motif with a female protagonist: she dies for love. In some cases, such as that of José Dolores, a love triangle results in death after betrayal.

Water

An undercurrent of water motifs is quietly insistent in folk saint myths and rituals. San La Muerte meditates beside a river; Niño Fidencio travels in spirit to cure sailors; Víctor Apaza buried his wife beside an irrigation ditch; Niño Compadrito's skeleton was discovered beside a creek; and the corpses of other folk saints, such as Carballito (from Tucumán) and Juana Figueroa, are similarly found beside water. Enriquito's tears drip from a tree that grew beside his tomb; bottles of water are the traditional offering to Difunta Correa, who died of thirst; and María Lionza is a water goddess (sometimes associated with Yemayá, a Santería water goddess of African origin). Rosita de Pachacutec miraculously saved a friend from drowning in a ditch, God saved Sarita Colonia from the same, and Sarita later escaped rape by walking into the ocean or throwing herself from a bridge.

Water is also prominent in ritual healings and cleansings. Leading curanderos such as Niño Fidencio, Pancho Sierra, and Don Pedrito Jaramillo all
made frequent and varied use of water in their cures. Today devotees conduct
healing rituals in Espinazo's mud pool and drink water that has absorbed
spiritual power from Fidencio's tomb. Rites of offering in the Fidencist
Christian Church also include water, "which is the symbol of life and purity."
The water that irrigates flowers at the tomb of Sarita Colonia and many other
saints is widely used for cleansings, healings, and the blessing of homes,
businesses, and people. Holy water can also be imported from Catholic churches for similar purposes, as it is at the shrines of José Dolores and Víctor
Apaza.[12]

Water is similarly used in expressions of folk Catholicism not affiliated
with folk saints. The most prominent examples include the domestic use of
holy water and the drinking of water from the flower vases near Christ and
saints. During the pilgrimage to the Lord of Qoyllur Rit'i, a bath for ritual
purification is required in a spring at Unupata ("water of the Lord"). In the
highlands above Piura, also in Peru, sacred lakes known as Las Huaringas are
used in ways similar to folk saint shrines. Curanderos and their patients visit
the lakes for cleansing and healing rituals, but the waters are also used for
love magic and for solving problems—such as poverty—that are commonly
presented to folk saints as well.[13]

Water is an ideal complement to folk saint devotions owing to its purity
and cleansing properties, but also to its associations with death. Many Spanish
Americans believe that after death a black dog leads one across a great river
(some say three rivers) to the realm of the dead (some say heaven). In some
areas, the appearance of water in dreams—drawing water from a well, entering
a well, or walking along a river or lake—is the announcement of imminent
death. The ocean, as in Sarita Colonia's myth, has allusions of suicide, with its
creepy black surface sucking one into an underworld and then covering over in
wait for the next victim. The tomb water that devotees' drink at so many
shrines likewise reaffirms the link between water and death, but now with the
idea that death water carries life-affirming graces and powers.

Skulls, Bones, and Skeletons

The connection between death and the supernatural is also represented in folk
devotion by skulls, skeletons, and bones. Two folk saints—San La Muerte
and Mexico's Santísima Muerte—are personifications of death and have the
corresponding skeletal form. San La Muerte is unique because his Grim
Reaper image, which is empowered as an amulet, is carved in human bone.

Elsewhere one finds Day of the Dead imagery, bone relics, miraculous skulls, and candles in the form of skeletons and skulls. Niño Compadrito and Miguelito are themselves skeletons, and—in unwitting homage to these themes— Pedrito Sangüeso's name is often distorted to the homonymic San Hueso (St. Bone).

The Guatemalan folk saint known as Rey Pascual (rey means "king") is commonly depicted as a skeleton holding a scythe and wearing a crown, much the same as San La Muerte. And just as San La Muerte is identified as a Jesuit or Franciscan and associated with care of indigenous lepers, so Rey Pascual is represented as a Franciscan and associated with indigenous Guatemalans dying of a plague. (The latter identity is derived from the belief that Pascual Bailón, now a canonized Catholic saint, appeared in 1650 and ended the plague in exchange for conversion.) Both devotions are syncretic and partially derived from indigenous veneration of skeletal remains. Today Rey Pascual, like San La Muerte, has dominion over death. The related folk saint in neighboring Chiapas, San Pascualito, collects the souls of the dead.[14]

The inherent power of bone is indexed by its many magical uses in northern Argentina. If you are having bad luck in love, try grinding baby bone and mixing it up with some wax to make an amulet. To protect yourself from curses, "go to the cemetery at midnight, get a bone from any skeleton, and take it to mass on Christmas eve." After mass, draw the sign of the cross in the dirt, saying "I am cured of all evil, and no more evil can be done to me." A prominent curandero in Santa Lucía, named Coco, healed by making the sign of the cross with the bone amulet inside his thumb.[15]

In the Andes, the meanings of skulls and bones in folk saint devotions are preceded by belief in the benevolent and malevolent powers of pre-Colombian graves. Contact with some ancient bones results in illness and death, but other bones—or even the same bones under other circumstances—are miraculous to positive ends. Niño Compadrito is the most apparent beneficiary of these traditions. His ambidextrous miraculousness—for good and for evil— echoes the dual potency of pre-Columbian bones.

Devotion at the graves that are beneficently miraculous is quite similar to devotion at folk saint shrines. Near Puno, for example, collective graves at the summit of a mountain respond to miracle requests made ritually. At least one of these graves is open, exposing multiple skulls and bones, and the site is associated with an apu (mountain spirit). The graves also have specialties, like folk saints. Musicians leave their broken instruments beside one grave, and after two days they are restored to perfection.

Bones are a tangible presence that embody the powers of life beyond death. They authenticate folk saint shrines, where the principal devotion occurs precisely at the tomb, as close to the bones as possible. When the actual bones are missing, as in the case of Difunta Correa (and perhaps Sarita Colonia), they are claimed to be present all the same, and the claim compensates for the absence.

Che Guevara's remains were buried secretly in 1967, and then discovered, disinterred, and transferred to Cuba in 1997. That removal was traumatic for some residents of Vallegrande and consequently was denied so that the bones could stay where they belonged. Susana, the nurse who washed Che's corpse, related that the wrong remains were taken. When I asked her how she knew, she explained that she put pajamas on Che's body prior to his burial, and the skeleton that was disinterred was not wearing pajamas.

Rosa, who runs a small restaurant in Vallegrande, was more adamant. She was one of the few people I could locate who believed in Che's miraculous powers, and she was positively disturbed by the removal of his remains. Rosa wiped away tears to relate that Che was a gift that God had given to Valle-grande. His grave was opened at night, in secret, to perpetuate a deception, because the bones that were taken were not his. "He is here, he lives here with us, he wanted to die and be buried here, and he is still here." The same is said of Pancho Villa: when soldiers came to relocate his remains to Mexico City, locals believed that the wrong remains were taken. Villa wanted to remain forever in Parral.[16]

Safe Journey

In 1939 the taxi driver Nicolas Florencio Caputo, known as the Taxista Caputo, was hired to take a fare to the Difunta Correa shrine. He was robbed and murdered on the way. Caputo soon became a patron saint of drivers. The offerings at his shrine, almost exclusively car parts, pay homage to his history and his specialty. In Venezuela, the folk saint known as Anima de Guasare was a truck driver killed in a traffic accident around 1960. His roadside shrine, like Caputo's, is visited by drivers—particularly truckers—to beseech a safe journey. The same is true of another Venezuela folk saint, Anima de la Yaguara.

Like St. Christopher, such folk saints protect devotees from the perils of the road. Sarita Colonia was widely recognized as a patron of taxi and bus drivers in Lima, but the best example is Difunta Correa. She died while journeying and now protects others from that tragic fate. The folk saint's misfortune becomes the devotees' salvation. Anything negative in the folk saint's life is inverted to positive gains for the community. Tragedy becomes miracles. Travel is interpreted broadly, encompassing road trips but also the daily journey into the strange world of risks and challenges. It's best to leave home with a San La Muerte in your pocket, a flower from Sarita's tomb in your purse, or some Niño Fidencio water sprinkled on your body. Commend yourself to Gaucho Gil on three consecutive Mondays. Because folk saints get you wherever you are going. They get you through life.

Notes

INTRODUCTION

1. The Niño Fidencio passage is quoted in Dore Gardner, *Niño Fidencio: A Heart Thrown Open* (Santa Fe: Museum of New Mexico Press, 1992), 105.

2. INILFI, n.d. [1940 or 1950], Corrientes, no town, 8.

3. Acknowledgments occasionally do recognize God as the source of miracles. For examples, see Milciades Aguilar and Ulises Aguilar, *La Cruz Gil: el culto popular al gauchito Gil, testimonios y documentos* (Buenos Aires: Camino Real, 1999), 69–70.

4. The María Lionza passage is quoted in Nelly García Gavidia, *Posesión y ambivalencia en el culto a María Lionza* (Maracaibo: Universidad del Zulia, 1987), 83; and the Niño Compadrito passage is appended to Takahiro Kato, "Historia tejida por los sueños: formación de la imagen del Niño Compadrito," in Luis Millones, Hiroyasu Tomoeda, and Tatsuhiko Fujii, eds., *Desde afuera y desde adentro: ensayos de etnografía e historia del Cuzco y Apurímac* (Osaka: National Museum of Ethnography, 2000), 186.

5. The quoted passage and details on Morillo are from Angelina Pollak-Eltz, *Las ánimas milagrosas en Venezuela* (Caracas: Fundación Bigott, 1989), 42.

6. The two quoted passages are from folkloric sources quoted in Susana Chertudi and Sara Josefina Newbery, *La Difunta Correa* (Buenos Aires: Editorial Huemul, 1978), 55 and 79, respectively.

7. The version of Difunta Correa's myth is from a 1944 report in Chertudi and Newbery, *La Difunta Correa*, 77–79.

8. The two López versions are from, respectively, INILFI, n.d., "Francisco López," Corrientes (capital), Escuela 44, 2; and INILFI, n.d., "Francisco López," Corrientes (capital), Escuela 207, 2.

9. From a prayer card quoted in James S. Griffith, *Folk Saints of the Borderlands: Victims, Bandits, and Healers* (Tucson, Ariz.: Rio Nuevo Publishers, 2003), 98–99.

10. INAPL, 1921, Chaco 144, Resistencia, 5.

11. On the rapacious police and soldiers, see Alejandro Ortiz Rescaniere, "Expresiones religiosas marginales: el caso de Sarita Colonia," in Marcel Valcárcel C., *Pobreza urbana: interrelaciones económicas y marginalidad religiosa* (Lima: Pontificia Universidad Católica del Perú, 1990), 175. See 173–174.

12. A report from Córdoba quoted in Susana Chertudi and Sara Josefina Newbery, "La Difunta Correa," *Cuadernos del Instituto Nacional de Antropología* 6 (1966): 109.

13. The information on Apaza is from Teresa María Van Ronzelen García Rosell, "Víctor Apaza: la emergencia de un santo" (master's thesis, Pontificia Universidad Católica del Peru, 1984), 58–59. See 172 and 177. The quoted passage is on 83. See also Jordán Rosas Valdivia, "Victor Apaza Quispe: o del fusilamiento a la santificación," *Revista ciencias sociales* 1 (1982): 52.

14. The information on La Chavela is from Lorenzo Jesús Peñalva Suca, "Consideraciones sociales acerca del mito de 'La Chavela' " (master's thesis, Universidad Nacional de San Agustín), 67–75, and unpaginated Anexo 1. See Vladimiro Bermejo, *La Chabela/Polvora* (Arequipa, Peru: Editorial UNSA, 1997), 19–55; and Nanda Leonardini and Patricia Borda, *Diccionario iconográfico religioso peruano* (Lima: Rubican Editores, 1996), 55.

15. Health-related miracles are also prominent in devotions to canonized saints. In a typology derived from medieval processes of canonization, 90.2% of miracles were related to cures between 1201 and 1300, and 79.3% between 1301 and 1417. André Vauchez, *Sainthood in the Later Middle Ages*, trans. Jean Birrell (Cambridge: Cambridge University Press, 1997), 468.

16. The Madre María passages are quoted in Andrea Maurizi, "Entre la duda y la fe: la Madre María," *Todo es historia* 2/9 (January 1968): 9 and 16, respectively. The Corrientes report is from INILFI, 1950, Corrientes, La Britania, 11. For another example of "healing with words," see INILFI, n.d. [1940 or 1950], Corrientes, Esquina, 1.

17. Abraham Valencia Espinoza, *Religiosidad popular: el Niño Compadrito* (Cuzco: Instituto Nacional de Cultura, 1983), 40.

18. The quoted passages from the Egyptian document are in Jan Ehrenwald, ed., *The History of Psychotherapy* (Northvale, N.J.: Jason Aronson, 1991), 31.

19. The Niño Fidencio passages are quoted in Pedro Angel González Valdés, *Vida y milagros del Niño Fidencio* (Saltillo, Mexico: N.p., 1970), 34. The Don Pedrito Jaramillo passage is quoted in Fernando Garza Quirós, *El Niño Fidencio y el fidencismo* (Mexico City: Ediciones Oasis, 1970), 66 n. 1.

20. Regarding Niño Fidencio, see Barbara June Macklin, "El Niño Fidencio: un estudio del curanderismo en Nuevo León," *Anuario Humánitas* (1967): 544.

21. For examples of the San La Muerte myths, see versions 8 and 10 in José Miranda Borelli, *San La Muerte: un mito regional del nordeste* (Resistencia, Argentina: Editorial Región, 1979), 19.

22. García Gavidia, *Posesión y ambivalencia*, 60; Pollak-Eltz, *Las ánimas milagrosas*, 22; and Angelina Pollak-Eltz, *María Lionza: mito y culto venezolano* (Caracas: Universidad Católica Andrés Bello, 1972), 31.

23. The San La Muerte passage is quoted in Elena María Krautstofl, *San la Muerte* (Posadas, Argentina: Editorial Universitaria, Universidad Nacional de Misiones, 2002), 139. The Sarita Colonia passage is from Uchcu Pedro, "Oraciones líricas a Sarita Colonia Zambrano," in Francis G. Johann, ed., *Sarita Colonia: la santa ungida por el pueblo* (Lima: Editorial San Marcos, 2003), 55.

24. The Sarita Colonia passage is available at http://socrates.berkeley.edu/ ~dolorier/sarita/testimonios/html.

25. Regarding Niño Compadrito's eyes, see Kato, "Historia tejida," 180.

26. For myth versions stressing San La Muerte among the poor, see Miranda Borelli, *San La Muerte*, 17–19. The quoted passage is on 19. The Sarita Colonia passage is quoted in Francis G. Johann's preface to Johann, *Sarita Colonia*, 9.

27. The Gaucho Gil passage is from a 1973 newspaper article in Federico R. Rainero, ed., *La cruz de Gil* (Corrientes: N.p., 1990), 20. On Sarita Colonia's burial, see the Radio Sol Armonía program transcript in Johann, *Sarita Colonia*, 18. The Difunta Correa passage is from *Difunta Correa: una historia que se hizo leyenda* (San Juan: Administración Difunta Correa, n.d. [2002]), 3.

28. The Difunta Correa passage is from "¿Qué es la 'Fundación Cementerio Vallecito'?" *Difunta Correa* 1/4 (April 1972): 4.

29. The first suggestion and response are available at http://groups.msn.com/ arcanoparapsicologo/tenermuyencuenta.msnw and http://boards1.melodysoft.com/ app?ID=cultoasanlamuerte&msg=243&DOC=81. The second exchange is available at http://boards1.melodysoft.com/app?ID=cultoasanlamuerte&msg=380 and http:// boards1.melodysoft.com/app?ID=cultoasanlamuerte&msg=382.

30. Quoted in Kato, "Historia tejida," 188.

31. Testimony appended to Heliodoro González Valdés, *Cabalgando con Fidencio: el despertar a una nueva vida espiritual* (N.p.: N.p., 1998), n.p.

32. Quoted in Manuel M. Marzal, *Los caminos religiosos de los inmigrantes en la Gran Lima: el caso de El Agustino* (Lima: Pontificia Universidad Católica del Perú, 1989), 159.

33. Quoted in José Luis Berlanga et al., *Las fiestas del dolor: un estudio sobre las celebraciones del Niño Fidencio* (Monterrey: Fondo Estatal Para La Cultura y las Artes de Nuevo León, 1999), 181.

34. Quoted in Gardner, *Niño Fidencio*, 50.

35. Uchcu Pedro, "Oraciones líricas," 61.

36. Juan V. Nuñez de Prado Béjar, "El mundo sobrenatural de los Quechuas del Sur del Perú a través de la comunidad de Qotobamba," *Allpanchis Phuturinqa* 2 (1970): 103–104. Folk saints are the preference for patronage of criminal activities, but the Catholic Church actually has one canonized saint who looks out for thieves. Dimas, "the good thief," was one of the two criminals crucified with Christ. Holy Week in Catacaos (in Bajo Piura, Peru) includes devotion to the "good thief" Dimas along with his negative counterpart, the "bad thief" Gestas. Rafael León, "Dimas, el

santo ladrón," *Caretas* 1562 (April 8, 1999): 44–48. In Colombia, the contract killers known as *sicarios* commend themselves to the Virgin.

37. Quoted in Tránsito Galarza, *Los poderes del Gauchito Gil: nuestro primer santo telúrico* (Buenos Aires: Libro Latino, 1999), 99.

38. Quoted in Gardner, *Niño Fidencio,* 50.

39. The litany to Sarita is available at http://socrates.berkeley.edu/~dolorier/sarita/testimonios/html. The two Gaucho Gil passages are quoted in Aguilar and Aguilar, *La Cruz Gil,* 53 and 56, respectively.

40. INILFI, 1950, Corrientes, Las Garzas, 19.

41. The Niño Fidencio story is in Gardner, *Niño Fidencio,* 106; and the Sarita story is in Ana María Quiroz Rojas, "Cuando Dios dijo que no, Sarita dijo quién sabe," in Gonzalo Portocarrero, ed., *Los nuevos limeños: sueños, fervores y caminos en el mundo popular* (Lima: Sur, 1993), 154.

42. Regarding Sarita, see Hipólito Colonia Zambrano, *Sarita Colonia Zambrano: una biografía familiar* (Lima: N.p., 1999), 78–79.

43. The Venezuelan example is from Pollak-Eltz, *Las ánimas,* 42.

44. Quoted in Ortiz Rescaniere, "Expresiones religiosas marginales," 181. See 180. In the cemetery in Callao there was a Cemetery of Broken Saints, until it was demolished to build new pavilions.

45. The three examples are from, respectively, http://boards1.melodysoft.com/app?ID=cultoasanlamuerte&msg=420; http://boards1.melodysoft.com/app?ID=cultoasanlamuerte&msg=371; and http://boards1.melodysoft.com/app?ID=cultoasanlamuerte&msg=192&DOC=121.

46. Quoted in Antonio Villasante A., "Religiosidad andina en un medio urbano," *Boletín del Instituto de Estudios Aymaras* 2/20 (1985): 39.

47. The information on Tio is from Gerardo Fernández Juárez, "El culto al 'tio' en las minas bolivianas." *Cuadernos hispanoamericanos* 597 (2000): 26–28; and Hans Van Den Berg, *Diccionario religioso aymara* (Iquitos: CETA-IDEA, 1985), 186.

48. INILFI, 1951, San Juan, Marquesado, n.p.

49. The quoted passage is from Chertudi and Newbery, "La Difunta Correa," 141.

50. On Telesitas, see Félix Coluccio, *Cultos y canonizaciones populares de Argentina* (Buenos Aires: Biblioteca de Cultura Popular/Ediciones del Sol, 1986), 25–29 and 147–151. In 1950, the government of Santiago del Estero prohibited Telesitas and other prayer dances. See Antonio Paleari, *Diccionario mágico jujeño* (San Salvador de Jujuy: Editorial Pachamama, 1982), 470.

51. INILFI, 1950, Corrientes, Colonia J.R. Vidal, n.p.

52. INILFI, 1950, Corrientes, Cerrito-Batel, 14.

53. The quoted passages are from, respectively, Garza Quirós, *El Niño Fidencio,* 76, and Gardner, *Niño Fidencio,* 45 (see 90).

54. The quoted Gaucho Gil passage is from Aguilar and Aguilar, *La Cruz Gil,* 70.

55. Colonia Zambrano, *Sarita Colonia Zambrano,* 60.

56. The Sarita Colonia passage is from Quiroz Rojas, "Cuando Dios dijo que no," 158. Regarding Hernández, see Pollak-Eltz, *Las ánimas milagrosas,* 53.

57. Takahiro Kato, "Breve Historia del Niño Compadrito del Cuzco," in Hiroyasu Tomoeda and Luis Millones, eds., *La tradición andina en tiempos modernos*, Senri Ethnological Reports 5 (Osaka: National Museum of Ethnology, 1996), 41.

58. The Argentine bishops' document is in Chertudi and Newbery, *La Difunta Correa*, 209–211. The article by the lay Catholics is Hector Dario Franco and Ana María Rosciani, "Sobre San la Muerte," *Norte* (August 24, 1986): N.p. Denial of recognition of San La Muerte's cult is described in "No inscriben a una entidad devota de San La Muerte, *Clarín* (April 12, 1997): 56.

59. The quoted passages are from Quiroz Rojas, "Cuando Dios dijo que no," 153. For the bishop's second statement, see *Sarita*, a documentary film by Judith and Marisol Vélez. Lima: Nómade Producciones, 2001.

60. Peñalva Suca, "Consideraciones socials," 67–75 and unpaginated Anexo 1. See Bermejo, *La Chabela/Polvora*, 19–55.

61. The quoted passages are from INILFI, n.d. [1940 or 1950], Corrientes (capital), n.p. The other details are from INILFI, "Francisco López," Corrientes (capital) n.p.; INILFI, "Leyenda de Francisco López," Corrientes (capital) 3; INAPL, Chaco 92, Puerto Bastiani, 4–5; and INAPL, Chaco 97, Resistencia, 1–4.

62. The three quoted clerical opinions are from, respectively, José Luis González Martinez, *La religión popular en el Perú: informe y diagnóstico* (Lima: Instituto de Pastoral Andina, 1987), 227 and 231; and Obispado de Goya, "Discernimiento sobre el fenómeno de religiosidad popular llamado 'Cruz Gil'" (May 3, 1984): 1.

63. The first quoted passage is from INILFI, 1950, Corrientes, Puerto Boca, n.p. The observation regarding spiritual contracts is from INILFI, 1950, Corrientes, Curtiembre, 12. The last quoted passage is from INILFI, 1950, Corrientes, Goya, n.p.

64. The quoted passage is from INILFI, 1950, Corrientes, El Rubio, 3. See INILFI, 1950, Corrientes, Algarrobos, 10.

65. Oronzo Giordano, *Religiosidad popular en la alta edad media* (Madrid: Editorial Gredos, 1983), 31 and 35.

66. The quoted passages are from, respectively, Burcardo di Worms appended to Giordano, *Religiosidad popular*, 185–186; and St. Cesáreo de Arles appended to Giordano, *Religiosidad popular*, 194 and 196.

67. Kato, "Breve Historia," 37 and 44.

68. Quoted in June Macklin, "Folk Saints, Healers, and Spiritist Cults in Northern Mexico," *Revista/Review Interamericana* 3/4 (1974): 363.

SAN LA MUERTE

1. [Maria Elsa ("Pelusa") Paniagua], *San la Muerte* (Posadas, Argentina: N.p., 2003), 12–13. The passage on the scythe as a shield is from a prayer on 37.

2. The 1917 text is by Juan Bautista Ambrosetti, quoted in Emilio Noya, *Imaginería religiosa y santoral profano de Corrientes* (Corrientes: Subsecretaría de Cultura de la Provincia de Corrientes, 1994), 67. For fictional adaptation of Ambrosetti's report, see Julio Vignola Mansilla, "San La Muetre," in *La noche de robar* (Buenos Aires: N.p., 1935), 71–80.

3. The quoted passage is from INILFI, 1950, Corrientes, Estación M.F. Mantilla, n.p.

4. The quoted passage is from INAPL, Chaco file 10, Desvío, 5.

5. The quoted passage is from Elena María Krautstofl, *San la Muerte* (Posadas, Argentina: Editorial Universitaria, Universidad Nacional de Misiones, 2002), 122.

6. For examples of the myths that have fallen out of circulation, see José Miranda Borelli, *San la Muerte: un mito regional del nordeste* (Resistencia, Argentina: Editorial Región, 1979), 16–19.

7. The Posadas version is in Krautstofl, *San la Muerte*, 15.

8. These two versions are in Miranda Borelli, *San la Muerte*, 17 and 16, respectively.

9. For examples, see 1 Chronicles 21:15; Psalms 78:49; Isaiah 37:36; and 2 Kings 19:35.

10. The quoted passage is from José Miranda, "San la Muerte," *Cuadernos del Instituto Nacional de Antropología* 4 (1963): 84.

11. The 1950 report is INILFI, 1950, Corrientes, Las Garzas, 2.

12. The quoted passages are from [Paniagua], *San la Muerte*, title page and 2, respectively.

13. Ibid., 40 and 2, respectively. A similar message is conveyed by a sign in the chapel to folk saint San Simón in San Andrés Itzapa, Guatemala.

14. The first quoted passage is from INILFI, 1940, Corrientes, Pueblo, n.p. The other two are from INILFI, 1950, Corrientes, Tablada Norte, 1.

15. The friendship payé is from Juan B. Ambrosetti, *Supersticiones y leyendas* (Buenos Aires: Ediciones Siglo Veinte, 1976), 9. The passages on San Son and San Marco are from INAPL, 1921, Formosa 1, Buen Lugar, 2 and 3, respectively. The invulnerability payé is from INAPL, 1921, Chaco 96, Vedia, 2. The longer quoted passage is from INAPL, 1921, Chaco 80, Resistencia, 2.

16. The first quoted passage is from Krautstofl, *San la Muerte*, 119. The 1975 study is Félix Coluccio, "El culto a San la Muerte," *Revista venezolana de folklore* 6 (October 1975): 100–101.

17. The example with the father's bone is from Miranda Borelli, *San La Muerte*, 28.

18. The quoted passage is from INAPL, 1921, Misiones 3, Candelaria, 23. On the same page, another report clarifies: "Have it baptized beforehand in three churches."

19. INILFI, "Francisco López," Corrientes (capital), n.p.

20. The example regarding the brides of Christ is from Krautstofl, *San la Muerte*, 142.

21. The quoted passage is from Martha Blanche, *Estructura del miedo: narrativas folklóricas guaraníticas* (Buenos Aires: Plus Ultra, 1991), 181. Regarding the bone relics, see Oronzo Giordano, *Religiosidad popular en la alta edad media* (Madrid: Editorial Gredos, 1983), 102.

22. For an example of the hermit bones, see William A. Christian, Jr., *Local Religion in Sixteenth-Century Spain* (Princeton, N.J.: Princeton University Press, 1981), 110.

23. *El culto a San la Muerte: leyendas, historias, oraciones y ritos* (N.p.: Editorial Alberto S. Bellanza, 1997), 7. For a scholarly account of San La Muerte's syncretic origins, see Ertivio Acosta appended to Félix Coluccio, *Cultos y canonizaciones populares de Argentina* (Buenos Aires: Biblioteca de Cultura Popular/Ediciones del Sol, 1986), 193–195.

24. The quoted passages are from Antonio Ruiz de Montoya, *Conquista espiritual hecha por los religiosos de la Compañía de Jesús en las provincias de Paraguay, Paraná, Uruguay y Tape* (Buenos Aires: Equipo Difusor de Estudios de Historia Iberoamericana, 1989), 77. Regarding the absence of religious imagery in Guaraní culture, see Gauvin Alexander Bailey, *Art on the Jesuit Missions in Asia and Latin America, 1542–1773* (Toronto: University of Toronto Press, 1999), 148 and 150.

25. Ruiz de Montoya, *Conquista espiritual hecha por los religiosos*, 131 and 132, respectively. See 135.

26. The quoted passages are from Barbara Anne Ganson, "Better Not Take My Manioc: Religion, Society, and Politics in the Jesuit Missions of Paraguay, 1500–1800" (Ph.D. diss., University of Texas, Austin, 1994), 375. See Bailey, *Art on the Jesuit Missions*, 154.

27. Fernando Martínez Gil, *Muerte y sociedad en la España de los Austrias* (Mexico: Siglo Veintiuno Editores, 1993), 321 and 325.

28. Jean Delumeau, *Sin and Fear: The Emergence of a Western Guilt Culture, 13th-18th Centuries*, trans. Eric Nicholson (New York: St. Martin's Press, 1991), 38; see 89–90. The two Montaigne quotes are on 36; see 54. The Spanish passage is from a novel by J. de Alcalá Yáñez, quoted in Martínez Gil, *Muerte y sociedad*, 320. The last passage is from Delumeau, 93.

29. On the Andean imagery, see Teresa Gisbert, *El paraíso de los pájaros parlantes* (La Paz: Plural Editores, 2001), 207–209. The Mexican example is from Mardith K. Schuetz-Miller, "Survival of Early Christian Symbolism in Monastic Churches of New Spain and Visions of the Millennial Kingdom," *Journal of the Southwest* 42/4 (2000): 790 and 795. The church was built in the 1770s; the frescoes are from the early nineteenth century.

30. Guillermo Furlong, *Misiones y sus pueblos de guaraníes* (Buenos Aires: N.p., 1962), 586–587.

31. The quoted passages are from Bailey, *Art on the Jesuit Missions*, 145 and 149, respectively.

32. The quoted passage is from Daisy Rípodas Ardanaz, "Pervivencia de hechiceros en las misiones guaraníes," *Folia histórica del nordeste* 6 (1984): 209. Regarding the magicians, see Ruiz de Montoya, *Conquista espiritual hecha por los religiosos*, 80.

33. The quoted passages are from Archivo General de la Nación, Criminales, Legajo 9, no. 2, 9–32–1–6, pp. 3, 4, and 5, respectively. The other details are on 3 and in Rípodas Ardanaz, "Pervivencia de hechiceros," 214; see n. 91. See also Ganson, "Better Not Take My Manioc," 154 and 210. Caté found the remains of an infant killed by a wild dog and "kept the child's arm in his house and distributed parts of the infant's body to other Indians" (Ganson, 162).

34. Bailey, *Art on the Jesuit Missions*, 169. See Rípodas Ardanaz, "Pervivencia de hechiceros," 213, and Martínez Gil, *Muerte y sociedad*, 266–269.

35. The quoted passage is from INILFI, 1950, Corrientes, Colonia El Porvenir, n.p. Regarding Niño Nakaq, see Juan José García Miranda, "Los santuarios de los Andes centrales," in Luis Millones, Hiroyasu Tomoeda, and Tatsuhiko Fujii, eds., *Historia, religión y ritual de los pueblos ayacuchanos* (Osaka: National Musueum of Ethnology, 1998), 73.

36. The quoted passage, in revised translation, is from Ganson, "Better Not Take My Manioc," 356. The second referenced letter is from the same source, 356.

37. The quoted passage is from Mario Polia Meconi, *La cosmovisión religiosa andina en los documentos ineditos del Archivo Romano de la Compañía de Jesús, 1581–1752* (Lima: Pontificia Universidad Católica del Peru, 1999), 419. The Pueblo example is from John L. Kessell, *Kiva, Cross and Crown: The Pecos Indians and New Mexico, 1540–1840* (Tucson, Ariz.: Southwest Parks and Monuments Association, 1987), 111. See Louis-Vincent Thomas, *El cadáver: de la biología a la antropología* (Mexico: Fondo de Cultura Económica, 1989), 96–98; and Lawrence E. Sullivan, *Icanchu's Drum: An Orientation to Meaning in South American Religions* (New York: MacMillan, 1988), 489–491.

38. See the Jesuit Martín Dobrizhoffer quoted in Miranda Borelli, *San la Muerte*, 11. See also Emilio Noya, "Corrientes entre la leyenda y la tradición," *Todo es historia* (October 1987): 5.

39. Dilma Iliana Meza, "Religiosidad Popular," Archivo Histórico, Provincia del Chaco, Monografías de Mitos y Leyendas, 1976, 3. The myth is in Miranda Borelli, *San la Muerte*, 17.

40. Regarding the Lord of Humility and Patience, see Miguel Raúl López Breard, *Devocionario Guaraní* (Santa Fe, Argentina: Ediciones Colmegna, 1973), 17–18; and Miranda Borelli, *San la Muerte*, 12. There is a good, Guaraní-carved example of this Christ image in the Museo de Arte Hispanoamericano Isaac Fernández Blanco in Buenos Aires (ID #1412).

41. Giordano, *Religiosidad popular*, 122.

42. Version 8 in Miranda Borelli, *San la Muerte*, 19. Version 10 on the same page offers a variation.

43. The first quoted passage is from "Carta del Cabildo de San Miguel," quoted in Bartomeu Melià, *El Guaraní conquistado y reducido* (Asunción, Paraguay: Centro de Estudios Antropológicos de la Universidad Católica, 1993), 191. The second and third quoted passages are from Ganson, "Better Not Take My Manioc," 402. The complete document is appended on 402–403. See Ruiz de Montoya, *Conquista espiritual hecha por los religiosos*, 98. For an example of St. Michael in mission art, see Bailey, *Art on the Jesuit Missions*, fig. 7, and the corresponding text on 168.

44. The first two quoted passages are from *San la Muerte*, produced by La Buena Gente Producciones Periodísticas for Elida López's Channel 9 program "Chaco: Palmo a Palmo," 1995.

45. Version 7 in Miranda Borelli, *San la Muerte*, 18. See 17.

46. The first quoted passage is from Martínez Gil, *Muerte y sociedad*, 335. See 323–326 and 333–337. For other variations on this common theme, see Delumeau, *Sin and Fear*, 72–77.

47. The first quoted passage is from an unidentified and unpaginated document in the Archivo Histórico, Provincia del Chaco, Monografías de Mitos y Leyendas. San La Muerte as an advocation of Christ is in Miranda Borelli, *San la Muerte*, 19. The prayer is quoted in Noya, *Imaginería religiosa*, 68. The last quoted passage is from Miranda Borelli, *San la Muerte*, 23.

48. Regarding the songbook, see Marta de París, *Corrientes y el santoral profano* (Buenos Aires: Editorial Plus Ultra, 1988), 69.

GAUCHO GIL

1. The background on social banditry is derived from Eric Hobsbawm, *Bandits* (New York: New Press, 2000), 20 and 47; Richard W. Slatta, "Images of Social Banditry on the Argentine Pampa," in Richard W. Slatta, ed., *Bandidos: The Varieties of Latin American Banditry* (New York: Greenwood Press, 1987), 49; and Hugo Chumbita, *Bairoletto: el último bandido romántico* (Buenos Aires: *Todo es historia*, supp. 10, n.d.), n.p.

2. The quoted passage is from *Difunta Correa: una historia que se hizo leyenda* (San Juan: Administración Difunta Correa, n.d. [2002]), 10.

3. INILFI, 1950, Corrientes, Tiro Federal, 2.

4. INAPL, Colección de Folklore, Chaco 92, Puerto Bastiani, 4–5. On López, see also INAPL, Colección de Folklore, Chaco 97, Resistencia, 1–4.

5. The same foreclosure story is told of Jesse James and, in Argentina, of Mate Cocido (sometimes spelled "Cosido"). The latter, whose real name was Segundo David Peralta, was a notorious thief in the late 1930s who attracted postmortem devotion in Chaco Province. See Hobsbawm, *Bandits*, 48–49.

6. The quoted phrase is from Hugo Chumbita, *Jinetes rebeldes* (Buenos Aires: Vergara, 2000), 240. See 214 and 241.

7. In this and the previous paragraph, I follow Oronzo Giordano, *Religiosidad popular en la alta edad media* (Madrid: Editorial Gredos, 1983), 47–49 and 53.

8. For an example, see INILFI, 1950, Corrientes, Tiro Federal, n.p. The same prayer-for-food exchange obtains in cemetery offerings.

9. INILFI, 1940, Corrientes, Mercedes, 34–35.

10. The quoted passage is from INILFI, n.d. (1940 or 1950), Corrientes (capital), n.p.

11. The 1973 newspaper article from Mercedes is in Federico R. Rainero, ed., *La cruz de Gil* (Corrientes: N.p., 1990), 20.

12. "Vida y muerte de José Dolores," n.d., 10. This typescript is at the José Dolores shrine in Rawson, San Juan.

13. The quoted passages are from, respectively, INILFI, 1950, Corrientes, Desvío, n.p.; and the chamamé "Injusta condena," quoted in Milciades Aguilar and Ulises

Aguilar, *La Cruz Gil: el culto popular al gauchito Gil, testimonios y documentos* (Buenos Aires: Camino Real, 1999), 87.

14. The quoted passages are from, respectively, INILFI, n.d., Corrientes (capital), 2; and INILFI, 1946, Corrientes (capital), "El Gaucho Lega," 5.

15. The song lyrics are quoted in Chumbita, *Jinetes rebeldes*, 242. In this and the previous paragraph, I also follow Félix Coluccio, *Devociones populares: argentinas y americanas* (Buenos Aires: Corregidor, 2001), 127–131; and documents in an unnumbered box labeled "Mitos y leyendas" in the Archivo Histórico, Provincia del Chaco, Resistencia.

16. The quoted passages are from Cristian Alarcón, "En una villa veneran a un adolescente muerto por la policia," available at www.pagina12,com.ar/2001/01–06/ 01–06–17/pag19.htm. Regarding the Venezuelan criminal saints, see Angelina Pollak-Eltz, *Las ánimas milagrosas en Venezuela* (Caracas: Fundación Bigott, 1989), 47–48.

17. The paragraphs on Frente Vital follow Cristian Alarcón, *Cuando me muera quiero que me toquen cumbia: vidas de pibes chorros* (Buenos Aires: Grupo Editorial Norma, 2003), 15–19, 29–35, 39–40, 59–63, and 79–81. The girlfriend is quoted on 81.

18. INILFI, 1940, Empedrado-Arroyo Solis, Corrientes, "Fusilamiento de Pedro Perlaitá," 2–4. The quoted passage are on 2, 3, 4, and 4, respectively.

19. The otherworldly passage is quoted in Paul J. Vanderwood, *Juan Soldado: Rapist, Murderer, Martyr, Saint* (Durham, N.C.: Duke University Press, 2004), 266. See 174 and 176.

20. The lawyer is quoted in "Los santos inocentes," chap. 1, "Historia de dos fusilados," *El Comercio, Revista Somos* (March 16, 1991): S24. The inmate is quoted in Teresa María Van Ronzelen García Rosell, "Víctor Apaza: la emergencia de un santo" (master's thesis, Pontificia Universidad Católica del Peru, 1984), 34. See Nanda Leonardi and Patricia Borda, *Diccionario iconográfico religioso peruano* (Lima: Rubican Editores, 1996), 248.

21. Van Ronzelen García Rosell, "Víctor Apaza," 52–53. For press accounts regarding the murder as a result of suspected infidelity, see Lolo Juan Mamani Daza, "Sobre los acontecimientos en torno a Víctor Apaza Quispe," *Antropus UNSA* 2 (2000): 71–72.

22. Van Ronzelen García Rosell, "Víctor Apaza," 195; and Mamani Daza, "Sobre los acontecimientos," 83. See Jordán Rosas Valdivia, "Víctor Apaza Quispe: o del fusilamiento a la santificación," *Revista ciencias sociales* 1 (1982): 47–50.

23. The quoted passages are from Van Ronzelen García Rosell, "Víctor Apaza," 69 and 91, respectively.

24. The three quoted passages are from, respectively, Rosas Valdivia, "Víctor Apaza Quispe," 54; Van Ronzelen García Rosell, "Víctor Apaza," 55 (see 53–55); and "Los santos inocentes," S24.

25. The quoted passages are from Van Ronzelen García Rosell, "Víctor Apaza," 96 and 172, respectively. See Mamani Daza, "Sobre los acontecimientos," 80–81.

26. Oreste Plath, *L'Animita: hagiografía folklórica* (Santiago, Chile: Editorial Pluma y Pincel, 1993) 56–63; the quoted passage is on 59.

27. The quoted passage is from Mario Guillermo Quinteros, "Impresionante devoción popular convocó el Gauchito Gil," *Norte* (Resistencia), January 8, 1995: 39.

28. The mentioned press reports are in Rainero, *La cruz de Gil*, 18, 31, 33, and 52.

29. See Mark 6:30–44. The same scene is in Matthew 14:13–21; Luke 9:10–17; and John 6:1–13.

30. Available at http://www.el-litoral.com.ar/leer_noticia.asp?IdNoticia=15827.

31. Obispado de Goya, "Discernimiento sobre el fenómeno de religiosidad popular llamado 'Cruz Gil'" (May 3, 1984): 1–2.

32. Luis T. Stöckler, "La veneración a la Cruz Gil: Carta Pastoral" (May 3, 1992), n.p.

33. Luis T. Stöckler, Obispo de Goya, "Mensaje Radial" (January 7, 2001), 1.

34. The quoted passages are from an unpublished survey conducted by the Mercedes parish on January 4–8, 1999, and summarized on February 16, 1999.

SARITA COLONIA

1. In this and the previous paragraphs, I follow Hipólito Colonia Zambrano, *Sarita Colonia Zambrano: una biografía familiar* (Lima: N.p., 1999), 20–21, 26, 29, and 43–44; and the transcribed Radio Sol Armonía interview with Hipólito Colonia Zambrano in Francis G. Johann, ed., *Sarita Colonia: la santa ungida por el pueblo* (Lima: Editorial San Marcos, 2003), 13–21. The dates are inconsistent in these sources.

2. Colonia Zambrano, *Sarita Colonia Zambrano*, 81. See Gonzalo Rojas Samanez, "Vida y milagros de Sarita Colonia," *Debate* 20 (1983): 20, and Alejandro Ortiz Rescaniere, "Expresiones religiosas marginales: el caso de Sarita Colonia," in Marcel Valcárcel C., *Pobreza urbana: interrelaciones económicas y marginalidad religiosa* (Lima: Pontificia Universidad Católica del Perú, 1990), 172.

3. The quoted passage is from Colonia Zambrano, *Sarita Colonia Zambrano*, 59. See Ortiz Rescaniere, "Expresiones religiosas marginales," 176.

4. Ortiz Rescaniere, "Expresiones religiosas marginales," 177.

5. Prayer at Ubilberto's tomb is discussed in "Los santos inocentes," chap. 2, "El nacimiento de un santo," *El Comercio, Revista Somos* (March 23, 1991): S26.

6. The stevedores are discussed in Ortiz Rescaniere, "Expresiones religiosas marginales," 176. Esther is quoted in Claudio Cano Paredes, "Un culto todavía oculto," in Johann, *Sarita Colonia*, 82. The last quoted passage is from Abel Maldonado in the Radio Sol Armonía program transcript in Johann, 27.

7. See Carlos Franco, *Imágenes de la sociedad peruana: la 'otra' modernidad* (Lima: Centro de Estudios Para el Desarrollo y la Participación, 1991), 117–123, esp. 120.

8. The quoted passage is from Eloy Jauregui, "Rezando en jerga," *El comercio, Suplemento dominical* 194 (November 3, 2002): R4. See Luise Freire Sarria, "Sarita, patrona de las buenas elecciones," *El comercio* (November 10, 2002): A20. On the similarity between Sarita and her migrant devotees, see Ortiz Rescaniere, "Expresiones religiosas marginales," 172 and 201.

9. The first two quoted passages are from Colonia Zambrano, *Sarita Colonia Zambrano*, 44 and 61, respectively. The song lyrics, the prostitute, and Sarita are quoted in Ortiz Rescaniere, "Expresiones religiosas marginales," 199–200, 173, and 172, respectively.

10. Franco, *Imágenes de la sociedad peruana*, 112–113; and Ortiz Rescaniere, "Expresiones religiosas marginales," 175–177 and 192–195. See Colonia Zambrano, *Sarita Colonia Zambrano*, 59.

11. The examples and quoted passages in this paragraph are from devotees in Ortiz Rescaniere, "Expresiones religiosas marginales," 174. See 175. Regarding abuse of domestic workers, see the comments of Soledad Minera de Avalos in the Radio Sol Armonía program transcript in Johann, *Sarita Colonia*, 21–22. Narratives by abused domestic workers in Peru are collected in Sindicato de Trabajadores del Hogar, *Basta: testimonios* (Cuzco: Centro de Estudios Rurales Andinos Bartolomé de Las Casas, 1982).

12. "Antes de robar rezaban ante Sarita Colonia . . . y así los capturó la policía," *El comercio* (December 1, 1994): A16.

13. The 1978 article is Martha Hinostroza, "Olor de santidad," *Caretas* 544 (August 14, 1978): 54.

14. The details from Sarita's life are from Colonia Zambrano, *Sarita Colonia Zambrano*, 26.

15. See ibid., 42 and 44–45, respectively, for quoted passages. I am also following 25–26; 28, and 34.

16. Ibid., 35.

17. Ibid., 33, 38, 40–41, and 51–52.

18. The quoted passages are from, respectively, Uchcu Pedro, "Oraciones líricas a Sarita Colonia Zambrano," in Johann, *Sarita Colonia*, 65; and Hinostroza, "Olor de santidad," 54.

19. The quoted passage is from a devotee in Ortiz Rescaniere, "Expresiones religiosas marginales," 173.

20. See ibid., 173–174, for quoted passages and examples cited here.

21. This version was first published in Fernando Ampuero, "¿Milagros con censura?" *Caretas* 804 (June 18, 1984): 46. Subsequent print repetitions of this version include Eloy Jauregui, "Rezando en jerga," *El comercio, Suplemento dominical* 194 (November 3, 2002): R4; and Luis Freire Sarria, "Sarita, patrona de las buenas elecciones," *El comercio* (November 10, 2002): A20. I have heard this version told by nondevotee Peruvian immigrants in New York City.

22. Colomba's story is in Rudolph M. Bell, *Holy Anorexia* (Chicago: University of Chicago Press, 1985), 152–154.

23. Casimir's story is in Donald Weinstein and Rudolph M. Bell, *Saints and Society: The Two Worlds of Western Christendom, 1000–1700* (Chicago: University of Chicago Press, 1982), 29.

24. I am grateful to Jean-Jacques Decoster for calling to my attention this relation of transgenders to Sarita's missing genitalia.

25. The quoted passages and narrative details are from Marina Warner, *Alone of All Her Sex: The Myth and the Cult of the Virgin Mary* (New York: Alfred A. Knopf, 1976), 71.

26. In these paragraphs on Rosita, I follow *Historia de Rosita de Pachacutec* (N.p.: N.p., n.d.), and my interview with Rosita's mother, Juana Gloria Milos Carhuayo.

27. The prostitute example is from Ortiz Rescaniere, "Expresiones religiosas marginales," 187.

28. The curandera quote and details are from Rojas Samanez, "Vida y milagros de Sarita Colonia," 21.

29. The bishop is quoted in Rojas Samanez, "Vida y milagros de Sarita Colonia," 20.

30. The ritual-exchange quotes are from Ortiz Rescaniere, "Expresiones religiosas marginales," 189.

DIFUNTA CORREA

1. This version is based on my interview with Zevallos's grandson, Rolando, in Santa Lucía, San Juan. For a version of the miracle attributed to Flavio Zevallos himself, see Félix Romualdo Alvarez, *Una nueva versión sobre la Difunta Correa* (San Juan, Argentina: Editorial Sanjuanina, 1967), 23–31. See also INAPL, 1921, San Juan 30, Pocito, 11; and Susana Chertudi and Sara Josefina Newbery, *La Difunta Correa* (Buenos Aires: Editorial Huemul, 1978), 89–94. A similar story is told of a northern Mexican folk saint, Jesús Malverde, in James S. Griffith, *Folk Saints of the Borderlands: Victims, Bandits, and Healers* (Tucson, Ariz.: Rio Nuevo Publishers, 2003), 68.

2. The first and second quoted passages, respectively, are from Pedro D. Quiroga, quoted in Susana Chertudi and Sara Josefina Newbery, "La Difunta Correa," *Cuadernos del Instituto Nacional de Antropología* 6 (1966): 120; and in Chertudi and Newbery, *La Difunta Correa*, 88 (see 128–129). The last quoted passage is from Alvarez, *Una nueva versión sobre la Difunta Correa*, 16.

3. Horacio Videla, *Historia de San Juan*, Vol. 4 (San Juan: Universidad Católica de Cuyo, 1976), 256.

4. Both quoted passages are from INAPL, 1921, San Juan 46, Caucete, 5.

5. INAPL, 1921, San Juan 14, Desamparados, 8.

6. "Prohiben templetes de la Difunta Correa," *El Diario de San Luis* (March 24, 1982): 3.

7. "Difunta Correa: Complace al Obispo de San Luis la reciente medida del gobierno provincial," *El Diario de San Luis* (March 30, 1982): n.p.

8. Regarding the international folk motifs, see Chertudi and Newbery, *La Difunta Correa*, 105–106, which follows motif T611 in Stith Thompson, *Motif-Index of Folk-Literature* (Bloomington: Indiana University Press, 1955–1958).

9. The Tintoretto painting is reproduced in Peter Humphrey, *Painting in Renaissance Venice* (New Haven, Conn.: Yale University Press, 1995), 234–235. See Marilyn Yalom, *A History of the Breast* (New York: Alfred A. Knopf, 1997), 21.

10. See ibid., 24–25. The quoted phrase, on 25, is from Pliny the Elder.

11. Alonso Cano's *St. Bernard and the Virgin*, also in El Prado, is a good example. Regarding Nut, see Anne Baring and Jules Cashford, *The Myth of the Goddess: Evolution of an Image* (Arkana/Penguin Books, 1993), 557.

12. The quoted passages are from, respectively, Stephen Benko, *The Virgin Goddess: Studies in the Pagan and Christian Roots of Mariology* (Leiden: E. J. Brill, 1993), 231; and Mechthild von Magdeburg, *Flowing Light of the Divinity*, trans. Christiane Mesch Galvani, ed. Susan Clark (New York: Garland Publishing, 1991), 15. Regarding Mary's title, see Marina Warner, *Alone of All Her Sex: The Myth and the Cult of the Virgin Mary* (New York: Alfred A. Knopf, 1976), 220. See also Caroline Walker Bynum, *Holy Feast and Holy Fast: The Religious Significance of Food to Medieval Women* (Berkeley: University of California Press, 1987), 270 and plates 17, 18, 19, and 23. Some advocations of the Virgin have been used by mothers to beseech good lactation.

13. Catalina Teresa Michieli, *Los Huarpes protohistóricos* (San Juan, Argentina: Instituto de Investigaciones Arqueológicas y Museo, 1983), 208–209. The myth is known only through a Catholicized transcription and later elaboration.

14. Jacobus de Voragine, *The Golden Legend: Readings on the Saints*, trans. William Granger Ryan (Princeton, N.J.: Princeton University Press, 1993), 1: 377–379; the quoted passage is on 379. See Susan Haskins, *Mary Magdalen: Myth and Metaphor* (New York: Harcourt, Brace, 1993), 223–224.

15. "La imagen de la Difunta," *Difunta Correa*, 1/6 (June 1972): 6.

16. Oscar Romero Giacaglia, "Historia de Difunta Correa," in the program for the 2003 Truckers' Day fiesta, published by the Difunta Correa Administration. The mentioned book is Cacho Romero, *La Difunta Correa: su mensaje, el sentido de amor, de su vida y de su muerte* (San Juan, Argentina: N.p., n.d.).

17. INILFI, 1946, San Juan, Los Hornos, Argentina, n.p.

18. The quoted passage is from Romero Giacaglia, "Historia de Difunta Correa," n.p.

19. Versions with a child present but with no miraculous breast-feeding include INAPL, 1921, San Juan 163, Trinidad, 5; INAPL, 1921, San Juan 90, Desamparados, 7 (this one has a daughter instead of son); and Chertudi and Newbery, "La Difunta Correa," 111 (see 108–111). Versions with no child present include INAPL, 1921, San Juan [no number], Concepción, 21; INAPL, 1921, San Juan 14, Desamparados, 8; and INAPL, 1921, San Juan 30, Pocito, 11. The quoted passages are from INILFI, n.d., San Juan, n.p.

20. An example of mother and son dead together is INILFI, n.d. [1940s], San Juan, n.p. (In this version it is an older son, not the husband, who is recruited into the troops.) The example with the hunter is INILFI, 1946, San Juan, Los Hornos, n.p.

21. The four versions are in *Difunta Correa*, no number, n.d. [1987], 3, 7, 9, and 10.

22. The Cavicchia painting has inventory number 64 in the Casa Natal de Sarmiento: Museo y Biblioteca, San Juan. The image of another folk saint, María Lionza, also appears to be derived from a painting. The original is a portrait of Eugenia María de Montijo (1826–1920), wife of Napoleon III. See Bruno Manara, *María*

Lionza: su entidad, su culto y la cosmovisión anexa (Caracas: Universidad Central de Caracas, 1995), 44.

23. The details and quoted passage in this and the previous paragraph are from "La Difunta es buena pagadora,"in *Difunta Correa*, 1/3 (March 1972): 6–7.

24. A reproduction of the billboard is in Chertudi and Newbery, *La Difunta Correa*, 171; see 165.

25. The quoted phrase is from *Difunta Correa: una historia que se hizo leyenda* (San Juan: Administration Difunta Correa, n.d. [2002]), 24.

26. The quoted phrase is from INILFI, 1951, San Juan, Alto de Sierra, n.p.

27. The Ekeko details are from Federico Arnillas Lafert, "Ekeko, alacitas y calvarios: la fiesta de Santa Cruz en Juliaca," *Allpanchis* 47 (1996): 130–133. In poorer regions, the desired objects are represented by stones. Regarding Qoyllur Rit'i miniatures, see Carlos Flores Lizana, *El Taytacha Qoyllur Rit'i* (Sicuani, Peru: Instituto de Pastoral Andina, 1997), 71–72.

NIÑO FIDENCIO

1. The biographical information on Fidencio follows Barbara June Macklin, "El Niño Fidencio: un estudio del curaderismo en Nuevo León," *Anuario Humánitas* (1967): 531–533; and Joseph Spielberg and Antonio Zavaleta, "Historic Folk Sainthood along the Texas-Mexico Border," Niño Fidencio Research Project Web site, http://vpea.utb.edu/elnino/researcharticles/historicfolksainthood.html.

2. Regarding Tatita, see Spielberg and Zavaleta, "Historic Folk Sainthood." The details on Niño Juanito are from Fernando Garza Quirós, *El Niño Fidencio y el fidencismo* (Mexico City: Ediciones Oasis, 1970), 111–113.

3. Regarding Von Wernich's vow and retreat, see June Macklin, "Folk Saints, Healers and Spiritist Cults in Northern Mexico," *Revista/Review Interamericana* 3/4 (1974): 358.

4. Regarding Von Wernich, see Macklin, "El Niño Fidencio," 534; and Pedro Angel González Valdés, *Vida y milagros del Niño Fidencio* (Saltillo, Mexico: N.p., 1970), 28.

5. Macklin, "El Niño Fidencio," 541–542; and Carlos Monsiváis, "El Niño Fidencio," in José Manuel Valenzuela Arce, ed., *Entre la magia y la historia: tradiciones, mitos y leyendas de la frontera* (Tijuana: El Colegio de la Frontera Norte and Mexico: Plaza y Valdés Editores, 2000), 116.

6. The summary of Fidencio's relations with medicine and the law is derived from Macklin, "El Niño Fidencio," 542 and 553; Garza Quirós, *El Niño Fidencio y el fidencismo*, 36–41; and Antonio N. Zavaleta, "El Niño Fidencio and the *Fidencistas*," in William W. Zellner and Marc Petrowsky, eds., *Sects, Cults, and Spiritual Communities: A Sociological Analysis* (Westport, Conn.: Praeger, 1998), 103–105.

7. The 1930 passage is from Francisco Vela González quoted in Garza Quirós, *El Niño Fidencio y el fidencismo*, 141. See 79, 125, and 141 regarding the possible profiteering. The last quoted passage is from Olimpia Farfán Morales, *El Fidencismo: la curación espiritista* (Monterrey, Mexico: Archivo General del Estado de Nuevo León, Serie Orgullosamente Bárbaros, 1997), 10–11.

8. The quoted passage from the brother, Joaquín Constantino Síntora, is from an interview in Garza Quirós, *El Niño Fidencio y el fidencismo*, 117. Regarding the archbishop, see 36–38.

9. The heart case and quoted passage are from testimony appended to Heliodoro González Valdés, *Cabalgando con Fidencio: el despertar a una nueva vida espiritual* (N.p.: N.p., 1998), n.p.

10. The quoted passages are from, respectively, Zavaleta, "El Niño Fidencio and the *Fidencistas*," 109; and Joaquín Constantino Síntora, quoted in Garza Quirós, *El Niño Fidencio y el fidencismo*, 117.

11. The quoted passage is from Heliodoro González Valdés, *Cabalgando con Fidencio*, 18.

12. Zavaleta, "El Niño Fidencio and the *Fidencistas*," 109–110.

13. See Heliodoro González Valdés, *Cabalgando con Fidencio*, 19–20.

14. The news passage is quoted in Macklin, "El Niño Fidencio," 544.

15. The virgin phrase is quoted in Garza Quirós, *El Niño Fidencio y el fidencismo*, 84. Regarding the genitalia, see Pedro Angel González Valdés, *Vida y milagros del Niño Fidencio*, 52–54. Many of the other details are from Macklin, "Folk Saints," 353. See Macklin, "El Niño Fidencio," 546.

16. Regarding Pancho Villa, see James S. Griffith, *Folk Saints of the Borderlands: Victims, Bandits, and Healers* (Tucson, Ariz.: Rio Nuevo Publishers, 2003), 100–101; and Ruth Behar, *Translated Woman: Crossing the Border with Esperanza's Story* (Boston: Beacon Press, 1993), 207–214.

17. Angelina Pollak-Eltz, *María Lionza: mito y culto venezolano* (Caracas: Universidad Católica Andrés Bello, 1972), 28 and 43.

18. Madre María's follower is quoted in Andrea Maurizi, "Entre la duda y la fe: la Madre María," *Todo es historia* 2/9 (January 1968): 12.

19. Brianda Domecq, "Un collage," in Valenzuela Arce, ed., *Entre la magia y la historia*, 55–66.

20. INILFI, 1940, Corrientes, Mercedes, n.p. See INILFI, 1950, Corrientes, Mercedes, 30.

21. The quoted passages are from Heliodoro González Valdés and Fabiola López de la Fuente Villareal, *Una luz en el desierto, el campo del dolor, vida del Niño Fidencio* (N.p.: n.p, 1997), 86 and 83, respectively. Von Wernich reportedly subscribed to the idea of Fidencio as a resurrection of Christ. See Garza Quirós, *El Niño Fidencio y el fidencismo*, 87.

22. Regarding the Mexican students, see José Luis Berlanga, et al., *Las fiestas del dolor: un estudio sobre las celebraciones del Niño Fidencio* (Monterrey: Fondo Estatal Para la Cultura y las Artes de Nuevo León, 1999), 107.

NIÑO COMPADRITO

1. The Pisac example (in the previous paragraph) is from Juvenal Casaverde Rojas, "El mundo sobrenatural en una comunidad," *Allpanchis Phuturinqa* 2 (1970): 191. Regarding Niño Compadrito's growth, see Abraham Valencia Espinoza,

Religiosidad popular: el Niño Compadrito (Cuzco: Instituto Nacional de Cultura, 1983), 29. The offering preferences are from Takahiro Kato, "Historia tejida por los sueños: formación de la imagen del Niño Compadrito," in Luis Millones, Hiroyasu Tomoeda, and Tatsuhiko Fujii, eds., *Desde afuera y desde adentro: ensayos de etnografía e historia del Cuzco y Apurímac* (Osaka: National Museum of Ethnography, 2000), 162 and 177.

2. Eliana Paliza C. and Mario Gallegos C., "El Niño Compadrito: ¿Milagroso? . . . o creencia popular." *Revista regional ilustrada* 2 (Cusco, 1987): 43. A variation is related in a 2002 news article by Toño Angulo Daneri, "Nino Compadrito: entre la religión y la herejía," Part 2: "Prohibido para los miedosos," *El comercio* (November 3, 2002): A40. See Kato, "Breve historia del Niño Compadrito del Cuzco," in Hiroyasu Tomoeda and Luis Millones, eds., *La tradition andina en tiempos modernos*, Senri Ethnological Reports 5 (Osaka: National Museum of Ethnology, 1996), 33.

3. Regarding Apu Ausangate, see Rosalind Gow and Bernabé Condori, *Kay Pacha* (Cuzco: Centro de Estudios Rurales Andinos Bartolomé de Las Casas, 1976), 38.

4. Nanda Leonardini and Patricia Borda, *Diccionario iconográfico religioso peruano* (Lima: Rubican Editores, 1996), 190. Advocations of the Christ child are on 183–191. See Valencia Espinoza, *Religiosidad popular*, 12, 18–19, and 22.

5. David Gow, "Taytacha de Qoyllur Rit'i: rocas y bailarines, creencias y continuidad," *Allpanchis* 7 (1974): 54–55; and Carlos Flores Lizana, *El Taytacha Qoyllur Rit'i* (Sicuani, Peru: Instituto de Pastoral Andina, 1997), 30–33.

6. The 1983 source is Valencia Espinoza, *Religiosidad popular*, 45.

7. María Belén is quoted in Kato, "Historia tejida," 172. See 181 n. 1. On duendes generally, see Casaverde Rojas, "El mundo sobrenatural," 176–179; Efraín Morote Best, "Estudio sobre el Duende," *Archivos peruanos de folklore* 2/2 (1956): 67 and 78; and Luis Alberto Aguilar, "Acompañar a los difuntos en el mundo minero andino," *Eco andino* 3/5 (1998): 101. For similar ideas in antiquity, see Elena Cassin, "The Death of the Gods," in S. C. Humphreys and Helen King, eds., *Mortality and Immortality: The Anthropology and Archaeology of Death* (London: Academic Press, 1982), 321: "The young dead person, unhappy and unsatisfied, becomes as a result virtually a demon."

8. The quoted passages are from, respectively, a seventeenth-century Jesuit quoted in Mario Polia Meconi, *La cosmovisión religiosa andina en los documentos ineditos del Archivo Romano de la Compañia de Jesús, 1581–1752* (Lima: Pontificia Universidad Católica del Peru, 1999), 506; and Pablo Joseph de Arriaga, *La extirpación de la idolatría en el Perú*, intro. and notes by Henrique Urbano (Cuzco: Centro de Estudios Regionales Andinos Bartolomé de Las Casas, 1999), 34.

Regarding mallquis generally, see Arriaga, *La extirpación de la idolatría en el Perú*, cxiii, 21, 34–35, 58; Polia Meconi, *La cosmovisión*, 21, 123, 125–126, 180–182, 329, 409, 419, 506–508, 539–540; Luis E. Valcárcel, *Historia del Perú antiguo*, Vol. 3 (Lima: Editorial Juan Mejía Baca, n.d.), 226–230; and Edmundo Guillén, "El enigma de las momias incas," *Boletín de Lima* 28 (1983): 29–42.

9. The quoted passage is from Arriaga, *La extirpación de la idolatría en el Perú*, 39. See Ladislao H. Landa V, "Chuchos o curis y otros nacimientos" [no editor], *Actas del*

IV Congreso Internacional de Etnohistoria (Lima: Pontificia Universidad Católica del Perú, 1998), 103; and Pierre Duviols, *Cultura andina y represión: procesos y visitas de idolatrías y hechicerías, Cajatambo, siglo 17* (Cuzco: Centro de Estudios Rurales Andinos Bartolomé de Las Casas, 1986), 381–382. The Lauramarca details are from Flores Lizana, *El Taytacha Qoyllur Rit'i*, 110.

10. The quoted passage is from Jean Delumeau, *Sin and Fear: The Emergence of a Western Guilt Culture, 13th–18th Centuries*, trans. Eric Nicholson (New York: St. Martin's Press, 1990), 448. See Louis-Vincent Thomas, *El cadáver: de la biología a la antropología*, trans. Juan Damonte (Mexico: Fondo de Cultura Económica, 1989), 59–65. See also Fernando Martínez Gil, *Muerte y sociedad en la España de los Austrias* (Mexico: Siglo Veintiuno Editores, 1993), 170–172; Jacobus de Voragine, *The Golden Legend: Readings on the Saints*, trans. William Granger Ryan (Princeton, N.J.: Princeton University Press, 1993), 2: 82–83; and Marina Warner, *Alone of All Her Sex: The Myth and the Cult of the Virgin Mary* (New York: Alfred A. Knopf, 1976), 78 and 252.

11. Regarding Golgotha (also known as Calvary), see Matthew 27.33, Mark 15:22, Luke 23.33, and John 19:17. Skulls appear in the iconography of Saints Jerome, Bruno, Paul, Mary Magdalene, Francis of Assisi, Catherine of Siena, Francisco de Borja, Vicente Ferrer, Teresa de Avila, and Mariana de Jesús, among others.

12. The quoted passage is from Kato, "Historia tejida," 182 n. 6; see 166–167. For a transcultural overview of skull relics, see Thomas, *El cadaver*, 147–152. See also Mario Polia Meconi, *Las lagunas de los encantos: medicina tradicional andina del Perú septentrional* (Piura: Central Peruana de Servicios, 1988), 79–80.

13. Regarding protection of Isabel's house, see Kato, "Historia tejida," 172.

14. Both examples are from Leonardini and Borda, *Diccionario iconográfico religioso peruano*, 45–46.

15. Regarding Tilcara, see Antonio Paleari, *Diccionario mágico jujeño* (San Salvador de Jujuy: Editorial Pachamama, 1982), 73–74. Details on the skulls in Salta are from Pablo Fortuny, *Supersticiones calchaquíes: ensayo e interpretación* (Buenos Aires: Editorial Huemul, 1965), 196.

16. In this and the previous paragraph, I follow Orlando Acosta, "La muerte en el contexto uru: caso Chipaya," in *Eco andino* 3/5 (1998): 32–37 and 8–9, respectively. For uses of skulls to bring rain, see Polia Meconi, *Las lagunas*, 95–96.

17. The prayer is in [Maria Elsa ("Pelusa") Paniagua], *San la Muerte* (Posadas, Argentina: N.p., 2003), 34.

18. The Aymara example is from Hans Van Den Berg, *Diccionario religioso aymara* (Iquitos: CETA-IDEA, 1985), 44, 83, and 174. The northern Peruvian example is from Polia Meconi, *Las lagunas*, 33 and 80.

19. The remedies are from an unpaginated narrative in Gow and Condori, *Kay Pacha*; Casaverde Rojas, "El mundo sobrenatural," 164; and Valencia Espinoza, *Religiosidad popular*, 46–47. The example with the two girls is from Hiromi Hosoya, "El Inca y el Apu: invención de la historia," in Hiroyasu Tomoeda and Jorge A. Flores Ochoa, *El Qosqo: antropología de la ciudad* (Cuzco: Miniserio de Educación del Japón y Centro de Estudios Andinos Cuzco, 1992), 97.

20. The quoted passages are from Gow and Condori, *Kay Pacha*, 8, and the unpaginated narrative in the same source, respectively.

21. The details regarding pregnancy are from Jorge A. Flores Ochoa, "La viuda y el hijo de Soq'a Machu," *Allpanchis Phuturinqa* 5 (1973): 49–53 (see 45–55). For additional information on soq'a, see Casaverde Rojas, "El mundo sobrenatural," 150–166.

22. Valencia Espinoza, *Religiosidad popular*, 2–3 and 69.

23. Ibid., 68 and 70–71; and Kato, "Breve Historia," 38–43. The monkey face is in José Vilca, "El feto sagrado," *Caretas* 1326 (August 25, 1994): 47. For some nondevotees, conversely, Vallejos Santoni's tragic death made him a miraculous soul worthy of devotion. See Rossano Calvo C., *La tradición: representación de la urbe andina cusqueña en el siglo 20* (Cuzco: Municipalidad de Santiago, 1999), 168. A 1699 Jesuit document reports that an Incan mummy was used in magical rituals intending to murder the parish priest. Polia Meconi, *La cosmovisión*, 149 and 548.

24. Regarding black-candle rituals, see Kato, "Breve historia," 36 and 44; and Toño Angulo Daneri, "Nino Compadrito: entre la religión y la herejía," part 1, "El Señorito de los Milagros," *El comercio* (November 2, 2002): A16.

25. The last example is from Angulo Daneri, "El Señorito," A16.

26. Regarding growth of the cult, see Kato, "Breve historia," 37. An anti-Protestant tract was approved by Vallejos Santoni in 1982 and was published in a Spanish/Quechua format. See Julio Francisco Macutela C. Masciotti, *Las sectas o iglesias separadas* (Cusco: N.p., 1986).

27. The decree is included in Valencia Espinoza, *Religiosidad popular*, 58–61.

28. The Cuzco headline is in Angulo Daneri, "Prohibido," A40. The devotees' concerns are quoted in Kato, "Breve historia," 38–43. See Valencia Espinoza, *Religiosidad popular*, 62.

29. The quoted passage is in Valencia Espinoza, *Religiosidad popular*, 71; see 2–3 and 58–61.

30. I follow Valencia Espinoza, *Religiosidad popular*, 2 and 63–64. In the New Testament, the Holy Family flees to Egypt and escapes Herod's massacre of the innocents thanks to a dream, then returns safely to Israel when a dream reveals that Herod is dead. See Matthew 2:12 and 2:19–20. Dream revelations are also prominent in the Old Testament. For a list of examples, see Jacques Le Goff, *The Medieval Imagination*, trans. Arthur Goldhammer (Chicago: University of Chicago Press, 1988), 229–231.

31. Kato, "Breve historia," 38–43; and Kato, "Historia tejida," 159.

32. The quoted passage is from Valencia Espinoza, *Religiosidad popular*, 59; see 58–61.

33. See, for example, Toño Angulo Daneri, "Nino Compadrito: entre la religión y la herejía," Part 3, "Los devotos ya tienen cura," *El comercio* (November 4, 2002): A7. This account reports two masses; Mora says he celebrated only one.

34. The quoted passage is from Manuel M. Marzal, *El mundo religioso de Urcos* (Cuzco: Instituto de Pastoral Andina, 1971), 224.

35. The quoted phrase is in Valencia Espinoza, *Religiosidad popular*, 59.

36. The quoted passage is appended to Kato, "Historia tejida," 185–186; see 174 and 184 n. 18. The remainder of the paragraph follows the same source, 167.

37. The debate and decision regarding the eyes is in Kato, "Historia tejida," 174–175.

38. In this and the previous paragraph, I follow Kato, "Historia tejida," 168–169. In the version that Juan tells, the woman was single and lonely, and Niño Compadrito married her so she would not grow old alone.

39. Regarding changes to the effigy and dream revelations "mutually reproducing one another in a process of interactions" (170), see Kato, "Historia tejida," 178–181.

CONCLUSION

1. Pastor Aguilar quoted in Adys Cupull and Froilán González, De Ñacahuasú a La Higuera (Havana: Editora Política, 1989), 424. An article by Pablo Guadarrama González, "San Ernesto de La Higerua," Casa de las Américas 206 (1997): 37–38, also mentions devotion to Che.

2. The anarchist examples are from Hugo Chumbita, Jinetes rebeldes (Buenos Aires: Vergara, 2000), 221 and 225.

3. The details on María Lionza devotion are from Angelina Pollak-Eltz, María Lionza: mito y culto venezolano (Caracas: Universidad Católica Andrés Bello, 1972), 29; and Bruno Manara, María Lionza: su entidad, su culto y la cosmovisión anexa (Caracas: Universidad Central de Caracas, 1995), 7. The other two examples are from Angelina Pollak-Eltz, Las ánimas milagrosas en Venezuela (Caracas: Fundación Bigott, 1989), 39 and 42, respectively.

4. INILFI, n.d., Corrientes (capital), n.p.

5. The Niño de las Chutas example is from Nanda Leonardini and Patricia Borda, Diccionario iconográfico religioso peruano (Lima: Rubican Editores, 1996), 187.

6. The quoted passage is from a report in Berta Elena Vidal de Battini, Cuentos y leyendas populares de la Argentina, Vol. 8, Leyendas (Buenos Aires: Ediciones Culturales Argentinas, 1984), 252. The other details on López are from INILFI, n.d., "Francisco López," Corrientes (capital), 2.

7. The quoted passage is from Milciades Aguilar and Ulises Aguilar, La Cruz Gil: el culto popular al gauchito Gil, testimonios y documentos (Buenos Aires: Camino Real, 1999), 62.

8. June Macklin, "Folk Saints, Healers, and Spiritist Cults in Northern Mexico," Revista/Review Interamericana 3/4 (1974): 362.

9. The forms of dream apparition are from Abraham Valencia Espinoza, Religiosidad popular: El Niño Compadrito (Cuzco: Instituto Nacional de Cultura, 1983), 29–31; and Takahiro Kato, "Historia tejida por los sueños: formación de la imagen del Niño Compadrito," in Luis Millones, Hiroyasu Tomoeda, and Tatsuhiko Fujii, eds., Desde afuera y desde adentro: ensayos de etnografía e historia del Cuzco y Apurímac (Osaka: National Museum of Ethnography, 2000), 162–163. The quoted passage is from Carlos Flores Lizana, El Taytacha Qoyllur Rit'i (Sicuani, Peru: Instituto de

Pastoral Andina, 1997), 88. God also appeared in a dream as a policeman ("who told me what I must do") in a narrative in Manuel Marzal, "La imagen de Dios en Urcos," *Allpanchis Phuturinqa* 2 (1970): 48. In Cajamarca folklore, the appearance of a policeman in one's dream is a sign that a wish will be fulfilled. Luis Iberico Mas, *El folklore mágico de Cajamarca* (Cajamarca: Universidad Nacional de Cajamarca, 1981), 244.

10. The María Catalina details are from Pollak-Eltz, *Las ánimas*, 46.

11. Regarding the last three Niños, see Olimpia Farfán Morales, *El Fidencismo: la curación espiritista* (Monterrey, Mexico: Archivo General del Estado de Nuevo León, Serie Orgullosamente Bárbaros, 1997), 10–11.

12. The quoted passage is from Heliodoro González Valdés, *Cabalgando con Fidencio: el despertar a una nueva vida espiritual* (N.p.: N.p., 1998), 32.

13. The Qoyllur Rit'i quote and details are from Flores Lizana, *El Taytacha Qoyllur Rit'i*, 74. Regarding the miraculous lakes, see Mario Polia Meconi, *Las lagunas de los encantos: medicina tradicional andina del Perú septentrional* (Piura: Central Peruana de Servicios, 1988), 35 and 87–89.

14. See Jim Pieper, *Guatemala's Folk Saints: Maximon/San Simon, Rey Pascual, Judas, Lucifer, and others* (Los Angeles: Pieper and Associates, 2002), 169–195.

15. The two magical uses are from, respectively, INAPL, n.d., Chaco 96, Vedia, 2; and Pablo Fortuny, *Supersticiones calchaquíes: ensayo e interpretación* (Buenos Aires: Editorial Huemul, 1965), 167.

16. Regarding Pancho Villa, see James S. Griffith, *Folk Saints of the Borderlands: Victims, Bandits, and Healers* (Tucson, Ariz.: Rio Nuevo Publishers, 2003), 104.

Bibliography

ARCHIVES

The research archives are itemized in the acknowledgments. The two principal sources, the Instituto Nacional de Investigaciones Lingüísticas y Filológicas (INILFI) in San Juan, Argentina; and the Instituto Nacional de Antropología y Pensamiento Lationamericano (INAPL) in Buenos Aires, Argentina, are identified in the endnotes by their acronyms.

BOOKS

Aguilar, Milciades, and Ulises Aguilar. *La Cruz Gil: el culto popular al gauchito Gil, testimonios y documentos.* Buenos Aires: Camino Real, 1999.

Aguilar Peña, Pastor. *Cuentos y tradiciones vallunas.* Vallegrande, Bolivia: Fondo Editorial de la Casa Municipal de Cultura, 2000.

Alarcón, Cristian. *Cuando me muera quiero que me toquen cumbia: vidas de pibes chorros.* Buenos Aires: Grupo Editorial Norma, 2003.

Alvarez, Félix Romualdo. *Una nueva versión sobre la Difunta Correa.* San Juan, Argentina: Editorial Sanjuanina, 1967.

Ambrosetti, Juan B. *Supersticiones y leyendas.* Buenos Aires: Ediciones Siglo Veinte, 1976.

Americas Watch and Centro de Estudios Legales y Sociales. *Police Violence in Argentina: Torture and Police Killings in Buenos Aires.* New York: Americas Watch and Centro de Estudios Legales y Sociales, 1991.

Arriaga, Pablo Joseph de. *La extirpación de la idolatría en el Perú.* Introduction and notes by Henrique Urbano. Cuzco: Centro de Estudios Regionales Andinos Bartolomé de Las Casas, 1999.

Bailey, Gauvin Alexander. *Art on the Jesuit Missions in Asia and Latin America, 1542–1773.* Toronto: University of Toronto Press, 1999.

Baring, Anne, and Jules Cashford. *The Myth of the Goddess: Evolution of an Image.* London: Arkana/Penguin Books, 1993.

Baumgarten, Albert I., ed. *Sacrifice in Religious Experience.* Leiden: Brill, 2002.

Behar, Ruth. *Translated Woman: Crossing the Border with Esperanza's Story.* Boston: Beacon Press, 1993.

Bell, Rudolph M. *Holy Anorexia.* Chicago: University of Chicago Press, 1985.

Berlanga, José Luis, et al. *Las fiestas del dolor: un estudio sobre las celebraciones del Niño Fidencio.* Monterrey: Fondo Estatal Para la Cultura y las Artes de Nuevo León, 1999.

Bermejo, Vladimiro. *La Chabela/Polvora.* Arequipa, Peru: Editorial UNSA, 1997.

Bibondo Carrizo, Raúl Oscar. *"Almita" Sivila.* San Salvador de Jujuy: Imprenta Minerva, 1973.

Blanche, Martha. *Estructura del miedo: narrativas folklóricas guaraníticas.* Buenos Aires: Plus Ultra, 1991.

Bogni, Carlos Victor. *Difunta Correa Santa . . .* San Juan, Argentina: Selecciones Sanjuaninas, 1994.

Bottasso, Juan. *Las religiones amerindias: 500 Años después.* Quito: Ediciones Abya-Yala, 1992.

Bravo, Benjamín, ed. *Diccionario de religiosidad popular.* Mexico: N.p., 1992.

Brooks County Historical Survey Committee. *The Faith Healer of Los Olmos: Don Pedrito Jaramillo.* [Falfurrias, Tex.]: Brooks County Historical Survey Committee, 1990.

Brozzi, Abel. *San la Muerte.* N.p.: N.p., n.d.

Calvo C., Rossano. *La tradición: representación de la urbe andina cusqueña en el siglo 20.* Cuzco: Municipalidad de Santiago, 1999.

Castelli, Eugenio, ed. *Antología cultural del litoral argentino.* Buenos Aires: Ediciones Nuevo Siglo, 1995.

Chapp, M. E., et al. *Religiosidad popular en la Argentina.* Buenos Aires: Centro Editor de America Latina, 1991.

Christian, William A., Jr. *Local Religion in Sixteenth-Century Spain.* Princeton, N.J.: Princeton University Press, 1981.

Chertudi, Susana, and Sara Josefina Newbery. *La Difunta Correa.* Buenos Aires: Editorial Huemul, 1978.

Chumbita, Hugo. *Bairoletto: el último bandido romántico.* Buenos Aires: *Todo Es Historia,* Supp. 10, n.d.

———. *Jinetes rebeldes.* Buenos Aires: Vergara, 2000.

Cipolletti, M. S., and E. J. Langdon, eds. *La muerte y el más allá en las culturas indígenas latinoamericanas.* Quito: Ediciones Abya-Yala, 1992.

Colonia Zambrano, Hipólito. *Sarita Colonia Zambrano: una biografía familiar.* Lima: N.p., 1999.

Coluccio, Félix. *Cultos y canonizaciones populares de Argentina.* Buenos Aires: Biblioteca de Cultura Popular/Ediciones del Sol, 1986.

———. *Devociones populares: argentinas y americanas*. Buenos Aires: Corregidor, 2001.

El culto a San la Muerte: leyendas, historias, oraciones y ritos. N.p.: Editorial Alberto S. Bellanza, 1997.

Cupull, Adys, and Froilán González. *De Ñacahuasú a La Higuera*. Havana: Editora Política, 1989.

Daman, Frans, and Esteban Judd Zanon. *Cristo crucificado en los pueblos de América Latina: antología de religión popular*. Cuzco: Instituto de Pastoral Andina, and Quito: Editorial Abya-Yala, 1992.

Delumeau, Jean. *Sin and Fear: The Emergence of a Western Guilt Culture, 13th-18th Centuries*. Translated by Eric Nicholson. New York: St. Martin's Press, 1990.

Difunta Correa: una historia que se hizo leyenda. San Juan: Administración Difunta Correa, n.d. [2002].

Duviols, Pierre. *Cultura andina y represión: procesos y visitas de idolatrías y hechicerías, Cajatambo, siglo 17*. Cuzco: Centro de Estudios Rurales Andinos Bartolomé de Las Casas, 1986.

Ehrenwald, Jan, ed. *The History of Psychotherapy*. Northvale, N.J.: Jason Aronson, 1991.

Farfán Morales, Olimpia. *El Fidencismo: la curación espiritista*. Monterrey, Mexico: Archivo General del Estado de Nuevo León, Serie Orgullosamente Bárbaros, 1997.

Flores Lizana, Carlos. *El Taytacha Qoyllur Rit'i*. Sicuani, Peru: Instituto de Pastoral Andina, 1997.

Fortuny, Pablo. *Supersticiones calchaquíes: ensayo e interpretación*. Buenos Aires: Editorial Huemul, 1965.

Franco, Carlos. *Imágenes de la sociedad peruana: la 'otra' modernidad*. Lima: Centro de Estudios Para el Desarrollo y la Participación, 1991.

Furlong, Guillermo. *Misiones y sus pueblos de guaraníes*. Buenos Aires: N.p., 1962.

Galarza, Tránsito. *Los poderes del Gauchito Gil: nuestro primer santo telúrico*. Buenos Aires: Libro Latino, 1999.

Ganson, Barbara Anne. "Better Not Take My Manioc: Religion, Society, and Politics in the Jesuit Missions of Paraguay, 1500–1800." Ph.D. diss., University of Texas, Austin, 1994.

García Gavidia, Nelly. *Posesión y ambivalencia en el culto a María Lionza*. Maracaibo: Universidad del Zulia, 1987.

Gardner, Dore. *Niño Fidencio: A Heart Thrown Open*. Santa Fe: Museum of New Mexico Press, 1992.

Garza Quirós, Fernando. *El Niño Fidencio y el fidencismo*. Mexico City: Ediciones Oasis, 1970.

Giménez, Miguel E. *La Difunta y el niño (Difunta Correa)*. San Juan, Argentina: N.p., 1996.

Giordano, Oronzo. *Religiosidad popular en la alta edad media*. Translated by Pilar García Mouton and Valentín García Yebra. Madrid: Editorial Gredos, 1983.

Gisbert, Teresa. *El paraíso de los pájaros parlantes*. La Paz: Plural Editores, 2001.

Gómez Balzarena, Odilia R. *Vida y muerte de Antonio Gil*. Mercedes. Corrientes: N.p., 1966.

González, José Luis, and Teresa María Van Ronzelen. *Religiosidad popular en el Perú: bibliografía*. Lima: Centro de Estudios y Publicaciones, 1983.

González Martinez, José Luis. *La religion popular en el Perú: informe y diagnóstico*. Lima: Instituto de Pastoral Andina, 1987.

González Valdés, Heliodoro. *Cabalgando con Fidencio: el despertar a una nueva vida espiritual*. N.p.: N.p., 1998.

————, and Fabiola López de la Fuente Villareal. *Una luz en el desierto, el campo del dolor, vida del Niño Fidencio*. N.p.: N.p., 1997.

González Valdés, Pedro Angel. *Vida y milagros del Niño Fidencio*. Saltillo, Mexico: N.p., 1970.

González Viaña, Eduardo. *Sarita Colonial viene volando*. Lima: Mosca Azul Editores, 1990.

Gow, Rosalind, and Bernabé Condori. *Kay Pacha*. Cuzco: Centro de Estudios Rurales Andinos Bartolomé de Las Casas, 1976.

Griffith, James S. *Folk Saints of the Borderlands: Victims, Bandits, and Healers*. Tucson, Ariz.: Rio Nuevo Publishers, 2003.

Haskins, Susan. *Mary Magdalen: Myth and Metaphor*. New York: Harcourt, Brace, 1993.

Hernández, José. *Martín Fierro*. Edited by Carlos Alberto Leumann. Buenos Aires: Angel Estrada, 1945.

Historia de Rosita de Pachacutec. N.p.: N.p., n.d.

Hobsbawm, Eric. *Bandits*. New York: New Press, 2000.

Hopgood, James F., ed. *The Making of Saints: Contesting Sacred Ground*. Tuscaloosa: University of Alabama Press, 2005.

Hoyos, María de, and Laura Migale. *Almas milagrosas: santos populares y otras devociones*. Buenos Aires: Equipo Naya, 2000. CD-ROM.

Hudson, Wilson M., ed. *The Healer of Los Olmos and Other Mexican Lore*. Austin: Texas Folklore Society, and Dallas: Southern Methodist University, 1951.

Huertas Vallejos, Lorenzo. *La religión en una sociedad rural andina (siglo 17)*. Ayacucho: Universidad Nacional de San Cristóbal de Huamanga, 1981.

Iberico Mas, Luis. *El folklore mágico de Cajamarca*. Cajamarca: Universidad Nacional de Cajamarca, 1981.

Ignotus. *Pancho Sierra: el gaucho santo de Pergamino*. Buenos Aires: Colección Esotérica Universal, 1974.

Johann, Francis G., ed. *Sarita Colonia: la santa ungida por el pueblo*. Lima: Editorial San Marcos, 2003.

Kohut, Karl, and Albert Meyers, eds. *Religiosidad popular en América Latina*. Frankfurt: Vervuert Verlag, 1988.

Larraburu, Luis Angel. *Del Yasy, del Pombero, del Maestro, y de otras emociones*. Posadas, Argentina: N.p., 1995.

León, Luis D. *La Llorona's Children: Religion, Life, and Death in the U.S.-Mexico Borderlands*. Berkeley: University of California Press, 2004.

Leonardini, Nanda, and Patricia Borda. *Diccionario iconográfico religioso peruano*. Lima: Rubican Editores, 1996.

López Breard, Miguel Raúl. *Devocionario guaraní*. Santa Fe, Argentina: Ediciones Colmegna, 1973.

Manara, Bruno. *María Lionza: su entidad, su culto y la cosmovisión anexa*. Caracas: Universidad Central de Caracas, 1995.

Martínez Gil, Fernando. *Muerte y sociedad en la España de los Austrias*. Mexico City: Siglo Veintiuno Editores, 1993.

Martos, Miguel Cristóbal. *Las reducciones jesuítas*. Buenos Aires: Editorial Argenta Sarlep, 1996.

Marzal, Manuel M. *El mundo religioso de Urcos*. Cuzco: Instituto de Pastoral Andina, 1971.

———. *Estudios sobre religión campesina*. Lima: Pontificia Universidad Católica del Perú, 1977.

———. *Los caminos religiosos de los inmigrantes en la gran Lima: el caso de El Agustino*. Lima: Pontificia Universidad Católica del Perú, 1989.

Melià, Bartomeu. *El Guaraní conquistado y reducido*. Asunción, Paraguay: Centro de Estudios Antropológicos de la Universidad Católica, 1993.

Michieli, Catalina Teresa. *Los Huarpes protohistóricos*. San Juan, Argentina: Instituto de Investigaciones Arqueológicas y Museo, 1983.

Miranda Borelli, José. *San La Muerte: un mito regional del nordeste*. Resistencia, Argentina: Editorial Región, 1979.

Mó, Fernando F. *Cosas de San Juan*. Vol. 4. San Juan, Argentina: N.p., 1990.

Moffatt, Alfredo. *Psicoterapia del oprimido: ideología y técnica de la psiquiatría popular*. Buenos Aires: Editorial Librería ECRO, 1974.

Montenegro, René. *Fogón de mi Taragüí*. Corrientes, Argentina: N.p., 1994.

Morales Segovia, Marily. *Manual de folklore de Corrientes*. Corrientes, Argentina: Fondo Editorial Sade Corrientes, 1984.

Morote Best, Efraín. *Aldeas sumergidas: cultura popular y sociedad en los Andes*. Cuzco: Centro de Estudios Rurales Andinos Bartolomé de Las Casas, 1988.

Noya, Emilio. *Imaginería religiosa y santoral profano de Corrientes*. Corrientes, Argentina: Subsecretaría de Cultura de la Provincia de Corrientes, 1994.

Nugent, José Guillermo. *El laberinto de la choledad*. Lima: Fundación Friedrich Ebert, 1992.

Ochoa Zazueta, Jesús Angel. *La muerte y los muertos: culto, servicio, ofrenda y humor de una comunidad*. Mexico City: SEP/SETENTAS, 1974.

Orsi, Robert A. *Between Heaven and Earth: The Religious Worlds People Make and the Scholars Who Study Them*. Princeton: Princeton University Press, 2005.

Paleari, Antonio. *Diccionario mágico jujeño*. San Salvador de Jujuy, Argentina: Editorial Pachamama, 1982.

[Paniagua, María Elsa ("Pelusa")]. *San la Muerte*. Posadas, Argentina: N.p., 2003.

París, Marta de. *Corrientes y el santoral profano*. Buenos Aires: Editorial Plus Ultra, 1988.

Pasteknik, Elsa Leonor. *Mitos vivientes de Misiones*. Buenos Aires: Editorial Plus Ultra, 1977.

Peñalva Suca, Lorenzo Jesús. "Consideraciones sociales acerca del mito de 'La Chavela.'" Master's thesis, Universidad Nacional de San Agustín, Arequipa, Peru, n.d.

Pérez Pardella, Agustín. *La Difunta Correa*. Buenos Aires: Plus Ultra, 1975.

Pieper, Jim. *Guatemala's Folk Saints: Maximon/San Simon, Rey Pascual, Judas, Lucifer, and others*. Los Angeles: Pieper and Associates, 2002.

Plath, Oreste. *Folklore religioso chileno*. Santiago: Ediciones Platur, 1966.

———. *L'Animita: hagiografía folklórica*. Santiago, Chile: Editorial Pluma y Pincel, 1993.

Polia Meconi, Mario. *Las lagunas de los encantos: medicina tradicional andina del Perú septentrional*. Piura, Peru: Central Peruana de Servicios, 1988.

———. *La cosmovisión religiosa andina en los documentos ineditos del Archivo Romano de la Compañia de Jesús, 1581–1752*. Lima: Pontificia Universidad Católica del Peru, 1999.

Pollak-Eltz, Angelina. *María Lionza: mito y culto venezolano*. Caracas: Universidad Católica Andrés Bello, 1972.

———. *Las ánimas milagrosas en Venezuela*. Caracas: Fundación Bigott, 1989.

Quinones, Sam. *True Tales from Another Mexico: The Lynch Mob, the Popsicle Kings, Chalino, and the Bronx*. Albuquerque: University of New Mexico Press, 2001.

Rainero, Federico R., ed. *La cruz de Gil*. Corrientes, Argentina: N.p., 1990.

Romero, Cacho. *La Difunta Correa: su mensaje, el sentido de amor, de su vida y de su muerte*. San Juan, Argentina: N.p., n.d.

Ruiz de Montoya, Antonio. *Conquista espiritual hecha por los religiosos de la Compañía de Jesús en las provincias de Paraguay, Paraná, Uruguay y Tape*. Buenos Aires: Equipo Difusor de Esudios de Historia Iberoamericana, 1989.

Scaraffia, Lucetta, and Gabriella Zarri. *Women and Faith: Catholic Religious Life in Italy from Late Antiquity to the Present*. Cambridge: Harvard University Press, 1999.

Serrano Martín, Eliseo, ed. *Muerte, religiosidad, y cultural popular: siglos 13–18*. Zaragoza: Institución Fernando el Católico, 1994.

Sindicato de Trabajadores del Hogar. *Basta: testimonios*. Cuzco: Centro de Estudios Rurales Andinos Bartolomé de Las Casas, 1982.

Slatta, Richard W., ed. *Bandidos: The Varieties of Latin American Banditry*. New York: Greenwood Press, 1987.

Sullivan, Lawrence E. *Icanchu's Drum: An Orientation to Meaning in South American Religions*. New York: MacMillan, 1988.

Susnik, Branislava. *Artesanía indígena: ensayo analítico*. Asunción: Asociación Indigenista del Paraguay, 1986.

Thomas, Louis-Vincent. *El cadáver: de la biología a la antropología*. Mexico: Fondo de Cultura Económica, 1989.

Torre, Juan L. de la. *La Difunta Correa*. San Juan, Argentina: Editorial Sanjuanina, 1973.

Torres, Amanda C. *La verdadera muerte de Visitación Sivila*. San Salvador de Jujuy: N.p., 1983.

Valcárcel, Luis E. *Historia del Perú antiguo*. 6 vols. Lima: Editorial Juan Mejía Baca, 1971.

Valencia Espinoza, Abraham. *Religiosidad popular: el Niño Compadrito*. Cuzco: Instituto Nacional de Cultura, 1983.

Valenzuela Arce, José Manuel, ed. *Entre la magia y la historia: tradiciones, mitos y leyendas de la frontera*. Tijuana: El Colegio de la Frontera Norte, and Mexico: Plaza y Valdés Editores, 2000.

Vallejo, Román Anselmo. *Antonio Gil Mercendeño*. Buenos Aires: Ediciones Camino Real, 1995.

Van Den Berg, Hans. *Diccionario religioso aymara*. Iquitos: CETA-IDEA, 1985.

Van Ronzelen García Rosell, Teresa María. "Víctor Apaza: la emergencia de un santo." Master's thesis, Pontificia Universidad Católica del Perú, 1984.

Vanaya, Marta, ed. *Mitos y leyendas guaraníes*. Buenos Aires: Jamkana, 1986.

Vanderwood, Paul J. *Juan Soldado: Rapist, Murderer, Martyr, Saint*. Durham, N.C.: Duke University Press, 2004.

Vauchez, André. *Sainthood in the Later Middle Ages*. Translated by Jean Birrell. Cambridge: Cambridge University Press, 1997.

Vidal de Battini, Berta Elena. *Cuentos y leyendas populares de la Argentina*, Vol. 8: *Leyendas*. Buenos Aires: Ediciones Culturales Argentinas, 1984.

Videla, Horacio. *Historia de San Juan*. Vol. 4. San Juan: Universidad Católica de Cuyo, 1976.

Vivante, Armando, and Nestor Homeo Palma. *Magia, daño y muerte por imagenes*. Salta, Argentina: Gofica Editora, 1999.

Voragine, Jacobus de. *The Golden Legend: Readings on the Saints*. Translated by William Granger Ryan. 2 vols. Princeton, N.J.: Princeton University Press, 1993.

Vrijhof, Pieter Hendrik, and Jacques Waardenburg, eds. *Official and Popular Religion: Analysis of a Theme for Religious Studies*. The Hague: Mouton, 1979.

Warner, Marina. *Alone of All Her Sex: The Myth and the Cult of the Virgin Mary*. New York: Alfred A. Knopf, 1976.

Westheim, Paul. *La calavera*. Mexico: Fondo de Cultura Económica, 1983.

Yalom, Marilyn. *A History of the Breast*. New York: Alfred A. Knopf, 1997.

Zapata Gollán, Agustín. *Supersticiones y amuletos*. Santa Fe, Argentina: Ministerio de Educación y Cultura, 1960.

Zarauz López, Héctor L. *La fiesta de la muerte*. Mexico City: Conaculta, 2000.

ARTICLES

Acosta, Ertivio. "Culto a San la Muerte." *Clarín*, August 15, 1985: 46.

Acosta, Orlando. "La muerte en el contexto uru: caso Chipaya." *Eco andino* 3/5 (1998): 7–40.

Aguilar, Luis Alberto. "Acompañar a los difuntos en el mundo minero andino." *Eco andino* 3/5 (1998): 89–122.

Agurto, Gastón "Santa Sarita." *Caretas* 1546, December 10, 1998: 90–92.

Ampuero, Fernando. "¿Milagros con censura?" *Caretas* 804, June 18, 1984: 46–49.

Angulo Daneri, Toño. "Nino Compadrito: entre la religión y la herejía," Part 1: "El Señorito de los Milagros." *El comercio* (Lima), November 2, 2002: A16.

———. "Nino Compadrito: entre la religión y la herejía," Part 2: "Prohibido para los miedosos." *El comercio*, November 3, 2002: A4.

———. "Nino Compadrito: entre la religión y la herejía," Part 3: "Los devotos ya tienen cura." *El comercio*, November 4, 2002: A7.

"Antes de robar rezaban ante Sarita Colonia...y así los capturó la policía." *El comercio*, December 1, 1994: A16.

Aranguren Paz, Angélica. "Las creencias y ritos mágicos religiosos de los pastores puneños." *Allpanchis* 8 (1975): 103–132.

Arnillas Lafert, Federico. "Ekeko, alacitas y calvarios: la fiesta de Santa Cruz en Juliaca." *Allpanchis* 47 (1996): 119–136.

Buntinx, Gustavo. "Sarita iluminada: de ícono religioso a héroe cultural." Available at www.fas.harvard.edu/~icop/gustavobuntinx.html

Cachay A., Raúl. "Colonia Sarita: de culto clandestino a ícono popular. *El Comercio* (Lima), *Somos* 788 (January 12, 2002): 46–49.

Casaverde Rojas, Juvenal. "El mundo sobrenatural en una comunidad." *Allpanchis Phuturinqa* 2 (1970): 121–244.

Cassin, Elena. "The Death of the Gods." In *Mortality and Immortality: The Anthropology and Archaeology of Death*, ed. S. C. Humphreys and Helen King, 317–325. London: Academic Press, 1982.

Chertudi, Susana, and Sara Josefina Newbery. "La Difunta Correa." *Cuadernos del Instituto Nacional de Antropología* 6 (1966): 95–178.

Coluccio, Félix. "Folklore en América: el niño en la muerte; el velorio del angelito," *Tradición: revista peruana de cultura* 5/12–14 (1953): 149–152.

———. "El culto a San La Muerte." *Revista venezolana de folklore* 6 (October 1975): 100–104.

Fernández Juárez, Gerardo. "El culto al 'tio' en las minas bolivianas." *Cuadernos hispanoamericanos* 597 (2000): 25–31.

Figgen, Kathleen L. "Bottles of Water on the Road: Material Symbols of an Argentine Popular Saint's Cult." *Women's Studies International Forum* 9/3 (1986): 281–285.

Flores Ochoa, Jorge A. "La viuda y el hijo de Soq'a Machu." *Allpanchis Phuturinqa* 5 (1973): 45–55.

———. "La *missa* andina." In *Homenaje a María Rostworowski: arqueología, antropología e historia en los Andes*, ed. Rafael Varón Gabai and Javier Flores Espinoza, 717–728. Lima: Instituto de Estudios Peruanos and Banco Central de Reserva del Perú, 1997.

Franco, Francisco. "El culto a los muertos milagrosos en Venezuela: estudio etnohistórico y etnológico." *Boletín antropológico*, 2/52 (2001): 107–144.

Freire Sarria, Luise. "Sarita, patrona de las buenas elecciones." *El comercio*, November 10, 2002: A20.

García, Silvia. "Algunos aspectos de la religión popular correntina." In *Cultura tradicional del área del Paraná medio*, ed. Instituto Nacional de Antropología, 269–281. Buenos Aires: Fundación Federico Guillermo Bracht, 1984.

García Miranda, Juan José. "La muerte en la cosmovisión andina: los presagios." In *Al final del camino*, ed. Luis Millones and Moisés Lemlij, 116–125. Lima: SIDEA, 1996.

———. "Los santuarios de los Andes centrales." In *Historia, religión y ritual de los pueblos ayacuchanos*, ed. Luis Millones, Hiroyasu Tomoeda, and Tatsuhiko Fujii, 51–85. Osaka: National Museum of Ethnology, 1998.

Glazer, Mark. "Faith and Saints in Mexican-American Folk Religion." In *More Studies in Brownsville History*, ed. Milo Kearney, 275–283. Brownsville: Pan American University, 1989.

Gow, David. "Taytacha de Qoyllur Rit'i: rocas y bailarines, creencias y continuidad." *Allpanchis* 7 (1974): 49–100.

Guadarrama González, Pablo. "San Ernesto de La Higuera." *Casa de las Américas* 206 (1997): 34–38.

Guillén, Edmundo. "El enigma de las momias incas." *Boletín de Lima* 28 (1983): 29–42.

Hinostroza, Martha. "Olor de santidad." *Caretas* 544, August 14, 1978: 54–55.

Hosoya, Hiromi. "El Inca y el Apu: invención de la historia." In *El Qosqo: antropología de la ciudad*, ed. Hiroyasu Tomoeda and Jorge A. Flores Ochoa, 83–108. Cuzco: Ministerio de Educación del Japón y Centro de Estudios Andinos, 1992.

Irarrazaval, Diego. "Mutación en la identidad andina: ritos y concepciones de la divinidad." *Allpanchis* 31 (1988): 11–83.

Jauregui, Eloy. "Rezando en jerga." *El comercio, Suplemento dominical* 194, November 3, 2002: R4.

Jeri, Rosa. "Sarita Colonia en la imaginación popular." *Ccantu* 6 (1983): 19–21.

Kato, Takahiro. "Breve Historia del Niño Compadrito del Cuzco." In *La tradición andina en tiempos modernos* (Senri Ethnological Reports 5), ed. Hiroyasu Tomoeda and Luis Millones, 31–47. Osaka: National Museum of Ethnology, 1996.

———. "Historia tejida por los sueños: formación de la imagen del Niño Compadrito." In *Desde afuera y desde adentro: ensayos de etnografía e historia del Cuzco y Apurímac*, ed. Luis Millones, Hiroyasu Tomoeda, and Tatsuhiko Fujii, 159–190. Osaka: National Museum of Ethnography, 2000.

Landa V., Ladislao H. "Chuchos o curis y otros nacimientos." *Actas del IV Congreso Internacional de Etnohistoria*, no editor, 76–106. Lima: Pontificia Universidad Católica del Perú, 1998.

León, Rafael. "Dimas, el santo ladrón." *Caretas* 1562, April 8, 1999: 44–48.

Macklin, Barbara June. "El Niño Fidencio: un estudio del curanderismo en Nuevo León." *Anuario Humánitas* (Centro de Estudios Humanísticos, Universidad de Nuevo León) (1967): 529–563.

———. "Folk Saints, Healers, and Spiritist Cults in Northern Mexico." *Revista/Review Interamericana* 3/4 (1974): 351–367.

Mamani Daza, Lolo Juan. "Sobre los acontecimientos en torno a Víctor Apaza Quispe." *Antropus UNSA* 2 (2000).

Mannheim, Bruce. "A Semiotic of Andean Dreams." In *Dreaming: Anthropological and Psychological Interpretations*, ed. Barbara Tedlock, 132–153. Cambridge: Cambridge University Press, 1987.

Mariluz Urquijo, José M. "Los guaraníes después de la expulsión de los jesuítas." *Estudios americanos* 25 (October 1953): 323–330.

Marzal, Manuel. "La Imagen de Dios en Urcos." *Allpanchis Phuturinqa* 2 (1970): 35–56.

Maurizi, Andrea. "Entre la duda y la fe: la Madre María." *Todo es historia* 2/9 (January 1968): 8–18.

Miranda, José. "San la Muerte." *Cuadernos del Instituto Nacional de Antropología* 4 (1963): 81–93.

Morote Best, Efraín. "Dios, la Virgen y los Santos (en relatos populares)." *Tradición: revista peruana de cultura* 5/12–14 (1953): 76–104.

———. "Estudio sobre el Duende." *Archivos peruanos de folklore* 2/2 (1956): 55–80.

Navarro Román, Julio, et al. "Devoción popular a la 'Animita' de la estación central." In *Religiosidad y fe en America Latina*, no editor, 189–193. Santiago, Chile: Ediciones Mundo, 1975.

Noya, Emilio. "Corrientes entre la leyenda y la tradición." *Todo es historia* (October 1987): 3–13.

Nuñez de Prado Béjar, Juan V. "El mundo sobrenatural de los Quechuas del Sur del Perú a través de la comunidad de Qotobamba." *Allpanchis Phuturinqa* 2 (1970): 57–120.

Ortiz de Zevallos, Pilar. "Algunas creencias prehispánicas sobre la maternidad y la primera infancia." In *Homenaje a María Rostworowski: arqueología, antropología e historia en los Andes*, ed. Rafael Varón Gabai and Javier Flores Espinoza, 527–544. Lima: Instituto de Estudios Peruanos and Banco Central de Reserva del Perú, 1997.

Ortiz Rescaniere, Alejandro. "Expresiones religiosas marginales: el caso de Sarita Colonia." In *Pobreza urbana: interrelaciones económicas y marginalidad religiosa*, ed. Marcel Valcárcel C., 169–201. Lima: Pontificia Universidad Católica del Perú, 1990.

Paliza C., Eliana, and Mario Gallegos C. "El Niño Compadrito: ¿Milagroso? . . . o creencia popular." *Revista regional ilustrada* 2 (1987): 40–43.

Perkins Hidalgo, Guillermo. "Supersticiones recogidas en la provincia de Corrientes." *Cuadernos del Instituto Nacional de Investigaciones Folklóricas* 1 (1960): 159–167.

Portocarrero Maisch, Gonzalo. "Un mediodía con Sarita." *Quehacer* 77 (1992): 96–99.

Quiroz Rojas, Ana María. "Cuando Dios dijo que no, Sarita dijo quién sabe." In *Los nuevos limeños: sueños, fervores y caminos en el mundo popular*, ed. Gonzalo Portocarrero, 143–160. Lima: Sur, 1993.

Riley, Luisa. "Fidencio, el Niño Fidencio." *Luna Córnea* 9 (1999): 5–14.

Rípodas Ardanaz, Daisy. "Pervivencia de hechiceros en las misiones guaraníes." *Folia histórica del nordeste* 6 (1984): 199–217.

Rodríguez, Marcelo. "'Apacita': de criminal a santón milagrero." *El comercio*, September 24, 1998: B8.

Rojas Samanez, Gonzalo. "Vida y milagros de Sarita Colonia." *Debate* 20 (1983): 19–21.

Romano V., Octavio Ignacio. "Charismatic Medicine, Folk-Healing, and Folk-Sainthood." *American Anthropologist* 67 (1965): 1151–1173.

Rosas Valdivia, Jordán. "Victor Apaza Quispe: o del fusilamiento a la santificación." *Revista ciencias sociales* 1 (1982): 42–57.

Rozas Alvarez, Jesús Washington. "Sana, sana, patita de rana. . ." In *El Qosqo: antropología de la ciudad*, ed. Hiroyasu Tomoeda and Jorge A. Flores Ochoa, 199–224. Cuzco: Ministerio de Educación del Japón y Centro de Estudios Andinos, 1992.

Sánchez Usón, María José. "El Niño-Mártir Dominguito de Val: a la santidad a través de la leyenda." In *Muerte, religiosidad, y cultural popular: siglos 13–18*, ed. Eliseo Serrano Martín, 119–150. Zaragoza: Institución Fernando el Católico, 1994.

Schuetz-Miller, Mardith K. "Survival of Early Christian Symbolism in Monastic Churches of New Spain and Visions of the Millennial Kingdom." *Journal of the Southwest* 42/4 (2000): 763–800.

Siles, Juan Ignacio. "San Ernesto de La Higuera." In *El Che en Bolivia: documentos y testimonios*, Vol. 3, ed. Carlos Soria Calvarro, 363–372. La Paz: CEDOIN, 1994.

Silva Santiesteban, Rocío. "Sarita Colonia viene a salvarnos." *El comercio, Revista Somos*, September 1, 1990: S16.

———. "Los santos inocentes," chap. 1: "Historia de dos fusilados." *El Comercio, Revista Somos*, March 16, 1991: S24.

———. "Los santos inocentes," chap. 2: "El nacimiento de un santo." *El Comercio, Revista Somos*, March 23, 1991: S26.

Spielberg, Joseph, and Antonio Zavaleta. "Historic Folk Sainthood along the Texas-Mexico Border." Niño Fidencio Research Project. http://vpea.utb.edu/elnino/researcharticles/historicfolksainthood.html.

Turner, Kay F. "Because of This Photography: The Making of a Mexican Folk Saint." In *Niño Fidencio: A Heart Thrown Open*, Dore Gardner, 120–134. Santa Fe: Museum of New Mexico Press, 1992.

Vanderwood, Paul. "Juan Soldado: Field Notes and Reflections." *Journal of the Southwest* 43/4 (2001): 717–727.

Vega-Centeno, Imelda. "Sistemas de creencia: entre la oferta y demanda simbólicas." *Nueva sociedad* 136 (1995): 56–69.

Vilca, José. "El feto sagrado." *Caretas* 1326, August 25, 1994: 44–48.

Villasante A., Antonio. "Religiosidad andina en un medio urbano." *Boletín del Instituto de Estudios Aymaras* 2/20 (1985): 32–48.

Wilde, Guillermo. "Los guaraníes después de la expulsión de los jesuitas: dinámicas políticas y transacciones simbólicas." *Revista complutense de historia de América* 27 (2001): 69–106.

Yoder, Don. "Toward a Definition of Folk Religion," *Western Folklore* 33/1 (1974): 2–15.

Zavaleta, Antonio N. "El Niño Fidencio and the *Fidencistas*." In *Sects, Cults, and Spiritual Communities: A Sociological Analysis*, ed. William W. Zellner and Marc Petrowsky, 95–115. Westport, Conn.: Praeger, 1998.

Index